BOX OFFICE POISON
by Alex Robinson

ISBN 1-891830-19-8
1. Fiction
2. Graphic Novels

 Edited by Chris Staros. Art direction and design by Brett Warnock. Color cover painting by Bwana Spoons. Published by Top Shelf Productions, PO Box 1282, Marietta, GA 30061-1282, USA. Publishers: Brett Warnock and Chris Staros. Visit our online catalog at www.topshelfcomix.com. Third Printing, July 2005. Printed in Canada.

For Kristen... the best.

PROLOGUE
I'M JANE PEKAR AND I FIND MYSELF POWERFULLY ATTRACTED TO A MAN IN A DRESS.
I'M SHERMAN DAVIES AND A PHONE CALL RUINS MY LIFE.
I'M IRVING FLAVOR AND I WEAR FOUR DIFFERENT TOUPEES THROUGHOUT THE BOOK.
I'M ED VELASQUEZ AND I AM BETRAYED -- TWICE IN ONE DAY.
I'M DOROTHY LESTRADE AND I'M NOT THE BAD GUY.
I'M STEPHEN GAEDEL AND YOU GET TO SEE ME NAKED MORE THAN YOU PROBABLY LIKE.
I'M HILDY KIERKEGAARD AND I BECOME MORE IMPORTANT IN THE END.

HI! WOULD YOU LIKE TO SIGN THIS PETITION AGAINST THE CHIMPANZEE TESTING IN THE LABS?
HUH?
OH, SURE.
GREAT!
UM.
I REALLY LIKED THAT THING YOU DID IN BASTIAN'S CLASS, THE ONE ON TRUMAN.
THANKS, UH...
SALLY, RIGHT?
RIGHT!
WELL, THANKS... I GUESS I'LL SEE YOU IN CLASS.
I...
I GUESS.
The Bohemian Girl

ALL I'M SAYING IS THAT IF I HAVE TO SPEND ANOTHER WEEK AT MY AUNT'S, I'LL GO CRAZY.
574
BZZZ!
BROOKLYN, N.Y. 1994
YES?
I'M SHERMAN DAVIES, I CALLED ABOUT THE ROOM FOR RENT?
C'MON UP!
SEEMS CLEAN ENOUGH.
IT'S GONNA BE A BITCH GETTING THAT DESK UP THESE STAIRS.
I'M WILLING TO CLIMB STAIRS IF IT'LL SAVE ME MONEY.
NOK NOK
IT'D BE CHEAPER TO LIVE IN QUEENS, Y'KNOW.
ARE YOU KIDDING? $250.00 A MONTH IS GREAT FOR THIS AREA!
YEAH, I READ THAT PARK SLOPE IS GOING TO BE THE NEXT SEATTLE.
JEEZ, I HOPE NOT!
THE FIRST FLANNEL SHIRT I SEE, I'M SPLITTIN'.
I WONDER WHY IT'S SO CHEAP?

3
HI, MY NAME'S STEPHEN.
YOU'RE HERE ABOUT THE ROOM?
Uh.
Yeah.
GREAT! GREAT! WELL, I'M ALREADY LATE, SO JANE HERE WILL HAVE THE HONOR OF SHOWING YOU THE PLACE, RIGHT?
SURE.
PLEASED TO MEET YOU HERMAN.
WELL, I HOPE YOU LIKE IT, SEE YA!

UH, IT'S SHERMAN, ACTUALLY.
OH, SORRY! SO WHAT DO YOU DO, SHERMAN?
WELL, FOR NOW I WORK IN A BOOKSTORE, BUT I WANT TO BE A WRITER.
A WRITER?! THAT'S GREAT!
OUR LAST ROOMMATE WAS A WRITER BUT WE... SHE HAD TO LEAVE.
THIS IS THE KITCHEN.
WOW! SO WHAT KIND OF STUFF DO YOU WRITE? STORIES?
UH, SOMETIMES. ACTUALLY, I MOSTLY WRITE -- I DON'T KNOW -- LIKE JOURNAL, OP-ED KIND OF STUFF.
COULD I READ SOME OF IT SOMETIME?
SURE! I'LL TRY TO BRING SOME TO CLASS.
I WOULD LIKE THAT VERY MUCH.

SO, DO YOU LIVE IN THE DORMS TOO?
NO, LAST SEMESTER WE -- MY FRIEND ZOOEY AND I -- GOT A PLACE DOWN ON AVENUE "A" AND 12th STREET.
REALLY? MY FRIEND GLEN LIVES ON 12th AND "B".
OR IS IT 13th AND "B"?
TAP TAP TAP
WOW, WELL IF YOU'RE EVER IN THE NEIGH-BORHOOD STOP ON BY!
YEAH, LIVING IN THE DORMS IS A PAIN IN THE ASS.
PLUS THEY'RE CLOSED DURING THE SUMMER, SO I HAVE TO GO LIVE WITH MY AUNT PHIN EVERY...
OH!! THAT REMINDS ME!! DO YOU LIKE LAUREL AND HARDY?
Uh. "WHO'S-- W-WHO'S ON FIRST" RIGHT?
NO, YOU UNCULTURED BOY!
YOU KNOW...
"HERE'S ANOTHER NICE MESS YOU'VE GOTTEN ME IN TO"...
OH YEAH!
Heh.
ANYWAY, NEXT MONTH THEY'RE HAVING A LAUREL AND HARDY FESTIVAL AT THE UNION, SO... DO YOU WANT TO...

IS IT MY IMAGINATION OR IS IT REALLY HOT IN HERE?
YEAH, THIS KITCHEN GETS REALLY HOT IN THE SUMMER.
DID I MENTION UTILITIES ARE INCLUDED?
C'MON, I'LL SHOW YOU YOUR ROOM...
SO, JANE, WHAT DO YOU DO? YOU GO TO SCHOOL?
NAW, I GRADUATED. I'M A CARTOONIST, ACTUALLY.
OH MY GOD, WHAT A COINCIDENCE!!
ED HERE'S A CARTOONIST TOO!
REALLY? WHAT KIND OF STUFF DO YOU DO?
Uh. WELL YOU KNOW, JUST DIFFERENT, LIKE, OF... KINDA, Uh, STUFF...
Uh. YOU KNOW.
WELL, Uh.
HERE'S THE ROOM!

UH.
UM.
HUH.
WHAT'S --UH. WHAT'S UP WITH THIS CEILING?
I KNOW, IT'S WEIRD, ISN'T IT? I GUESS THE PREVIOUS OWNER USED IT FOR SOME WEIRD STORAGE OR SOMETHING.
BUT IT HAS A SKY LIGHT!
DOES THAT DOOR UP THERE OPEN?
WHERE'S IT GO?
HMM...
UPSTAIRS, I GUESS. BUT IT'S... LOCKED.
THE SKYLIGHT OPENS, THOUGH.
I HAVE TO SAY, THIS IS ONE OF THE ODDEST ROOMS I'VE EVER SEEN.
I GUESS I'LL TAKE IT!

Y'KNOW... I NEVER WOULD'VE GUESSED, SHERM.
Hmm?
I NEVER WOULD'VE THOUGHT YOU WERE A...
Y'KNOW, THAT YOU'D NEVER...
"WELL I PRACTICE ALOT WHEN I'M ALONE."
HA HA!
BESIDES, YOU WEREN'T SO BAD YOURSELF, SAL.
I REALLY ENJOYED THAT "SONS OF THE DESERT" MOVIE, TOO.
MMM. WELL I SAW TAKING YOU TO THAT AS MY CIVIC DUTY.
THE FACT THAT YOU COULD BE A SENIOR AT COLLEGE...
HAVING NEVER SEEN A LAUREL AND HARDY MOVIE...
IS AS DAMNING AN INDICTMENT AS I CAN IMAGINE OF THE PUBLIC SCHOOL SYSTEM...
I CAN'T HELP IT, SAL. I GREW UP IN NEW JERSEY, WE...UM...WE DIDN'T HAVE FILM REVIVALS AT....
AT...Gulp
AT THE MALL.
MMM.....
SPEAKING OF REVIVALS...
SHERMAN
C--
CAN'T WE REST
FOR AWHILE
I'M GONNA
HAVE A
HEART ATTACK!

OKAY, OKAY. WE'LL GET THIS ONE UP AND THEN TAKE A REST. COME ON: HEAVE!
Ho...
SO IS THAT GIRL HERE TODAY? THAT, UH... JANE?
I DON'T THINK I'VE EVER MET A FEMALE CARTOONIST, ACTUALLY.
I DON'T KNOW IF SHE'S HOME.
DON'T GET ANY IDEAS, THOUGH: I THINK SHE'S GOING OUT WITH THAT GUY STEPHEN.
WHAT? REALLY?
HOW COME HE HAS A CUTE CARTOONIST GIRL-FRIEND AND I DONT? IT'S NOT FAIR I TELLS YA!
(WATCH THIS CORNER, ED.)
WHY? YOU THINK SHE'S CUTE?
SHE'S OKAY...
I GENERALLY LIKE 'EM WITH A BIT MORE MEAT ON THEIR BONES.
BUT I WOULDN'T KICK HER OUT OF BED.

HAVE YOU EVER MET A CHICK YOU WOULD KICK OUT OF BED?
HMM... LET ME THINK... OH YEAH! YOUR MOM!
YOU OKAY JAMES? I DON'T WANT YOU TO STRAIN YOURSELF OR ANYTHING.
Fiction H-P
MEOW.
SORRY, BUT AFTER HAULING UP TWO HUNDRED BOXES OF BOOKS I HAD TO CHECK OUT THIS PRECIOUS CARGO.
ALL THESE BOOKS! YOU MIGHT AS WELL STAY AT WORK.
sugar
1,137 OF THEM. "THEY'RE MY WIFE AND THEY'RE MY LIFE."
OKAY, DICKWEED, THE VAN'S EMPTY. I LEFT THE REST OF YOUR CRAP IN THE HALLWAY DOWNSTAIRS.
I'M GONNA GET OUTTA HERE.
PRIVATE BEACH
IT'S BECAUSE I'M FAT. GIRLS DON'T LIKE FATSOS.
UGH! LOOKIT THIS! BLURB*
THANKS, JOE. I GUESS I'LL SEE YOU AT PHIN'S ON TUESDAY, RIGHT?
SEE YA. THANKS.
Whew! OKAY, BREAK TIME.
WHO NEEDS A BEER?
*FAT SQUEEZING SOUND

YOU KNOW WHAT YOU NEED? YOU KNOW WHAT WOULD DO YOU GOOD?
QUITTING THE BOOKSTORE AND GETTING A REAL JOB?
AS YOU CAN SEE, NORM, THE FOUNDATION HERE IS JUST STARTING TO CRACK...
SMOKE!
Rolling Stone
YOU SHOULD GET A PSYCHIC CLEANSING.
YEAH, OR I COULD JUST EMPTY MY WALLET OUT A WINDOW.
NO, REALLY, ZOOEY'S GIRLFRIEND HAD ONE AND IT REALLY HELPED HER NEGATIVITY.
YOU'RE SERIOUS, AREN'T YOU.
I'VE GONE TO A LOT OF PSYCHICS. A PSYCHIC CLEANSING'S ONLY FIFTY DOLLARS.
FIFTY DOLLAR$?!?
YOU COULD GET FOUR C.D.S FOR THAT!!
WELL... YEAH.
BUT A CLEANSING WILL DO YOU A LOT MORE GOOD THAN FOUR MORE BILLY JOEL C.D.S.
YEAH, A LOT MORE GOOD FOR THE PSYCHIC CHARLATAN WHO GETS MY FIFTY BUCKS.

ED, I GOTTA SAY I'M NOT LOOKING FOWARD TO UNPACKING ALL THIS JUNK.
THIS LOOKS LIKE THE LAST SCENE IN "RAIDERS OF THE LOST ARK".
MAYBE I'LL JUST LIVE OUT OF THE BOXES.
SHERM, CAN I USE YOUR BATHROOM?
SURE, GO AHEAD.
Fragili
Fiction
Uh.
YOU DON'T KNOW WHICH BOX THE DOOR IS PACKED IN, DO YOU?
HMM. MAYBE WE COULD SAW THROUGH THE FLOOR.
OH MY GOD?! WHAT IS IT?!
IT'S A FAIRY TALE I WROTE WITH YOU AND ME AND ZOOEY AND ED AND EVERYBODY AS THE CHARACTERS.
OH MY GOD!! THIS MUST'VE TAKEN FOREVER!

WELL, YOU DESERVE IT, MY LITTLE BANANA FISH.
OOOH, YOU BIG SWEETIE!
OKAY! OKAY! NOW CLOSE YOUR EYES AND I'LL GIVE YOU MY ANNIVERSARY PRESENT!
RABBIT
MMM. THIS DOESN'T HAPPEN TO INVOLVE REDI-WHIP™ AND A CATHOLIC SCHOOL-GIRL UNIFORM, DOES IT?
OKAY, READY, LOOK!
TA-DAHH!
COME AND SEE
EUROPE
HOME OF DWEEBS!!
A BROCHURE ABOUT EUROPE! IT'S JUST MY SIZE, TOO!
NO, YA DOPE, WE'RE GOING TO EUROPE FOR THE SUMMER!
SURPRISE!
HAWKLINE MONSTER
EUR--SAL, I CAN'T AFFORD THIS, I'VE GOT $35,000 IN LOANS TO PAY OFF!
YOU DON'T HAVE TO PAY FOR IT! I'M GONNA ASK MY PARENTS AND THEY'RE GONNA PAY!
WHAT?

I ASKED YOU WHEN YOU GRADUATED.
OH, JUST THIS PAST JUNE. ENGLISH MAJOR.
ED HERE WENT TO HUNTER, TOO.
REALLY? THEY HAVE A CARTOONING DEPARTMENT AT HUNTER, ED?
NO, UH, MY...
MY PARENTS MADE ME MAJOR IN BUSINESS.
SO WHAT DO YOU DO NOW?
TO MAKE MONEY I MEAN.
I WORK IN A HARDWARE STORE.
BUT I'M SENDING MY STUFF OUT TO COMIC COMPANIES AND STUFF TOO.
THAT'S THE SPIRIT.!
SAY, SHERMAN, DID YOU GO TO EUROPE?
HUH?
OH, UH.
NO.

WHAT DO YOU MEAN "NO"? WHY CAN'T YOU GO?
SAL, I REALLY APPRECIATE THE OFFER
BUT
AND I'D LOVE TO
THEN WHY CAN'T YOU?
I... I'D JUST FEEL AWKWARD, I JUST... WITH YOUR PARENTS PAYING, I CAN'T ACCEPT IT.
OH, THAT'S BULLSHIT, SHERMAN. WHAT DIFFERENCE DOES THAT MAKE?!
I'M THE ONE WHO ASKED YOU!
I KNOW,
OKAY, SO YOU'RE GOING, RIGHT?
NO, I'M NOT. I'M SORRY, SAL
WHAT THE FUCK, SHERMAN?! IS IT ME?!
NO, UH, I ALMOST WENT THIS SUMMER.
BUT IT DIDN'T WORK OUT.
HEY, GUYS!!
I'M BACK! WHADDAYA SAY WE GET SOME DINNER?
ME FEEL STUPID!
OH HERE WE GO AGAIN. I'M NOT
JUST SHUT UP!

ED COULD'VE COME ALONG, HE DIDN'T HAVE TO GO.
OH, HE KNEW, HE JUST... HAD TO WORK EARLY TOMORROW.
GENERAL TSO'S
YEAH, I WORKED AT THE SAME BOOKSTORE AS YOU, ABOUT... CHRIST! TEN YEARS AGO!
HOW LONG HAVE YOU BEEN THERE?
LET'S SEE, I STARTED IN MY SOPHMORE YEAR, SO THAT'S ABOUT THREE, THREE AND A HALF YEARS.
RETAIL BITES.
"When Love Puts in, friendship is Gone"
YEAH, I REALLY HAVE TO LOOK FOR A NEW GIG.
Thank you!!!
HAVE YOU HAD ANY OF YOUR WRITING PUBLISHED OUTSIDE OF SCHOOL?
NO.
I MEAN, THE BOOKSTORE USED TO BE OKAY. BUT IN THE PAST... I MEAN THE PAY'S ALWAYS BEEN CRAP, BUT IN THE PAST FEW MONTHS THEY'VE BEEN CRACKING DOWN.
DRESS CODES AND SHIT.
I'M SORRY, SHERM...
BUT IT LOOKS AWFUL.

THANKS.
YOU'RE JUST TRYING TO MAKE ME FEEL BETTER.
HOW CAN YOU EVEN WORK AT A PLACE THAT WOULD MAKE YOU CUT YOUR HAIR AS PART OF SOME "DRESS CODE"?
I GUESS IT'S THIS WEIRD OBSESSION OF MINE ABOUT HAVING MONEY TO BUY FOOD AND THINGS.
YEAH, BUT YOU'RE BARELY MAKING MINIMUM WAGE.
YOU SHOULD QUIT. ALL YOU EVER DO IS COMPLAIN ABOUT HOW SHITTY IT IS.
GREAT ADVICE FROM SOMEONE WHO'S NEVER HAD TO WORK A DAY IN HER LIFE.
FUCK YOU! I'VE WORKED!
THAT'S RIGHT, I FORGOT ABOUT THOSE INFAMOUS THREE DAYS AT "MOONBEAM'S GRANOLA AND TOFU HUT."
WHY DID YOU QUIT AGAIN? OH YEAH!
"IT SUCKED."

WELL, SORRY, SAL, WE CAN'T ALL JUST RUN BACK TO MOMMY AND DADDY WHEN LIFE ISN'T ALL ROSEY AND WE NEED MORE ALLOWANCE.
SOME OF US HAVE TO HAVE **SOME** SENSE OF RESPONSIBILITY.
SO I'D APPRECIATE IT IF YOU'D **MIND YOUR OWN BUSINESS.**
YOU
YOU'RE SO MEAN
I KNOW
SORRY, HON, I PROMISED CATTON I'D HELP HIM WITH HIS THESIS.
WHAT?! I WAS HOPING WE COULD HAVE A NI ONE--
I KNOW! I KNOW!
P.S
ELI
BUT ONCE THIS SUMMER SESSION IS OVER, I'LL GIVE YOU MY UNDIVIDED ATTENTION!
OH, YOU A
YOUR GENE
SPIRIT!
IF
I

I Once Had a Girl or should I Say She once Had Me. She Showed Me...
...lends you a hand
Doesn't Have a point of view, Knows not where he's going to, isn't he a bit like you and me? Nowhere Man, please...
MMMF!
it's the Word, Love! Everywhere I go, I hear it said, in the good and the bad books that I have read.
Say the word and you'll be free...
all the times I've tried So hard to leave her, she would turn to me and start to cry, and she promises the earth to me and I belive her...
after all this time I don't know why...
...places have their moments with lovers and friends I still can recall, some are dead and some are living...
In My Life, I Loved them all...
... Hide your head in the sand. little girl, I Catch you with another man, that's the end little girl
No, no, no
no, no, no,

KNOCK, KNOCK.
SHERMAN?

UH... YEAH, COME IN.
WELL, IT LOOKS LIKE YOU'RE ALMOST DONE IN HERE.
I DON'T KNOW.
I'M STARTING TO FEEL LIKE I'LL NEVER GET THROUGH ALL THIS SHIT...
SO, WHAT'S UP?
WELL, YOU DON'T KNOW WHAT YOU GOT UNTIL YOU MOVE IT.

I RENTED A MOVIE. D'YA WANNA JOIN ME?
WHAT IS IT.
"THE BOHEMIAN GIRL"
...?
WHAT'S IT ABOUT?
IT'S A LAUREL AND HARDY MOVIE.
LAUREL HARDY
THE BOHEMIAN GIRL
REALLY?!
I LOVE LAUREL AND HARDY!
WOW, ME, TOO!

SALLY?
SHERMAN.
WHAT'S WRONG WITH YOUR HAIR?
NOTHING... EVERYTHING WILL BE OKAY...
I'M SORRY I HAD TO GO.
THAT BUZZING...
I'LL ALWAYS BE WITH YOU ...
THAT NOISE?!
WHAT'S WRONG?
WHY'RE YOU STOPPING?
WHAT THE FUCK IS THAT BUZZING?!
BZZZZZZZZZZZZZZZZZZZZZZZZZ

BZZZZZZZ!
7:30
•UGLY MOLES
•ANAL WARTS
•HAIRY BACKS
AIDS
1•900•LOVE CAT
VANESSA
DAILY NEWS
YANKS WIN!
Subway
F 1/9 2 3 L
KA CHUNGA!
DAVIES SHERMAN
VANESSA
ANNMARIE
REBECCA
MARGARITA
LAURA
VICKY
12 1 2 3 4 5 6 7 8 9 10 11

Boiling Frog
CAN I HELP SOMEONE?
DOES ANYONE NEED HELP?
DOUBLE CROSS
T. CONSIGLIO
DEATH OF A CLOWN
IN HIS OWN WRITE
TIME QUAKE
YES, DO YOU WORK HERE?
NOW WHY ELSE WOULD I BE ASKING IF ANYONE NEEDED HELP, YOU STUPID OLD BAT?
YES, CAN I HELP YOU?

I NEED A BOOK
WELL, I GUESS YOU'VE COME TO THE RIGHT PLACE.
SURE, WHAT'S THE BOOK?
I DON'T KNOW THE TITLE, BUT IT'S BY SOME-ONE SMITH.
OH JESUS.
DO YOU KNOW WHAT IT'S ABOUT?
NO.
IT HAS A BLUE COVER. WHERE CAN I FIND IT?
I'M SORRY, BUT I NEED MORE INFORMATION
WHAT DO YOU MEAN? YOU'RE HERE TO HELP ME!
LET ME TALK TO THE MANAGER!!
I'LL BE RIGHT BACK, MISS.
FUCKING OLD HAG!! "IT HAS A BLUE COVER!"
I'M SURPRISED SHE CAN EVEN READ A BOOK!
I HAVE A COLLEGE DEGREE, I DON'T NEED THIS!!!
SHERMAN!!
JANICE! HOW'RE YA DOING?
WHERE'RE YOU STORMIN' OFF TO?
OH, SOME STUPID OLD LADY WANTS TO SEE THE DRAGON.
HMM. I THINK I SAW HER IN THE BASEMENT YELLING AT JAMES.
BUT WAIT! I HAVE TO TELL YOU SOMETHING!

OKAY, READY? READY?
DUANE'S STOPPING BY TODAY!!
REALLY? YOU MEAN WE FINALLY GET TO MEET THE ELUSIVE FUTURE MR. JANICE SINK?
WHAT'S THIS?!
WE'RE GONNA GONNA SEE ROMEO DREAMBOAT LOVER-BOY HIMSELF?
THAT'S RIGHT, RAY. HE'S COMING BY AROUND ONE AND WE'RE GETTING SOME LUNCH.
'AN I'M SURE AFTER SIX MONTHS IN THE ARMY HE'S GONNA WANNA GET A LITTLE SOMETHIN' ELSE, TOO, ANH? ANH?
HeeHee! OH, RAY, STOP!
JESUS.
DO YOU WORK HERE?
YES?
I'M A SOPHMORE AT N.Y.U. AND MY TEACHER, PROFESSOR CALLE, ASSIGNED US A BOOK "INTRODUCTION TO ECONOMICS, 5th ed," BY IMMORDINO AND I DIDN'T SEE IT ON THE SHELF, SO I AXED A CLERK -- A SKINNY CHINESE GIRL -- AND SHE CHECKED THE SHELF TOO, THEN SHE CHECKED THE STOCKROOM AND THEN SHE CHECKED THE COMPUTER AND SHE SAID YOU GUYS WAS OUT OF IT, SO I AXED ANOTHER CLERK -- A TALL, BLACK GUY WITH A SHAVED HEAD -- AND HE ALSO CHECKED, TOO, AND HE ALSO SAID YOU WAS SOLD OUT AND YOU SHOULD GET IT IN ABOUT TWO WEEKS OR SO.
Uh. SO YOU WANT ME TO...?
WELL, COULD YOU JUST SEE IF YOU COULD FIND IT FOR ME?
Uh, NO, I'M SORRY, BUT IF TWO CLERKS TOLD YOU WE DON'T HAVE IT, THEN WE DON'T HAVE IT.
IS THERE SOMEONE ELSE WHO CAN HELP ME?
EXCUSE ME, DO YOU HAVE "THE ANNOYED" BY VIRGIL?
I'M DOUBLE PARKED.
I'M SORRY, I'M BUSY, YOU'LL HAVE ASK ANOTHER CLERK!
IT HAS A PURPLE COVER!

EMPLOYEES ONLY
HMM... NOW WHY DID I COME DOWN ...?
NO SMOKING
HEY, SHERMAN!
PURA VIDA
PURA VIDA
PURA VIDA
HEY, JAMES HOW'S IT GOING?
YOU HEAR ABOUT JANICE'S BOYFRIEND?
YEAH. I WONDER WHAT HE LOOKS LIKE?
I BET HE'S REAL UGLY.
CUTE GIRLS ALWAYS HAVE UGLY BOYFRIENDS.
RANDOM HOUSE
YOU'RE A BITTER GUY, JAMES, BUT I HAVE MORE FAITH IN JANICE THAN THAT.
WE'LL SEE ...
DEAD BOYS
OH YEAH! DO YOU HAVE PLANS FOR THIS FRIDAY?
NO, WHY?
WELL, MY ROOMMATES ARE GOING AWAY FOR THE WEEKEND SO I'M GOING TO HAVE A LITTLE HOUSE WARMING.
SURE, WILL THERE BE ANY GIRLS?
I'M WORKING ON IT, I'M WORKING ON IT.

HEY, AREN'T YOU AND LISA STILL GOING OUT?
JAMES!! NELLIE WANTS TO SEE YOU UP IN HER OFFICE!
SHIT.
WELL, BACK TO THE DRAGON'S LAIR FOR ME, SHERMAN.
?
Heh, SORRY. WELL, I'M GONNA GO AND USE THE EUPHEMISM.
GOOD LUCK.
AND SO...
AHHH... NOTHING IS QUITE AS SATISFYING AS A SHIT ON COMPANY TIME.
JAMES BETTER BE CAREFUL, HE'S REALLY BEEN PUSHING HIS LUCK LATELY.
I WONDER WHY SHE WANTED TO SEE HIM NOW? PROBABLY FOR NOT SHAVING AGAIN.
THE DRAGON'S BEEN REALLY HOUNDING HIM LATELY. SHE'S--
THE DRAGON!!!
I TOTALLY FORGOT ABOUT THAT OLD LADY WHO WANTED TO SEE THE MANAGER!!!
THAT WAS LIKE TWENTY MINUTES AGO!!

AND SO...
HMM... I DON'T SEE THAT OLD LADY OR THE DRAGON...
SHE MUST'VE...
AHHHH!!!
GOTCHA!!!
HAHA!
JESUS, JANICE! YOU'RE GONNA GIVE ME A HEART ATTACK!
OH, TAKE IT EASY.
SAY, YOU DIDN'T NOTICE SOME OLD LADY COMPLAINING ABOUT ME, DID YOU? TO THE DRAGON OR ANYONE?
... NO. WHY? WHAT DID YOU DO TO HER?
AWHILE AGO I TOLD HER I'D GET THE MANAGER FOR HER BUT I TOTALLY FORGOT!
WELL, I'M SURE YOU WOULD'VE HEARD BY NOW IF YOU WERE IN TROUBLE. DON'T WORRY.
YEAH... YEAH I GUESS YOU'RE RIGHT.
WHAT TIME IS IT? I WANT TO TAKE MY BREAK.
WELL, GUYS...
Uh...
IT LOOKS LIKE NELLIE THE DRAGON WON'T BE GIVING ME ANY MORE HEADACHES.
WHY? DID YOU FINALLY KILL HER?

NOPE.
I QUIT.
WHAT?!
"WELL, THE DRAGON HAD CALLED ME TO THE CARPET YET AGAIN. SHE WAS RANTING ABOUT MY SLOVENLY APPEARANCE AND
AND YOU WERE TWENTY-FIVE MINUTES LATE. THAT'S THE SAME AS STEALING.
I'M GIVING YOU A WRITTEN WARNING.
IN OTHER WORDS, NEXT TIME WE HAVE A PROBLEM WE'LL HAVE TO LET YOU GO.
UNDERSTAND?
DO YOU UNDERSTAND, JAMES?
NELLIE?
FUCK.
OFF.

OH MY GOD!! YOU DID NOT!
B-BUT YOU CAN'T! WHAT'RE YOU GONNA DO? HOW'RE YOU GONNA SURVIVE?!
IT'S NOT LIKE I'M RESIGNING AS CHAIRMAN OF IBM OR SOMETHING. I'M SURE I CAN FIND SOMEPLACE ELSE WILLING TO PAY ME $5.50.
MAYBE MORE.
FOR NOW, I'LL JUST HAVE TO SWALLOW MY PRIDE AND BORROW SOME MONEY FROM MY DAD.
THE BEST PART IS THAT I WON'T HAVE TO TAKE SHIT FROM THAT MONSTER ANYMORE!
NO SPITTING
WELL, JANICE, SORRY I WON'T GET TO MEET YOUR FIANCÉE AFTER ALL...
OH, YOU'LL BE AT SHERMAN'S PARTY RIGHT? MAYBE YOU'LL SEE HIM THERE!
MEMO
WE'LL SEE.
I'LL CALL YOU, SHERM.
'KAY.
KA-CHUNGA!

SO BILL IN THE HISTORY SECTION WENT OUT FOR DRINKS WITH SHANNON--BUT! HE HAS A GIRLFRIEND AT COLLEGE!
AND JOE IN SCIENCE PAPERBACK HAS HIS EYE ON SUZY IN POETRY! BUT HE'S SHY.
NOT THAT SHE'D GO OUT WITH HIM ANYWAY--SHE'S WAY OUT OF HIS LEAGUE --AND SHE LIVES WITH HER BOYFRIEND.
DIONNE UP IN THE FRONT JUST BROKE UP WITH HER BOYFRIEND SO ROBBIE IN PETS WANTS TO MAKE A MOVE.
COFFEE
SNACKS
HOW COULD HE DO THIS TO ME? LEAVING ME ALONE IN THIS HELLISH PLACE.
EVERYONE'S GOING GAGA OVER THAT NEW GIRL IN REFERENCE. I GUESS THEY DON'T KNOW SHE'S ONLY SIXTEEN!
EXCEPT RAY, OF COURSE, HE WANTS HER EVEN MORE NOW.
OH, SURE, I'D LIKE TO QUIT. WHO WOULDN'T? BUT WITH NOTHING TO FALL BACK ON? IMPOSSIBLE. NEVER.
I HEARD THAT JAMES HAS BEEN FIGHTING WITH HIS GIRLFRIEND AND SHE WAS REALLY MAD HE QUIT HIS JOB.
STILL, HOW MUCH MORE OF THIS CRAP DO I HAVE TO TAKE BEFORE I FINALLY GET OFF MY ASS AND GET A BETTER GIG?
TIME TO GO BACK...
EXCUSE ME, DO YOU WORK HERE? I'M LOOKING FOR "A STREETCAR NAMED DESIRAY WILLIAMS" BY SIGNET?
IT HAS A RED COVER.
CONFEDERACY OF DUNCES
J.K. TOOLE
INFERNO
JOB THING

DO YOU CARRY NON-FICTION BOOKS?
CAN I USE A XEROX MACHINE TO COPY A FEW PAGES?
I DON'T WANT TO HAVE TO BUY THE BOOK.
USED
I COULDN'T FIND ANY BOOKS ON LIONS IN THE PETS SECTION.
NY
DO YOU WORK HERE?
CAN I USE MY LIBRARY CARD?
Uh... DO YOU... uh... DO YOU HAVE BOOKS ON HOW TO HYPMOTIZE GIRLS?
DO YOU HAVE ANY BOOKS ON BUILDING A SIMPLE ROBOT?
Genesco
U of C
WHERE ARE BOOKS BY SHERLOCK HOLMES?
DO YOU HAVE ANY BOOKS ON HOW TO FILL OUT MONEY ORDERS?
Uh., HEH, DO YOU HAVE ANY BOOKS ABOUT, LIKE, HERBS?
LET ME GUESS: MARIJUANA.
WHOA-HO-HO! HOW DID YOU GUESS THAT?
DO YOU HAVE "FINDING AN ANGEL FOR YOUR CO-DEPENDENT INNER CHILD"?
IT'S A PAPERBACK ABOUT 120 PAGES.
DO YOU WORK HERE? DO YOU WORK HERE? CAN I AXE YOU SOMETHING? DO YOU WORK HERE?
Heh.!
WHAT DO YOU MEAN "WE DON'T CARRY SOMETHING CALLED BOX OFFICE POISON"?!?
FOOLS!! I'LL BE FAMOUS!!!

(ALL QUESTIONS 100% GENUINE!!!)

Uh...DO YOU HAVE THE CLIFF'S NOTES TO "BRIDGES OF MADISON COUNTY"?
IT HAS A YELLOW COVER.
Pearl Jam
WOODSTOCK 94
CAN I GET A DISCOUNT ON THIS DAMAGED BOOK?
IT'S A GIFT FOR MY HUSBAND.
OUR BODIES OUR SELVES
HOW COULD YOU BE SOLD OUT?!
BUT MY CLASS STARTS TOMORROW!!
THESE ARE ALL THE BOOKS YOU HAVE ON NORWEGIAN TREE FROGS?!
WHAT OTHER STORES WOULD CARRY MORE?
DO YOU CARRY, LIKE, NOVELS?
DO YOU HAVE "AN INTERRUPTION OF DREAM" BY SIGMUND FROOD?
COULD YOU RECOMMEND A BOOK FOR MY AUNT?
SHE'S EIGHTY FIVE.
DO YOU HAVE "YOU CAN BREAK THE CYCLE OF ADDICTION AND LIVE LIFE HAPPILY EVER AFTER SIMPLY BY READING ONE SELF HELP BOOK BY T.P. PHARNUM?
I SAW IT ON "OPRAH"
CAN YOU FIND THESE BOOKS FOR ME?
I DON'T WANT TO HAVE TO LOOK FOR THEM.
OCCULT?
WHY DO YOU KEEP BOOKS ON TAROT CARDS IN "OCCULT"?
WARNING: THE BIGGER THE FRAMES, THE SMALLER THE BRAINS
EH, EH, EH, PLEASE YOU ARE, EH, DO YOU VERK IN...EH, FIND FOR US BOOKS PLEASE, EH, DO YOU HEV?
SHERMAN, THIS IS DUANE, ...MY FIANCEE

HI, HOW YOU DOING, SHERMAN.
HEY, DUANE. WE FINALLY GET TO MEET YOU.
JANICE'S TOLD US ALL SO MUCH ABOUT YOU.
MY GOD! JAMES WAS RIGHT!!
IT AIN'T TRUE I SWEAR! HUH HEH.
JANICE HAS FALLEN UNDER THE SPELL OF AN UGLY BOYFRIEND!
Heh. WELL...
'SCUSE ME, DO YOU GUYS SELL ROPE?
DID YOU JUST ASK IF WE SOLD ROPE? ROPE?
Uh, YEAH,
WHERE WOULD IT BE?
SHERMAN?
NELLIE WANTS TO SEE YOU IN HER OFFICE.
HOOBOY, THAT CAN'T BE GOOD!

MANAGER
I QUIT!!
Uh... YOU WANTED TO SEE ME?
SURE, SHERMAN. CLOSE THE DOOR AND SIT.
WELL...?
GET ON WITH IT, YOU STUPID OLD BAT.
SHERMAN... WE'VE HAD A COMPLAINT ABOUT YOU FROM A WOMAN THIS MORNING. SHE SAID YOU WERE RUDE TO HER, AND THEN YOU JUST WALKED AWAY.
SHIT! SHIT! SHIT!
WELL, WHAT HAPPENED WAS I
FRANKLY, SHERMAN, I DON'T CARE WHAT HAPPENED.
YOU'RE A GOOD CLERK AND WE THINK HIGHLY OF YOU, IN OTHER WORDS, WE'RE GOING TO HAVE TO WRITE YOU UP.
UNDERSTAND?
OF COURSE I UNDERSTAND, YOU FRIGGIN' TROLL! I UNDERSTAND THAT I QUIT!!!
UH-HUH.
ALRIGHT, THEN, IN OTHER WORDS, YOU KNOW WHAT THAT MEANS, SO NO MORE TROUBLE, OKAY?
OKAY, YOU UGLY BITCH! I QUIT, OKAY? OKAY?! IS IT OKAY IF I SPLIT YOUR HEAD OPEN WITH A FUCKING AXE?!
OKAY.
OKAY. OH, ALSO...

I'M SURE YOU'VE HEARD THAT WE HAD TO LET JAMES GO...
WHAT?!
...SO I'M ASSIGNING YOU TO TAKE CARE OF ALL OF HIS SECTIONS.
JUST ME? B-BUT THAT'S-- MY WORK-LOAD WILL BE DOUBLED!!
WELL, I'M REALLY SORRY IT'LL BE CUTTING IN TO YOUR SOCIAL HOUR, BUT WE CAN'T AFFORD TO HIRE A NEW CLERK.
NOW YOU'LL BE ABLE TO 'CUZ I QUIT!!
I'M SURE YOU UNDERSTAND THIS'S BEEN A SLOW SEASON FOR ALL RETAIL JOBS. WE ALL WILL JUST HAVE TO TIGHTEN OUR BELTS A BIT.
I'D LIKE TO TIGHTEN MY BELT AROUND YOUR GOD DAMNED STUPID LYING NECK! I QUIT!!
Uh-Huh.
MEIN KAMPF
SO UNLESS YOU HAVE ANYTHING ELSE TO SAY...?
I QUIT
NO

¡KA-CHUNGA!
THAT'S IT! I'VE HAD ENOUGH!
TONIGHT I'M PICKING UP THE PAPER AND I'M GOING TO LOOK THROUGH THE WANT-ADS AND I'M FINDING ME A JOB-- TONIGHT!!!
THAT IS $3.50, PLEASE, SIR.
TODAY, A NEW CHAPTER BEGINS IN THE LIFE OF SHERMAN DAVIES!
NO MORE MR. RETAIL SCHMUCK!
"WHAT ARE CHESTNUTS?"
AH! IS THAT THE SOUND OF JEOPARDY I HEAR?
SO, HOW'RE THINGS IN THE WILD AND WOOLY WORLD OF BOOK SALES?
IT SUCKS, OF COURSE.
"WHO IS JAMES WILSON?"

"WHO IS ETTA JAMES?"
"WHO IS BILLIE HOLIDAY?"
IS THIS YOUR COPY OF TODAY'S "TIMES?"
HUH?
OH, YEAH.
ARE YOU DONE WITH IT? I'D LIKE TO DO THE PUZZLE.
I MEAN, UNLESS YOU'RE STILL..
UH...
The New York Times
NAH. YOU CAN HAVE IT.
I WON'T BE USING IT.

YOU GALS READY? LET'S FIND OUT WHO OUR NEXT LUCKY BRIDE WILL BE!!
LET'S HAVE IT GERTS!
READY!
READY!
C'MON, JANE LET ME GET IT!
EVERBODY BETTER GET OUT OF MY WAY!
Ballad of Jane and Stephen
HYAH!

I GUESS I WAS WHAT YOU'D CALL A LATE BLOOMER.
I HAD FRIENDS IN HIGH SCHOOL, BUT I NEVER WENT ON DATES OR ANYTHING.
IRON MAIDEN
ART SCHOOL WAS DIFFERENT. I WAS THE ONLY GIRL IN THE WHOLE CARTOONING DEPARTMENT.
X
THE FIRST GUY I EVER WENT OUT WITH WAS RUFUS KONIGSBERG, A MEDIA ARTS MAJOR.
AFTER A FEW DATES WE BOTH DECIDED TO "JUST BE FRIENDS" AND WE ACTUALLY WERE, TOO.
THE SECOND GUY I WENT OUT WITH WAS HUNT STRATHMORE, A CARTOONIST. WE ONLY WENT OUT ONCE.
WE WENT AND SAW "BATMAN" AND OVER DINNER HE ASKED ME WHO I THOUGHT WAS STRONGER: THE HULK OR SUPERMAN?
SPAWN
IT WAS ALL HE TALKED ABOUT! HE WAS OBSESSED WITH SUPER-HERO COMICS!
AND--ALTHOUGH I HADN'T PLANNED ON IT-- A LOUSY FIRST KISS.

I DECIDED TO THROW MYSELF IN TO MY WORK.
DURING MY SOPHMORE YEAR, MY OLDER SISTER KIM GOT MARRIED, THE SECOND PEKAR SISTER TO DO SO.
ONE NIGHT THAT YEAR, RUFUS AND I WERE DRINKING AND LONELY AND HORNY AND WE DID IT...
IT WAS BREATHTAKINGLY PERFUNCTORY.
THEN THERE WAS "DUKE", A PAINTER AND MY UNREQUITED OBSESSION. I WORKED MYSELF UP TO ASK HIM OUT AND HE WORKED HIMSELF UP TO TELL ME HE WAS BUSY.
MY FIRST REAL "BOYFRIEND" WAS ACTUALLY ANOTHER CARTOONIST. MICHAEL HAD AN ENORMOUS IMPACT ON MY WORK, TOO. HE LEAD ME AWAY FROM ELVES AND FANTASY STUFF TO MORE REALISTIC STORIES.

AND THE SEX WAS AMAZING ...
WHEN MICHAEL TRANSFERRED TO ANOTHER SCHOOL WE BOTH AGREED IT WOULD BE FOR THE BEST TO BREAK UP
THAT SUMMER, MY NEXT OLDEST SISTER JOYCE TIED THE KNOT. THREE DAUGHTERS DOWN, TWO TO GO.
HALLOWEEN OF MY JUNIOR YEAR, RUFUS HAD A PARTY. MY ROOM-MATE JEOPARDY DIRECTED MY ATTENTION ACROSS THE ROOM TO SOME GUY-- A CROSS BETWEEN JESUS CHRIST AND PAUL BUNYAN --IN A DRESS!

THE UNDERTOW OF HIS PRESENCE DRAGGED ME THROUGH THE SEA OF MASKS...
I LISTENED AS HE DEBATED SOME KID ABOUT-- OF ALL THINGS --ABRAHAM LINCOLN'S ATTITUDES TOWARDS BLACKS AND SLAVERY.
I JUST LISTENED TO HIM TALK, TO HIS VOICE. I WASN'T MUCH OF A HISTORY BUFF BUT HE MADE IT SOUND SO ... EXCITING, SO VITAL.
HE HAD A PASSION THAT I FOUND VERY--
UH, HI.
MISS OYL, I PRESUME?
Heh
YOU IDIOT!! I LATER LEARNED FROM RUFUS THAT THE JESUS GUY-- WHOSE NAME WAS--IS-- **STEPHEN GAEDEL** -- THOUGHT I WAS "REALLY CUTE BUT SEEMED STUCK UP"

EVENTUALLY, IN A PAINFULLY HIGH SCHOOLISH WAY, RUFUS PLAYED MATCHMAKER AND THERE WE WERE... OUT FOR DINNER AND A MOVIE.
H'LO
HI
IT WAS AWFUL.
MAYBE WE WERE BOTH NERVOUS OR WHATEVER BUT HE SEEMED LIKE A TOTALLY DIFFERENT PERSON. AWKWARD SILENCES WERE THE RULE OF THE NIGHT.
IMAGINE MY SURPRISE WHEN TWO WEEKS LATER HE CALLS ME.
SURE.
IN THE AFTERNOON?
UH-HUH. OKAY!
YARD SALE
IT WAS GREAT. WE JUST WALKED AROUND THE VILLAGE, GOT A BITE TO EAT AND CHATTED UP A STORM. WE EVEN WENT BOWLING!
BEFORE WE PARTED, STEPHEN EXPLAINED IT ALL TO ME. HE WAS IN ONE LONG-TERM RELATIONSHIP MOST OF HIS ADULT LIFE -- HE WAS TWENTY SEVEN -- AND IT ENDED ABOUT A YEAR AGO.

I WAS THE FIRST GIRL HE'D GONE OUT WITH SINCE THEN. THAT'S WHY HE WAS SO NERVOUS ON OUR "BIG DATE" LAST TIME. HE WAS REALLY RUSTY AT SOMETHING HE NEVER FELT TO GOOD AT ANYWAY...
OUBLE ROSS!
BUT JANE... YOU SEEM LIKE YOU'RE SMART AND FUNNY AND, WELL, BEAUTIFUL AND I REALLY LIKE YOU SO I HOPE YOU'LL GIVE ME A CHANCE...
Uh-- I HOPE I'M NOT EMBARRASSING YOU.
AT THAT MOMENT I WOULD'VE DONE ANYTHING FOR HIM
TODAY MY OLDER SISTER GERTRUDE GOT MARRIED, LEAVING ME THE SINGLE SINGLE PEKAR GIRL...
WE'VE BEEN TOGETHER FOR... WOW, ALMOST FOUR YEARS. AFTER I GRADUATED FROM SCHOOL WE GOT A PLACE TOGETHER

STEPHEN GOT A JOB TEACHING U.S. HISTORY AT CAROL COLLEGE HERE IN THE CITY. THE MONEY ISN'T GREAT, BUT THERE'S NOTHING ELSE HE'D RATHER DO.
AND ME, I'M STRUGGLING TO GET MORE OF MY COMICS PUBLISHED. IT'S A DOG EAT DOG WORLD.
Sigh... EVEN A REJECTION LETTER IS BETTER THAN AN EMPTY MAILBOX...
SO ANYWAY, TODAY AT MY SISTER'S WEDDING THE QUESTION ON EVERYONE'S LIPS IS "SO, WHEN ARE YOU TWO CRAZY KIDS GOING TO GET MARRIED?" MY REPLY IS USUALLY A NON-COMMITTAL SHRUG...
BUT I HAVE A SECRET: TWO WEEKS AGO STEPHEN ASKED ME TO MARRY HIM.
I SAID NO.
I'VE GOT IT!!

WOO-HOO! WATCH OUT, PATRICK CUZ YER ASS IS MINE NOW!
WE'D DANCED AROUND THE IDEA BEFORE. HE MUST'VE KNOWN MY FEELINGS ON THE SUBJECT...
DON'T WORRY, JANE. MAYBE NEXT TIME!
OH WELL, MAYBE.
DON'T GET ME WRONG-- I LOVE STEPHEN AND I'M IN LOVE WITH HIM AND AT THIS POINT IT'S EASY AND PLEASANT TO IMAGINE SPENDING THE REST OF MY LIFE WITH HIM....
ANDREW AND I ARE MARRIED BUT WE'RE JUST AS HAPPY AS EVER*
...BUT MARRIAGE? MAYBE IT JUST SEEMS TOO ADULT FOR ME.
FIRST MARRIAGE... THEN KIDS... THEN OLD AGE... THEN DEATH. I REALIZE THE LATTER TWO WILL HAPPEN RING OR NO RING BUT...
SO I HAD TO SAY NO.
JANEY! WHEN'RE YOU AND THAT LONG HAIRED MAN OF YOURS GONNA GET MARRIED?
I DON'T KNOW, GRAMS.

* BERTRAND RUSSELL

HAVING A GOOD TIME, HUN?
YEAH.
I REALLY THOUGHT YOU HAD THAT DAMN BOUQUET.
MMM.

ED.. THE INK STUD

HOW'S IT GOING, ED?
:GROAN: TERRIBLE. THESE GIRLS ARE DRIVING ME CRAZY.
NO LUCK, huh?
IT'S NOT EVEN THAT! I'M SO AFRAID OF BEING REJECTED, I JUST ASSUME THEY'LL SAY NO SO I DON'T EVEN TRY.
IT'S DOWNRIGHT PATHETIC!
IF THAT'S YOUR ATTITUDE, YOU'RE RIGHT, IT IS PATHETIC!
ED, YOU HAVE TO HAVE CONFIDENCE! GO IN THERE THINKING: "I'M A GREAT CATCH! SURE I HAVE MY FLAWS, BUT WHO DOESN'T? I'M SMART AND I'M COOL AND I'M FUNNY AND IF SHE CAN'T SEE THAT, FUCK'ER! FUCK HER AND HER SHALLOW SUPERFICIAL MALL RAT VALUES!! I'M ED VELASQUEZ, CARTOONIST, STUD... AMERICAN!!!! DAMMIT!"
Uh, ACTUALLY, I WAS BORN IN COSTA RICA.
BUT YOU LIVE IN AMERICA!
NOW GO GET LAID, ED!

THIS IS CRAZY! WHAT AM I DOING?! WOMEN AREN'T INTERESTED IN ME. WHAT WAS IT JAMES SAID I NEEDED...?
OH YEAH! CONFIDENCE!
HEY, BABY, HOW'S IT GOING?
WHAT WOULD YOU SAY IF I TOLD YOU THAT YOU WERE THE MOST BEAUTIFUL WOMAN IN THE ROOM?
HMM. I WOULD LAUGH NERVOUSLY AND TELL YOU THAT YOU'VE HAD TOO MUCH TO DRINK.
WHAT WOULD YOU SAY IF I SAID I WANTED TO BRING YOU HOME, COVER YOU IN TAPIOCA PUDDING AND WE MAKE HOT STEAMY LOVE 'TIL SUNRISE?
I'D SAY "LET'S GO."

REALLY?! EVEN THOUGH I'M FAT?
SURE.
EVEN THOUGH I'M KINDA SHORT?
YOU BET.
EVEN THOUGH I SNORE?
CERTAINLY.
EVEN THOUGH I STILL LIVE WITH MY PARENTS?
YEP.
IN QUEENS?
NO PROBLEMO.
EVEN THOUGH MY FEET SMELL LIKE DORITOS?
UH HUH.
EVEN THOUGH I SWEAT AT THE SLIGHTEST PROVOCATION?
FINE.
EVEN THOUGH I'M A VIRGIN?
DAMN RIGHT.
EVEN THOUGH I HAVE EXCESSIVE FLATULENCE?
HUH?
I FART ALOT?
YOU GOT IT, JACK.
EVEN THOUGH I'VE GOT PIMPLES ON MY BUTTOCKS?
YES.
WOW!! I CAN'T BELIEVE IT! YOU'VE MADE ME THE HAPPIEST CARTOONIST IN THE WORLD!!
CART--?
UH.
EXCUSE ME, I HAVE TO GO OVER THERE NOW.

IF YOU COULD HAVE BRUNCH WITH ANY FICTIONAL CHARACTER, WHO WOULD IT BE?
HOLDEN CAULFIELD.
KILGORE TROUT.
JESUS H. CHRIST.
THE VAMPIRE LESTAT.
DR. JOHN H. WATSON
ADRIAN MOLE, AGE 13¾.
HOMER SIMPSON.
DOES HE COUNT?

WELL, IT'S GETTING LATE, SO...
ONES TO LEAVE AGAIN?
SHIT! I GOTTA BE AT WORK IN FIVE HOURS!
WELL, THANKS FOR COMING GUYS.
THANK YOU SHERMAN
YEAH, SHERM IT WUZ FUN!
UH, IS SHE GONNA BE ALRIGHT?
DON'T WORRY, SHE'S LIKE THIS EVERY FRIDAY, RIGHT, KEL?
GONNA PUKE...
WELL, THANKS AGAIN, SHERMAN. IT WAS A BLAST!
WELL, SEE YOU AT WORK ON SUNDAY.
SURE, WE'LL HAVE TO DO IT AGAIN!
OKAY, SEE YA. BYE!
BYE! 'NIGHT.
whew.
SURRENDER DOROTHY or BANG! ZOOM!
IF I NEVER HOST ANOTHER PARTY IN MY LIFE IT'LL BE TOO SOON FOR ME.

YOU WANT ME TO STAY AND HELP YOU CLEAN UP, SHERM?
MMMM....? OH, NAH. I'LL DO IT TOMORROW. JANE AND STEPHEN DON'T GET HOME UNTIL AROUND SIX.
WELL, OKAY. I'LL TALK TO YOU TOMORROW THEN.
SAY, ARE YOU GOING TO SHOW JANE YOUR PAGES BEFORE THE BIG INTERVIEW?
Uh, NO. I DON'T THINK SO.
OKAY.. 'NIGHT ED. THANKS FOR COMING.
THANKS FOR INVITING ME.
G'NIGHT.
YAWN
KLANGA
KKLANG!
??

Uh...MISS? DO YOU NEED HELP?
I'M AFRAID THE PARTY'S OVER AND YOU'RE GONNA HAVE TO...
I'M STUCK.
"STUCK."
:SIGH: I WAS OUT HERE SMOKING A CIGARETTE --ABOUT 2 HOURS AGO-- AND MY LEGS GOT CAUGHT BETWEEN THESE BARS.
CHATEAU Le Cheap
WAIT A MINUTE...
:UMF:
HMM. IT LOOKS LIKE YOU'RE RIGHT. YOU'RE REALLY STUCK.
VERY GOOD, WATSON! NOW, HOW ABOUT GETTING A SAW OR SOMETHING AND GETTING ME OUT OF HERE, HM?

WELL, OKAY, BUT IF THAT LEG'S COMING OFF I BETTER GET SOME CLEAN TOWELS AND PEROXIDE.
OOOOH! YOU MEAN FOR... OKAY, I GET IT. BUT I THINK I'VE GOT A BETTER IDEA.
I'LL BE RIGHT BACK. DON'T GO AWAY!
HA.
VOILA!
Vaseline
PETROLEUM JELLY
CAN I ASK YOU WHAT YOU INTEND TO DO WITH THAT?
WE'LL JUST GREASE YOU UP AND SLIP YOU RIGHT OUT!
Vaseline

WE'LL HAVE YOU OUT IN A JIFFY.
I HAVE TO SAY, IF I HAD THOUGHT I WOULD BE USING LUBRICATION TONIGHT IT WASN'T FOR THIS.
WELL, THE NIGHT'S STILL YOUNG.
OH IT IS, IS IT?
OKAY, LET'S TRY IT.
Uh, PULLING YOU OUT, I MEAN.
ERF
OWOW OWOW!
OOOF! I'M FREE!
OUCH!
MY HERO! NEXT TIME I GO TO A PARTY I'LL BRING MY OWN VASELINE.
Whew!
Heh.

OC!! WHERE THE
L ARE YOU
OING?!?
I'VE GOTTA FIND ARYSA! STAY HERE AND WATCH THE KIDS!
BUT WHERE ARE--
"TO THE COMPUTER ROOM... I THINK I'VE FIGURED OUT WHO RATTED US OUT!"
I'M DEACTIVATING THE LAUNCH SYSTEM NOW... IN A MINUTE I.M.P.'S MISSLE COMMAND WILL BE USLESS.
MILADY... WE HAVE TO GO.
ARYSA, I CAN'T LET YOU DO THAT. WE HAVE
WHA-- MIHO, WHAT ARE YOU DOING?!
WELL? WELL? WHAT DO YOU THINK?

HUH? OH, YEAH, IT'S GREAT STUFF.
GOOD.
"GOOD?" I SPEND A HUNDRED PAGES BUILDING UP SUSPENSE ABOUT WHO THE TRAITOR IS AND WHEN I FINALLY REVEAL IT, IT'S "GOOD"?
I MEAN, WAS IT TOO OBVIOUS WHO IT WAS?
CUD
HMMM? OH, NO, THE INKING LOOKS FINE.
CUD
YOU'RE NOT EVEN PAYING ATTENTION ARE YOU? YOU'RE STILL THINKING ABOUT THAT FIRE ESCAPE GIRL I BET.
UH... YEAH, I GUESS I AM, SORRY.
IT'S OKAY, BUT DID SOMETHING GO ON THAT YOU'RE NOT TELLING ME?
NO, LIKE I SAID, AS SOON AS SHE WAS FREE, SHE SAID THANKS AND GOODBYE AND SHE LEFT.
I NEVER EVEN GOT HER NAME.
SO WHAT'S THE MATTER, THEN?
CUD

THERE WAS THIS ONE MOMENT WHERE I... YOU KNOW THAT FEELING? WHERE ALL THE LITTLE HAIRS ON YOUR NECK STAND UP AND YOUR STOMACH'S ALL...
I DON'T KNOW. I JUST HAVEN'T FELT THAT SENSATION SINCE SALLY AND I FIRST MET.
WELL, LET'S HOPE IT WORKS OUT BETTER THAN THAT DID.
SO WHY DON'T YOU CALL HER UP AND ASK HER OUT OR SOMETHING?
HEY, GUYS.
CUD
MILK
HEY, JANE, WHAT'S UP?
OH, NOT MUCH.
SORRY TO INTERRUPT, BUT IS THIS YOUR STUFF IN THE LIVING ROOM, ED?
BLESS This MESS
OH, YEAH. SORRY TO LEAVE A MESS.
NO! NO, IT'S REALLY GOOD. IT'S BEEN A LONG TIME SINCE I'VE READ ANY SCI-FI, BUT THIS SEEMS GREAT.
WHO'S YOUR PUBLISHER?
Pg 32
UH, WELL, NO ONE, ACTUALLY. I HAVE AN INTERVIEW AT ZOOM COMICS TOMORROW.

WOW! ZOOM! THE BIG BOYS! WELL, GREAT! GOOD LUCK!
THANKS, JANE. I'VE BEEN WORKING ON THIS STORY, WITH THE SAME CHARACTERS, SINCE LIKE EIGHTH GRADE.
CUD
ALL MY LIFE I'VE DREAMED OF WORKING FOR ZOOM COMICS!
BLESS this MESS
I'M JUST SO NERVOUS ABOUT IT. I HOPE IT WORKS OUT.
WELL, YOU COULD ALWAYS PUBLISH IT YOURSELF.
HEY, JAMES, WHAT'S UP?.... YEAH, NOTHING MUCH...
OH, THANKS FOR COMING, I'M GLAD YOU HAD A GOOD TIME... NO, NO, I RUBBED SOME SELTZER ON IT AND THE STAIN CAME RIGHT OUT. LISTEN, THERE WAS THIS GIRL AT THE PARTY... SHORT BROWN HAIR, REALLY CUTE... A BLACK SKIRT, DRESS TYPE THING. DID SHE COME WITH YOU?... DO YOU KNOW HER NAME OR ANYTHING?
NO, SORRY, SHERMAN. I THINK I REMEMBER HER, BUT SHE WASN'T WITH ME. YOU ASK JANICE?
EDWIN DROOD
UMM... NOPE. DOESN'T SOUND LIKE ANYONE I KNOW, SORRY.
WHATSAMATTER, THIS CHICK GIVE YOU CRABS OR SOMETHING?... NAH, I NEVER EVEN SAW HER.

WOW! I CAN'T BELIEVE HOW PERFECT WE ARE FOR EACH OTHER! WE BOTH LIKE LAUREL AND HARDY, RAYMOND CARVER, BILLY JOEL AND GYROS, WE BOTH HATE ROD STEWART, AND WE SHARE THE SAME INTELLIGENT, CYNICAL, YET HUMOROUS APPROACH TO LIFE! IT'S **AMAZING!**
LET'S HAVE SEX FOR HOURS, SOULMATE!
WOW! ISN'T THAT ED VELASQUEZ, THE CARTOOING GENIUS BEHIND THE Star Raiders™ THE NEWEST COMIC FROM ZOOM?
OH, ED, I'M SORRY I IGNORED YOU IN HIGH SCHOOL.
THAT'S OKAY, BABY. Heh Heh!
ED, I REPRESENT CADBURY FILMS AND WE'D LIKE TO MAKE A MAJOR MOTION PICTURE BASED ON YOUR COMIC!
Star Raiders
VOLUME TEN

DO YOU WORK HERE, PAL?
YES?
DO HAVE THE NEW ISSUE OF "REFRIGERATOR MAGNET COLLECTOR" MAGAZINE? IT'S $3.95.
NO, I'M SORRY, WE DON'T CARRY MAGAZINES
SO LIKE I WAS SAYING, I TRIED CALLIN
COULD YOU TELL ME WHERE I CAN FIND THEM?
MAGAZINES?
THERE'S A BIG MAGAZINE SHOP AT 22nd AND PARK AVENUE. MAYBE THEY WOULD HAVE IT.
OH? OKAY.
ANYWAY I TRIED TO CALL EVERY WHO WAS A PARTY AN
WHY COME YOU GUYS DON'T CARRY MAGAZINES? I'VE COME ALL THE WAY FROM UP TOWN.
WELL, I'M SORRY YOU TRAVELLED ALL THIS WAY, SIR, BUT WE STILL DON'T CARRY MAGAZINES.
NOT AT ALL?
NO.
ANYWAY, NO ONE SEEMS TO HAVE SEEN THIS MYST GIRL. I'M BEGI THINK I IMA WHOLE...
DO YOU THINK YOU COULD CALL THAT MAGAZINE STORE FOR ME? THE CURRENT ISSUE HAS AN INTERVIEW WITH RICK MORANIS.'
SIR, I -- UT!!

COMICS
EDITOR
TH--
AHEM!
THIS STUFF IS FUCKING GREAT, ED!

IT IS?!
ED, I'VE BEEN AN ASSISTANT EDITOR AT ZOOM FOR FIVE WEEKS NOW, AND THIS WORK IS ONE OF THE TOP SIX I'VE SEEN!
YOU MEAN -- I'M HIRED?
OF COURSE!
WELL, PROBABLY.
uh.
ED, I JUST HAVE TO RUN YOUR WORK BY THE SUIT-AND-TIE BOYS UP-STAIRS FOR THE FINAL GO AHEAD.
SO CAN YOU COME BY...FRIDAY SO WE CAN MAKE UP THE CONTRACTS?
SURE!
ED, IT'S BEEN A PLEASURE AND I LOOK FOWARD TO WORKING WITH YOU.

???
OH, RIGHT, RIGHT! THAT GUY FROM THAT PARTY!
THAT'S RIGHT, WITH THE FIRE ESCAPE AND EVERYTHING.
AND EVERYTHING, YES. SO YOU WORK AT THIS STORE?
YEAH, YEAH, AT LEAST UNTIL I CAN GET A WRITING GIG.
A WRITER! THAT MUST BE MARVELOUS
YEAH, WELL, SO WHAT ABOUT YOU? WHAT DO YOU DO?
OH, ME? I'M A WRITER.
BULLY
M. SERVINSKAS
TIME AND AGAIN AND AGAIN AND AGAIN
JACK FINNEY
CRAP
DANIELLE STEEL
OPEN WIDE!!
PAUL IS DEAD!
REALLY?! I MEAN YOU WRITE FOR A LIVING?
UH-HUH. I'M AN ASSISTANT EDITOR AT METRO-CHIC.
WOW, THAT MUST BE GREAT!
YEAH, IT'S OKAY
LET'S SEE, FIFTEEN, TWENTY TWO... SIX...
GROUCHO
...
SAY, UM, I HOPE YOU DON'T THINK THIS IS TOO, UH, FOWARD OF ME (I MEAN I DON'T EVEN KNOW YOUR NAME), BUT, UM, MAYBE, IF YOU'RE NOT TOO BUSY, YOU AND I CAN GET TOGETHER AND, UH, YOU KNOW, HAVE A CUP OF LUNCH OR A BITE TO COFFEE OR SOMETHING, HEH...
I MEAN IF YOU AREN'T TOO BUSY, I MEAN...

SURE, WHY NOT?
GREAT! GREAT! SO, UH, WHEN ARE...
WELL, HOW ABOUT WE DO IT -- GET TOGETHER -- ON FRIDAY... HOW'S 7:30 FOR YOU?
THAT WOULD BE GREAT.
MARVELOUS. HERE'S MY NUMBER. GIVE ME A CALL AND WE'LL SET IT UP.
WELL, I HAVE TO GET BACK TO WORK NOW, SO, UH, THANKS AND I'LL CALL YOU ABOUT FRIDAY!
OKAY, I'M LOOKING FOWARD TO IT.
AND SHERMAN, WAIT!
I FEEL WEIRD ASKING THIS BUT...
YOU GET AN EMPLOYEE DISCOUNT, RIGHT?

WHATCHA DOIN', BALLOO?
OH, RE-RE-READING CATTON'S THESIS FOR HIM. HE HANDS IT OVER TOMORROW.
HOW'S THE DRAWING GOING?
GROAN TERRIBLE. MY HANDS ARE REALLY SHAKEY FOR SOME REASON, I CAN'T INK.
HEY! I'VE GOT AN IDEA! LET'S TAKE A TWENTY MINUTE BREAK!
A BREAK? I ONLY STARTED TEN-- UT! MISSPELLED "GIDEON WELLES".
C'MON, STEPHEN, I REALLY THINK I NEED A QUICK, FAST BREAK.... JUST TO CALM MY NERVES...
JUST TO CALM YOUR NERVES, HM?
YEAH, I REALLY NEED THEM CALMED SOMETHING AWFUL...
WELL, AS LONG AS IT'S STRICTLY FOR THERA-PUTIC PURPOSES...

WAS SO NERVOUS! BUT I COULDN'T BELIEVE IT! SHE SAID YES! AND SHE'S CUTE, TOO. CUTER THAN SALLY!
3
AS SOON AS SHE LEFT, I REALIZED I STILL DON'T KNOW HER NAME!
OH YEAH?
3
SOMETIMES I FEEL LIKE I LIVE IN SOME SIT-COM.

HEY GUYS. YOU WANT TO GO TO DINNER?
IT'S ON ME...
DINNER? SURE.
HEH HEH...
YOUR FIRST DATE SINCE YOU AND SALLY BROKE UP? WOW!
YOU MUST BE EXCITED.
I WAS, AT FIRST. THEN I REALIZED I HAVE TO ACTUALLY GO ON THE DATE. NOW, IT'S MORE LIKE PANIC.

NOW, ED, YOU MUST BE EXCITED! GETTING HIRED BY ZOOM COMICS!
TAINS
I KNOW, AS LONG AS I'VE KNOWN YOU, YOUR LIFE'S DREAM HAS BEEN TO GET PAID TO DRAW COMICS!
YEAH, BUT I ALMOST HATE TO TALK ABOUT IT. I DON'T WANT TO JINX MYSELF.
YEAH, BUT THAT EDITOR GUY MADE IT SOUND AS IF IT WAS JUST A MATTER OF DOTTING THE AYES AND CROSSING THE TEES ON THE CONTRACT, RIGHT?
I GUESS SO... IT'S HARD FOR ME TO BELIEVE. I'LL FINALLY BE ABLE TO QUIT MY DAD'S STORE, MAYBE FINALLY GET MY OWN APARTMENT...
Uh, ED, I HAVE SOME BAD NEWS...
M

ED, I RAN YOUR PROJECT PAST THE BIG WIGS UPSTAIRS AND, Uh, THEY PUT THE KIBOSH ON IT...
I'M AFRAID WE WON'T BE HIRING YOU AT THIS JUNCTURE.
ZOOM
ED, I HOPE THIS DOESN'T...
BUT... BUT YOU MADE IT SOUND LIKE IT WAS A CINCH! LIKE IT WAS JUST A MATTER OF DOTTING THE TEES AND CROSSING THE AYES ON THE CONTRACT!
ED, I'M SORRY IF YOU MISUNDERSTOOD, BUT I'M A LOW MAN ON THIS TOTEM POLE. I CAN'T MAKE THIS KIND OF DECISION.
SWELL
ED... YOU'RE A GREAT CARTOONIST WHO DESERVES TO BE WORKING...
SO I'M GIVING YOU THIS.
A COFFEE FILTER?

A COFFEE FILTER WITH A NUMBER ON IT, ED, A TELEPHONE NUMBER OF A CARTOONIST LOOKING TO HIRE AN ASSISTANT.
OH, YEAH? WHO IS IT?
IRVING -- Uh, WAIT -- FLAVOR! IRVING FLAVOR.
WHO?
ACTUALLY, ED, HE'S AN OLD TIMER WE DON'T USE MUCH ANYMORE, BUT THE EXPERIENCE YOU'LL GET WORKING WITH HIM WILL BE INVALUABLE.
ALOT OF THE HOTTEST TALENT AROUND TODAY STARTED OUT AS ASSISTANTS. BILLY McKENICA STARTED AS A
ROBBIE GAR
"HERO SQUA
HELPED WIT
BACKGROUNDS
THIS ISN'T HAPPENING.
OH, YEAH?
SO NOT ONLY ARE THEY NOT GOING TO PUBLISH MY BOOK, BUT HE'S OFFERING ME A JOB SHARPENING PENCILS FOR SOME DINOSAUR.
ELPED INK NICKY AMENDOLA'S STUFF AT GHOSTED CHRIS C. ECKER FOR TWO YEARS! APPRENTICESHIP TO GET ILLS YOU NEED TO GET G IN THE FIELD. YOU WON'T GET ANYWHERE WITHOUT NETWORKING KISSING ASS OF EDITORS AND PUTTING IN YOUR
I GUESS SO.
SO, E
MAY
DAY
GOO
ENOU
WORK
ZOOM. BU OOKS. NOW, I GUESS RE NOT READY. BUT YOU'V GOT A LOT OF POTENTIAL, ED, SO DON'T GIVE UP!
THIS IS A NIGHTMARE. I SHOULD NEVER HAVE COME HERE. I'LL NEVER GET A CARTOONING JOB.
THANKS ALOT.
CAN I GO JUMP OUT THE WINDOW NOW?

ZOOM
271
U.S. MAIL
SIGH

HEY HEY HEY!
LOOKING SHARP, MR. MAN! YOU READY?
CIVIL WAR
I HOPE SO. GOD, I'M SO NERVOUS I FEEL LIKE I'M GOING TO PUKE.
DID YOU PUT ON NICE CLEAN KNICKERS? ARE YOU BRINGING ANY CONDOMS?
Uh, YES AND YES. WHY?
GOOD. IT MEANS YOU'RE GOING INTO THIS DATE WITH SELF-CONFIDENCE. YOU'LL DO FINE.
CIVIL WAR
WELL, I HOPE YOU'RE RIGHT. I HAVEN'T DONE THIS DATING THING IN --
SHIT!
I GOTTA GO, I'M MEETING HER AT THE THEATRE AT 7:30. I CAN'T BE LATE!
GOOD LUCK!

NIGHTSTALKE
ED WOOD
THEATR
TALKER 4
PLAYING
NIGHTSTALKER 4
ED WOOD
FJÖRD'S
THEATRE

SHERMAN!
HUH? OH, YOU MADE IT.
HI! WERE YOU JUST ABOUT TO LEAVE? I'M REALLY SORRY I'M LATE! REALLY, MY DOG WAS SICK.
MM, NOTHING SERIOUS, I HOPE.
OH, NO, JUST SOME HAIRBALL THING. GROMIT GETS THEM ALL THE TIME.
ARE WE TOO LATE FOR THE MOVIE?
WELL, THE MOVIE STARTED FIFTEEN MINUTES AGO, SO...
OOH, I'M REALLY SORRY. OKAY, HOW ABOUT WE JUST SKIP THE MOVIE AND EAT SOMEWHERE?
HOW ABOUT SLAGGER'S? IS THAT OKAY WITH YOU?
SLAGGER'S? SURE. OH, AND I GOT YOU THIS.
A ROSE! HOW PERFECTLY CHARMING! THANKS, SHERMAN.
YOU'RE WELCOME ...
I HAVE TO FIND OUT HER NAME!

GOOD EVENING, AND WELCOME TO SLAGGER'S...
LAST ZO
OMD
PRETTY CROWDED. DO YOU COME HERE OFTEN?
SOMETIMES AFTER WORK WE'LL -- OH! THERE'S A TABLE!
I HOPE THIS IS OKAY. IS IT? OKAY?
SURE. THIS IS FINE.
OKAY! NOW, I'LL BE RIGHT BACK, I HAVE TO USE THE CAN.
ACTUALLY, I HAVE TO USE THE TELEPHONE BUT I'M TO EMBARRASSED TO SAY SO. BACK IN A SEC!
HAVE A GOOD TIME.
SWILL

DRIVER'S LICENSE DRIVER'S LICENSE DRNER'S LICENSE HURRY BEFORE SHE GET'S BACK WHAT'S HER NAME HURRY BEFORE--UT!
!
WHAT IF SHE DOESN'T HAVE ONE? WHAT IF SHE BUSTS ME GOING THROUGH HER-- AHHA!
(YEESH, WHAT A PHOTO)
BEATRICE! HER NAME IS BEATRICE LESTRADE!
BEATRICE. BEATRICE. BEA. AUNT BEA. BEATRICE! BEATRICE!
CONDOM
READY TO EAT, SHERMAN?
I SURE AM ... BEATRICE.
WHY DID YOU CALL ME **THAT**?!

WHAT, HE DIDN'T GIVE YOU A REASON? HE HAD TO HAVE GIVEN YOU A REASON AT LEAST.
THE REASON WAS THAT I SUCKED, DAD, WE PLEASE TALK ABOUT ANYMORE
EDDIE, DON'T USE THAT LANGUAGE AT THE TABLE!
SORRY, MA.
OH YEAH, THAT REMINDS ME: I'M SCHEDULING YOU FOR AN EXTRA EIGHT HOURS AT THE STORE STARTING NEXT WEEK. YOU'LL--
EIGHT HOURS?! THAT'S A WHOLE 'NOTHER DAY! I WON'T HAVE TIME TO DRAW.
DRAW? EDDIE WE HAVE A STORE TO RUN. DRAWING DOESN'T PUT BREAD ON THE TABLE. HARDWARE DOES.
MARIA, WHERE'S THAT CHICKEN?
WELL, NOT YET IT DOESN'T BUT--
ONCE IT DOES YOU CAN DO WHATEVER THE HELL YOU WANT, BUT UNTIL THEN, AS LONG AS YOU'RE UNDER **MY** ROOF, EATING **MY** FOOD, WATCHING **MY** CABLE, YOU'RE **MINE** FOR AT LEAST THIRTY-TWO HOURS A WEEK... FORTY STARTING AS OF NEXT WEEK.

NOW PASS THE PEAS, PLEASE.
I TALKED TO MRS. TROUT YESTERDAY. HER SON, LEON, IS GOING INTO THE MARINES NEXT MONTH.
PURA
HUH, ABOUT TIME. THAT KID WAS A MESS.
I KNOW, I KNOW. HE GOT THAT POOR SLUT PREGNANT TOO!
IS SHE KEEPING IT?
EXCUSE ME, I HAVE TO GO TO THE BATHROOM.
SHE DOESN'T KNOW YET.
HELLO?
FLAVOR 555-1014
HELLO, MY NAME IS ED VELASQUEZ AND I WAS TOLD TO CALL YOU ABOUT THE ASSISTANT JOB?

WHAT I MEAN IS WHO TOLD YOU THAT WAS MY NAME?
(AND WHERE THE HELL IS THAT FUCKING LIGHTER?)
Uh, SOMEONE...
!!
SOMEONE WHO?
SOMEONE... AT THE PARTY?
WELL THAT ISN'T MY NAME, OKAY? I GO BY MIDDLE NAME, DOROTHY, OKAY? AND NOT "DOT" OR "DOTTIE" OR "DOR", DOROTHY.
GREAT! FINE! NO PROBLEM, DOROTHY.
Heh.
NOW, LET'S EAT!

THAT WAS GREAT.
MMM...MAN, IF I WASN'T ALWAYS SO BROKE, I'D EAT SLAGGER'S SPAGHETTI EVERY-NIGHT.
CAN I GET YOU SOMETHING ELSE?
YES, I'LL HAVE AN ALABAMA SLAMMER, PLEASE.
OH, UH, JUST A SCREWDRIVER FOR ME.
SO. I READ SOMEWHERE THAT METROCHIC HAD A BIG EDITORIAL SHAKE UP LATELY. IS THIS TRUE?
:SIGH: YEAH, A FEW MONTHS AGO THEY HIRED THIS NEW WOMAN TO REVAMP THE MAGAZINE.
IT'S A PUBLICITY STUNT MORE THAN ANYTHING ELSE. SHE ACTS LIKE SOME BIG QUEEN BEE BUT WE ALL HATE HER. SHE WON'T LAST.
STILL, IT'S WRITING, RIGHT?
A LITTLE. MOST OF IT IS PETTY OFFICE POLITICAL BULLSHIT.

HAVE YOU EVER HAD ANYTHING PUBLISHED, SHERMAN?

UH, I'VE TRIED SUBMITTING SOME -- UH, NO, I HAVEN'T, REALLY.

IT'S A TOUGH RACKET.

YEAH. ACTUALLY, I HAVEN'T BEEN ABLE TO WRITE AS MUCH AS I'D LIKE TO LATELY. THE DAMN BOOKSTORE WEARS ME DOWN.

HOW LONG HAVE YOU BEEN WORKING THERE?

HMM. IT WILL BE FOUR YEARS THIS OCTOBER. OY. I STARTED MY SOPHMORE YEAR.

WHAT SCHOOL DID YOU GO TO?

HUNTER, HERE IN THE CITY. ENGLISH MAJOR.

ME, TOO. ABOUT THE ENGLISH, I MEAN. I WENT TO SARAH LAWRENCE.

UH, ISN'T THAT A GIRL'S SCHOOL?

IT USED TO BE. I DID GO TO AN ALL-GIRL'S HIGH SCHOOL, THOUGH, AND AN ALL-GIRL COLLEGE MY FRESHMAN YEAR. IT WAS THE ONLY SCHOOL MY DAD WOULD PAY FOR, AT FIRST.

THAT MUST'VE BEEN ROUGH.

IT WAS, AT FIRST. THEN I GOT MYSELF KICKED OUT.

THEY KICKED YOU OUT? WHAT FOR?

WELL, IT SEEMS I WAS HAVING THIS LITTLE FLING WITH THE DEAN'S SON.

THEY KICKED YOU OUT FOR THAT?

WELL, IT ALSO SEEMS THIS DEAN'S SON WAS SIXTEEN YEARS OLD.

AAAH. THE JOEY BUTTAFUOCO OF THE SORORITY SET, eh?

MM. OR HUMBERT HUMBERT.

DID YOU GROW UP IN THE CITY?

YES. AND I WAS SUPPOSED TO BE BORN HERE, TOO, BUT I WAS BORN TWO WEEKS EARLY, WHILE MY PARENTS WERE ON VACATION IN JERSEY. IT WAS THE LAST TIME I WAS EARLY FOR ANYTHING.

HEY, I FROM NEW JERSEY, TOO!

IMAGINE THAT. DO YOU LIKE LIVING IN BROOKLYN?

YEAH. PARK SLOPE'S A GREAT NEIGHBORHOOD. BUT THE SAY IT'S GOING TO BE THE NEXT SEATTLE.

REALLY? I HEARD IT WAS GOING TO BE DES MOINES. DO YOU LIKE YOUR ROOMMATES?

YEAH, THEY'RE PRETTY COOL. JANE WANTS TO BE...

A CARTOONIST.

WOW. HOW DID YOU KNOW THAT?

HAHA. WELL, IT'S KIND OF FUNNY, BUT I USED TO BE THEIR ROOMMATE.

JESUS! YOU'RE KIDDING! WHAT A COINCIDENCE! WHEN WAS THIS?

I JUST MOVED OUT ABOUT SIX MONTHS AGO.

MAN. I CAN'T BELIEVE IT. WHY DID YOU MOVE OUT?

WELL, I NEEDED MORE SPACE AN

I WANTED TO LIVE IN MAN

HOW LONG HAVE YOU

NOW?

"LONGEST GIRLFRIEND?
Y MY ONLY SERIOUS RELATIONSHIP.
HER NAME WAS SALLY. WE BROKE UP THIS
ST FEBRUARY.
SIX MONTHS AGO? WHO DUMPED WHO?
SHE DUMPED ME FOR SOME LOSER. BUT IT WAS A LONG TIME COMING. I MEAN, WE'D BEEN SLOWLY DRIFTING APART FOR AWHILE. BUT WE WERE GOING OUT FOR ALMOST TWO YEARS.
WERE YOU IN LOVE WITH HER?
UM,.. I SUPPOSE I WAS. AT LEAST IN THE BEGINNING.
WOULD YOU GO OUT WITH HER AGAIN IF YOU COULD?
NO. WE'RE TOO DIFFERENT NOW. WE DIDN'T HAVE TOO MUCH IN COMMON TO BEGIN WITH, AND IT ONLY GOT WORSE. NO, I WOULDN'T. GO OUT WITH SALLY AGAIN, I MEAN. WHAT ABOUT YOU?
NAH, SALLY'S NOT MY TYPE.
HA HA, NO, I MEAN WHAT'S YOUR LONG-EST RELATIONSHIP?
HMMM, ACTUALLY, I GUESS IT WAS ONLY FOUR MONTHS, PRETTY SAD, eh? I'VE GONE OUT WITH MY SHARE OF GUYS, BUT THEY ALL TURNED INTO ASSHOLES SOONER OR LATER.
I'LL BEAR THAT IN MIND. YOU DON'T BELIEVE IN ASTROLOGY, DO YOU?
ASTROLOGY? NO.
THANK GOD.
SHERMAN, DO YOU HAVE ANY BROTHERS OR SISTERS?
I HAVE A YOUNGER BROTHER, JOE.
DOES HE WRITE, TOO?
JOE? JEEZ, NO, HE'S A MECHANIC. HE NEVER EVEN FINISHED HIGH SCHOOL BUT HE'LL PROBABLY MAKE MORE THAN EITHER OF US. AND YOU?
ONLY CHILD. WELL, ACTUALLY, I HAVE A HALF-BROTHER AND A HALF-SISTER.
WHAT WAS HE, A TRANS-SEXUAL?
NO, MY FATHER REMARRIED AFTER MY MOTHER DIED.
OH. UM, SORRY I BROUGHT IT UP.
NO, NO, I BROUGHT IT UP. GREAT SMALL TALK FOR A FIRST DATE, HUH?
ACTUALLY, UH, MY MOM DIED, TOO. WHEN I WAS FOURTEEN.
REALLY? WHAT WAS HER NAME?
HER NAME? JOANNE, WHY?
JUST CURIOUS, GEORGE.
WHY? WHAT WAS YOUR MOTHER'S NAME?
BEATRICE.
OH.

RESERVOIR DOGS WAS BETTER.
? HUH. I SAW "PULP FICTION" SEVEN TIMES.
SEVEN TIMES?! MAN, THAT'S FIFTY-SIX DOLLARS! FIVE C.D.S.
ACTUALLY, I SNUCK IN THE LAST FOUR TIMES. WHAT CAN I TELL YOU? IT WAS A GREAT MOVIE.
OKAY, HERE YOU GO: SUPPOSE THEY MADE A MOVIE OF YOUR LIFE, OKAY? WHO WOULD YOU WANT TO PLAY YOU?
YOU MEAN WHO LOOKS LIKE ME OR WHO WOULD PLAY ME BEST OR...?
YEAH, WHO WOULD PLAY YOU BEST.
HMMM... LINDA LAVIN.
LINDA LAVIN?! YOU MEAN T.V.'S "ALICE"?
SURE! WELL, A YOUNG LINDA LAVIN. SHE'S A FINE ACTRESS.
THAT'S HYSTERICAL. "KISS MAH GRITS!"
THAT WAS POLLY HOLIDAY, FLO, WISE GUY. WHY? WHO DO YOU THINK SHOULD PLAY ME?
UMMM... WINONA RYDER?
HA!
EITHER HER OR NELL CARTER.
OH, FUCK YOU. OKAY, YOU KNOW WHO SHOULD PLAY YOU? MR. SMARTY PANTS? RICK MORANIS!
WHAT? YOU'RE KIDDING. I HOPE YOU'RE KIDDING OR ELSE I'M GOING HOME.
HAHAHA! OKAY, OKAY, NO REALLY, YOU KNOW WHO CAN PLAY YOU? REALLY?
I HAVE A FEELING I DON'T WANT TO KNOW, BUT WHO?
JIMMY STEWART.
HA HEH, YEAH, RIGHT...
NO, REALLY...

SURE, A YOUNG JIMMY STEWART, WITH GLASSES, THE RIGHT HAIRCUT, I COULD SEE THAT.
WELL, HEH, MAYBE,
UM. I SHOULD PROBABLY GET GOING. IT'S LATE, RIGHT?
KISS HER YOU ASSHOLE! IT'S THE PERFECT TIME! KISS HER!!
Uh... Uh... I GUESS IT IS....
WHICH TRAIN ARE YOU GOING TO? I'LL WALK YOU THERE.
I'M GOING TO THE "F," BUT YOU DON'T...
NO, IT'S OKAY, I'M JUST GOING TO TAKE A CAB AFTER THAT.
THANKS AGAIN FOR THE FLOWER, SHERMAN.
DOROTHY! HOLD ON A SECOND!
HUH?

ED, THIS WORK IS AMAZING! I SHOULD BE THE ONE ASSTING YOU!
AH, YOU'RE JUST SAYING THAT TO GET IN PANTS, MISS FLAVOR.
NO, ED, I MEAN IT, YOU'RE ONE OF FINEST COMIC BOOK ARTISTS I'VE EVER SEEN!
BUT YOU'RE RIGHT, I DO WANT TO GET IN YOUR PANTS!
THIS IS MARCY AVENUE, LAST STOP IN BROOKLYN!
CRACKLE
SUCKERS!
PLAY LOTTO
1865/
MARCY AVE
APT 2
TAKE M/ TRAIN
2 BLOCKS

3L
bing bong!
COMING! HOLD YER DAMN HORSES!
Uh, I'M ED VELASQUEZ. I'M HERE FOR THE ASSISTANT JOB.
YER DAMN RIGHT YOU ARE!!

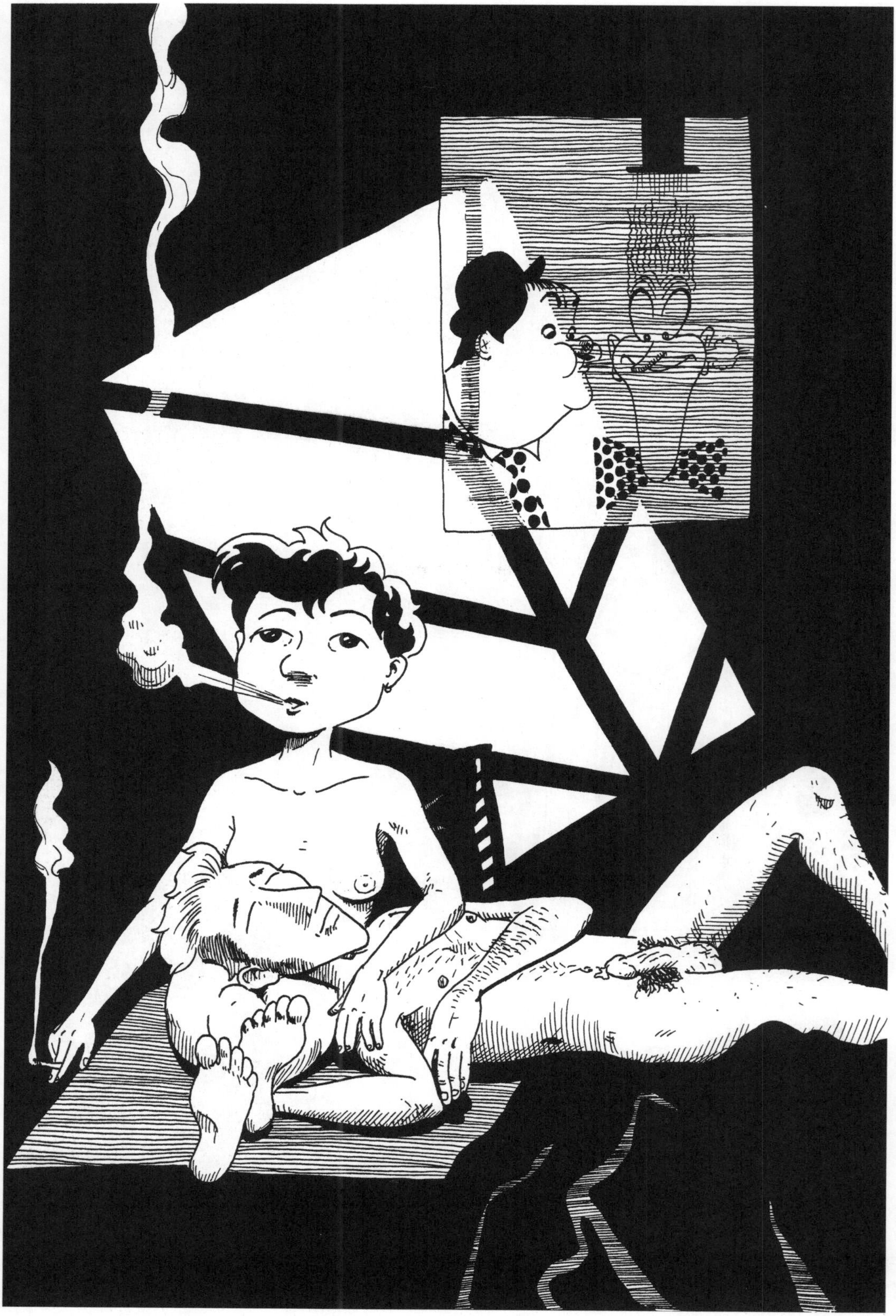

1030 KS
'MORNING MRS. TWEED.
GRUNT
HORRIBLE
AS
ARE
THE
DEAD
...
HONEY! I'M HOME!

WHAT HAPPENED? HOW'D IT GO?
WOOHOO!
THEY WENT FOR IT! THEY'RE GOING TO PUBLISH MY BOOK!!
GLORIOUS BURDEN
WOW! THAT'S GREAT!!
OOOH! I'M SO HAPPY!
HEY, LET'S GO OUT TO BRUNCH TO CELEBRATE!
MMM... CHAMPAGNE BRUNCH?
CHAMPAGNE? AS LONG AS WE'RE CELE--

IS SHE HERE AGAIN?
C'MON, HON, THEY'RE PUBLISHING YOUR EMMA GOLDMAN BOOK!
DON'T GET ALL IN A HUFF OVER A STUPID THING LIKE THIS! JUST PRETEND YOU NEVER SAW HER HERE.
YOU'RE RIGHT, YOU'RE RIGHT. IT DOESN'T AFFECT ME AT ALL, IT'S NONE OF MY BUSINESS.
GREAT. NOW LET ME GET MY SHOES ON AND WE'LL EAT.
BUT SHOULDN'T WE AT LEAST SAY SOMETHING TO SHERMAN? THEY'VE BEEN GOING OUT FOR LIKE TWO MONTHS AND IF SHE--
GROAN
JANE, IT'S NOT OUR BUSINESS!
BUT SHERMAN'S OUR FRIEND SO DOESN'T THAT MAKE IT OUR BUSINESS, STEPHEN?
YEAH, BUT...

I CAN JUST SEE IT! SHE'S BEING ALL NICE AND SWEET AND PURE, UNTIL SHE'S GOT HIM WHERE SHE WANTS AND THEN...
HER TRUE EVIL, DEMONIC, USING MESSY NATURE WILL TAKE OVER AND DRIVE POOR SHERMAN INSANE!
JUST LIKE SHE DID WITH US!
JANE, SHE WASN'T ALL THAT BAD, AN
"WASN'T THAT BAD?!" SHE..
AND... AND THAT WAS OVER A YEAR AGO. MAYBE SHE CLEANED UP HER ACT.
IT WAS TEN MONTHS AGO!
BUT MORE IMPORTANTLY, SHERMAN'S A BIG BOY WHO CAN TAKE CARE OF HIMSELF. IF HE WANTS OUR ADVICE, HE'LL ASK FOR IT.
NOW, C'MON, LET'S SCARF DOWN SOME PANCAKES AND MIMOSAS, HUH?
MMM... OKAY, OKAY, YOU'RE RIGHT. BUT IF HE DOES ASK, I WON'T LIE TO HIM, I'LL TELL HIM EVERYTHING!
FINE, FINE. CAN WE GO NOW?

...GLITTERING CROWDS AND SHIMMERING CLOUDS... IN CANYONS OF STEEL... THEY'RE MAKING ME FEEL... I'M HOME...
*"AUTUMN IN NEW YORK" PERFORMED BY BILLIE HOLIDAY
INK-B-GON
DOUBLE CROSS!! BRAND PEN NIBS
IT'S AUTUMN IN NEW YORK THAT BRINGS THE PROMISE OF NEW LOVE ...AUTUMN IN NEW YORK... IS OFTEN MINGLED WITH PAIN...
DREAMERS WITH EMPTY HANDS... MAY SIGH FOR EXOTIC LANDS... IT'S AUTUMN IN NEW YORK
IT'S GOOD TO LIVE IT AGAIN... AUTUMN IN NEW
KLK
GOOD MORNING, ED.
'MORNING MR. FLAVOR.

Grant knew he should've called out sick. "Do you work here?" the two hundred and fifty seventh customer asked.

"Yes, can I help you with something?" Grant replied for the two hundred and fifty seventh time.

"Do you have a book called Basic Reading and Writing Skills? It's for a class. My teacher said you should have it and it's definitely in stock."

How would your teacher know that you moron? "It should be in aisle five, all the way in the back of the store."

"Really? Where's that?" the student asked with a vacant stare.

Grant let out an audible contemptuous sigh. "All the way in the back of the store. Aisle five." What kind of world is this where idiots are going to college to learn Basic Reading and Writing Skills anyway? Shouldn't that--

"And it would definitely be there?" the student asked skeptically. "Could you show it to me?"

"You'll have to ask a clerk back in aisle five, sir." Grant responded in his iciest voice possible, and he'd had alot of practice lately so it was near absolute zero. The thick headed moron finally started walking away. "Can I help someone find a book?" Grant called to the swarming mob.

It was textbook season at Matthew's books again. Every year, Grant swore it would be his last. A cute girl approached Grant for help, which was trouble. As one of his co-workers pointed out, cute girls are the worst kind of customers because the only time they come into a bookstore is when they are forced to. When Chris told him this, Grant shook his head at the sexist and yet true nature of the comment.

"Do you work here?" the girl asked.

"Yes, can I help you with something?" Grant replied.

"Yeah, um, do you have...uh, Don Quick-sote? It's for my literature class?"

Ah. Don Quixote. "Hmmm. Do you know the author?" Grant couldn't wait.

"Uhhh..." the girl stammered as she scanned her syllabus. No one told her college would be this tough! "Servants?"

Yow, Grant thought, another one to tell everyone in the stockroom. Grant indicated ten feet to his left. "That would be on the fiction wall under the author's last name."

The girl smiled helplessly. "I looked but I couldn't find it. Could you maybe show it to me?" As she said this, Grant could sense her shifting into the If-I-Act-Cute-He'll-Give-Me-What-I-Want mode. Most guys fell for it like suckers, but Grant had been around long enough to know better. The hidden, sometimes deeply sometimes barely at all, subtext of the young girl's posturing was "If you find it for me I'll think you're cute and have sex with you." As stated, at this point, most guys would let their hormones do the thinking and show this girl everything, but Grant knew. She was just another stupid customer. He would show her all the books on her list and then she'd be gone.

When it came down to it, Grant just wasn't a people person.

"No, I'm afraid if it wasn't on the shelf then we are sold out." Grant smiled limply. Why doesn't your Monday Night Football asshole boyfriend find it for you?

IT'S... WELL, I DON'T GET IT. I MEAN, I UNDERSTAND IT... BUT...
WHAT DO YOU MEAN? JAMES READ IT AND HE SAID IT WAS HYSTERICAL.
THAT'S PROBABLY BECAUSE JAMES WORKED AT THE BOOKSTORE WITH YOU. IT'S ALMOST LIKE AN INSIDE JOKE
HAVE YOU SHOWN IT TO ANYONE ELSE?
NAH... I DON'T KNOW. I GUESS IT WAS JUST SOMETHING I NEEDED TO GET OFF MY CHEST. I HATE THAT FRIGGIN' PLACE.
YOU SHOULD QUIT.

NOW WHY DIDN'T I THINK OF THAT!
OH! SPEAKING OF QUITTING!
I WAS TALKING TO LARRY VIVRON AT WORK YESTERDAY AND HE TOLD ME THAT THAT CUNT STILL BLAMES ME FOR LOSING THAT ROLLERBLADING PIECE!
CAN YOU BELIEVE IT?!
CHRIST! I'M THE ONE WHO SHOULD QUIT!
DICTIONARY
WAS THIS THE ARTICLE THAT YOU GAVE TO THAT CABBIE TO GIVE TO HER DOORMAN THAT SUNDAY NIGHT?
EXACTLY. CAN YOU BELIEVE IT? I MEAN I AM RIGHT, RIGHT?
UM.
WHAT?
SHE PROBABLY LOST IT AFTER HER DOORMAN GAVE IT TO HER AND NOW SHE'S TRYING TO SET ME UP AS HER OSWALD.
YEAH, YOU'RE PROBABLY RIGHT.
OH YEAH. ON FRIDAY I'M SUPPOSED TO GO TO THE MOVIES WITH ED. DO YOU WANT TO GO?
WHO'S ED? THAT TALL BLACK GUY FROM YOUR STORE?
NO, ED'S THE GUY WE SHOT POOL WITH LAST MONTH. SHORT, SHAVED HEAD?
OH, OKAY.

WHAT MOVIE?
"NIGHTSTALKER FOUR". THAT SUPER HERO MOVIE.
MMM... NAH. WHY DON'T YOU JUST MAKE IT A BOY'S NIGHT OUT?
I'LL STILL GET TO SEE YOU NEXT WEEKEND, RIGHT?
SURE, I'LL COME OVER SATURDAY.
HEY, I'VE GOT AN IDEA. WHY DON'T I COME TO YOUR PLACE SATURDAY?
M-MY PLACE? WHY?
CUZ I'VE ONLY BEEN THERE ONCE. AND BESIDES, WOULDN'T IT BE GREAT TO HAVE A WHOLE PLACE TO OURSELVES?
WE COULD RUN AROUND NAKED!
SATURDAY NIGHT? ARE YOU SURE?
YEAH. ALSO THAT WAY I COULD JUST WALK TO WORK ON SUNDAY.
I GUESS SO. OKAY.
GREAT!
MAN, I HAVEN'T SEEN ED IN AGES.

NO.... NONONONO.
WHAT? WHAT'S WRONG WITH IT? IT LOOKS FINE!
NO, NO, IT DOESN'T LOOK FINE. HE LOOKS LIKE HE'S ON HIS WAY TO A DAMNED FUNERAL!
YOU GOT TO MAKE HIM SILLY! WACKY!
NO. NO.
MR. FLAVOR, WHAT COMIC BOOK IS THIS FOR, ANYWAY?
COMIC BOOK? KID, THIS IS FOR SOME DAMN CEREAL BOX.
"ZIGGY FLAKES OR "SICKY CHIPS" OR SOMETHING...
SUGAR
CEREAL BOX?!
I THOUGHT I WAS SUPPOSED TO BE ASSISTING YOU ON COMICS!
WHAT, YOU'RE SO GREAT YOU THINK YOU CAN JUST JUMP RIGHT IN MR. HOTSHOT O'BIG TIME? YOU THINK YOU CAN DO IT, HUH?
SURE!
FUCK YOU.
DO THAT "SNOOKY" BOX AGAIN AND MAYBE I'LL LET YOU DO A PAGE
COMICS

A CEREAL BOX!
HAHAHA! KID, YOU KNOW WHO YOU REMIND ME OF? YOU REMIND--HEH HEH -- YOU REMIND ME OF TOMMY JANGKOWSKI BACK IN THE OLD DAYS! HAHA! GOOD OLD TOMMY!
WHO'S TOMMY JANGKOWSI?
YOU DON'T KNOW TOMMY JANGKOWSI? HE INKED MY WORK ON "CAPTAIN COMPOUND" FOR ZOOM COMICS FROM '59 TO '63...
BEST INKER IN THIS DAMNED BUSINESS.
OH YEAH? IS HE STILL WORKING?
NAH... HE'S PASSED AWAY. ZOOM GAVE HIM THE AXE IN '74.
IMAGINE THAT? HE WORKS FOR THEM FOR TWENTY-TWO YEARS, THEN FFT! THOSE SONS OF BITCHES FIRE HIM. NO PENSION, NO THANK YOU, NO NOTHING.
I TOLD HIM... YOU KNOW WHY THEY FIRED HIM? A UNION. SOME YOUNG UPSTART FELLAS WERE TRYING TO START A UNION. HE THOUGHT IT WAS A GOOD IDEA...
I TOLD HIM, I TELL HIM "TOMMY, ZOOM WON'T LIKE IT, THE COMPANY DON'T LIKE THIS UNION STUFF."
"DON'T ROCK THE BOAT!"

HE STARTED TALKING ABOUT HOW IT WAS SOMETHING WE ALL HAD TO DO. WE COULD GET ALL SORTS OF, LIKE, BENEFITS: HEALTH CARE, RETIREMENT PLANS. WE WOULD EVEN GET TO KEEP OUR ARTWORK.
DID... DID YOU JOIN?
OF COURSE NOT!
YOU KNOW WHY? EVEN THEN, I KNEW YOU CAN'T FIGHT CITY HALL, ED. AND YOU KNOW WHAT HAPPENED, RIGHT? WHAT HAPPENED TO TOMMY?
THEY FIRED HIM.
ZOOM FIRED MOST OF 'EM. MOSTLY OLDER GUYS WHO WEREN'T AS POPULAR ANYMORE. LIKE TOMMY.
HE TRIED GETTING WORK AT OTHER COMIC COMPANIES, BUT NO ONE WOULD TOUCH HIM. AND THERE AREN'T TOO MANY OTHER THINGS SUPER-HERO GUYS CAN DO.
LIKE I SAID, HE'S DEAD NOW.
THE POINT I'M TRYING TO TELL YOU, KID, IS... THIS IS A TERRIBLE BUSINESS. THEY'LL CHEW YOU UP AND THROW YOU OUT LIKE YESTERDAY'S CABBAGE. SO YOU ALWAYS GOTTA LOOK OUT FOR NUMBER ONE: YOU!
I GUESS SO...
BUT WOULDN'T THE UNION HAVE WORKED IF EVERYONE JOINED? THEN IT WOULD HAVE...
INK

THEN THEY WOULD'VE FIRED EVERYONE!! THEY'LL FIRE ALL OF US!!
THEY CAN'T FIRE EVERYONE, THEY STILL NEED TO PUBLISH COMICS TO...
NO, NO. YOU'RE WRONG. YOU'RE WRONG. THEY...
I MEAN, AS LONG AS NO ONE CAVED IN, THE COMPANY WOULD HAVE--
NO! NO! YOU'RE WRONG! YOU DON'T KNOW WHAT THE HELL YOU'RE TALKING ABOUT!!
NOW, DO THAT DAMN BOX COVER AGAIN AND DON'T BOTHER ME AGAIN!!!
YES, SIR
SLAM
STUPID OLD GOAT

THANKS, SPIKE, GOOD WORK!
ALRIGHT, AM I GOING TO ... OR WILL YOU ... NASTY OR WILL YOU ... WHO SENT YOU?
L-LORD FYRE...
DAMN!
MAN! YOU REALLY BEAT THE TAR OUTTA THAT GUY! HAHA!
HAHAHA!
HMM! HOW DID LORD FYRE KNOW WHERE WE WERE? IN ANY CASE WE OBVIOUSLY HAVE TO GET MOVING!
C'MON, BOYS!
YOU DID ALL OF THIS YOURSELF?
WHO'D YOU DO IT FOR?
OH, IT'S SOMETHING I'VE BEEN WORKING ON FOR YEARS.
YEAH, HUH?
WELL I HATE TO BE THE ONE TO BREAK IT TO YOU, KID, BUT NO ONE BUYS SCI-FI ANYMORE.
YOU WON'T GO ANYWHERE WITHOUT DOING SUPER-HEROES.
I GUESS SO.
BUT THIS GIRL I KNOW, JANE, WAS TELLING ME ALL ABOUT SOME OF THESE, UH, "ALTERNATIVE" PUBLISHERS?
SOME OF THEM DON'T EVEN PUB-LISH SUPERHEROES!

YEAH, WHAT DO THEY DO? WESTERNS? ROMANCE? YOU PROBABLY GOT SOME OF YOUR WAR COMICS?
YOUR KIDDIE BOOKS AND WHAT NOT?
ACTUALLY FROM WHAT I'VE SEEN, THEY PUBLISH ALL KINDS OF WEIRD STUFF. HUMOR, AUTOBIOGRAPHY, SEX COMICS, SOME SCI-FI STUFF.
THERE'S EVEN A BOOK CALLED "SERBIA", BY A CARTOONIST WHO SPENT TIME THERE.
YOU KNOW, "REAL LIFE."
SAFFRON
"REAL LIFE?" THESE ARE COMIC BOOKS, FOR CHRIST'S SAKE! NO ONE WANTS TO READ ABOUT THAT!
AND BESIDES, IF ALL THIS STUFF WAS SO GOOD, HOW COME THEY DON'T MAKE 'EM ANYMORE, HANH?
THEY DO STILL MAKE THEM!
SOME OF THOSE BLACK AND WHITE ALTERNATIVE COMICS ARE --
WAIT A MINUTE, DID YOU SAY THESE COMICS ARE IN BLACK AND WHITE?! HOW MANY COPIES DO THEY SELL EVERY MONTH?
WHAT, IT CAN'T BE MORE THAN, WHAT, 100? 150 THOUSAND?
UM. I THINK SHE SAID THE MOST POPULAR ONE, "BILE" SELLS ... UH....
30,000 COPIES...
AND IT COMES OUT ONLY THREE -- MAYBE FOUR -- TIMES A YEAR.
YEAH, SO LIKE I WAS SAYING:
YOU WON'T GO ANYWHERE IN COMICS UNLESS YOU DRAW SUPERHEROES.

YES, YES.
YES! THAT'S IT, ED, YOU GOT THAT DAMN KOOKINESS!
WELL, THIRD TIME'S THE CHARM, I GUESS.
SO NOW CAN I DO A REAL COMIC BOOK PAGE?
ENHHHHH...
SURE.
OKAY, SO IN THIS LAST PANEL, CAPTAIN FORCE TURNS AND HE SAYS, HE SAYS, "KIDS! BEATING UP VILLAINS IS MY JOB. YOUR JOB IS TO SAY NO TO DRUGS!"
OKAY. I'VE ROUGHED IN THE PENCILS HERE, SO NOW ALL YOU GOT TO DO IS TIGHTEN THEM UP, LETTER THE PAGE AND THEN INK THE DAMN THING, OKAY?
GOTCHA.
OH, AND HERE LET ME GIVE YOU THESE.

WHAT IS THIS? A BUNCH OF RIPPED UP OLD COMICS?
THESE ARE YOUR "MORGUE" SHOTS. THESE ARE COMIC PANELS I WANT YOU TO COPY, TO SWIPE. FOR THE STORY AND EVERYTHING.
?? SWIPE THEM? YOU MEAN PLAGIARISM?
AAGH
IT'S NOT "PLAGIARISM." YOU'RE USING REFERENCE. EVERYONE DOES IT.
I GUESS SO...
OF COURSE. NOW GET TO WORK.
I GOTTA USE THE CAN.
OOOF!
DON'T LOOK NOW, TOUGH GUY! YOUR TIME IS UP!
MR. FLAVOR, YOU EVER WORK WITH JACK KIRBY?

JACK? SURE. HE DID A TURN WITH US AT ZOOM AFTER HE FIRST LEFT MARVEL.
DECENT GUY. HELL OF A GUY. HELL OF AN ARTIST, TOO.
YEAH.
I CAN'T BELIEVE HOW BADLY MARVEL TREATED HIM. HE CREATED ALL OF THEIR BIG CHARACTERS AND THEY TREATED HIM LIKE SHIT.
VINCENT PRICE DEAD
YEAH, WELL, JACK WAS A BIG BOY. HE KNEW WHAT HE WAS GETTING INTO. HE KNEW THAT THE COMPANY OWNED WHATEVER HE DID.
OCTOBER 26, 1994 50¢ CLOUDY, RAINS
BROOKLYN POST
VINCENT PRICE DEAD
HORROR STAR DEAD AT 82
YEAH, BUT HE HAD NO WAY OF KNOWING THAT MARVEL WOULD MAKE MILLIONS OFF OF HIM! I'M SURE HE WOULD'VE --
HE STILL WOULD'VE WORKED FOR THEM! IN THOSE DAYS IT WAS THEIR WAY OR THE HIGHWAY.
I GUESS SO.
STILL, I THINK WILL EISNER PROBABLY HAD THE RIGHT IDEA. HE WORKED OUT A DEAL TO OWN ALL HIS WORK. I KNOW MARVEL MADE MORE, BUT I'M SURE EISNER MADE A PRETTY PENNY.
EISNER'S A SCHMUCK.

EISNER? WILL EISNER?! GET OUT OF HERE?
HE'S A GENIUS!
A GENIUS? NO.
BEETHOVEN IS A GENIUS. PICASSO IS A DAMNED GENIUS. THAT GUY, GATE, WHO INVENTED COMPUTERS IS A GENIUS.
EISNER'S SOME CARTOONIST.
SO, WHAT, BECAUSE HE'S A CARTOONIST HE CAN'T BE A GENIUS?
THAT'S RIGHT, THAT'S RIGHT.
WHY?
ED. LOOK AT THE BUSINESS WERE IN. COMICS ARE NOT SOMETHING YOU ASPIRE TO. MOST CARTOONISTS REALLY WANT TO DO SCI-FI BOOK COVERS AND OTHER SERIOUS ILLUSTRATION WORK.
HOW CAN YOU SAY THAT?! THERE ARE A LOT OF CARTOONISTS WHO LOVE CARTOONING, WHO LOVE COMICS!
YEAH, AND YOU KNOW WHAT THEY'RE CALLED? LOSERS.
WHAT?!
WHO ELSE WOULD SPEND EIGHT HOURS DOING A PAGE OF DRAWINGS FOR $50 WHEN THEY COULD DO A SERIOUS ILLUSTRATION IN HALF THAT TIME AND GET PAID TEN TIMES AS MUCH?
NOT TAKE INTERNALLY
JITTER COFF
MAYBE BECAUSE THEY LOVE DOING IT AND IT GIVES THEM A SATISFACTION THAT ILLUSTRATION DOESN'T.
YEAH, WELL SO DOES JERKING OFF BUT YOU'D BE A FOOL TO TURN DOWN A GOOD PAYING JOB FOR THAT.

"JERKING --?!"
later...
Z Z Z Z
MR. FLAVOR. WAKE UP.
MR. FLAVOR, I'M LEAVING AND I NEED MY MONEY.
SNFX WHA..
LEAVING? IT'S ONLY 6:00, ED, YOU'RE SUPPOSED TO STAY UNTIL 7:30.
MR. FLAVOR, I TOLD YOU, I NEEDED TO LEAVE EARLY TODAY, REMEMBER?
SO CAN I HAVE MY MONEY?
DAMN, YOU'RE RIGHT, I'M SORRY. LET ME GET IT NOW.
SO HOW MANY HOURS DO I OWE YOU?
FORTY FOUR.

OKAY, OKAY. WHAT'RE YOU LEAVING EARLY FOR? YOU GOT A BIG HOT DATE OR SOMETHING?
NO. I'M GOING TO THE MOVIES WITH A FRIEND.
WHAT'RE YOU SEEING? THAT NEW STALLONE MOVIE? THAT'S SUPPOSED TO BE GOOD, RIGHT?
NO. WE'RE SEEING "NIGHTSTALKER IV".
UH... YEAH, YEAH, I HEARD THAT WAS SUPPOSED TO BE GOOD...
YEAH.
HERE YOU GO ED.
THANK YOU.
WELL... I'LL SEE YOU ON MONDAY. DON'T BE LATE, HEH.
I WON'T.
HEY, AND BRING IN THOSE COMICS TO SHOW ME! MAYBE I CAN GIVE YOU SOME POINTERS!
HEH HEH!
I WILL.

URE EVIL!
IF I EVER SEE YOU AROUND HERE AGAIN,
BRIDGMAN
HOGARTH

WHO DIRECTED "HALLOWEEN"?
JOHN CARPENTER.
I THINK
WHERE'S SHERMAN TONIGHT? OH, WAIT, LET ME GUESS:
HE'S OUT WITH HER.
BUZZZ TRY AGAIN.
ACTUALLY, HE SAID HE WENT TO THE MOVIES WITH ED.
REALLY? GOOD. MAYBE HER VOODOO SPELL ON HIM ISN'T AS STRONG AS WE FEARED.
ANARCHY
WELL, HE DID SAY HE WAS GOING TO HER PLACE TOMORROW.
WHAT'S A FIFTEEN LETTER WORD FOR "CINEMATIC BOMB ELEMENT"?
FIRST LETTER IS "B".
ANARCHY
WAIT, HE'S GOING TO HER HOUSE?
THAT'S WHAT I WAS LED TO BELIEVE.
EXCELLENT...

SECRET OF THE NIGHTSTALKER
NOW PLAYING NIGHTSTALKER
THIS GUY FLAVOR SOUNDS LIKE A REAL BASTARD.
I KNOW. IF I WANTED THIS KIND OF ABUSE I'D STAY AT MY DAD'S SHOP. I SHOULD HAVE TOLD HIM OFF RIGHT THEN AND THERE.
BUT I'M NOT GOING BACK, THAT'S FOR SURE.
NIGHT STALKER
SO, WHAT NOW? BACK TO THE HARDWARE STORE?
UGH. I DON'T KNOW. MAYBE I'LL TRY SOMETHING DIFFERENT. IS YOUR BOOK STORE HIRING?
ED, I WOULDN'T WISH THAT ON ANYONE.
SIGGY THE MOVIE
DEADMAN
GOOF

I HEARD THIS "NIGHTSTALKER" IS SUPPOSED TO BE THE BEST OF THE FOUR.
IT SHOULD BE. WHAT, DID IT MAKE SEVEN BILLION DOLLARS SO FAR?
BEATLES
YEAH, BUT I'M GLAD A MOVIE BASED ON A COMIC IS DOING WELL.
OH YEAH? WHY'S THAT?
BEATLES
WELL, IT'LL PROBABLY GET MORE PEOPLE TO READ COMICS. IT'LL PUT US ONE STEP CLOSER TO BEING ACCEPTED AS REAL ART.
A MOVIE STARRING A GUY IN MOLDED RUBBER MUSCLES IS GOING TO ELEVATE COMICS TO "REAL ART"?
GO AHEAD! THEY LAUGHED AT ED WOOD, TOO, Y'KNOW!
IF THIS MOVIE IS ONE-TENTH AS GOOD AS ED WOOD I'LL BE HAPPY.
MAN, LOOK AT THEM...
ED, I KNOW I'M A MARRIED MAN, BUT THERE ARE SOME DYNAMITE CHICKS IN THIS TOWN.
YOU DON'T HAVE TO TELL ME...
THAT REMINDS ME, HOW'S IT GOING WITH THAT GIRL, WHAT WAS HER NAME, BE... BEATRICE?
DOROTHY. IT'S DOROTHY. THINGS ARE GOING PRETTY WELL. I'M SUPPOSED TO GO TO HER PLACE TOMORROW NIGHT.
OH, WELL EXCUSE ME!

FUCK YOU, AND YOUR LITTLE "OH-I'M-GOING-TO-MY-LITTLE-GIRLFRIEND'S-HOUSE-TONIGHT," YOU SON OF A GOD DAMNED BITCH!
HAHAHA! YOU JEALOUS BASTARD.
I KNOW, I KNOW. YOU'RE RIGHT. :UGH: I NEED A GIRLFRIEND. THIS VIRGINITY IS KILLING ME. IF I DON'T GET A GIRLFRIEND SOON, I'LL GO CRAZY.
AT THIS POINT, I SHOULD JUST GO TO A--
Welcome! to VIVRON CINEMAS
UT! IT'S STARTING!
I HOPE THERE'S GOOD PREVIEWS.
SHH!
ONCE IN EVERY GENERATION THERE COMES A FILM LIKE NO OTHER... COMING THIS SPRING FROM FAMILY FILMS, TOMMY BRAD IN..."CATCHER"
BUD
BUT DON'T YOU WONDER WHERE THE DUCKS GO IN WINTER, PHEBE?
OH, HOLDEN! :giggle:
IF YOU LOVED HIM ON "SATURDAY NIGHT LIVE", YOU'LL LOVE TWO HOURS OF HIM IN..."FAT GUY"!
DONNIE DEDVED CALLED IT: "PULP FICTION WITHOUT ALL THAT DIALOGUE"... IT'S "DEAD MEAT"
IT'S THE END OF THE WORLD, ED...
HEY BUDDY, SHUT UP!
SHHH! IT'S STARTING!

WELL, DOC, IT DOESN'T LOOK LIKE ADMIRAL ARMOR WILL BE BOTHERING US AGAIN.
COME ON, LET'S GO HOME AND TAKE A LONG HOT BATH...
JESUS... IS IT FINALLY OVER? ARE WE ALLOWED TO GO HOME NOW?
OH, COME ON, IT WASN'T THAT BAD. YOUR STANDARDS ARE TOO HIGH.
DOUBLE CROSS
YEAH, SOMEHOW I PICKED UP THIS CRAZY IDEA THAT MOVIES SHOULD HAVE JUNK LIKE PLOTS AND GOOD CHARACTERIZATION.
WELL, THIS WASN'T THAT KIND OF A MOVIE. YOU CAN'T JUDGE A ROLLER-COASTER BY THE SAME STANDARDS AS--
OHMYGOD! SHERMAN! LOOK AT THE CREDITS!
WHAT? "NIGHSTALKER IS A REGISTERED TRADEMARK OF ZOOM COMICS INTERNATIONAL, A DIVISION OF BEHEMOTH BANKS?" SO WHAT?
F BEHEMOT
NIGHTSTALKER CREATED BY IRVING FLAVOR
NO! UNDER THAT!
MR. FLAVOR...

SEE THAT'S JUST IT: I'M SURE MR. FLAVOR DOESN'T MAKE A NICKEL ON ANY OF IT. THE MOVIES, THE TOYS, THE T-SHIRTS, EVEN THE COMICS. ZOOM OWNS NIGHTSTALKER LOCK, STOCK AND BARREL.
MAMF, DAF SHUCKS... gulp
BUT CAN'T HE SUE OR ANYTHING?
PROBABLY NOT. EVEN IF HE'S IN THE RIGHT, IT MEANS SUING A HUGE CORPORATION WITH TONS OF LAWYERS. HE COULDN'T AFFORD TO FIGHT.
YEAH, BESIDES, HE PROBABLY TRIED EVERYTHING HE COULD.
MAN. I USED TO LOVE THAT NIGHTSTALKER COMIC BOOK.
"JUSTICE COMES BY NIGHT."
WELL, I GUESS WE'LL CALL IT A NIGHT.
HMMM. IT'S STILL KIND OF EARLY.
DOROTHY JUST LIVES UP ON 23rd MAYBE I'LL PAY HER A SURPRISE VIST. YOU WANT TO COME?
IT'S TEMPTING, BUT I'LL LEAVE YOU LOVEBIRDS ALONE.
SEE YOU LATER.

MA, I'M HOME!
SHHH! I FINALLY GOT YOUR FATHER TO SLEEP! TRY NOT TO MAKE SO MUCH NOISE.
OH, SORRY.
WHILE YOU WERE OUT YOUR BOSS CALLED, THAT ARTIST...
MR. FLAVOR? WHAT DID HE SAY?
HE SAID YOU DON'T HAVE TO BE AT THE STUDIO UNTIL NOON ON MONDAY.
ARE YOU HUNGRY? DO YOU WANT SOME RICE?
NAH, I'VE HAD A LONG DAY. I'M JUST GOING TO GO TO BED.
'NIGHT, MA.
GOODNIGHT, EDUARDO.
Soda
"JUSTICE COMES BY NIGHT"...

WHAT'S THE STRANGEST PLACE YOU'VE MADE WHOOPEE ?
ON THE ROOF OF MY GIRLFRIEND'S APARTMENT BUILDING.
WHOOPEE?
YOU MEAN, LIKE, CHEWBACCA?
HMMM...
PROBABLY ON THE "M" TRAIN,
CHRISTMAS EVE, 1989
UH, ON MY PARENT'S KITCHEN TABLE.
EVERYONE ELSE WAS ASLEEP.
CORPORATE COMICS SUCK
UP THE BUTT. HA HA!
ACTUALLY, IN THE MOVIES. DURING "THREE AMIGOS."
WHAT A SHITTY MOVIE!
THE WOODS?
YOU KISS YOUR MOTHER WITH THAT MOUTH?
GET YOUR DAMNED MIND OUT OF THE GUTTER.
A WHORE-HOUSE IN TORONTO.

PEEP SHOW
SHERMAN! WHAT ARE YOU DOING HERE?
WHAT A PLEASANT SURPRISE...
ARE YOU SURE? I HAVE A FEELING I CAUGHT YOU AT A BAD TIME.
NO, NO, I WAS JUST IN THE MIDDLE OF SOME CLEANING.
IT'S MARVELOUS TO SEE YOU.
MMM....

SO...
SO. HehHeh.
UH, DOROTHY, I'M GETTING THE IMPRESSION YOU DON'T WANT ME TO COME INSIDE.
WHAT?! OH, NONONONO! No. NO! I DO. I DO.
SO...?
WELL, LIKE I SAID I WAS IN THE MIDDLE OF CLEANING, SO IT'S A BIT OF A MESS.
MY STUDIO.
I DON'T CARE ABOUT THAT!
BELIEVE ME, THE DORM I LIVED IN IN COLLEGE WAS CONDEMNED BY THE NUCLEAR REGULATORY COMMISSION.
NO, REALLY, IT'S A MESS.
I'M SURE I'VE SEEN WORSE. LET'S GO IN.
OKAY, OKAY. BUT JUST SO YOU KNOW, IT'S ONLY BECAUSE I'VE BEEN SO BUSY AT THE MAGAZINE THAT I HAVEN'T CLEANED.
I DON'T NORMALLY LET IT GET THIS FAR OUT OF HAND, OKAY?
THIS BETTER CAUSE CANCER IN LAB RATS FOR ALL THE FUSS YOU'RE MAKING.
AND NO WISE-ASS COMMENTS, OKAY?

SIGGLY CHIPS
DR. P SICIAN'S SALTED TREATS
SIGGLY CHIPS
BEE
BARK! BARK! BARK! BARK! BA
NO WISE ASS COMMENTS...
GROMIT, SHUT-UP!
UH.
HEY! I'VE GOT AN IDEA! LET'S GO OUT FOR A DRINK!
WHY DON'T YOU RUN DOWNSTAIRS AND PICK UP A BOTTLE OF ABSOLUT TO KICK THINGS OFF?
SURE, OKAY.
BUT I'LL GET POPOV OR SOMETHING. THAT ABSOLUT'S OUT OF MY BUDGET.
GREAT! I'LL GET READY WHILE YOU'RE GONE!
METRO

CLOSED
YANKOV VODKA
QUICK! IS HE LOOKING? NOW? NOW?
WAIT... OKAY! DO IT! HE'S NOT LOOKING!
UNDER 21
Jackie Marlon BEER
OH YEAH!
BIFF TOUC
HURRY UP! HE'S RINGIN' UP SOME GUY!
JUST THIS PLEASE.
WAIT! IS HE LOOKING?
NO! HURRY-UP!
DR. PHYSICIAN
OLD TIME GIN
SHIT!
YOU AGAIN!!
RUN!
HAHA! FUCK YOU, ASSHOLE!
YOU FUCKIN' BITCHES! I'LL BREAK YOUR FUCKING LEGS!!
UNDER 21
DRINK BEER!
DON'T DRIVE DRUNK
OH YEAH

DRINK!
SALE!
DRINK BEER!
YANKOV
Majestic GOLD Vodka
80 PROOF 1 LITER
MAJESTIC GOLD VODKA $35 99 1 LITER
SPECIAL $2 99
Majestic GOLD Vodka
Made from the finest ingredients this side of the Mississippi
Majestic Gold Vodka is

U.P.S.! I HAVE A DELIVERY FOR A MISS DOROTHY LESTRADE!
COME ON IN, IT'S OPEN...
HEY, YOU WOULDN'T BELIEVE WHAT HAPPENED! I WAS BUY-AI-AI-YI!
READY TO GO... LOW-VAIR?
WELL, LET'S NOT MAKE ANY HASTY DECISIONS... WE COULD ALWAYS JUST STAY IN!
Heh Heh!
LOOK, I EVEN BOUGHT US SOME MAJESTIC GOLD!
OH NO YOU DON'T!
IF YOU'RE GOING TO PLY ME WITH LIQUOR UNTIL I PASS OUT SO YOU CAN HAVE YOUR WAY WITH ME I WANT IT TO BE IN A NICER DUMP THAN THIS.
AFTER TWO MONTHS, I'D THINK YOU WOULD HAVE MORE REALISTIC EXPECTATIONS BY NOW.

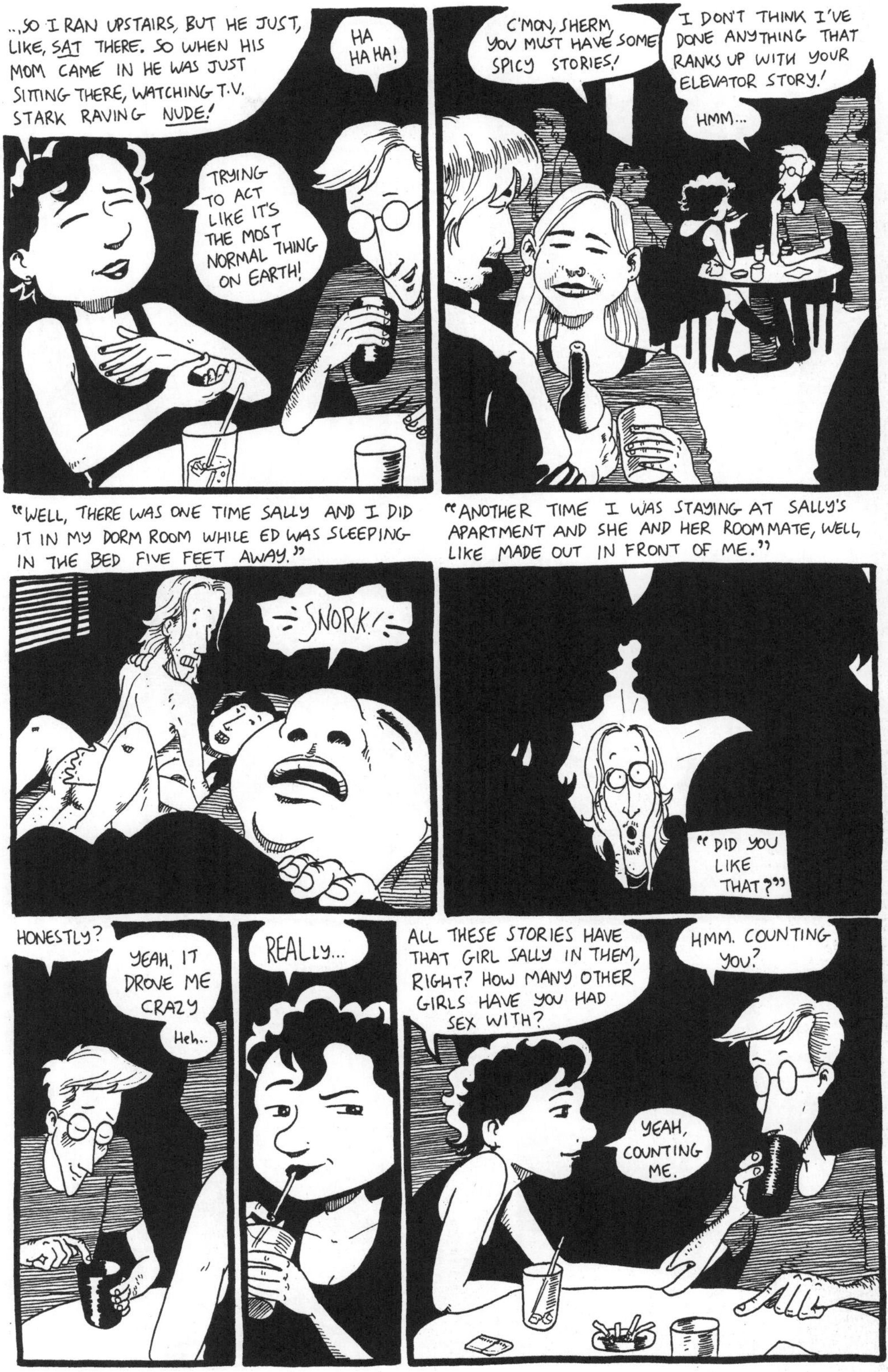
...SO I RAN UPSTAIRS, BUT HE JUST, LIKE, SAT THERE. SO WHEN HIS MOM CAME IN HE WAS JUST SITTING THERE, WATCHING T.V. STARK RAVING NUDE!
HA HA HA!
TRYING TO ACT LIKE IT'S THE MOST NORMAL THING ON EARTH!
C'MON, SHERM, YOU MUST HAVE SOME SPICY STORIES!
I DON'T THINK I'VE DONE ANYTHING THAT RANKS UP WITH YOUR ELEVATOR STORY!
HMM...
"WELL, THERE WAS ONE TIME SALLY AND I DID IT IN MY DORM ROOM WHILE ED WAS SLEEPING IN THE BED FIVE FEET AWAY."
SNORK!
"ANOTHER TIME I WAS STAYING AT SALLY'S APARTMENT AND SHE AND HER ROOMMATE, WELL, LIKE MADE OUT IN FRONT OF ME."
"DID YOU LIKE THAT?"
HONESTLY?
YEAH, IT DROVE ME CRAZY
Heh..
REALLY...
ALL THESE STORIES HAVE THAT GIRL SALLY IN THEM, RIGHT? HOW MANY OTHER GIRLS HAVE YOU HAD SEX WITH?
HMM. COUNTING YOU?
YEAH, COUNTING ME.

HMMM...
ONE.
REALLY?! I'M ONLY THE SECOND GIRL YOU'VE HAD SEX WITH?!
JESUS! KEEP IT DOWN, WOULD YOU?!
WHAT CAN I TELL YOU? I WAS A LATE BLOOMER. I DIDN'T HAVE SEX UNTIL MY... JUNIOR YEAR.
THAT'S SO CUTE.
YOU'RE NOT SO BAD YOURSELF.
YEAH, RIGHT. I'M SURE AFTER HEARING ME TALK ABOUT SEX ALL NIGHT YOU THINK I'M SOME NYMPHO.
IT'S THE ALCOHOL, REALLY.
NO, ACTUALLY, I LIKE THAT ABOUT YOU. IT'S... I DON'T KNOW... REFRESHING TO HEAR A GIRL BE SO CANDID ABOUT STUFF LIKE THAT.
YOU KNOW, SEX STUFF.
REALLY? SO.... WHAT ELSE DO YOU LIKE ABOUT ME?

YOU'RE FUNNY, YOU'RE SMART, YOU'RE RAVISHINGLY CUTE, YOU PICK UP THE BAR TAB EVERY NOW AND AGAIN...
WOULD YOU SAY... THAT YOU LOVED ME?
I THOUGHT YOU SAID YOU DIDN'T BELIEVE IN LOVE.
I DON'T.
BUT I KNOW YOU DO.
UH...
....
HA HA...
OKAY, STUDLY, LET'S FLY. AND I'LL EVEN PAY THE CHECK, HOW ABOUT THAT?
OH, DOROTHY, YOU ALWAYS KNOW JUST WHAT TO SAY.
I JUST WANT TO MAKE ONE STOP, OKAY?
SURE. WHERE?

WHERE THE HECK ARE WE GOING? IT'S A LITTLE CHILLY AIN'T IT?
COME ON, I JUST HAVE TO SHOW YOU THIS.
C'MERE, GIVE ME YOUR HAND.
HUH?
SAY! YOU'RE NOT WEARING ANY...
ANY...
MY HEAVENS!
MISS LESTRADE, I BELIEVE... MMM... I BELIEVE YOU HAVE THE... THE ADVANTAGE... OF... OF

MAN, I SHOULD GOT ZONK TO COME OVER.
ZONK'S A ASSHOLE, MARL.
YEAH, I KNOW, BUT HE GOT SOME GREAT MONKEY AND I COULD SURE AS SHIT NEED SOME.
YOU CHECK THAT SKO HE'S SHIMMIN' WITH? SHIT.'
YEAH, SHE BE CRAWLIN'.
SHE GOT ALL SORTS OF POX IN ''ER BOX.' HAHA!
YEAH.
HE'S AN ASSHOLE.

HOLY SHIT!
HOLY FUCKING SHIT! LOOK!!
WHOA! SHIT!
YO, GET A FUCKIN' ROOM, BITCH!
HAHA!
SHIT, THEY'RE FUCKIN' LIKE CATS!
THAT REMINDS ME THAT TIME WE BE AT THE RATKELLER AN' TELLY TELLS SOME SHITHEAD HE CAN GET --
SHIT!
GET DOWN! HE SEES US!
FUCK THAT SHIT!
WHOOOO!
GO BOY! GO BOY!
MORE

BALLOO...
WHAT DO YOU THINK ABOUT WHEN YOU MASTURBATE?

Verbal Intercourse

SIGH
HUN, YOU KNOW THAT THAT'S CLASSIFIED INFORMATION.
I KNOW, I KNOW, I JUST THOUGHT IT'D BE A NICE ANNIVERSARY PRESENT FROM YOU.
SORRY, SWEETIE, THAT'S BETWEEN ME AND MISS ROSIE PALMS.
OH, YOU'LL TELL HER BUT YOU WON'T TELL ME, HUH?
DO... DO YOU HAVE ANY ... ARE THERE ANY THINGS THAT YOU'VE EVER WANTED TO TRY, YOU KNOW,
IN BED...
THAT YOU'VE NEVER DONE?
UH... NOT THAT I CAN THINK OF. NOT RIGHT NOW.
WHY? DO YOU?

C'MON, THERE MUST BE SOMETHING!
BECAUSE, Y'KNOW, IF THERE WAS ANYTHING YOU EVER WANTED TO TRY, I'M WILLING TO, LIKE, EXPERIMENT
TO MAKE YOU, YOU KNOW, HAPPY.
REALLY?
OH, NOW THAT YOU MENTION IT, I WOULD LIKE TO SODOMIZE A DONKEY CORPSE IN FRONT OF MY DAD WEARING A LEATHER TU-TU AND 8" SPIKED HEELS.
C'MON, I'M SERIOUS!
SO AM I!
NO, REALLY, I CAN'T THINK OF ANYTHING.
BUT IF THERE'S ANYTHING YOU WANT TO TRY, JUST SAY THE WORD.
OH, SPEAKING OF PARENTS, YOUR SCHOOL HAS OFF FOR THANKS-GIVING, RIGHT?
YEAH, WE GET A WEEK OFF. WHY?
IT SEEMS MY PARENTS ARE GOING TO BE IN TOWN AND THEY WANT TO HAVE DINNER WITH US.
ON THANKSGIVING DAY? I GUESS THAT'S OKAY. MY FOLKS'RE GOING TO BE IN FLORIDA, SO I HAVE NO PLANS.
FLORIDA? WHAT ON EARTH FOR?
I DON'T KNOW, SOMETHING ABOUT A PLUMBERS CONVENTION...

OH! THAT REMINDS··
OH, WAIT, SO THAT MEANS YOU TALKED TO YOUR DAD?
NAH. HE JUST LEFT A MESSAGE. ON THE MACHINE. WHAT WERE YOU GOING TO SAY?
REALLY GOOD NEWS! I TALKED TO HERA AND SHE SAYS I CAN HAVE A $500 ADVANCE AS SOON AS I HAND IN THE FIRST FIFTY PAGES! ISN'T THAT SUPER?
THAT'S GREAT! WHEN DO YOU THINK THAT'LL BE?
MMM... PROBABLY NOT UNTIL AROUND JANUARY. I STILL HAVE SOME RESEARCH ON BERKMAN.
MAYBE WE CAN GO ON A LITTLE TRIP BEFORE SCHOOL RESUMES?
THAT WOULD BE GREAT! MAYBE GO BACK TO THAT PLACE WITH THE FIREPLACE IN LICHTFIELD?
I WAS ON THE L-TRAIN TODAY? MAN, IT WAS LIKE THE TRAIN OF THE DAMNED!
SHEESH!
THERE WAS THIS WOMAN WITH A GAGGLE OF BRATTY LITTLE SHITS AND THEY'RE RUNNING AROUND SCREAMING AND CRY-ING AND YELLING AND BUMPING IN TO PEOPLE...
AT ONE POINT TWO OF THEM WERE ROLLING AROUND OF THE FLOOR!
I'M THINKING: "HOMELESS PEOPLE PISS ON THOSE FLOORS, GUYS."
EECH. I SOAK MY SNEAKERS IN ALCOHOL FOR TWENTY-FOUR HOURS IF I EVEN STEP IN THE L-TRAIN!
I KNOW. BUT DON'T THEY... WHY ON EARTH WOULD YOU LET YOUR STUPID KID DO THAT, YOU KNOW?

PEOPLE ARE AWFUL, WHAT CAN I TELL YOU?
YOU KNOW WHAT ONE OF MY BRILLIANT YOUNG MINDS WROTE IN AN ESSAY THIS WEEK?
I GIVE UP. WHAT?
THAT ABRAHAM LINCOLN FREED THE SLAVES IN 1964 WHEN HE SIGNED THE "EMASCULATION PROCLAMATION".
OOH BOY, FREED THE SLAVES OF WHAT?
IT AMAZES ME. AND THESE ARE COLLEGE KIDS. ARE THEY LEARNING ANYTHING IN HIGH SCHOOL?
COME ON, YOU SAID YOU HATED HISTORY UNTIL YOU WENT TO COLLEGE.
HAVE TO KEEP TRYING, BALLOO. MAYBE YOU'LL BE THE ONE TO TURN THEM ON TO IT.
I MEAN, IF YOU COULD CONVERT ME, ANYTHING IS POSSIBLE.
I KNOW. I GUESS I JUST WORRY THAT IT'S... IRRELEVANT. WHO THE HECK CARES ABOUT ELIHU ROOT OR CRISPUS ATTUCKS OR WILLIAM McKINLEY IN THE AGE OF THE INFOTAINMENT SEWER HIGHWAY?
McKINLEY... HE INVENTED THE COTTON GIN, RIGHT?
NO, HE WAS PRESID-- OH, HA HA HA. VERY AMUSING.

I'M GOING TO GET UP AND HAVE A DRINK.
YOU WANT ANYTHING?
NAH. I MEAN, I'LL COME WITH YOU.
HAPPY FIVE YEAR-IVERSARY, CUTEST OF PIES!
MM HMM!
KLNK

OKAY, I'LL SEE YOU GUYS LATER.
WISH ME LUCK.
SEE YOU, ED.
HEY
WHATTA YOU DO IN MY HOUSE, ANH?
WHAT? I WAS JUS VISITING MY FRIEND ON
YOU KNO LEEV HERE! YOU GO HOME! MY HOUSE!
·Come on Knock on our Door!·
WHAT'R YELLING FOR?! I
YOU GO!! I AMA BOSS! YOU NO LEEVERE! YOU GO!! GO!
YOU GET OUT! I CALL A POLICE! GO!
GO! GO!
OKAY! OKAY! JEEZ!
3
THUMP THUMP

WHY MRS. TWEED, I THOUGHT THAT WAS YOUR RANTING I HEARD. TO WHAT DO WE OWE...
TWO DAYS! YOU NOA PAY VRENT! YOU VRENT PAY NOW! AHN! AHN!
OH! THAT'S RIGHT! TODAY'S THE THIRD. IT MUST'VE SLIPPED OUR MINDS.
ANH! YOU PAY VRENT I CALL POLICA!
OKAY, OKAY, DON'T LET'S GET ALL EXCITED. I'LL HAVE MY HUSBAND BRING THE MONEY UP AS SOON AS HE GOES TO THE BANK.
WHYA YOU NO PAY? WHY? WHY?! NO!! NO! YOU PAY! MY HOUSE!
OKAY, WE'RE DONE. STEPHEN WILL BE UP IN A BIT, OKAY?
BYE!
BYE!
ALDA TINE YOU HAVE PEOPLE COMOVER! UP DOWN STAIRS! BOOM BOOM BOOM!
DON'T FALL DOWN THE STAIRS AND BREAK YOUR NECK OR ANYTHING.

WAS THAT OUR FAVORITE PSYCHO BALKAN LAND-LADY?
"I CALL POLICE! I CALL POLICE! MY HOUSE!!"
OH PLEASE PLEASE PLEASE CAN WE MOVE OUT IN MARCH?
DID YOU HEAR HER IN THE HALLWAY LAST NIGHT? SHE WAS SCREAMING AT THE YOSSARIANS AT THREE A.M.!
SHE HAS BEEN BAD LATELY. I THINK SHE NEEDS HER DOSAGE INCREASED.
UGH, WHY DOESN'T HER STUPID FAMILY PUT HER IN A RUBBER ROOM ALREADY?
MAO?
HEY, BIG NOSE!
NOW THAT YOUR BOOK IS COMING OUT MAYBE WE CAN AFFORD A NEW PLACE.
OH, YEAH, THE TIMES' BESTSELLER LIST IS FULL OF COMICS ABOUT TURN-OF-THE CENTURY FEMINIST ANARCHISTS!
ISN'T IT?
:sigh: LET ME GET SHERMAN AND PAY VRENT NOW.
BLOPPO

BOY, YOU'RE GOING TO CARRY THAT WEIGHT A LONG TIME

As John Lennon tuned his guitar, part of him wanted to throw up.

Ever since the Beatles officially broke up in 1970, they had been pestered by the question: When Will You Get Back Together? Paul McCartney's shocking assassination by a lone nut working for the IRA in 1980 seemed to put the question at last to rest. What will it take to have a Beatles reunion? The joke went. Three more bullets.

Yet, here they were, in a recording studio. Three old men trying desperately to sound like they did thirty years ago.

They all had solo careers, of course, with varying degrees of failure and success. But as time went on and McCartney's ghost loomed larger and larger, it seemed hopeless to compete. Sure, John had had some hits (notably his 1981 tribute to McCartney "And Now You Sleep") but more and more the comparisons came up: Paul ha genius behind the Beatles. Paul took John's cranky tirades and made them prese

Everybody loves you when y round, a wise young man once sang...

It seemed with every intervie defend himself. Sure, Paul w ind Sgt. Pepper, but without John's psychede 've went nowhere. Sure, Pa ne who welded together the "good parts" of Abbey Road, but hadn't John...broken

"All right, let's get this fucker started." Lennon sighed to Brian Eno in the he tape started. It was a rough (very rough) demo tape of an unfinished McCartney so Check My Machine." Lennon winced inside. Even by Paul's standards, this song was pur rubbish. But after years of Linda, Paul's' hated widow, scraping the barrel of "Unreleased" and "Never before heard demos" this was all that was left.

Lennon's recent recordings were going virtually straight into the bargain bins nowadays, but this piece of garbage was going to be the centerpiece of the NEW BE M. All three surviving Beatles were hoping it would give their sales a much need nnon couldn't quite see the logic in that. He stopped touring in 1989 for exactly t e him crazy that the crowd would leap to its feet when he dragged out a Beatles so crap like "Run For Your Life" but he could practically taste the disappointment when the opening cords of "Serve Yourself" from his 1987 album "Europe on Five C e would put on a brave face about it, saying he didn't care what people liked and all br side it was killing him.

He has once told a journalist that he could 'She L was thirty. Thirty! He was nearly twice that

"For Christ's sake, " he muttered, in rt.

"What's wrong, John?" said Eno fro

Lennon sighed again.

SHERMAN?
YEAH, COME ON IN.
HOW'S IT COMING?
AH, I'M JUST SCREWING AROUND.
WHAT'S UP? READY FOR ME TO KICK YOUR ASS AT CHESS AGAIN?
HAHA, YEAH, RIGHT. ACTUALLY, I'M HERE FOR THE RENT.
MRS. TWEED'S ON THE RAMPAGE AGAIN.

OH. UH. WELL...
Y'SEE, I LENT DOROTHY $75 LAST WEEK. SHE SWORE SHE WOULD PAY ME BACK BY MONDAY BUT
WAIT A MINUTE, TO DOROTHY?
YEAH,
I'M REALLY SORRY. I CAN GET IT TO YOU ON THURSDAY WHEN I GET...
TRUMAN
DAVID McCULLOUGH
Uh, DOES SHE... TELL ME IF IT'S NONE OF MY BUSINESS, BUT, Uh, DOES SHE OWE YOU MORE MONEY? I MEAN, DOES SHE... BORROW FROM YOU, Uh, ALOT?
NO. WHY?
THIS IS THE FIRST TIME I'VE LENT HER A PENNY.
WELL, THAT'S GOOD.
SO YOU'LL DEFINITELY HAVE THE MONEY ON THURSDAY?
DEFINITELY. AS SOON AS I GET PAID.
OKAY, I SUPPOSE WE COULD SPOT YOU UNTIL THEN. I DON'T THINK MRS. TWEED CAN WAIT.
THANKS ALOT, STEPHEN!
BUT IF IT HAPPENS AGAIN I'LL BUST YOUR FUCKING KNEECAPS!!
Heh Heh!

THE UNKNOWN LINCOLN
GOLDMAN·L
JAMES! IT'S SHERMAN... YEAH, FINE... UH, LISTEN: COULD I BORROW, LIKE, $75?
OKAY, SHERMAN'S ALL PAID UP, SO I'M OFF TO THE BANK FOR OUR SHARE.
HE PAID YOU?
HUH? OH, YEAH. IT WAS CLOSE BUT HE HAD IT.
YOU NEED ANYTHING WHILE I'M OUT? JUICE OR SPROUTS OR SOMETHING?
FLAKES
NAH, THANKS.
BETTER BRING AN UMBRELLA, I HEAR THERE'S A STORM-A-BREWIN'.
PLEAS

HEY!
HEY, BIG GUY! YOU WOIK HEAH?
NO. I DON'T--
GRID LOCK BEN ELTON
SECRET DIARY OF ADRIAN MOLE
HIGH FIDELITY NICK HORNBY
COLONEL ROOSEVELT JEFFERS
X-RAY
FUCK! YOU GOT ME THAT TIME, JAMES!
IT'S FUNNY, AS MUCH AS YOU HATE YOUR JOB YOU STILL ARRANGE FOR US TO MEET IN A GODDAMNED BOOKSTORE!
HIGH
WELL, I DON'T HATE BOOKS, JUST THE PEOPLE WHO BUY THEM.
AND THE PEOPLE WHO PAY YOU.
ahem
OH YEAH! SHERMAN, THIS IS MARTI MARTI, THIS IS SHERMAN, WE USED TO WORK AT MATTHEW'S BOOKS TOGETHER.
HEY.
PLEASED TO MEET YOU.
JAMES, HEY, I'M GONNA GO LOOK AT THE TAROT BOOKS, OKAY?
I'LL MEET YOU HERE, RIGHT?
SURE, SURE.
SO ANYWAY, WHAT'S THIS ABOUT YOU NEEDING SOME DOUGH?
YOU SON OF A BITCH. YOU LUCKY GODDAMED SON OF A BITCH.
WHERE'D YOU MEET HER? ONE OF THE FRESHMAN MIXERS AT N.Y.U.?
ACTUALLY, HehHeh... SHE'S STILL IN HIGH SCHOOL.
SHE'S FIFTEEN.
LOLITA VLADIMIR NABOKOV

WAITAMINUTE FIFTEEN?!
THIS GIRL IS HALF YOUR AGE!!
YOU COULD GO TO JAIL!!
I KNOW. IF HER FATHER FOUND OUT, HE'D KILL ME.
I'D GET FIRED, TOO.
FIRED? YOU FOUND ANOTHER JOB?
YEAH. ACTUALLY THAT'S HOW I MET MARTI. I'M TEMPING AT HER DAD'S BEER DISTRIBUTORSHIP.
I'M TAKING SOME WORD PROCESSING CLASSES AT NIGHT.
TEMPING, HUH? HOW MUCH'RE THEY PAYING?
OH, YOU DON'T WANT TO KNOW. DID THAT NEW VONNEGUT BOOK EVER COME OUT?
NO, REALLY COME ON, HOW MUCH?
SHERMAN, YOU DON'T WANT TO HEAR IT.
I DO. HOW MUCH?
$15.50 PER HOUR,
NO BENEFITS, THOUGH.
$15.50?!
THAT'S -- THAT'S TWICE WHAT I MAKE! AND I'VE BEEN AT MATTHEW'S FOR FOUR YEARS!!
$15.50?!?
FUCK YOU.
AWW, DON'T BE THAT WAY. ANYWAY, WHAT'S ALL THIS ABOUT YOU NEEDING SOME DOUGH?

SLAM!
....?
WHOO! JESUS, IT'S REALLY COMING DOWN OUT THERE!
OH, I'M SORRY, DID I WAKE YOU UP?
UM, NO, NO. IT'S OKAY. IT'S JUST THIS WEATHER. THE RAIN KNOCKS ME OUT. WHAT TIME IS IT?
QUARTER TO SEVEN, ALMOST TIME FOR THE SIMPSONS!
PLUS! I BRING TIDINGS OF GREAT JOY: I WENT AND BORROWED SOME MONEY FROM JAMES SO I CAN PAY YOU BACK TODAY INSTEAD OF ON THURSDAY!
YEESH, I SHOULD PROBABLY HANG THIS IN THE BATHROOM.
PAY ME BACK FOR WHAT?
THE RENT MONEY. THE $75 I WAS SHORT? I GOT IT FR--
YOU WERE $75 SHORT ON THE RENT?
HEY, GUYS. I'M STARVING, YOU GUYS WANT TO SEND OUT FOR CHINESE?
SURE! WE CAN USE THE $75 THAT SHERMAN HAS FOR YOU!
FUN FATS

GREAT, SO WHERE DO YOU WANT TO...
DUM FUKS
UM.
WHAT?
YOU TOLD ME SHERMAN PAID HIS RENT.
UH, HE... I MEAN..
NO, WAIT, IT'S MY FAULT...
I EXPLAINED TO STEPHEN THAT DOROTHY OWES ME..
"DOROTHY?"
BEATRICE LESTRADE IS SOMEHOW INVOLVED IN THIS?
SURE, SHE NEEDED TO..
GRRRRRR!!!
EVERY TIME I TRY TO GET OUT, SHE PULLS US RIGHT BACK IN!!
JANE, DON'T
DON'T "JANE, DON'T" ME! AS LONG AS SHE STAYED OUT OF OUR LIVES, I'D KEEP MY MOUTH SHUT!
BUT NOW SHE'S GOT US FIGHTING, SHE'S GOT YOU LYING TO ME, IT'S LIKE SHE NEVER LEFT!!

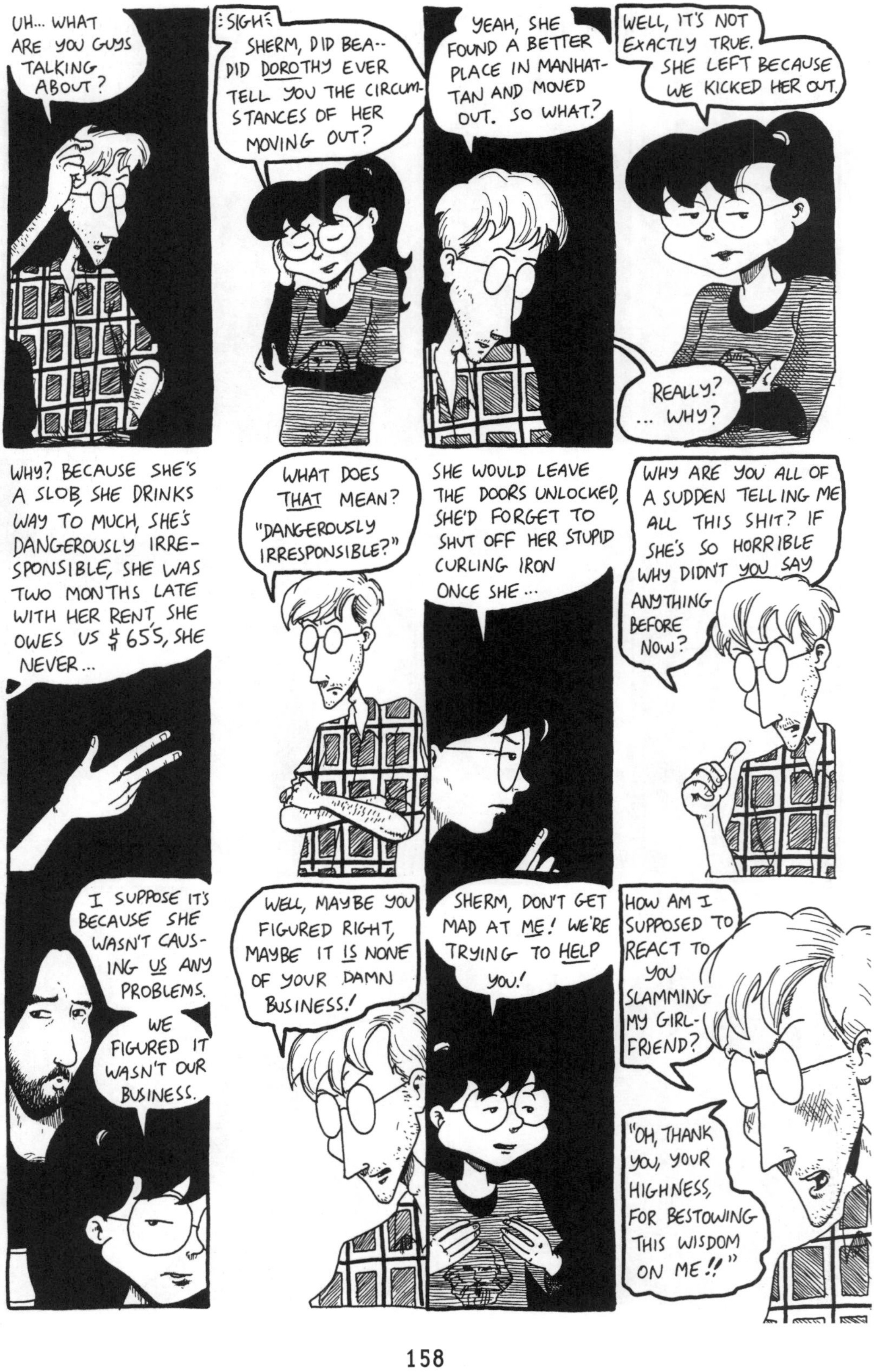
UH... WHAT ARE YOU GUYS TALKING ABOUT?
:SIGH:
SHERM, DID BEA-- DID DOROTHY EVER TELL YOU THE CIRCUMSTANCES OF HER MOVING OUT?
YEAH, SHE FOUND A BETTER PLACE IN MANHATTAN AND MOVED OUT. SO WHAT?
WELL, IT'S NOT EXACTLY TRUE. SHE LEFT BECAUSE WE KICKED HER OUT.
REALLY? ... WHY?
WHY? BECAUSE SHE'S A SLOB, SHE DRINKS WAY TO MUCH, SHE'S DANGEROUSLY IRRESPONSIBLE, SHE WAS TWO MONTHS LATE WITH HER RENT, SHE OWES US $655, SHE NEVER...
WHAT DOES THAT MEAN? "DANGEROUSLY IRRESPONSIBLE?"
SHE WOULD LEAVE THE DOORS UNLOCKED, SHE'D FORGET TO SHUT OFF HER STUPID CURLING IRON ONCE SHE...
WHY ARE YOU ALL OF A SUDDEN TELLING ME ALL THIS SHIT? IF SHE'S SO HORRIBLE WHY DIDN'T YOU SAY ANYTHING BEFORE NOW?
I SUPPOSE IT'S BECAUSE SHE WASN'T CAUSING US ANY PROBLEMS.
WE FIGURED IT WASN'T OUR BUSINESS.
WELL, MAYBE YOU FIGURED RIGHT, MAYBE IT IS NONE OF YOUR DAMN BUSINESS!
SHERM, DON'T GET MAD AT ME! WE'RE TRYING TO HELP YOU!
HOW AM I SUPPOSED TO REACT TO YOU SLAMMING MY GIRLFRIEND?
"OH, THANK YOU, YOUR HIGHNESS, FOR BESTOWING THIS WISDOM ON ME!!"

SO HERE'S YOUR FUCKING MONEY AND LET'S NOT BRING IT UP AGAIN!
SHERMAN, DON'T BE SUCH--
A BABY.
THAT WASN'T NEARLY AS FUN AS I THOUGHT IT WOULD BE.
WHY DIDN'T YOU TELL ME THE TRUTH TO BEGIN WITH?
I GUESS I WANTED TO AVOID A FIGHT.
DOROTHY, HI IT'S ME. CALL ME WHEN YOU GET IN. I'D LIKE TO MEET YOU FOR LUNCH TOMORROW. 'KAY SO CALL ME. SEE YA.

ED QUIXOTE
WHAT THE HELL'RE YOU TALKING ABOUT?
"RESCUE ME" FROM WHO?!
FROM...
FROM OBSCURITY, FROM YOURSELF...
FROM ZOOM COMICS.

"OBSCURITY?" WHO THE HELL'RE YOU TO TALK TO ME LIKE--
MR. FLAVOR...
MR. FLAVOR, I KNOW YOU CREATED NIGHTSTALKER.
YEAH.
YEAH. SO?
SO I WANT TO HELP YOU FIGHT ZOOM COMICS.
I WANT YOU TO GET WHAT'S COMING TO YOU.
PISS OFF ZOOM COMICS?! HA!
WHAT THE HELL FOR?!
MR. FLAVOR, THE NIGHTSTALKER MOVIES ALONE HAVE GROSSED NEARLY A BILLION DOLLARS.
PLUS MONEY FROM T-SHIRTS. PLUS MONEY FROM TOYS. PLUS FAST-FOOD TIE-INS, VIDEO GAMES, BED SHEETS AND WHATEVER ELSE THEY COULD SLAP A NIGHTSTALKER LOGO ON.
A LOT OF PEOPLE GOT-- ARE GETTING RICH OFF OF YOUR CREATION.
THEY OWE YOU.
FUCK YOU, HOT SHOT. HOW DO YOU KNOW I DIDN'T SIGN A DEAL ALREADY? HOW STUPID DO YOU THINK I AM, HUH?

I'M NOT SAYING YOU'RE STUPID. WHEN YOU MADE UP NIGHTSTALKER YOU HAD NO WAY OF KNOWING WHAT HE'D BE WORTH.
IT WAS A DIFFERENT WORLD THEN.
UH, WHY? DID YOU SIGN A DEAL?
OF COURSE I DID.
"IN 1944, I WAS TWENTY YEARS OLD."
"I SOLD THEM NIGHTSTALKER FOR $55."
BUY BONDS
BLOOP
BLOOP
MR. FLAVOR, I THINK WE CAN SHAME ZOOM COMICS INTO..
"SHAME THEM?"
WHAT AM I, SOME DAMN CHARITY CASE? AND HOW WILL IT LOOK, ME EMBARRASSING ZOOM IN PUBLIC?
I'LL NEVER WORK IN COMICS AGAIN!

UH, MR. FLAVOR, WITH ALL DUE RESPECT, THE LAST WORK YOU DID FOR ZOOM COMICS WAS EIGHT YEARS AGO.
A SIX PAGE "MAN-WOLF" BACK UP STORY IN "A.I.A.C. FORCE" # 247.
I...
I, UH,
CHECKED.
MR. FLAVOR, AFTER WE WIN, YOU'LL BE RICH, YOU'LL NEVER HAVE TO DRAW ANOTHER V.D. POSTER OR CEREAL BOX OR COLORING BOOK FOR THE REST OF YOUR LIFE!
YEAH, BUT THEY GOT HUNDREDS OF SHARKS, HUNDREDS OF LAWYERS WORKIN' FOR 'EM.'
I ONLY GOT TWO THINGS, JACK AND SHIT.
AND JACK JUST LEFT THE BUILDING.
SEE, THAT'S WHERE YOU'RE WRONG.
FIRST OF ALL, YOU'RE A SWEET OLD MAN, A LITTLE GUY DICKED OVER BY A BIG COMPANY.
THE MEDIA -- OR A JURY -- LOVE THAT KIND OF STUFF.

AND.
"YOU'VE GOT SOMETHING ON YOUR SIDE MORE POWERFUL THAN ANY MUSCLEBOUND STOOGE OR ATOM GUN, JUSTICE IS ON YOUR SIDE!"
WHERE THE HELL'D YOU GET THAT FROM?
IT'S FROM "NIGHTSTALKER" #115, 1953.
YOU TAUGHT ME THAT, MR. FLAVOR.
THAT'S THE CORNIEST LOAD OF HORSESHIT I EVER HEARD.
BUT YOU KNOW I'M RIGHT.
sigh
OKAY, OKAY.
SO WHAT DO WE DO?

Not guilty
SHE SAID WHAT?!
I KNOW, I KNOW I WAS A BIT AGOG MYSELF.
YOU DON'T BELIEVE HER, DO YOU?
SHIT, I ALWAYS KNEW SHE HATED ME, BUT I DIDN'T THINK THIS MUCH!
NO. SHHLRP
I DON'T BELIEVE HER.
CAREFUL, THIS IS STILL A BIT HOT.
FIRST OF ALL, AS FAR AS THE MONEY GOES, I TOLD HER I'D PAY THEM AS SOON AS I COULD!
I JUST SENT THEM A CHECK FOR $100 LIKE LAST MONTH!
AS FOR MY BEING AN "ALCOHOLIC" ...
DOROTHY, I SAID I DON'T BE..
MISS HIGH AND MIGHTY CLEAN-AND-SOBER THINKS ANY-ONE WHO'S EVER TAKEN A DRINK ANYWHERE AT ANY TIME IS A DRUNK!
HELL, SHE PROBABLY THINKS YOU'RE A DRUNK, TOO!

AND, YEAH, OKAY, I CAN BE A BIT MESSY FROM TIME TO TIME, BUT SHE MAKES HOWARD HUGHES LOOK LIKE FRED SANFORD!
SHE'S THE MOST ANAL RETENTIVE SOUL I'VE EVER MET!
YEAH, WELL DON'T LET IT BOTHER YOU. SHE WAS PROBABLY IN A BAD MOOD OR SOMETHING.
OH, NO, SHE REALLY DISLIKES ME. IT'S-- UM-- I DON'T KNOW IF I SHOULD,...
SHOULD WHAT?
NO, NO, I SHOULDN'T TELL YOU. NEVER MIND, IT'S IRRELEVANT.
TELL ME WHAT?
NO, IT WAS A LONG TIME AGO, IT WOULDN'T BE FAIR TO STEPHEN. FORGET IT!
HEH.
STEPHEN? WHAT'S HE GOT TO DO--
ONCE WHILE JANE WAS OVER HER FOLKS' HOUSE HE MADE A PASS AT ME.

STEPHEN?!
YOU'RE KIDDING!
NO, REALLY, IT'S TRUE!
IT WAS ONLY ONE TIME AND I GUESS IT'S KIND OF FLATTERING, IN A WEIRD WAY.
I DIDN'T LET HIM DO ANYTHING!
ACTUALLY, IT MADE THINGS REALLY AWKWARD, AS YOU CAN IMAGINE.
IT CERTAINLY WAS A BIG INCENTIVE TO MOVE OUT.
I WASN'T SURE IF I SHOULD TELL YOU, I DON'T WANT TO EMBARASS STEPHEN. I MEAN HE... I DON'T KNOW.
PANT! PANT!
I CAN'T BELIEVE IT.
STEPHEN?
JANE MUST'VE FOUND OUT SOMEHOW, OR MAYBE SHE JUST FELT IT, OR SOMETHING, I DON'T KNOW.
I MEAN, IT'S NOT LIKE WE WERE EVER CLOSE FRIENDS OR SOMETHING BEFORE, BUT I THINK THAT'S WHY SHE HATES ME NOW.
STEPHEN?
STEPHEN.
STEPHEN GAEDEL.
YES, STEPHEN GAEDEL, THE BIG JESUS LOOKING GUY!!
NOW COME ON, MY LUNCH BREAK IS OVER TEN MINUTES AGO.
SO WHAT DO YOU WANT TO DO ON FRIDAY?

WELL, THE FILM FORUM IS SHOWING THE MALTESE FALCON., HAVE YOU EVER SEEN IT?
UH, HUMPHREY BOGART, ACTUALLY, AND PETER LORRE... MARY ASTOR.
WHO'S THAT WITH? CARY GRANITE?
SOUNDS MARVELOUS, PICK ME UP AT WORK.
SHERM, I HOPE IT DOESN'T BOTHER YOU...
THAT STEPHEN THING I TOLD YOU.
IT'S JUST, I DON'T KNOW, EMBAR-RASSING OR... I DON'T KNOW.
BOTHER ME? NO, OF COURSE NOT. WHY SHOULD IT?
I'M SHOCKED, SHOCKED AND STUNNED, BUT, NO, IT DOESN'T BOTHER ME.
DON'T LET IT BOTHER YOU, MY LITTLE CUTTLEFISH.
TCH! SUCH A SWEETIE!
STEPHEN!
IMAGINE THAT!

IF YOU COULD HAVE BRUNCH WITH ANYONE LIVING OR DEAD, WHO WOULD IT BE ?
ABE LINCOLN.
NO WAIT! THEODORE ROOSEVELT!
NO WAIT!
A YOUNG FRANK SINATRA
SAMMY GECK.
THAT SON OF A BITCH OWES ME $18.
HAHA!
SUPERMODEL ANNA NICOLE SMITH.
GROWWWL!
UM
MY MOTHER
EMMA GOLDMAN.
MR. SNUFALUFAGUS.
OR JOHN TRAVOLTA.

OKEY-DOKE, SO NIGHTSTALKER WILL APPEAR IN THE SEVEN ISSUE CROSSOVER WITH RAZORBURN.
WE SHOULD GET GARNER TO INK THE COVER OF #22.
SILKO WILL GET HER NEW COSTUME IN "RAIDERS" #152, RIGHT AFTER TAZER COMES BACK FROM THE FORGOTTEN ZONE.
CAN WE GET THAT IN BEFORE "ATAC FORCE" #318?
UH, ACTUALLY J.C., I NEED TAZER FOR MY SHARKSKIN STORY IN "CAPTAIN COMPOUND" #13, SO COULD WE POSSIBLY--
I'M SORRY, J.C.?
PAULIE, MY LAD! WHAT IS IT, WHAT'S SO URGENT?
OOM
J.C., I JUST GOT OFF THE PHONE WITH TOM SALMON FROM "COLLECTOR'S WORLD." IT'S ABOUT IRVING FLAVOR.
IT COULD BE TROUBLE.
IRVING FLAVOR
IRVING FLAVOR.

WAIT!
I THINK THIS IS HIM.
YEP, HE'S COMING IN.
UH, MR. FLAVOR, ARE SURE YOU WANT TO... UM..
I MEAN, IS THAT WHAT YOU'RE...
WHAT? WHAT THE HELL ARE YOU MUMBLING ABOUT?
OKAY, LET HIM IN, I'M READY.
a Life in a DAY
The Nightstalker Interviews Part One

HELLO, MR. FLAVOR! MY NAME IS ARCHIE PUPKIN III, I'M A WRITER FOR "COMICS WORLD", COMICDOM'S NUMBER ONE NEWS MAGAZINE!
IT IS TRULY AN HONOR TO MEET YOU, SIR!
THIS IS MY LOVELY AND TALENTED ASSISTANT
HILDY KIERKEGAARD.
H'LO.
STAR WARS
KS

YEAH, HI THERE, MR. PUPKIN! A REAL PLEASURE!
UH, COULD I GET YOU GUYS ANYTHING BEFORE YOU START? SOME COFFEE? OR...
HOHO! PLEASE MR. FLAVOR, CALL ME ARCHIE!
NO, THANK YOU, WE STOPPED AT A LOVELY DOUGHNUT SHOP IN GLENDALE PRIOR TO OUR ARRIVAL.
SO, MR. FLAVOR, SHALL WE GET CRACKING?
HILDY?

I JUST TALK INTO THIS?
HELLO! HELLO! TESTING ONE--
UH, JUST TALK NORMAL, MR. FLAVOR.
NOW, THEN, MR. FLAVOR, THE PUBLICATION OF THIS INTERVIEW WILL BE YOUR FIRST STEP IN THE VOYAGE OF JUSTICE!
BZZZ!
OH! THAT'S PROBABLY JANE. I'LL GET IT!
"COMICS WORLD" HAS ALWAYS CHAMPIONED THE UNDERDOG! LAST YEAR WE PRINTED A BITING THREE PART EXPOSE ON REGGIE WICKER'S FIGHT WITH INKSTAIN PRESS!
HE BECAME OUR CAUSE CELEBRAE! WE ORGANIZED A MASSIVE BOYCOTT OF INK STAIN'S PRODUCTS!
A PETITION AGAINST THEIR RUTHLESS BARBARISM!
WE LOST HUNDREDS, NAY, THOUSANDS OF DOLLARS IN ADVERTISING BUT WE HAD TO KEEP UP THE FIGHT!
YOU ARE OUR FIGHT NOW, MR. FLAVOR!!
STAR WAPS
YOU GOT REGGIE WICKER HIS MONEY?
WHAT?

HI ED! I'M SORRY I'M LATE, BUT THAT M-TRAIN IS LIKE THE TOONERVILLE TROLLEY!
I KNOW, MOST PEOPLE DON'T EVEN KNOW THERE IS AN M-TRAIN.
IT'S OKAY, MR. PUPKIN'S JUST GETTING STARTED
I'LL TAKE YOUR COAT.
ARCHIE PUPKIN?
HE'S FROM "COMIC'S WORLD" ISN'T HE? WHAT, WOULDN'T "COLLECTOR'S GUIDE" COME?
NAH. ZOOM COMICS IS THEIR BIGGEST ADVERTISER. THEY WOULDN'T TOUCH THE STORY.
MMM, FREE PRESS INDEED.
WELL, "COMIC'S WORLD" HAS A LOWER CIRCULATION, BUT THEY DO HAVE A HISTORY OF HELPING LOST CAUSES...
THEY'LL HAVE TO DO ... FOR NOW.
KLIK
WHIRRRRRR
SO...
MR. FLAVOR
TELL US ABOUT THE NIGHTSTALKER.

JEEZ, WELL, LET'S SEE... I GUESS THE FIRST TIME I MET SIMON LEBLANC WAS 19... 1940? SOMEWHERE AROUND THERE. I WAS JUST A KID...SIXTEEN OR SOMETHING.
NOW, I DON'T KNOW IF YOU REMEMBER, BUT AT THE TIME, SIMON WAS A HOTSHOT EDITOR AT WORLD PRESS. THEY'RE DEFUNCT NOW, BUT AT THE TIME THEY WERE A VERY BIG, VERY POPULAR COMIC PUBLISHER.
HE WAS A CUSTOMER AT MY DAD'S SHOP.
WHY SHOULD WE BUTT IN? LET THE LIMEYS FIGHT THEIR OWN WAR!
YOU'RE PROBABLY RIGHT, MR. LEBLANC.
DO YOU WANT CUFFS?
SO ANYWAY, MY FATHER HAD TOLD HIM THAT I WAS INTERESTED IN BEING AN ARTIST SO SIMON ASKED TO SEE SOME OF MY WORK.
Flavberg FINE Tailoring
THIS STUFF AIN'T BAD! NOT BAD AT ALL, KID!
SAY, WHY DON'T YOU COME BY THE OFFICE NEXT WEEK AND MEET THE FELLAS!
HE DIDN'T HAVE TO ASK ME TWICE, THAT'S FOR DAMN SURE! SO, I GO DOWN AND I GET TO MEET ALL THESE ARTISTS! THEN SIMON TAKES ME ASIDE...
IRVING, I'M GOING TO TELL YOU SOMETHING NO ONE ELSE KNOWS: I'M LEAVING WORLD COMICS AND STARTING MY OWN COMPANY.
WHY SHOULD I SPEND MY LIFE MAKING SOMEONE ELSE RICH?
IRVING, I WANT YOU TO COME WORK FOR ME. I NEED A SIX PAGE STORY BY MONDAY. CAN DO IT?
MY FATHER HAD A SAYING: "WHEN OPPORTUNITY KNOCKS, DON'T KNOCK OPPORTUNITY!"

WHAT ELSE COULD I DO? I WENT HOME, MADE UP A CHARACTER, AND BAM! DID A SIX PAGE STORY! IT WAS... I'VE DONE A MILLION COMICS SINCE THEN, BUT THAT ONE... I THINK IT WAS MY FAVORITE. YOU ALWAYS REMEMBER YOUR FIRST TIME, AS THEY SAY.
I NEED YOU TO HELP ME OPEN THE STORE TOMORROW!
IRVING! GO TO BED, IT'S 1:30 IN THE MORNING!
SO THAT'S HOW YOU INVENTED NIGHTSTALKER, WITH THAT STORY?
OH, NO, NO, NO. THIS WAS A CHARACTER CALLED DR. INVISIBLE. I ONLY DID A FEW STORIES WITH HIM.
HURRY! THE COPS WILL BE COMING SOON! GIVE ME THE TOOLS!
I HOPE DR. INVISIBLE DOES NOT COME!
HE WAS A MAGICIAN WHO COULD TURN HIS BODY INVISIBLE TO FIGHT CRIME.
NO!!
HMMM. I LIKE IT, KID, IT'S ALL RIGHT.
WELCOME TO ZOOM COMICS!
YOU WON'T BELIEVE YOUR EYES!
ZOOM COMICS!
PLUS: MAJOR JUSTICE!
WHO IS DR. INVISIBLE?
IN THE BEGINNING, IT WAS FUNNY, EVERYONE WHO WORKED FOR SIMON AND HIS NEW COMPANY WAS EITHER REALLY OLD OR REALLY YOUNG!
IS THAT WHEN YOU WORKED WITH DICKIE SLAB?
YEAH, AND IT WAS AROUND THAT TIME -- BEFORE THE WAR -- THAT HE FIRST DID MAJOR JUSTICE.

ACTUALLY, IT WAS BECAUSE OF DICKIE THAT I ... THAT I MADE UP THE NIGHTSTALKER TO BEGIN WITH!
HE WAS WORKING ON HIS MAJOR JUSTICE COMIC -- THIS WAS IN 1942 AND WHAT WITH THE WAR GOING ON AND ALL, IT WAS A BIG HIT...
ANYWAYS, ONE TIME WE'RE SITTING AROUND ZOOM'S OFFICE -- I'D BEEN DOING VARIOUS BOOKS AT THE TIME, WORKING ON A LOT OF DIFFERENT CHARACTERS AND WHAT NOT, SO WE'RE TALKING AND...
GEE WHIZ, IRV! I FORGOT ABOUT THAT THREE PAGER SIMON GAVE ME TO DO FOR FRIDAY!
WHAT AM I GONNA DO FOR A VILLAIN?
ZOOM
AHH! QUIT YOUR BELLY-ACHING! HERE: HERE'S A BAD GUY FOR YOU!
AND THAT WAS IT, I MADE HIM UP, RIGHT ON THE SPOT!
SO DICKIE USED HIM FOR THAT ISSUE (I THINK IT WAS PUNCH OUT! #27) AND THAT WAS IT.
OF COURSE, HE WAS KIND OF DIFFERENT THEN, WHAT WITH HIS GUN AND ALL THAT NAZI STUFF AND EVERYTHING. BUT THE IDEA WAS THERE.
BUT LIKE I SAID THE STORY CAME AND WENT AND I DIDN'T REALLY THINK ABOUT IT UNTIL A FEW MONTHS LATER...
OH, BY THE WAY: NEXT MONTH WE'RE LAUNCHING ANOTHER TITLE. I'LL NEED A TEN PAGER BY THE FIFTEENTH.
GULP!
HAVE A GOOD WEEKEND, IRV!

NOW, YOU GOTTA UNDERSTAND, BACK IN THEM DAYS, IT WAS A LOT DIFFERENT. THEY DIDN'T GIVE A SHIT WHAT YOU DID, AS LONG AS KIDS KEPT BUYING IT AND IT MADE MONEY. OTHER THAN THAT, YOU HAD TOTAL FREEDOM.
SO SIMON DIDN'T CARE WHAT THE HELL WE DID, STORYWISE, WE SURE AS HELL HAD TO FILL UP A LOT OF PAGES QUICK! BUT I'LL BE DAMNED IF IT DIDN'T TEACH US ALL DISCIPLINE! YOU CAN'T DO THAT MANY PAGES AND NOT GET GOOD.
No. 1
SUMMER
10¢
'BEST' COMICS
BUY BONDS
CAPTAIN COMPOUND
SO SIMON TELLS ME I GOT TO DO THIS NEW STORY, I DO WHAT ALL GREAT ARTISTS DO FROM TIME TO TIME... I RECYCLED. I TOOK THE NAZI BAD GUY, CHANGED HIS COLORS A BIT, DITCHED THE NAZI SHIT AND THERE YOU GO.
EAT A JOE
I DID A COUPLE OF STORIES WITH THE NIGHTSTALKER WHEN
Uh, YOU WANTED TO SEE ME, SIMON?
IRV! COME ON IN, PAL!
THE NEWSGUYS ARE TELLING ME GOOD THINGS ABOUT THIS NIGHTS... NIGHT...
NIGHTSTALKER?
RIIIIIIGHT. RIGHT.
SO THIS CHARACTER'S PROVING TO BE KIND OF POPULAR FOR US. SO!
I'M GIVING YOU AND THE NIGHTSTALKER YOUR OWN BOOK
AND!
YOU'LL BE GETTING A TIDY LITTLE RAISE!
I WAS ONLY THE SECOND "ZOOMER" TO GET MY OWN BOOK
THANKS ALOT, SIMON!
I WAS ONE WEEK SHY OF MY NINETEENTH BIRTHDAY.

I REALLY WORKED HARD ON THE BOOK, TOO, TRYING TO KEEP IT FRESH AND EXCITING. I EVEN MADE MYSELF A PROMISE: I'D INTRODUCE A NEW VILLAIN EVERY OTHER ISSUE.
MOST OF 'EM WERE DUMB, BUT SOME WERE GREAT... THE BRAIN, RAE-GUARD, AND OF COURSE ADMIRAL ARMOR!
THE BOOK WAS A HIT. SIMON GAVE ME ANOTHER RAISE THE NEXT YEAR.
Y'KNOW, WHEN I THINK ABOUT IT ... WHEN I THINK ABOUT IT...
THOSE WERE PROBABLY THE HAPPIEST DAYS IN MY LIFE.
SO... WHAT WENT WRONG?
AROUND JUNE OF 1944, I TOOK MY GIRL SOPHIE TO THE PICTURES TO SEE "GASLIGHT" AT THE BROOKLYN SHOWPLACE.
(IT'S NOT THERE ANYMORE-- THEY TORE IT DOWN TO MAKE A SUPER-MARKET IN '72)
IS THIS TOO CLOSE?
BUT ANYWAYS, BACK IN THEM DAYS THEY USED TO SHOW NEWS REELS AND CARTOONS AND ALL SORTS OF SHIT BEFORE THE FEATURE.

SO, DID YOU TELL MARIA ABOUT US GETTING...
OHMYGOODNESS! IRVING, LOOK AT THE SERIAL!
ISN'T THAT YOUR SUPER HERO?!
SHHHH!
AND IT WAS.
I REMEMBER LOOKING UP AT THAT SCREEN... IT WAS LIKE SOMETHING OUT OF A DREAM, SEEING HIM, ALL THREE-DEE. IT ... I WAS GOD DAMNED HYPMATIZED, IN A TRANCE UNTIL SOPHIE TALKED. SHE SAID "MY GOODNE
COME ON, MOONBOY! WE'VE GOT TO GET TO THE MUNITIONS FACTORY!
MY GOODNESS, IRV! NOW THAT YOUR CHARACTER'S IN THE PICTURES YOU'LL BE RICH!
HUH?
THE NEXT MONDAY I WENT IN TO WORK AND ASKED SIMON WHAT WAS GOING ON...
AW, JEEZ, IRV, I REALLY WISH YOU HADN'T SEEN THAT.

UH. WHY? WHAT DO YOU MEAN?
BECAUSE I WANTED TO BE THE ONE TO TELL YOU ABOUT THE PICTURE DEAL!
THIS COMPANY, GOLD FILMS IS MAKING A TEN PART SERIAL WITH THE NIGHTSTALKER! AIN'T THAT TERRIFIC?
I... I SUPPOSE. BUT... WELL...
I KNOW, I KNOW, BEFORE YOU ANSWER, TAKE A LOOK AT THIS. HERE! LOOK!
SIMON, THIS IS FOR ME?
THAT'S RIGHT, MY FRIEND! DON'T LET IT BE SAID I DON'T TREAT MY BOYS RIGHT!
COME ON, LET'S GO OUT TO LUNCH AND CELEBRATE!
AHH, DON'T MENTION IT, KID! JUST KEEP ON WORKING YOUR MAGIC FOR ME!
THANKS! THANKS A LOT! LET ME GET MY JACKET!
OH, JEEZ, WAIT! I ALMOST FORGOT! I NEED YOU TO SIGN THIS!
HUH? WHAT IS IT?
DOUBLE CROSS
AHHH, JUST SOME RELEASE FORM THE BOYS AT THE STUDIO WANTED ME TO HAVE YOU SIGN?
YOU EVER SEEN TO CALIGU S? THEY GRE MANICO
CA...
CAN WE TAKE A BREAK OR SOMETHING?

OH, WHY CERTAINLY!
HILDY!
WOULD YOU BE A DARLING AND RUN DOWN TO GET SOME FOOD STUFFS FROM THE DELI?
STAR WARS
UH, I GUESS SO. WHAT DO YOU NEED?
CHECK IF THEY HAVE SESAME BAGELS. IF THEY DON'T HAVE SESAME, GET ONION...

MEANWHILE, AT A POST OFFICE ON THE ISLAND OF MANHATTAN...
NEXTSTEPDOWN.
NEXT.
6
UH, HI, I'D LIKE TO MAIL THESE FIRST CLASS.
SUBMISSIONS EDITOR
c/o NEW YORKER
20 W. 43rd St.
NEW YORK, N.Y.
10036-7441
EXCUSE ME, LOVELY LADY!
WHAT KIND OF COUNTRY WOULD IT BE IF EVERYONE'S CAR WAS PINK?
IT'D BE A PINK CAR-NATION!
HAHAHA!

NOW, WHAT IS THE BEST NATION ON EARTH?
A DONATION!
OKAY, YOU GOT ME. HERE YOU GO.
THANK YOU VERY MUCH, MY DEAR MADAM!
AND ENJOY YOUR STAY HERE IN THE BIG APPLE!
HEY, WHY DID THAT GUY THINK I WAS SOME TOURIST?
CUZ ANYONE WHO LIVES IN NEW YORK HAS HEARD THAT SCHTICK A MILLION TIMES.
Tony's DELI
YEAH, I GUESS A REAL NEW YORKER WOULD'VE STABBED HIM TO DEATH.
WELL, I DID IT. I CAN'T WAIT FOR THOSE REJECTION LETTERS TO COME POURING IN.
THAT'S GOOD. YOU'VE TAKEN YOUR FIRST STEP INTO A LARGER WORLD.

YEAH, WE REALLY GOT INTO QUITE A TIFF ABOUT IT. I'D NEVER SEEN HIM LIKE THAT.
MAN, YOU REALLY HATE HER, DON'T YOU?
I GUESS IF I HATE ANYONE IT'S HER.
WHY? YOU DON'T LIKE HER, DO YOU?
I DON'T EVEN KNOW HER ENOUGH TO SAY, SHE DOESN'T SEEM TO CARE FOR ME TOO MUCH, THOUGH.
THE ONLY TIME I EVER GOT TO MEET HER WAS THE ONE TIME THE THREE OF US WENT TO PLAY POOL OVER ON FLATBUSH AVE.
SHE BARELY SAID TEN WORDS TO ME THE WHOLE NIGHT.
TCH
TYPICAL.
SO I DON'T KNOW, I GUESS WHAT I DON'T LIKE ABOUT HER IS THAT I NEVER GET TO SEE SHERM ANYMORE.
HOW DOES THAT THING GO? "WEDDING BELLS ARE BREAKING UP THIS GANG OF MINE?"
I THINK WHAT YOUR FATHER'S DOING IS VERY BRAVE.
WELL LET'S NOT GO THAT FAR, LET'S HOPE.

Pssst! I THINK SHE'S TALKING TO YOU.
WHAT, ME? MY DAD?
THANKS, I GUESS.
UH.
WHAT FOR?
WHAT FOR? AFTER ALL THESE YEARS HE'S STANDING UP FOR WHAT'S HIS, RIGHT?
OH! OH, I GET IT!
YOU THINK MR. FLAVOR IS MY DAD!!
HE'S NOT? I THOUGHT ...
NO, NO. OH GOD NO!
I'M HIS... I GUESS ASSISTANT. I HELP HIM WITH HIS ARTWORK AND STUFF.
HOW LONG HAVE YOU BEEN WITH "COMICS WORLD", UH, HILDY, RIGHT?
RIGHT.
ACTUALLY, IT'S FUNNY, THIS IS ONLY MY SECOND INTERVIEW ASSIGNMENT.
I'VE BEEN INTERNING FOR ABOUT A MONTH BUT I THINK I'M GOING TO QUIT AFTER THIS.
AND LEAVE SHOW BIZ? WHY?

I DON'T KNOW.
I GUESS I THOUGHT MAYBE I'D BE INTERESTED IN A CAREER IN WRITING, OR JOURNALISM OR SOMETHING BUT I GUESS I'M NOT.
PLUS, MR. PUPKIN IS ALWAYS MAKING PASSES AT ME.
:SIGH: AND THEY WONDER WHY MORE WOMEN DON'T WORK IN COMICS.
YOU KNOW, HILDY, YOU DON'T HAVE TO QUIT JUST BECAUSE THIS PUPK..
HILDY?
ARE YOU ALMOST READY WITH THAT TEA, DARLING?
I BELIEVE WE ARE READY TO RESUME THE INTERVIEW.
IT'LL BE A COUPLE OF MORE MINUTES.
STAR WARS
DIXIE
SO... UH, WHERE WERE WE MR. PUPKIN?
LET'S SEE ...YOU'D JUST SIGNED THAT RELEASE FOR ZOOM.
OH YEAH... YEAH, THAT'S RIGHT.

YEAH, SO I CONTINUED TO WORK FOR SIMON, FOR ZOOM FOR MANY YEARS AFTER THAT. I MOSTLY WORKED ON THE NIGHTSTALKER, BUT I ALSO HELPED DEVELOP SOME OTHER TITLES, EVEN TWO NIGHTSTALKER SPIN-OFFS, "CAPTAIN KNOCKOUT" AND "MOONBOY ADVENTURE".
JUSTICE COMES BY NIGHT
NIGHT-STALKER
NOW I WILL SHOW YOU MY TRUE IDENTITY!
:GASP: DR. FIEND!
ZOOM
IN 1950, I GOT MARRIED, WITH SIMON AS MY BEST MAN.
WHO IS "X" MAN?
LIKE I SAID, THINGS WAS GOING REALLY GOOD. I WAS HAPPY, MAKIN' DECENT MONEY, MARRIED TO A GREAT GAL.
THEN, ON THE DAY AFTER THANKSGIVING IN 1951, IT ALL FELL APART...
VAL? WASN'T SIMON SUPPOSED TO BE IN L.A.?
THE LIGHT'S ON IN HIS OFFICE. WHAT GIVES?
MR. LEBL--?
oh my god..

STALKER
NOW, YOU'RE GONNA HEAR A LOT OF SHIT ABOUT WHAT HAPPENED, HOW SIMON WAS IN WITH THE MOB, HOW SIMON WAS SCREWING DICKIE'S WIFE, ALL SORTS OF CRAP. WELL, DON'T YOU BELIEVE A WORD OF IT!
SIMON WAS A GREAT MAN. HE BUILT THIS COMPANY UP FROM NOTHING. SURE, HE MADE A LOTTA ENEMIES, ALL SUCCESSFUL MEN DO. SO I JUST WANT TO SET THE RECORD STRAIGHT. HE WAS A DECENT GUY.
IF IT WASN'T FOR HIM, NONE OF US WOULD BE HERE TODAY.
SO AFTER SIMON PASSED ON, HIS BROTHER JOEY TOOK OVER ZOOM. HE REALLY WASN'T TOO CRAZY ABOUT THE IDEA, DIDN'T REALLY HAVE HIS HEART INTO IT, SO AFTER TWO YEARS...
HEY, FELLAS, THIS IS MY NEPHEW JULIUS, SIMON'S SON.
HELLO.
HOLY MOLEY! "LITTLE JULES?"
HEY! I AIN'T SEEN YOU SINCE YOU WAS THIS HIGH!

GENTLEMEN, I'VE ARRANGED THIS LITTLE MEETING TO LET YOU KNOW THAT, AS OF NOW, "LITTLE JULES" IS EDITOR-IN-CHIEF OF ZOOM COMICS!
JOEY, YOU'RE SHITTIN' ME!
WELCOME ABOARD JULES! THAT'S GREAT! HEY! CAN I HAVE A RAISE?
HAW HAW!
PLEASE, CALL ME J.C.
AND WE'LL TALK ABOUT RAISES LATER. I WANT A CHANCE TO MEET WITH EACH OF YOU ONE-ON-ONE.
WE HAD THE MEETINGS, THE USUAL NEW-BOSS-I-WANT-TO-BE-YOUR-FRIEND-LET'S-ALL-WORK-HARD-AS-A-TEAM-BULLSHIT. HE ALSO WAS BIG ON PUTTING OUT A LOT MORE KINDS OF BOOKS, CUZ AT THIS POINT WE WERE STILL DOIN' SUPERHERO STUFF AND SALES WERE A BIT SLOW.
I WANT YOU TO DO A 10 PAGE HORROR STORY FROM YOU BY THE FIFTEENTH, OKAY?
I'VE HEARD THESE "INJURY TO THE EYE" STORIES ARE BIG WITH THE KIDS.
10 PAGES? UH, BUT WHAT ABOUT "NIGHTSTALKER"? I WON'T HAVE TIME...
IRV, UNTIL WE KNOW WHAT WE'RE DOING, TRYING OUT THESE NEW DIRECTIONS, ALL THE SUPERHERO BOOKS ARE CUTTING BACK TO A BI-MONTHLY SCHEDULE.
DON'T WORRY, WE'LL GIVE YOU OTHER WORK TO KEEP YOU BUSY.

WHAT ELSE COULD I DO? I DID THE MURDER STORY THE BEST I COULD. NEXT THING YOU KNOW, CHOP! CHOP! CHOP! JULES HAS CANCELLED HALF THE SUPERHERO TITLES AND PUT HORROR AND SCI-FI AND "TRUE CRIME" STUFF IN THEIR DAMN PLACE. ONE DAY CHUCK NESTOR COMES TO ME AND SAYS...
IRV... IRV, THEY FIRED ME.
WHAT?!
THEY'RE REPLACING "MAJOR JUSTICE" WITH A MYSTERY BOOK "WHODUNNIT?"
TOMMY JANGKOWSKI'S DOIN' IT.
JANGKOWSKI?! YOUR SON-OF-A BITCH ASSISTANT?! HE JUST STARTED! YOU'VE BEEN AT ZOOM FOR TEN YEARS!! THEY --
I KNOW... HEY, DON'T WORRY! THEY'RE NOT THE ONLY GAME IN THE SEA! I'M SURE I'LL BE WORKIN' AGAIN BY YESTERDAY!
LUCKILY, "NIGHTSTALKER" WAS ONE OF ZOOM'S ONLY SUPERHERO BOOKS THAT WAS MAKING MONEY. IN FACT, IT WAS EVEN MADE INTO A WEEKLY T.V. SHOW!
I WOULD FIGHT MY ENEMIES FROM HERE TO SCHENECTADY FOR ONE PUFF OF A CHESTERBORO™!
OF COURSE I NEVER SAW A PENNY OF IT, BUT I WAS STILL PROUD, AND ZOOM WAS STILL PAYING ME WELL.
UNTIL...

UM. YOU WANTED TO SEE ME?
IRVING, COME ON IN, SIT DOWN.
J.C., IF THIS IS ABOUT THAT VAMPIRE STORY, I TOLD CAROL I'D HAVE IT IN BY--
IRVING.
IRVING, I'M AFRAID I HAVE... I HAVE SOME BAD NEWS.
I THOUGHT THE BI-MONTHLY SCHEDULE WOULD HELP YOU OUT, BUT...
WELL.
I'M AFRAID WE'RE TAKING YOU OFF OF THE "NIGHTSTALKER" AND REPLACING YOU WITH ABE RONKO.
WH--?
WHAT?
I'M SORRY, IRVING, BUT--
"BUT?" BUT I'VE BEEN DOING NIGHTSTALKER FOR TEN YEARS!

I CREATED NIGHTSTALKER! GOD DAMN IT, HE'S MINE IF YOU THINK I'LL..
IRVING, IF YOU WANT TO WORK HERE AGAIN, I ADVISE YOU TO SIT DOWN AND LISTEN.
BUT I WOULDN'T SIT! THIS KID WASN'T GOING TO TELL ME WHAT TO DO!
"WHAT MAKES YOU THINK I WANT TO WORK HERE?" I SAYS TO HIM.
I TELL HIM "YOU'RE NOT KICKING ME OFF "NIGHTSTALKER'. IN FACT, UNLESS YOU RETURN IT TO A MONTHLY SCHEDULE, I'M WALKING!"
HE ASKS ME TO PLEASE BE REASONABLE, HE OFFERS ME A DEAL.
IF I'LL DO THE HORROR BOOKS, I'LL GET A 15% RAISE.
"NO WAY" I SAY.

"EITHER I STAY ON THE NIGHTSTALKER, OR I'M GONE.'"
"A 30% RAISE AND MY OWN OFFICE?" HE OFFERS ME. HE STARTS SAYING HOW IMORTANT I AM TO ZOOM.
"NO DEAL" I SAY.
"IF YOU CHANGE YOUR MIND," I SAY
"YOU KNOW WHERE YOU CAN FIND ME!"
1213
GREAT! WE'LL WRAP THIS UP NEXT TIME!

WHAT ELSE IS IN THE NEWS THIS MORNING, ROBIN?
WELL, A 7-YEAR OLD BOY WAS FOUND STABBED TO DEATH IN RIDGEWOOD, QUEENS...
UHAWHAWHAW!
JACKIE, THAT'S NOT FUNNY.
UH... THE BOY'S BODY WAS FOUND IN HIS AUNT'S ATTIC. POLICE ARE--
HOLD ON A SECOND. WHAT IS IT, BABA BOOEY?
OKAY, LISTEN TO ME ASSWIPE!
glorious results of a misspent youth
WHEN ARE YOU IDIOTS GOING TO IT THROUGH YOUR THICK HEADS?! HE DOES NOT WANT TO DO IT! HOW CAN I MAKE IT-- WHAT?
THERE'S AN ANGRY HAITIAN WOMAN ON THE PHONE, SHE WANTS TO TALK TO YOU.
GREAT! HELLO?
YES. I KNOW. NO, I... NO! AND PLEASE DON'T CALL HERE AGAIN, GOT IT?
GOOD!
KLAK!
WHAT ON EARTH WAS THAT ALL ABOUT?
OH, THAT WAS SOMEONE FROM THAT STUPID DICK INLET SHOW,
TRYING TO SUCKER STEPHEN ONTO THEIR SHOW.
IF IT'S SO GREAT THEN WHY'D YOU LEAVE? YOU DON'T HAVE A JOB, DO YOU?
STEPHEN? WHY WOULD THEY WANT HIM ON THEIR SHOW?
IS HE AN ALIEN TRANS-VESTITE OR SOMETHING?
WHY YOU SAY THAT? I'M NOT GOING--

OH, YOU KNOW, ABOUT THE WHOLE BROWN THING. I TOLD THEM BEFORE THAT HE--
WAIT A SEC, WHAT'S A "BROWN THING?"
MA'AM, HOW MUCH DO YOU WEIGH? YOU'RE A BIG FAT PIG, I BET. RIGHT?
UH.
YOU THE PIG! I'M NO GOING TO TALK AT YOU THIS WAY!!
HOW CAN YOU LISTEN TO THAT HOWARD STERNS? WHILE YOU'RE EATING NO LESS!
LADY, I HAVE TO GO. JUST REMEMBER TO GO BACK TO HAITI
OH NO, YOU AREN'T GETTING AWAY THAT EASY. WHAT'S THIS "BROWN THING?"
ALL RIGHT, WE HAVE TO GO TO COMMERCIALS... WE'LL BE
KLK!
STEPHEN NEVER...? I THOUGHT YOU KNEW, I THOUGHT HE TOLD YOU.
COME ON! WHAT IS IT? JAMES BROWN? BROWN ACID? THE ST. LOUIS BROWNS?
I'M DYIN' HERE!
ERR... I GUESS HE WOULDN'T MIND... BUT YOU HAVE TO PROMISE NOT TO TELL HIM
OR ANYONE
THIS BETTER BE GOOD AFTER ALL THIS BUILD UP.
OKAY: REMEMBER THAT CEREAL FROM THE '70s, "BROWN-E-OS?"
OH, SURE! THE ONE WITH THAT ANNOYING LITTLE SNOT-FACED KID?
"MOMMY! I CAN TASTE THE BROWN!"
HAHA!
HUNTER

DIDN'T THAT CEREAL CAUSE TUMORS?
THAT SNOT-FACED KID WAS STEPHEN.
GET OUTTA HERE!
IT'S TRUE
NO WAY!
IT'S TRUE.
YOU LIE!
I SWEAR IT.
TER
HE WAS IN A TOY STORE AND A DIRECTOR OR PRODUCER OR WHATEVER DISCOVERED HIM.
HE'S A NATURAL!
DID HE EVER DO ANYTHING ELSE?
NAH, BUT HIS PARENTS TOOK ALL THE MONEY FROM IT AND PUT IT IN LIKE A TRUST FUND.
IT PAID FOR HIS COLLEGE AND HE STILL HAS SOME SACKED AWAY.
MOMMY! I CAN TASTE THE BROWN!
SO, EVERYNOW AND AGAIN ONE OF THESE TALK SHOWS DO ONE OF THESE "WHERE-ARE-THEY-NOW" SHOWS AND PESTER STEPHEN TO APPEAR.
HE ACTUALLY DID DO IT ONCE ON A WHIM AFTER COLLEGE...
COME ON, SAY IT FOR US...
UH..."MOMMY, I CAN TASTE THE BROWN."
WOOOOOOO!
WHO'S THE MAN?

"SO FOR A FEW WEEKS FOLLOWING THE BROADCAST, AN ALL-TOO FAMILIAR SCENE PLAYED ITSELF OUT..."
ARE YOU READY TO ORDER?
UH, YEAH. IF I ORDER THE SOUP, WILL I BE ABLE TO TASTE THE BROWN? HAHAHA!
HAHA
SO, SINCE THEN, HE'S TRYING TO KEEP THE BROWN THING UNDER RAPS.
MAN, STEPHEN IS FULL OF SURPRISES, ISN'T HE?
YOU DON'T KNOW THE HALF OF ..
UH, YEAH, SO I TOLD HER THAT IN MY EXPERIENCE, THERE WAS NO SUCH THING AS LUCK, THAT NO MATTER H
MORNING EVERYBODY.
THIS MESS
?
WHAT ON EARTH ARE YOU TA..
HUNTER
I DIDN'T KNOW YOU WERE STILL HERE.
AREN'T YOU GOING TO THE INTERVIEW?
MWAH!
JESUS, THAT REMINDS ME. I HAVE TO GET READY FOR WORK!
HUNTER
NAH. IT'S JUST TOO DEPRESSING.
IF YOU'RE MAKING TEA, MAKE ME SOME?

FLAVORS A BITTER, MEAN UNLIKABLE OLD MAN.
BUT ZOOM REALLY SCREWED HIM OVER WITH THIS NIGHTSTALKER THING. HE SHOULD BE A MILLIONAIRE, KICKING BACK, RETIRED IN FLORIDA.
INSTEAD, HE LIVES IN A ROACH INFESTED APARTMENT IN BROOKLYN, STILL HAVING TO DRAW WHEN HE'S NEARLY EIGHTY.
A SLOW DEATH AT THE HANDS OF BIG BUSINESS.
SO, WHAT'RE YOU GOING TO DO TODAY INSTEAD? WORK ON THE BOOK?
YOU MUST BE ALMOST DONE WITH CHAPTER SIX, RIGHT?
SOMETIMES I'M ASHAMED OF THIS INDUSTRY.
OH, STEPHEN! NO! NO! NO!
PANT PANT
I CAN TASTE THE BROWN...
SLOBBER

NIGHT STALKER INTERVIEWS PART II:
LIFE in EXILE AFTER ABDICATION
SO WHAT THE HELL ELSE COULD I DO?

AFTER J.C.--AFTER I QUIT ZOOM, I STILL HAD A WIFE AND KID TO SUPPORT, RIGHT?
SO FIRST THING I DO IS START PRYING MY WARES TO OTHER COMICS PUBLISHERS. SO, UH, THAT'S HOW I HOOKED UP WITH EAGLE EYE INC.
THEY WERE MUCH SMALLER, OF COURSE, AND THE MONEY WASN'T NEARLY AS GOOD, BUT I DID GET A CERTAIN DEGREE OF RESPECT, SEEING AS HOW I MADE UP THE NIGHT-STALKER AND ALL.
OKAY, WHAT I NEED YOU TO DO IS, COME UP WITH ANOTHER CHARACTER LIKE THAT, OKAY?
WE KNOW YOU GOT IT IN YOU, MERV!
I TRIED MY HAND AT A BUNCH OF DIFFERENT CHARACTERS -- GLADIATOR, DR. OBOT, THE GLAMOUROUS GHOST -- BUT NONE OF THEM CAUGHT ON TO BIG.
I GOTTA HUNCH J.C. PULLED IN SOME FAVORS WITH THE NEWS-STAND DISTRIBUTORS TO MAKE SURE THE BOOKS WOULD FLOP... BUT I CAN'T PROVE NOTHING.

AFTER MY TIME WITH EAGLE EYE WAS UP, I WENT TO WORK FOR ANOTHER SMALL PUBLISHER, FUN STUFF TIME, WHO WAS OUT IN DETROIT OR SOMETHING.
I DID A GREAT NEW CHARACTER CALLED ATOMIC GORILLA. HE WAS A ZOO KEEPER WHO'D BEEN HIT BY A RADIOACTIVE ASTEROID AND TURNED INTO A SUPER-SMART APE.
BUT THE PUBLISHER SKIPPED TOWN WITH MY ART BEFORE THE FIRST ISSUE EVEN SAW PRINT. IF I EVER FIND THAT SON OF A BITCH... AHH, THAT WAS FORTY YEARS AGO, HE'S PROBABLY DEAD. WHERE WAS I?
DETROIT...
OH YEAH!
SHOULD HAVE SEATBELTS!
WHEN I GOT BACK TO NEW YORK, MY WIFE HAD MET THIS WOMAN WHOSE HUSBAND RAN THE APEX NOVELTY CO. OUT OF BAYONNE. HE WAS LOOKIN' FOR SOME ARTIST TO DO SOME OF THOSE, Y'KNOW, HUMOROUS BAR NAPKINS.
THE MONEY WASN'T BAD, SO...
THANKS ALOT, IRV! THESE LOOK GREAT! WAIT A SEC, I'LL CUT YOU A CHECK.
AND, HEY, WHILE I'M DOING THAT, TAKE A LOOK AT THIS.
YOU USED TO DRAW COMICS, RIGHT? YOU SHOULD GET A KICK OUT OF THIS.
BLOPPO'S WILD RIDE!

BUT WHAT IF DAGWOOD FINDS -- OH MY STARS!
GOOD, MRS. BUMSTEAD!
SLURP!
WHAT..?
HOLY SHIT! THIS IS ... WHAT THE HELL KIND OF COMIC IS THIS?!
HAHA! MY FRIEND, THAT'S WHAT'S KNOWN AS A "TIJUANNA BIBLE". A REAL RIB TICKLER, HUH?
NOW, LEMME SEE HERE...
THEY'RE NOT ALLOWED TO MAKE COMICS LIKE THIS, ARE THEY?
HAHA. NO, THEY AREN'T.
BUT WE DO IT ANYWAY.
AND SAY, IRV, IF YOU'RE EVER LOOKING FOR SOME MORE WORK...
HUH?
WHAT, YOU MEAN THIS KINDA SHIT?! I... COULDN'T... WHAT THE HELL WOULD I TELL MY WIFE?!
HOLY SHIT.
TCH!
YOUR WIFE! TELL HER YOU'RE MAKING MORE BAR NAPKINS! WHO CARES?
LOOK, IF YOU DON'T WANT TO DO, IT'S OKAY WITH ME. STELLA JUST TOLD ME YOU NEEDED THE WORK IS ALL.
UH.
HOW MUCH DOES IT PAY?

SO... THAT'S WHAT I DID FOR THE NEXT TWO MONTHS OR SO: DREW ILLEGAL PORNO COMICS, STARRING A LOT OF FAMOUS CARTOON CHARACTERS AND (IF I COULD GET THE LIKENESS) THE OCCASIONAL MOVIE STAR.
IT WAS AN EXPERIENCE, I'LL SAY THAT MUCH. FIRST IT WAS DISGUSTING, DRAWING THAT KIND OF STUFF. BUT AFTER A WHILE, I DON'T KNOW, IT BECAME KIND OF FUN, KIND OF LIKE SOLVING A MATH PROBLEM. BUT THEN IT GOT BORING. I MEAN THERE'S ONLY SO MANY POSES, Y'KNOW?
JUSTICE COMES BY NIGHT!
I'M NOT ASHAMED OF DOING IT. I NEEDED TO MAKE SOME MONEY, RIGHT? SO WHY THE HELL NOT? NOW, I KNOW THAT WE WERE, WHAT YA CALLIT, INFRINGING ON SOME COPYRIGHTS. BUT YOU KNOW WHAT? FUCK'EM! IF IT WASN'T FOR ZOOM GIVING ME THE AXE I WOULDN'T BE HAVING TO DO THIS SHIT TO--
UH, WAIT A SECOND, DIDN'T YOU SAY YOU QUIT ZOOM COMICS, MR. FLAVOR?

YEAH, THAT'S RIGHT, I QUIT. THAT'S WHAT I JUST SAID.
SO ONCE I FINISHED --
HILDY...
YEAH, BUT JUST NOW YOU SAID YOU WERE FIRED.
THEY DIDN'T FIRE ME, MISSY. I QUIT, LIKE I JUST SAID THERE.
NO, NO, YOU SAID A SECOND AGO YOU WERE FIRED! YOU SAID "IF IT WASN'T --
HILDY.
HAHAHA...
I'M SORRY MR. FLAVOR, WHY DON'T WE JUST KEEP ON GOING.
YOU WERE ABOUT TO TELL US WHAT YOUR NEXT JOB WAS AFTER... ABOUT YOUR NEXT JOB.
WELL, AS LONG AS I CAN CONTINUE WITHOUT ANYMORE OUTBURSTS FROM THE PEANUT GALLERY. SHE SEEMS TO KNOW MY CAREER BETTER THAN ME, RIGHT?
HANH?
EXCUSE ME FOR A MOMENT, MR. PUPKIN.
HA!
WOMEN, RIGHT?
HEH HEH
RIGHT, WOMEN...

WHAT'RE YOU DOING, ED?
HMM? OH, I'M WORKING ON THIS FLYER FOR A VIDEO STORE OPENING.
WITH MR. FLAVOR DOING THE INTERVIEW, SOMEONE HAS TO PICK UP THE SLACK ON THE DRAWING END.
IT MUST BE REALLY TOUGH WORKING ALL THE TIME FOR HIM.
DON'T TAKE THIS THE WRONG WAY, BUT HE CAN BE REALLY OBNOXIOUS.
MMM...
OKAY, SO BIG DEAL, RIGHT? YOU CREATED THIS SUPER-HERO AND GOT RIPPED OFF!
DOES THAT MEAN YOU HAVE TO TAKE IT OUT ON EVERYONE ELSE?
I GUESS SO...
GRAND
RENT ON

OKAY, DO YOU WANT TO HEAR SOMETHING REALLY FUNNY?
ACTUALLY, IT'S NOT REALLY FUNNY, IT'S ACTUALLY KIND OF DEPRESSING, BUT ANYWAY.
MY FRIEND CARLA AND I HAD TICKETS TO ONE OF THOSE FREE SNEAK PREVIEWS.
YOU KNOW, WHERE THEY LET YOU IN FOR FREE? IT WAS THE NEW JACKIE CHAN MOVIE. SO, WE'RE SUPPOSED TO--
HOW DO YOU SPELL "SISKEL", LIKE SISKEL AND EBERT?
IS IT S-I-S-K-E-L OR S-I-S-K-L-E?
UH, E-L, I THINK.
THAT'S WHAT I THOUGHT
(THEY SPELLED IT WRONG IN THIS AD COPY).
UH.
SO ANYWAY, WE WERE SUPPOSED TO GO SEE THIS MOVIE, BUT NOW HER BOYFRIEND WON'T LET HER GO!
CAN YOU BEAT THAT? I DON'T HAVE A BOYFRIEND, BUT IF I DID...
BOY, OH BOY!
OPEN
RENT ONE
WOW.
THE WORST PART IS NOW I HAVE TO GO BY MYSELF.
MEET T.V.
I FEEL SO PATHETIC GOING BY MYSELF, BUT I JUST MOVED TO THE CITY A FEW MONTHS AGO, SO I DON'T REALLY KNOW ANYBODY, RIGHT?

REALLY? HUH.
SO... IT LOOKS LIKE I'LL BE GETTING BACK TO THE INTERVIEW NOW
GRAND OPENING
HUH? OH, YEAH. I GUESS SO.

TAVERN
AT GIMBEL'S IN THE MEN'S DEPARTMENT SELLING MEN'S SLACKS, BUT I GOTTA TELL YOU, IT JUST WASN'T WORKING OUT. ASIDE FROM THE FACT THAT THE MONEY WAS SHIT, I... I MISSED DRAWING.
THE LAST ART JOB I HAD WAS TWO YEARS AGO, DRAWING THOSE GOD DAMNED PORNO COMICS.
I WAS OUT OF OPTIONS. SO I DECIDED TO TAKE A CRAPSHOOT AND BITE THE BULLET...
ZOOM
UH. HELLO. I'M HERE TO APPLY FOR THE ARTIST'S POSITIONS I SAW IN THE PAPER.
MY NAME IS FLAVOR... IRVING FLAVOR.
CERTAINLY, SIR. JUST LEAVE YOUR PORTFOLIO WITH US OVERNIGHT AND WE'LL CALL YOU TOMORROW, MMMHM?
OH...UH.
SURE. SURE.
THIS IS SOMETHING SENATOR KENNEDY AND ALL AMERICANS MUST KNOW. WE TRIED IT WITH HITLER AND...
HELLO. MY NAME IS FLAVOR, I DROPPED OFF MY PORTFOLIO YESTERDAY?
OH, YES, THIRD ROOM ON THE LEFT, MR. NESTOR IS WAITING.

"NESTOR?" I WONDER IF THAT'S THE SAME --
IRV! GOOD TO SEE YOU!
I'LL BE DAMNED! CHUCK NESTOR!
HOW'D YOU WIND UP BACK HERE, YOU OLD BASTARD?
OH, I'VE BEEN HERE ABOUT TWO YEARS NOW. LET'S GO IN MY OFFICE.
"YOUR OFFICE!" LISTEN TO YOU, MR. BIGSHOT! WHEN--
J.C.!
IRVING! GOOD TO SEE YOU AGAIN!
WE WERE JUST IN THE MIDDLE OF A STORY CONFERENCE.
HAVE A SEAT.
SO, CHUCK HERE TELLS ME YOU'RE LOOKING FOR WORK.
UH. YES, SIR.
RELAX, IRV, RELAX.
I KNOW THERE'S BEEN SOME BAD BLOOD BETWEEN US, BUT AS FAR AS I'M CONCERNED THAT'S HISTORY.
AND I'M NOT WHAT YOU WOULD CALL A "HISTORY BUFF."

CHUCK'S SHOWN ME YOUR PORTFOLIO, AND IT LOOKS LIKE YOU STILL "GOT IT." SO AS LONG AS YOU'LL BEHAVE YOURSELF YOU'VE GOT A JOB, OKAY?
UH, OKAY, SURE.
OH! UH:
BUT J.C., WE DON'T NEED ANY PENCILLERS RIGHT NOW. MAYBE, IRV, WE COULD CALL YOU ONCE AN OPENING -- UH...
UH, ONCE WE HAVE AN OPENING. J.C.?
HMMM.
I THINK I HAVE AN IDEA. IRV, WHAT DO YOU THINK ABOUT STARTING OUT IN MECHANICAL?
MECHANICAL? YOU MEAN,.. DOWNSTAIRS MECHANICAL?
YES, YOU KNOW: PASTE UP, CORRECTIONS, WHAT HAVE YOU. WE REALLY DO NEED SOMEONE QUICK.
IT WOULD BE STRICTLY TEMPORARY, OF COURSE.
WHAT ELSE COULD I DO?
I TOOK IT.

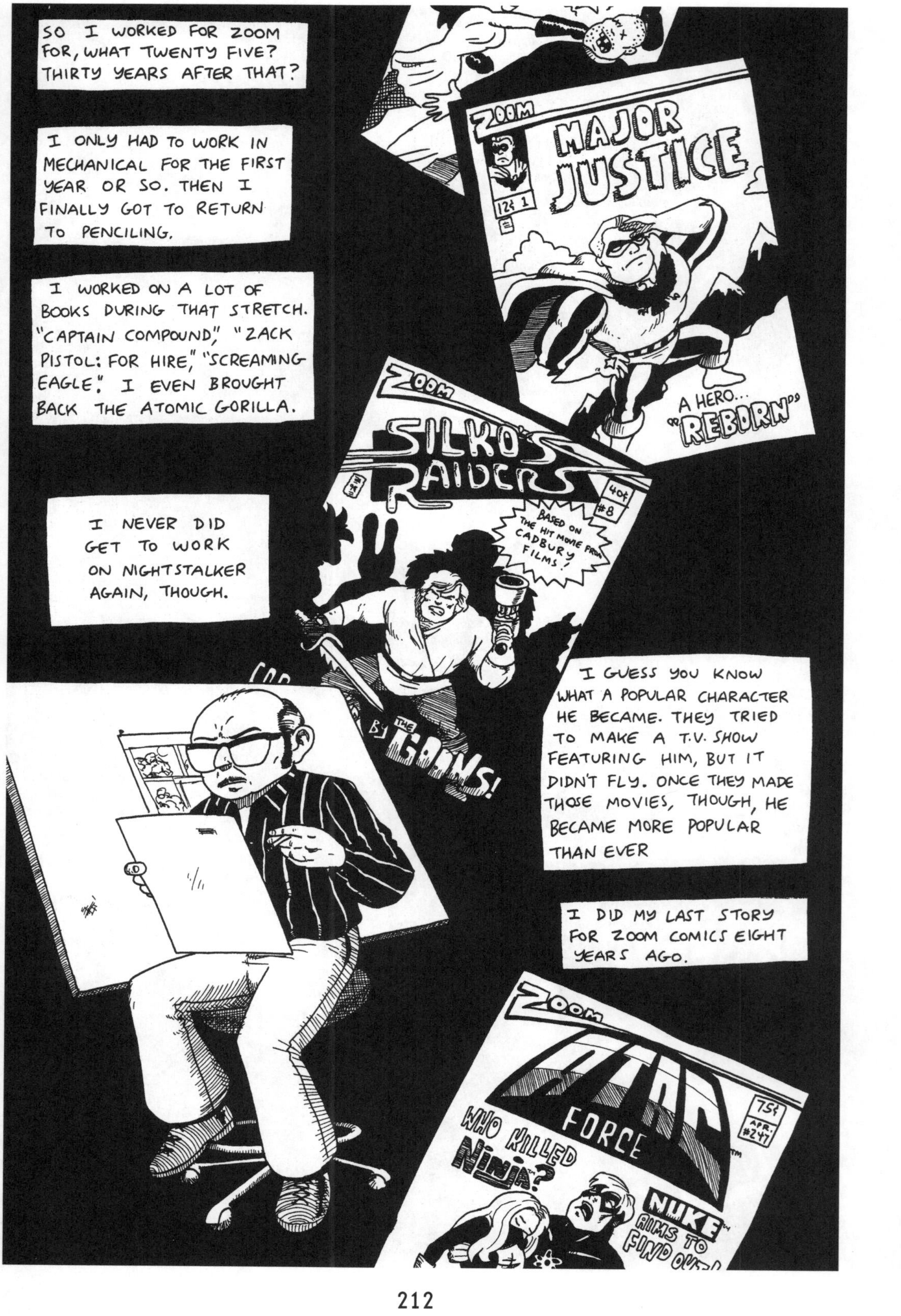
SO I WORKED FOR ZOOM FOR, WHAT TWENTY FIVE? THIRTY YEARS AFTER THAT?
I ONLY HAD TO WORK IN MECHANICAL FOR THE FIRST YEAR OR SO. THEN I FINALLY GOT TO RETURN TO PENCILING.
ZOOM
MAJOR JUSTICE
12¢ 1
A HERO... "REBORN"
I WORKED ON A LOT OF BOOKS DURING THAT STRETCH. "CAPTAIN COMPOUND," "ZACK PISTOL: FOR HIRE," "SCREAMING EAGLE." I EVEN BROUGHT BACK THE ATOMIC GORILLA.
ZOOM
SILKO'S RAIDERS
40¢ #8
BASED ON THE HIT MOVIE FROM CADBURY FILMS!
I NEVER DID GET TO WORK ON NIGHTSTALKER AGAIN, THOUGH.
BY THE GOONS!
I GUESS YOU KNOW WHAT A POPULAR CHARACTER HE BECAME. THEY TRIED TO MAKE A T.V. SHOW FEATURING HIM, BUT IT DIDN'T FLY. ONCE THEY MADE THOSE MOVIES, THOUGH, HE BECAME MORE POPULAR THAN EVER
I DID MY LAST STORY FOR ZOOM COMICS EIGHT YEARS AGO.
ZOOM
FORCE
75¢ APR. #247
WHO KILLED NINJA?
NUKE AIMS TO FIND OU

I...UH, GUESS THAT'S ABOUT IT.
SEEMS KINDA ANTI-CLIMATIC, DON'T IT?
HONESTLY? YES.
BUT IN REALITY?
NO!
FOR YOU SEE, WE HAVE SIMPLY SEEN THE FIRST TWO ACTS OF THE DRAMA THAT IS YOUR LIFE!
NOW! WHEN WE RETURN FROM THE INTERMISSION, WE SHALL BEAR WITNESS TO THE HEART RACING FINALE!
YEAH, HUH?
WE'RE GOING TO PUBLISH THIS INTERVIEW! RALLY THE COMICS COMMUNITY TO YOUR SIDE! WE WILL RECLAIM YOUR RIGHTFUL CLAIM TO THE NIGHTSTALKER!!
AN EXCITING NEW ERA IN THE HISTORY OF SEQUENTIAL ART!
THE RETURN OF IRVING FLAVOR!

IF YOU COULD CHANGE ONE ASPECT OF YOUR APPEARANCE WHAT WOULD IT BE?

PAINFUL GENITAL ITCHING? CALL US TODAY
THIS MEANS YOU! PUNCHING IN OTHER EMPLOYEES ARE GROUNDS FOR INSTANT
CHUNG
DO YOU WORK HERE, SIR?
WHERE ARE YOUR THREE DIMENSIONAL BOOKS?
IS THIS YOUR MOST RECENT LATIN DICTIONARY?
THIS CAME OUT IN 1969!
DO YOU KNOW WHO WON THE PULITZER PRIZE IN 1982? WHERE DO YOU KEEP THOSE BOOKS?
DO YOU BELONG TO THIS STORE? DO YOU HAVE THIS IN A SMALLER VERSION?
NUCLEAR PHYSICS
CAN I AXE YOU SOMETHING? YOU WORK HERE, RIGHT?
CAN YOU TALK TO MY DAUGHTER AND FIND OUT WHICH BOOKS SHE NEEDS?
IS THIS BOOK OUT IN PAPERBACK? DO YOU WORK IN THIS STORE?
IS THERE ANYONE HERE WHO REALLY KNOWS THE BOOKS?
WHEN WILL THIS COME OUT IN HARDCOVER?
WHITE AS SHE
YOU ARE WORKING HERE, PLEASE?
SHERMAN, I WANT TO TALK TO YOU IN MY OFFICE.

SHERMAN, THIS MORNING A CUSTOMER COMPLAINED ABOUT YOUR ATTITUDE.
NOW, NORMALLY WE'D LET IT SLIDE, BUT LATELY YOUR PERFORMANCE HAS BEEN... NOT WHAT IT COULD BE...
I SEE THAT YOU'VE BEEN LATE FOUR TIMES AND ALREADY MISSED TWO DAYS THIS MONTH.
I'M NOT GOING TO GIVE YOU A FORMAL WARNING, BUT OFF THE RECORD...
GET IT IN GEAR, OKAY?
HEY, YOU WORK HERE CHIEF? CAN YOU HELP ME?
WARNING!!
KA-CHUNG
BOILING FROG No. 2
Art of FRICTION
FUCKER
FUCKIN' PIECE OF SHIT ASS MOTHER FUCKER GOD DAMN FUCK ASS!!
PERFECT ENDING TO A PERFECT FUCKING DAY. WHERE THE HELL IS SHE?!
FUCK
MATTHEWS'

HI! HI! I'M SORRY I'M LATE! GROMIT WOULDN'T LET--
WHERE THE HELL'VE YOU BEEN?! I'VE BEEN STANDING OUT HERE IN THE COLD FOR HALF A FUCKING HOUR!
VOICE
HOMELESS HAVE AIDS PLEASE HELP GOD BLESS
WHY DIDN'T YOU WAIT INSIDE THE STORE WHERE IT WAS WARM? I WOULD'VE --
I CAN'T STAND TO BE IN THAT URINE SOAKED HELL HOLE A FUCKING SECOND MORE THAN I HAVE TO.
BESIDES, THAT'S NOT THE POINT.
OH? SO WHAT IS "THE
THE POINT IS THAT YOU'RE LATE. AGAIN.
WHAT THE HELL'S UP WITH YOU? I SAID I WAS SORRY!
YEAH, I KNOW, YOU SAY THAT EVERY TIME YOU'RE LATE AND I'M BEGINNING TO NOT BELIVE YOU.
I SWEAR, DOROTHY, I FEEL LIKE I'VE SPENT THE BETTER PART OF SIX LIFETIMES WAITING FOR YOU OUTSIDE MOVIE THEATERS AND WAITING FOR YOU OUTSIDE CONCERT VENUES AND WAITING FOR YOU OUTSIDE SUBWAY STATIONS AND-- UGH! I'M JUST GOD DAMNED SICK OF IT!
SHIT, SOUNDS LIKE SOMEBODY HAD A GOOD DAY AT WORK.

AS A MATTER OF FACT, I DID. ASIDE FROM THE USUAL HELLISHNESS, THE DRAGON YELLED AT ME FOR BEING LATE.
I DON'T KNOW WHY YOU DON'T GET ANOTHER JOB. ALL YOU EVER--
OH, THAT'S REALLY EASY FOR YOU TO SAY. YOU'VE GOT A GREAT JOB YOU LIKE DOING!
THIS IS THE N-TRAIN TO CONEY ISLAND MAKING ALL LOCAL STOPS STAND CLEAR OF...
WHO? ME?
MY EDITOR IS TEN TIMES WORSE THAN ANY RINKY DINK BOOKSTORE MANAGER! YOU WOULDN'T LAST FIVE MINUTES WITH HER!
?? OH, SO WHAT'S THAT SUPPOSED TO MEAN? YOU--
IT MEANS THAT YOU'RE ACTING LIKE A HELPLESS LITTLE BABY INSTEAD OF GETTING UP OFF YOUR ASS AND TRYING TO DO SOMETHING!
FUCKER!
FUCK YOU! THERE'S NOTHING I CAN--
"Oh, my boss is so mean! Those customers are so stupid! My life is so hard! Sob! Sob!"
IF YOU DON'T LIKE THE JOB THEN QUIT. IT'S A BOOKSTORE, NOT BRAIN SURGERY, YOU'LL FIND ANOTHER ONE.
SO, SHIT OR GET OFF THE POT, OKAY?

2187
OH, YOU REALLY HAVE THE ANSWERS TO EVERYONE ELSE'S PROBLEMS DON'T YOU? WHY DON'T YOU TAKE A LOOK AT YOUR OWN STUPID LIFE FOR A CHANGE.
HEY, I MAY HAVE PROBLEMS BUT AT LEAST I'M NOT FUCKING BELLY ACHING ABOUT THEM ALL THE TIME.
THAT'S TRUE. INSTEAD YOU SPREAD THEM AROUND SO THEY BECOME EVERY-ONE'S PROBLEMS.
WHA--?! LIKE WHAT? I DON'T--
"LIKE WHAT?" LIKE MONEY FOR INSTANCE. YOU STILL HAVEN'T PAID ME BACK THAT $100 YOU BORROWED FOR YOUR RENT LAST MONTH.
YEAH, AND YOU ONLY REMIND ME OF THAT TWICE A DAY.
YEAH, PLUS EVERY TIME I SEE YOU BLOW $200 ON SHOES YOU'LL NEVER FUCKING WEAR OR ANOTHER CASE OF GIN.

YOU.. GO FUCK YOURSELF, OKAY?
OH, WHAT'S THE MATTER? DID I..
SHERMAN! THERE'S SOME MAIL FOR YOU ON THE DESK.
BULL RUN!
IT'S FROM THE NEW YORKER.
OH MY GOD! OPEN IT!
WHAT... WHAT DOES IT SAY?
UM...
"DEAR CONTRIBUTOR..."

OH... DON'T WORRY ABOUT IT TOO MUCH, SWEETIE.
I HEARD THAT WILLIAM FAULKNER WALL-PAPERED HIS BED ROOM WITH ALL HIS REJECTION SLIPS.
BESIDES, THE NEW YORKER ISN'T EASY TO CRACK.
YEAH. YEAH, I KNOW.
I GUESS I WAS SECRETLY HOPING THAT ... I DON'T KNOW.
F. SCOTT FITZGERALD WAS MY AGE WHEN HE WROTE "THIS SIDE OF PARADISE".
DON'T WORRY, SWEETIE. JUST GIVE YOURSELF SOME TIME.
I BELIEVE IN YOU.
OH YEAH:
MY DAD'S COMING IN TO TOWN NEXT WEEK FOR THANKSGIVING AND HE WANTS TO HAVE DINNER WITH US, OKAY?
G'NIGHT.

ED'S BANTIA
SPECIALS
BACON SANDWICH
HOT DOGS
DELICIOUS COFFEES
SO WHEN IS THIS BIG INTERVIEW WITH THIS FLAVOR GUY SUPPOSED TO BE PUBLISHED?
WHERE HE TELLS HIS LIFE STORY AND ALL?
Brooklyn
I'M NOT SURE. I THINK IT COMES OUT IN TWO WEEKS OR SO.
WHY?
I DON'T KNOW... I'M JUST THINKING: THIS GUY'S STORY MIGHT BE A GOOD PIECE FOR OUR MAGAZINE.
REALLY?
WOULD "METRO-CHIC" DO AN ARTICLE LIKE THAT?
OF COURSE. I WOULD JUST HAVE TO CLEAR IT WITH MY EDITOR. DO YOU THINK I COULD INTERVIEW HIM?

SURE! I'LL TALK TO HIM ABOUT IT. THAT WOULD REALLY BE GREAT.
MARVELOUS. WELL, I'M GOING TO LEAVE YOU TWO FOR YOUR BOYS' NIGHT OUT.
YOU HAVE A KEY, RIGHT, SWEETIE?
UH-HUH.
STAY OUT AS LONG AS YOU WANT AND GET AS DRUNK AS YOU WANT, I WON'T WAIT UP.
SO LONG, BOYS! HAPPY BIRTHDAY, NED!
BYE.
LET'S GO, GROMIT! DID YOU LIKE YOUR LITTLE WALKY?
DINER
"NED?"
DO YOU THINK SHE WAS SERIOUS ABOUT DOING AN ARTICLE ON MR. FLAVOR?
THAT WOULD REALLY HELP HIM OUT.
I DON'T KNOW... LAST WEEK SHE WANTED TO INTERVIEW SOME JUGGLER IN UNION SQUARE PARK.
BEFORE THAT IT WAS SOME HOMELESS WOMAN ON THE F-TRAIN PLATFORM.
I WOULDN'T GET TOO EXCITED.
I GUESS SO. WE COULD REALLY USE THE PUBLICITY, THOUGH. I'M HOPING THAT EVEN IF HE CAN'T GET NIGHTSTALKER BACK, AT LEAST HE MAYBE COULD GET SOME STEADY WORK.
WHAT ABOUT YOU? ARE YOU STILL GETTING PAID?

SEE, THAT'S JUST IT: WE'VE HARDLY HAD ANY JOBS THE PAST FEW WEEKS AND HE HASN'T BEEN ABLE TO PAY ME.
THANK GOD MY AUNT DAISY GAVE ME SOME BIRTHDAY MONEY!
WELL, I SUPPOSE THAT'S MY CUE...
HAPPY BIRTHDAY, YOU LONG EARED GALLOOT!
Ed!
A FIFTY DOLLAR GIFT CERTIFICATE TO "UNCLE AL'S COMIC GALAXY OF FUN AND COLLECTABLES!"
OH BOY!
UNCLE
COMIC GALA
OF FUN AND COLLECTABLE
OPEN
HELL DID ALL COME FROM? ANSWER TO THAT!
WHAT TH--?!
SPACE CREATURE!™
YOU KNOW WHAT YOU'RE GOING TO GET?
ALMOST. WHICH ONE SHOULD I GET?
"THE COMPLEAT BLOPPO VOL. II"
OR "EAVESDROP: A CARTOON JOURNAL OF A PATHETIC BASTARD?"
NIGHTSTALKER V.S. SPACE CREAT

SPEAKING OF WHICH, DID YOU EVER WIND UP TALKING TO THAT BLONDE GIRL? ZELDA?
WHO? HILDY? THAT GIRL FROM "COMICS WORLD? NAH. SHE HAD NO INTEREST IN ME.
SHE WAS REALLY CUTE THOUGH. TALL ... AND THOSE BREASTS...
MAN.
COMPLEAT BLAPPO VOLUME 2
THESE PAST FEW WEEKS I'VE HAD A MAD CRUSH ON THIS PUERTO RICAN GIRL AT WORK.
I SEEM TO HAVE A THING FOR SPANISH GIRLS LATELY.
OH YEAH?
"I HAD ONE OF THOSE WEIRD MOMENTS WHERE I WAS TALKING TO HER AND I FELT LIKE 'If I was still single, I think this girl might have gone out with me. I could've kissed her.'"
"YOU KNOW HOW IT IS. AS SOON AS YOU'RE UNAVAILABLE, IT'S LIKE A MAGNET. I THINK IT'S THAT BOOST OF CONFIDENCE YOU GET--
WHAT?
FUCK YOU.
OKAY?
OH, COME ON, ED. YOU'RE TIME WILL COME!
AUGH.
IF I WASN'T SO POOR, I THINK I WOULD BLOW ALL MY MONEY ON A HIGH PRICED CALL GIRL AND GET IT OVER WITH.
PUD SQUAD
DOCTOR YANK!
DEATH GIRL
DO NOT TOUCH
YOU SHOULD! PUT IT ON YOUR CREDIT CARD!
OH, SCREW YOU. YOU JUST WANT TO SEE ME--
OH MY GOD. I'M IN LOVE.

$125.00
NO BOX GOOD COND.
WHAT THE HECK IS IT?
IT'S A BANTHA! THE TUSKEN RAIDERS RODE THEM IN "STAR WARS," REMEMBER?
UH.
THEY WERE SUPPOSED TO MAKE THESE AS PART OF THE TENTH ANNIVERSARY RELEASES, BUT BECAUSE OF A PRINTING ERROR, THEY ONLY MADE THREE THOUSAND!
ONLY?
ED, YOU KNOW THIS IS A SIDE OF YOU THAT SCARES ME, RIGHT?
I'VE GOT TO HAVE IT.
I DON'T KNOW, $125 IS A LITTLE STEEP.
YOU COULD PROBABLY GET AT LEAST A MID-PRICED CALL GIRL FOR THAT.
I KNOW... BUT...
SHE WOULD ONLY BE MINE FOR AN HOUR...
A BANTHA IS FOREVER.

HAHAHA!
LIKE YOU COULD LAST AN HOUR WITH A CALL GIRL!
VERY FUNNY, SMART GUY. COME ON, I GOT AN APPOINTMENT WITH THIS BANTHA!
I CAN'T BELIEVE I JUST SPENT $125 ON A TOY. I'M SO STUPID.
"HAPPY BIRTHDAY, NED!"
UNCLE AL'S COMIC GALAXY
MOM! I'M HOME! SORRY I'M LATE.
DID I MISS DINNER?
HMM? OH, NO, NO. YOUR FATHER HAD TO WORK LATE AT THE STORE SO WE WON'T EAT UNTIL 9:30, OKAY?
THERE'S SOME MAIL FOR YOU ON THE TELEVISION, AND DON'T FORGET TO CALL AUNT DAISY AND THANK HER.
YEAH, YEAH, YEAH...
I HOPE THIS IS BIRTHDAY MONEY...
JEEPERS!

NOV. '94
COMICS WORLD
Number 196
$5.95 U.S. $8.95 Can.
THIS ISSUE: SALES CONTINUE TO RISE INDUSTRY-WIDE!
PLUS THE WORST COMICS OF THE YEAR!
ZOOM COMICS VS. IRVING FLAVOR
PIONEER CREATOR CHALLENGES THE "PALACE OF DREAMS" FOR OWNERSHIP OF THE NIGHTSTALKER!

WHAT IS YOUR SECRET TALENT?
LA LA LA LA LA LA LA LA
I USED TO PLAY TRUMPET.
BACK IN THE FORTIES, I MEAN.
I CAN DO A MEAN MARLON BRANDO:
"EVERY TIME I TRY TO GET OUT, THEY PULL ME RIGHT BACK IN!"
WHEN I WAS YOUNGER, I COULD OPEN A BEER BOTTLE WITH MY TEETH.
NO, I WOULDN'T TRY IT NOW!
UH... I CAN JUGGLE.
I USED TO TAKE PIANO LESSONS. I COULD PROBABLY PLAY "DON'T LET IT END."
I KNOW EVERY INKER WHO EVER WORKED ON "BATMAN."

MADAM.
MADAM!
HUH? WHAT.
MADAM, TWENNYTIRD ANINTH AVENUE.
PLEASE, EYDOLLAR, FORTY CENT YOU WILL, PLEASE.
CENSE
HMET AMAPEDALON
MOKING
YOU C'N KEEP THE CHANGE...
gromit
318
EVENIN'
ZZZZ
ALL VISITORS MUST BE ANNOUNCED

GROMIT, SWEETIE, MOMMY'S HOME...
MOMMY'S REAL TIRED SO SHILL FEED Y' TOMORROW, KAY?
?!
GROMIT?

RING
RING
RING
RING
:GROAN: WHO THE HELL IS CALLING US AT THIS HOUR?
RING
RING
SHOULD WE GET IT? WHAT IF IT'S LIKE AN EMERGENCY?
RING
WHATEVER IT IS, IT CAN WAIT FIVE MORE HOURS.
I'M NOT GETTING IT.
RING
RING
UGH! I CAN'T STAND IT ANYMORE! I GONNA GO GET..
OW!
SORRY!
RIN-
HELLO?
SHERMAN? HELLO, IS SHERMAN THERE?
WHO..?! IS THIS DOROTHY?!
YEAH. CAN I TALK TO SHERMAN?

I THINK HE'S ASLEEP, SEEING AS HOW IT'S 2:30 IN THE--
CAN I PLEASE TALK TO SHERMAN, PLEASE?
HAHA HA!
SHERMAN
HAHA HEE!
HA HA!
SHERMAN
HAHA! HA!
SHERMAN
MUH.. WHAT?
DOROTHY'S ON LINE ONE.
AM I TO UNDERSTAND IT IS NOW 2:37 IN THE MORNING?
THAT'S RIGHT.
SHE INSISTED.
THIS HAD BETTER BE GOOD. I HAVE TO BE AT WORK IN--
SHERM? OH, SWEETIE! I DON'T KNOW WHAT TO DO! SHIT!
ABOUT WHAT? WAIT, WAIT, CALM DOWN, WHAT'S WRONG?!
IT'S GROMIT! I-- I CAME HOME, AND HE WAS, WAS ALL--
WAIT A MINUTE...YOU CAME HOME JUST NOW? WHERE WERE YOU ALL NIGHT?!

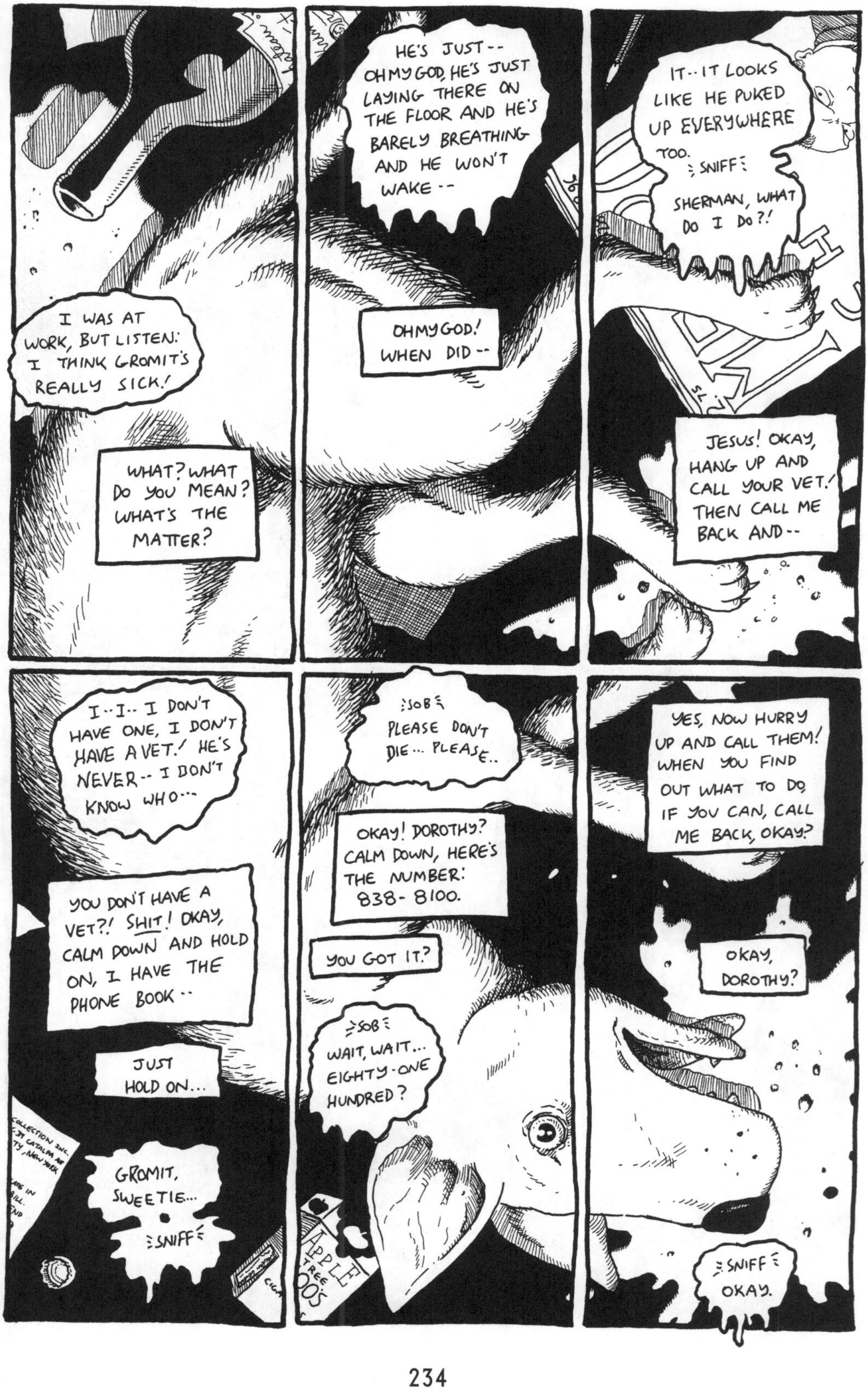
I WAS AT WORK, BUT LISTEN: I THINK GROMIT'S REALLY SICK!
WHAT? WHAT DO YOU MEAN? WHAT'S THE MATTER?
HE'S JUST-- OHMYGOD, HE'S JUST LAYING THERE ON THE FLOOR AND HE'S BARELY BREATHING AND HE WON'T WAKE--
OHMYGOD! WHEN DID--
IT--IT LOOKS LIKE HE PUKED UP EVERYWHERE TOO.
SNIFF
SHERMAN, WHAT DO I DO?!
JESUS! OKAY, HANG UP AND CALL YOUR VET! THEN CALL ME BACK AND--
I--I-- I DON'T HAVE ONE, I DON'T HAVE A VET! HE'S NEVER-- I DON'T KNOW WHO--
YOU DON'T HAVE A VET?! SHIT! OKAY, CALM DOWN AND HOLD ON, I HAVE THE PHONE BOOK--
JUST HOLD ON...
GROMIT, SWEETIE...
SNIFF
SOB
PLEASE DON'T DIE... PLEASE..
OKAY! DOROTHY? CALM DOWN, HERE'S THE NUMBER: 838-8100.
YOU GOT IT?
SOB
WAIT, WAIT... EIGHTY-ONE HUNDRED?
YES, NOW HURRY UP AND CALL THEM! WHEN YOU FIND OUT WHAT TO DO, IF YOU CAN, CALL ME BACK, OKAY?
OKAY, DOROTHY?
SNIFF
OKAY.

NOVEMBER
RIN--
YES? YES? HELLO?!
SHERMAN? I CALLED...

:SNIFF: THEY TOLD ME TO BRING HIM TO THE HOSPITAL, SO I'M GOING TO CATCH A CAB.
WILL YOU MEET ME THERE?
SURE.
I'LL BE THERE AS SOON AS I CAN. DON'T WORRY. HE'LL BE FINE.
I HOPE SO :SNIFF:
I LOVE YOU, SWEETIE.
... I LOVE YOU, TOO. BYE.
GOOD BYE.
THE SMOKING SECTION: LAST REFUGE OF THE OPPRESSED.
WH--?

OH, SHERMAN. I'M SO GLAD YOU'RE HERE...
SORRY IT TOOK ME SO LONG. YOU KNOW THE F-TRAIN.
DID YOU TALK TO THE DOCTOR?
ANI
THEY JUST TOOK HIM IN. THEY DON'T KNOW WHAT HAPPENED YET OR WHAT'S WRONG.
I'M SO SCARED.
DON'T WORRY, HE'LL BE FINE. HOWS ABOUT WE WAIT INSIDE? THAT WAY IF THE DOCTOR NEEDS YOU, HE CAN FIND YOU. OKAY?
OKAY.
MR. O'BRIEN?
YEAH? HOW IS SHE?
WE HAVE GOOD NEWS, MR. O'BRIEN. WE X-RAYED DIGGLES AND IT LOOKS LIKE THE TOY WILL PROBABLY PASS WITHOUT ANY PROBLEM.
LASSIE SA
"SPAY ME,
OH, THANK GOD! MY WIFE WAS WORRIED SICK!
MISS LESTRADE?

MISS LESTRADE?
WHAT? YES?
HI, I'M DOCTOR KLOSIG.
I'VE HAD A CHANCE TO TAKE A LOOK AT ...GROMIT, AND I THINK WE'VE FIGURED IT OUT.
FIX
WE THINK GROMIT IS SUFFERING FROM AN OVERDOSE OF A DEPRESSANT, MOST LIKELY ALCOHOL
IT'S JUST ABOUT THE SAME AS IT IS IN HUMANS, EXCEPT, OBVIOUSLY, A DOG GROMIT'S SIZE WOULD NOT HAVE TO DRINK ALOT BEFORE HE BECAME ILL.
JESUS.
DOES THIS SOUND PLAUSIBLE?
DID YOU NOTICE ANY BROKEN BOTTLES OR SPILLED LIQUOR...?
ANYTHING OF THAT NATURE?
MAYBE. I...
I DON'T KNOW.

IN ANY CASE, I'M GOING TO BE STRAIGHT WITH YOU: AT THIS POINT YOUR DOG GROMIT IS IN A COMA.
WE'RE DOING WHAT WE CAN, BUT UNFORTUNATELY, THERE ISN'T MUCH WE--
EX
I WANT YOU TO DO EVERYTHING YOU CAN DO! I DON'T CARE HOW MUCH IT COSTS, OR, OR,
JUST PLEASE MAKE SURE HE'LL BE OKAY!
UH...
WE WILL, MISS LESTRADE BUT I HAVE TO BE HONEST WITH YOU:
IT IS UNLIKELY GROMIT WILL COME OUT OF THIS COMA.
USUALLY WHEN AN ANIMAL THIS STAT ...UH, DEAT
OHMYGOD OHMYGOD OH MYGOD
WH...
CAN :SNIFF:
CAN I SEE HIM?
CERTAINLY.
I'LL BE RIGHT BACK, SWEETIE.

SO THIS GUY COMES IN AND SAYS TO ME "I'M LOOKING FOR A BOOK BY JOSE IGNJATOVIC."
I SAY "SURE. HOW DO YOU SPELL THAT LAST NAME?" AND THE GUY GOES "IGNJATOVIC. JOSE IGNJATOVIC."
ENJOY SNACKS
CAUTI
WET FL
SO I SAY, "OKAY, HOW DO YOU SPELL THAT?"
"IGNJATOVIC. IGNJATOVIC."
I ASK HIM "DO YOU KNOW THE TITLE OF THIS BOOK?
HE SAYS "IGNJATOVIC. JOSE IGNJATOVIC."
AT THIS POINT I'M BEGINNING TO FEEL LIKE BASIL FAWLTY -- YOU KNOW, FROM "FAWLTY TOWERS". I SAY, "CAN YOU SPELL THE LAST NAME?
I EVEN TRY TO HELP HIM ALONG: "I-G-?"
"IGNJATOVIC." HE TELLS ME.
"JOSE IGNJATOVIC."
I SWEAR, PEOPLE ARE SO STUPID.
WHAT AM I GOING TO DO IF HE DIES?
HE'S NOT -- HE'LL BE OKAY.
UH, YOU SURE YOU DON'T WANT A BITE?
IF I -- IT'S MY FAULT. IF I WASN'T SUCH A SLOB THIS WOULD NEVER HAVE HAPPENED.

COME ON, IT WAS AN ACCIDENT. YOU'VE DONE EVERYTHING YOU CAN TO HELP HIM.
STOP BEATING YOURSELF UP OVER IT.
LET'S GO OUTSIDE FOR A CIGARETTE, OKAY?
PARK
SHIT.
I'M SO TIRED. LOOKS LIKE I WON'T BE GOING TO THE OFFICE TODAY.
DO YOU WANT ME TO TAKE OFF FROM--
MISS LESTRADE.
YES?
I'M, UH.
I'M AFRAID I HAVE SOME BAD NEWS...

"ARE YOU SURE YOU DON'T WANT ME TO CALL OUT AND KEEP YOU COMPANY?"
"NAH. I'M JUST GOING TO GO HOME AND GO TO SLEEP."
"OKAY, I'LL CALL YOU WHEN I GET HOME FROM WORK."
"SEE YOU LATER"
"BYE"
CORSOKOFF
PREMIUM
VODKA

"OKAY, I'LL CALL YOU WHEN I GET HOME FROM WORK."
"SEE YOU LATER."
SHERMAN, I HAVE TO SPEAK TO YOU, PLEASE.
"BYE."
SHERMAN, I COULDN'T HELP BUT NOTICE YOU WERE TWO HOURS LATE.
YEAH, I'M SORRY. I CALLED MARIA AND TOLD HER TO TELL...
I DON'T CARE IF YOU SENT A TELEGRAM FROM KATMANDU. YOU WERE STILL LATE.
I HAVE WARNED YOU REPEATEDLY ABOUT YOUR RECENT ABSENCES, YOUR LATENESSES, BUT YOU DON'T SEEM TO...
SIGH
OKAY, I DON'T LIKE TO HAVE TO DO THIS, BUT I'M GIVING YOU A FORMAL, WRITTEN WARNING.
YOU ARE NOW ON PROBATION.
BOOK
IF YOU ARE MORE THAN FIFTEEN MINUTES LATE OR MISS ONE DAY WITHOUT A DOCTOR'S NOTE, WE'LL BE FORCED TO DISMISS YOU.
IS THIS ALL CLEAR, SHERMAN?
READ BANNED BOOKS
YEAH.

"BYE"

BELA
MR. FLAVOR! DID YOU SEE? OUR INTERVIEW CAME ...
UH. MR. FLAVOR?
EDDIE... EDDIE I CAN'T GO ON.
COMICS WORLD
IRV FLAVOR
PIONEER CREATOR CHALLENGES THE PALACE OF DREAMS FOR OWNERSHIP OF THE NIGHTSTALKER
THIS ISSUE: SALES CONTINUE TO RISE INDUSTRY-WIDE!
PLUS THE WORST COMICS OF THE YEAR!
UM... WHAT DO YOU MEAN? WHAT'S WRONG?
ED. I'M A FAILURE. MY WHOLE LIFE HAS BEEN GOD DAMN SHIT.
I'M NOTHING.
WORLD

AFT--
AFTER MY WIFE LEFT ME... SHE GOT REMARRIED TO THIS ITALIAN. GARGIOLA, GARGIOLA HIS NAME WAS.
YOU WANNA KNOW HOW I REMEMBER THIS ASSHOLE'S NAME SO WELL, EVEN THOUGH THIS SHIT HAPPENED SO LONG AGO?
EVEN THOUGH MY WIFE, GOD BLESS HER SOUL, IS BURIED IN THE COLD, HARD GROUND?
MY DAUGHTER'S NAME IS FLORENCE JEAN GARGIOLA.
WHAT HAPPENED WAS, AFTER SHE GOT REMARRIED, MY WIFE HAD FLOEY'S NAME CHANGED. FROM MY NAME TO HIS.
SEE, SHE DIDN'T WANT NOTHING TO DO WITH ME, DIDN'T EVEN WANT MY GOD DAMN NAME TO REMIND HER...

I HAVEN'T SEEN FLOEY SINCE SHE WAS SIXTEEN.
FIRST IT WAS CUZ SHE HATED ME. HER MOTHER DID THAT. THEN IT... THEN I DIDN'T WANT HER TO SEE ME.
UH. MR. FLAVOR. WHY ARE YOU TELL--
DON'T YOU GET IT YET, EDDIE?!
I'M A FUCKIN' FAILURE!
MR. FLAVOR, DON'T--
I READ THIS FUCKING INTERVIEW AND THERE IT IS IN GOD DAMN BLACK AND WHITE!
WHAT A SCHMUCK I AM! I HAD ONE GOOD IDEA IN MY WHOLE LIFE AND I LET THEM TAKE IT!
AVOR SPEAKS!
IRVING FLAVOR WORKS OUT OF A HUMBLE STUDIO IN BROOKLYN. IT DIDN'T HAVE TO BE THIS WAY. 50 YEARS AGO, FLAVOR CREATED AN AMERICAN ICON, WHO FORBES ESTIMATES IS WORTH NEARLY A BILLION DOLLARS. HOW DID THIS HAPPEN? IN HIS FIRST INTERVIEW, ARCHIE RUPKIN TALKS TO THIS COMICS PIONEER ABOUT HIS LONG CAREER IN THE INDUSTRY AND HIS LATEST QUEST FOR JUSTICE... THE OWNERSHIP OF THE HERO WHO RUNS AT NIGHT...
COMICS WORLD #197
22
IRVING FLAVOR
I FUCKIN' BLEW IT.

KNOCK KNOCK!
YOU WANTED TO SEE ME, J.C.?
HEY, PAULIE!
ZOOM
HEY. COME ON IN, RALPHIE.
I BROUGHT IN THOSE NEW COSTUME DESIGNS FOR DR. MORTE'S ACTION FIG--
RALPHIE, WHAT THE HELL IS THIS?
I, THE UNDERSIGNED wish to
register my shock and displeasure at
the disgraceful behavior of Zoom comics
treatment of one of its founding creators.
rightful return of the character
the NIGHTSTALKER to his
Creator, Irving Flavor, immediately.
SIGNED
COMICS
UH.
GEEZ, I DUNNO. LEMME SEE...
"I, THE UNDERSIGNED," BLAH BLAH BLAH...
"DISGRACEFUL BEHAVIOR," MMM...
"ZOOM COMICS."... YA DA DA DA...
"CHARACTER OF THE NIGHTSTALKER TO HIS CREATOR, IRVING FLAVOR, IMMEDIATELY," BLAH BLAH.
HUH!
I DUNNO, J.C., LOOKS LIKE SOME KIND OF PETIT
DON'T PLAY GAMES WITH ME, YOU LITTLE SHIT.

PAULIE FOUND THIS ON YOUR DESK, AND I WAS JUST CURIOUS AS TO WHAT THE HELL IT WAS DOING THERE.
I... I PICKED IT UP AT UNCLE AL'S COMIC GALAXY. I DIDN'T-- I WASN'T GOING TO SIGN IT, I WAS JUST--
YOU'RE DAMN RIGHT YOU WEREN'T GOING TO SIGN IT. YOU KNOW WHY?
THE NIGHTSTALKER IS WHOLLY AND LEGALLY OURS.
IF THAT CRAZY OLD BASTARD THINKS HE CAN BLACKMAIL US INTO GIVING HIM OUR GOLDEN GOOSE, HE'S GOT ANOTHER THOUGHT TO THINK!
AND IF ANYONE AT THIS COMPANY THINKS THIS CRANK DESERVES PENNY ONE FROM US, THEN MAYBE THAT PERSON WOULD FEEL BETTER WORKING FOR SOMEONE ELSE.
SO... WE UNDERSTAND EACH OTHER?
WE SURE DO, J.C.!
LISTEN, I'M REAL SORRY IT HAD TO--
FORGET IT.
JUST LEAVE ME THOSE ACTION FIGURE DESIGNS AND I'LL GET BACK TO YOU.
GOTCHA!

THAT SHOULD KEEP THEM QUIET. FOR A WHILE, ANYWAY.
SO.
WHAT ELSE HAVE YOU HEARD ABOUT THIS FLAVOR THING?
I HAVEN'T HEARD MUCH ELSE ABOUT IT. THE EXPECTED GRUMBLINGS FROM THE USUAL TROUBLEMAKERS. NOTHING IMPORTANT.
I TALKED TO TOM SALMON AND HE SAYS "COLLECTOR'S WORLD" WILL BACK US UP 100%. I DON'T THINK IT'S ANYTHING TO WORRY ABOUT.
J.C., "COMICS WORLD" HAS GIVEN SO MANY UNFAIR BAD REVIEWS AND TRASHED SO MANY PEOPLE THAT THEY HAVE NO CREDIBILITY.
STILL...
WITH THE BIG CAROLCO. MERGER ON DECK, I DON'T WANT THIS GETTING ANY STICKIER.
UH, WHO'RE YOU CALLING?

MR. FLAVOR, I TALKED TO AN EDITOR AT "METRO-CHIC" AND SHE WANTS..
RING!
DO ME A FAVOR AND ANSWER THAT, WILL YA?
RING!
HELLO, FLAVOR STUDIOS, THIS IS ED SPEAKING, HOW CAN I HELP YOU?
UH-HUH.
OKAY. I--UH-- THINK HE'S IN A MEETING RIGHT NOW, BUT I'LL CHECK. HOLD ON.
SHOULD I TELL HIM YOU'RE NOT IN, OR...
"LITTLE JEWELS?"
COMICS
IT'S SOME GUY FROM THE JAYCEES OR SOMETHING, TRYING TO SELL YOU SOME JEWELRY?
JEWELS?! WHY WOULD--
IRVING, DICKIE, THIS IS MY LITTLE BOY JULIUS!
HEY! LITTLE JULES!
YOUR FATHER TELLS US ALL ABOUT YOU! YOU'LL PROBABLY BE RUNNIN' THIS DUMP SOMEDAY! HA HA!
WELCOME ABOARD JULES! CAN I HAVE A RAISE? HAW HAW!
PLEASE, CALL ME J.C.
J.C.!
HOLY SHIT! GIMME THAT PHONE!

J.C.? WHO'S THAT?
J.C. LEBLANC!
UH, HELLO?
J.C. LEBLANC?! THE PUB--
THE PUBLISHER OF ZOOM COM--
SHHH!
I'M TRYING TO HEAR THE GUY FOR CHRIST'S SAKE!
NO, J.C., I'M HERE. NO, I DON'T KNOW WHY HE TOLD YOU THAT. YOU KNOW GODDAMNED KIDS...
HANH? OH FINE, FINE. DOIN' OKAY. YOU KNOW.
OH, YOU SAW THAT INTERVIEW, DID YA?
YEAH, WELL, I DIDN'T KNOW THEY WAS--
NO, NO. YOU'RE RIGHT ABOUT THAT.
WHAT DO YOU MEAN?
NO... NO, I THINK... NO, THAT WOULD BE OKAY.
YEAH, FINE.
YEAH, OKAY. G'BYE J.C.
WHAT? WHAT DID HE WANT?
THAT DAMN SON OF A BITCH WANTS TO MEET ME AT HIS OFFICE.
HE WANTS TO WORK ALL THIS OUT!

Her House
THE WINNER AND NEW CHAMPEEN!
I AM THE GREATEST!! WOO HOO!
HAHA HA!
HAHA!
OH, SO YOU'RE THE CHAMP? HUH? WELL--
AAHH! NO FAIR! HAHAHAA!
OKAY! OKAY! HAHAHA YOU'RE THE CHA-HAHA!
RRRRR!!
WHOMP
AHHHH!
HAHAHA HAHA!
Whew YOU ALMOST GOT--
SHHHH!
WAIT...
OH COME ON, IT'S 8:00! HOW COULD SHE--?

THAT WAS A LOT OF FUN, BALLOO, BUT I GOTTA GET BACK TO THE DRAWING BOARD.
AWW!
MAYBE LATER WE CAN HAVE A RE--
BANG! BANG! BANG!
SHIT. HERE WE GO.
WHO IS IT?
YOU MAKE A TOO MUCH NOISE! QUIET! QUIET! MY HOUSE, ANH?
WE'RE SORRY, MRS. TWEED. OUR KITTY KNOCKED--
ALDA TINE DE NOISE! WHY? WHY?! I CALL--
CLICK CLACK!
ANH? WHAT IS--?
CLOMP
SO I TOLD HIM I WOULDN'T DO IT, DUDE, "GET IT YOURSELF!"
NO WAY!
CLOMP
I SWEAR TO GOD! HE GOT REAL PISSED AND SHIT, SAYING HE--
HEY!
FUCK.

ON! STUPID FUCKING KEY...
HEY!
SHIT! DYLAN, HURRY! SHE'S COMING DOWN THE STAIRS!
WHAT YOU DO, ANH? WHY YOU DO HEAH, ANH?!
HE'S WITH ME, MRS. TWEED (GET INSIDE, SKEET). IT'S NOT A BIG DEAL, OK
NO! HE NO PAYA VRENT! HE NO LIVE A HEAH! I CALL POLICE!!
GO AHEAD, I WISH YOU WOULD. (SKEET, GET IN THE FUCKING APARTMENT)
MY HOUSE! HE NO LIVE HEAH! MY HOUSE! ANEEMAL!
HE'S NOT LIVING HERE, HE'S JUST VISITING! SO LEAVE US ALONE YOU DUMB BITCH!

WHEED! WHEED! WHEED! WHEED!
KRISH!
AROOOOO

$3.95 ISYOURCHANGE THANK YOUFORSHOPPINGAT BIGGO MART ENJOYYOURDAY NEXT.
33
NO, I ADMIT IT.
I NEVER WOULD'VE BELIEVED THAT THEY WOULD STILL BE GOING OUT AFTER FIVE MONTHS, NO.
SHERMAN TOLD YOU ABOUT THE DOG, RIGHT?
YEAH.
THE POOR THING'S PROBABLY BETTER OFF DEAD IF SHE'S AS BAD NOW AS SHE WAS WHEN SHE LIVED WITH US.
MEATS
DIDN'T GANDHI SAY SOMETHING LIKE YOU JUDGE A PERSON BY HOW THEY TREAT THEIR ANIMALS?
SOMETHING LIKE THAT. THEN AGAIN, EVEN HITLER LOVED HIS PUPPIES.
AFTERNOON, DYLAN.
HEY, YOU GUYS HEAR THE BIG THING WITH TWEED LAST NIGHT?
WE HEARD YOU CALL HER A WORD THAT RHYMES WITH "WITCH," THAT'S FOR SURE! HAHA!
NO! I MEAN THE PART WHERE LIKE THE AMBULANCE CAME!
Y'KNOW, AFTER SHE HAD HER FUCKIN' HEART ATTACK?!

JEESUM CROW!
YOU MEAN ... SHE'S DEAD?
YEAH, RIGHT! I WISH!
SHE'S JUST GONNA LIKE BE IN THE HOSPITAL FOR LIKE SIX WEEKS OR SOMETHING.
SHIT! MY RIDE! I GOTTA GO. BYE!
SEE YA.
♫ Ding Dong, the witch is dead...
AHHHH... NOW THIS IS CIVILIZED...
A SNOWY, WINTER NIGHT, CURLED UP WITH A GOOD BOOK, COCOA WITH MARSH-MALLOWS AND MY FAVORITE LOVER.
NOW ALL THAT WE NEED IS A CRACKLING FIRE PLACE. I BELIEVE YOU BEGIN THIS CHAPTER, SWEETIE PIE?
Ahem "GENESIS --"
"MY MOTHER NEVER TRUSTED THE KITCHEN CAB-INETS. SINCE THE FOUNDING OF THE COLONY IT HAD BEEN A TRADITION TO UNLOAD OOTHECAE -- EGG SACS -- IN THE CABINETS SO THE YOUNG-LINGS WOULD BE NEAR THE PRINCIPAL FOOD STOCKS."
"BUT, BLOATED WITH HER BROOD OF THIRTY-EIGHT, MY --"

WHAT THE HELL--?!
IT SOUNDS LIKE IT'S COMING FROM DOWN-STAIRS.
SOUNDS LIKE A BASS GUITAR OR SOMETHING.
IT MUST BE DYLAN AND HER MUSICIAN PALS.
MAYBE YOU SHOULD GO DOWN AND TELL HER TO KNOCK IT OFF.
WAIT A MINUTE! WHY SHOULD I GO? YOU TELL HER!
YEAH, BUT SHE LIKES YOU. SHE HASN'T LIKED ME AFTER THAT THING WITH THE WATERBUG LAST YEAR.
OH! SHE DOESN'T DISLIKE YOU CUZ OF THAT!
ANYWAY, IF I GO DOWN AND TELL HER THEN SHE'LL HATE BOTH OF US. AT LEAST THIS WAY ONE OF US WILL BE FRIENDLY!
IT'S LIKE A GOOD COP/ BAD THING, Y'SEE?
"GOOD COP/ BAD COP?" I DON'T GET--
COME ON, PLEASE? HOW ABOUT THIS: IF YOU GO, I'LL DO THE DISHES UNTIL FRIDAY, OKAY?
AND DO BIG NOSE'S LITTERBO ?
OKAY DEAL!

GOODLUCK, BALLOO.
BAD-UMB-DUM-DUM-BADUM--
YEAH, YEAH, YEAH.
HI. UH, WOULD YOU MIND KEEPING IT DOWN A WEE BIT?
WHAT? THE MUSIC? WERE WE TOO LOUD?
YEAH, A LITTLE. MY GIRLFRIEND HAS...UH... AN EAR INFECTION SO SHE'S REAL...UH, SENSITIVE.
MEOW?
SHHHH!
WELL, THAT'S THAT.
SO? WHAT DID THEY SAY?
WELL, I JUST ASKED THEM IF-- --I JUST TOLD THEM THAT THEY'D HAVE TO PLAY A LITTLE QUIETER AND THEY SAID THEY WERE SORRY AND THAT WAS THAT.
AND THEY DIDN'T GIVE YOU A HARD TIME OR ANYTHING?
NAH. THEY'RE NOT GOING TO--
BADUM

ARK! GRARK!
RARK!
RARARARK!
RARK! GRARK!
RARK! RARARK!
RRRRARK! RARK!
RARK!
GRARK!
GRARARK!
ARK!
KNOCK! KNOCK!
ARK! ARK! ARK! ARK! ARK! ARK! ARK!
YES? HOW CAN I HELP YOU?
UM, HI MR. YOSSARIAN. I'M SORRY TO BOTHER YOU, BUT I WAS WONDERING IF YOU COULD MAYBE, UH, STOP YOUR DOG FROM BARKING SO MUCH?
I'M TRYING TO WORK UP--
GRRR
WHO? SNOOPY? SHE AIN'T BEEN BARKIN'. SHE AIN'T BEEN BARKIN'.
ESERT STORM
RARK! ARK! RARK!

UH, HEH, I DON'T KNOW... IT SOUNDS LIKE SHE'S SORT OF BARKING TO, UH, SORT OF BARKING TO ME.
HEH.
SURE, OF COURSE SHE'S BARKING NOW.
SHE DOESN'T TAKE TO STRANGERS.
GRRRRRR
RORAR! RARK!
RARK!
I... I GUESS THAT MAKES SENSE.
I SWEAR, I THOUGHT HE WAS GOING TO SIC THAT MONSTER ON ME.
I WONDER IF SHE WOULD'VE EATEN ME OR JUST WENT FOR THE JUGULAR AND QUIT?
RARK! RARARARK!
ARARARK!
YOU MEAN THIS BITCH HAS BEEN BARKING SINCE NOON?!
THAT'S LIKE EIGHT HOURS!
RR! RARK!
DON'T WORRY, AFTER FOUR HOURS YOU HARDLY EVEN NOTICE.
RARK! ARARAR ARARAR ARARARK!
AAH, HOW MUCH LONGER COULD IT GO ON? RIGHT?
RARK!
RARK!

MARK!
MARAR ARARK!
GRRARK!
MARARK! MARK!
ARARARK! ARK! RRARK!
RARK!
RARARARK! RARARARARK! RARK! ARK!
AHHHHHHH....
READY?
ONE TWO THREE FOUR..

WHAT HAPPENED TO MY R2-D2? WHAT HAPPENED TO MY G.I. JOE? I CAN'T FIND MY EASY BAKE OVEN WHERE DID MY MAGIC 8-BALL GO?
DID SOMEONE SEE MY FRANKENBERRY? OR MY SIX MILLION DOLLAR MAN? GROOVY GHOULIES, I CAN'T SEE YOU AT CRAZY EDDIE'S OR THOM McCANN.
OH, GOD, WHERE ARE YOU? WHY DID YOU HAVE TO LEAVE ME THEN?
SWEATY NECK
OHMYGOD OHMYGOD OHMYGOD OHMYGOD...
JANE, I THINK I'LL LEAVE FOR WORK A LITTLE EARLY.
RATTLE!
THAT'S IT! I'VE SNAPPED! I CAN'T TAKE IT!
AAAAGH! SHUT UP!
JANE, WHAT'RE?!
QUIET!

JANE, WAIT.! DON'T--
SHUT UP!
SHUT THE FUCK UP!!
QUIET!
QUIET!
IF YOU DON'T GO BACK INSIDE AND SHUT UP YOU'RE GONNA FIND THAT FUCKING DOG DEAD IN THE HALLWAY!
JESUS! JANE!
WHAT THE HELL?!
HEY! WHAT'S WITH ALL THE DAMN RACKET UP THERE?!
WHAT THE FUCK DID SHE-- WHAT THE FUCK DID YOU SAY, YOU CUNT?!
PLEASE, EMIL, DON'T START WITH--
I'LL KICK YOUR FUCKIN' ASS, YOU FUCKIN' SKANK!
MARK!
GRRARK! MARKMARARK!
WAAAAAAAAH!!

C'MON UP, YOU PATHETIC, UNEMPLOYED COCKSUCKER!
JANE, ARE YOU NUTS OR SOMETHING?!
WHAT THE HELL'S GOING ON OUT HERE?
MARK! MARARARK!
FUCK YOU BITCH!
UH, HI, WE'RE SORRY TO BUG YOU AGAIN, HEH, BUT DO YOU THINK YOU COULD JUST BE A LITTLE BIT --
MARARK!
YOU BALD, DICKLESS FREAK!
LET GO OF ME, MONA! I GOTTA KICK THAT SLUT'S ASS!
EMIL, IF YOUR PAROLE OFFICER FINDS OUT THAT YOU'VE --
MARK! MARARK!
WAAAAAAH!
DUDE, WHAT'S WITH YOU? HOW THE FUCK ARE WE GONNA REHEARSE IF YOU KEEP TELLING --
GRARK! ARK! MARARARK!
HEY, ASSHOLE! WILL YOU KEEP THAT FUCKIN' MUTT QUIET FOR TWO SECONDS?!
YOU! IF YOU NO-TALENT JACK-OFFS DON'T KEEP IT DOWN, I'M GONNA SHOVE THAT GUITAR UP YOUR ASS!
AND SEND IN THAT DOG AFTER IT!
THAT'S IT! BOTH YOU BITCHES ARE FUCKIN' DEAD!
C'MON, SNOOPY!
WAAAAAAH!
MARARK! MARK! ARK!

DYLAN, MAN, WHAT'S GOIN' ON? WE GOTTA PRACTICE.
YOU BETTER NOT BE YELLING AT ME!
Y'SEE, WE DIDN'T GET MUCH SLEEP
YOU'RE DAMN RIGHT I'M YELLING AT YOU, RIOT GRRRRL!
I'VE HEARD BETTER MUSIC COMING FROM GRAVEL MIXERS!
AWRIGHT! SO WHICH OF YOU SMART MOUTHED BITCHES WANTED YOUR ASSES KICKED, HANH?
MARARK! GRR! ARK!
FUCK YOU, MAN!
YEAH, WHY DON'T YOU AND YOUR FAT HIPPY DAD THERE GO BACK UPSTAIRS AND PLAY WITH YOUR LOVE BEADS, OKAY?
I'D RATHER BE A FAT HIPPY THAN SOME PHONEY KURT COBAIN STARBUCKS SEATTLE GRUNGY TRENDOID WHO WOULDN'T KNOW A GOOD TUNE IF IT CAME OUT OF THE BARREL OF A SHOTGUN INTO HER GRUNGE HEAD!!
I'M SORRY, BUT WE SLEEP
ARE YOU PUSHING ME?! DID YOU JUST PUSH ME, FAGGOT ASS?!
COME BACK DOWN...
GARARARK!
ARK!
MARK!
ARK!
WAAAAAH!
OH MY GOD ... KURT....
DID I JUST HEAR YOU DIS KURT, MAN? I BETTER NOT'VE HEARD THAT CUZ KURT WAS A TRAGIC GENIUS, MAN!
OH, YEAH! "BOOHOO! I'M A RICH, WHITE ROCK STAR, NO ONE
URK
I DIDN'T TOUCH-- OW!
C'MON, SNOOPY! GET HIM! BITE HIS ASS!
Oh my God...
HHHHHHH
MARARK!
ARK!
HEY!

YOU GO INSIDE NOW... OR I AM CALL POLICA, ANH?
FUCK!
I'M GO FOR FIVE DAY, AND THIS IS HOW YOU ARE!
AH-NE-MALS.
AH-NE-MALS!
YOU NEED ME, ANH?
:sniff:
SWEATY NEC
YOU NEED ME.
YOU NEED SORA TWEED...
TO CONTROL OF ZOO, ANH?
CONTROL!
NOW... INSIDE... AND QUIET.

MARK!
Whimper.
SLAM!
CLOMP
CLOMP
CLOMP
CLOMP
CLOMP
CLOMP
CLOMP
CLOMP
CLOMP
CLOMP!
CLOMP!
CLOMP!
SLAM!
SLAM
MY HOUSE...
?

NO!
NO!!
YOU QUIET, OR I CALL POLICA! NO! ANH!
NO NOISE!!
QUIET!
BUT MRS. TWEED, HIS TEETH IS COMING IN, SO HE DON'T--
WAAH! WAAAH!
FUCK! FUCK! YOU DALK LIKE BARK! GET OUT!
GET OUT OF MY HOUSE! OUT!
SLAM!
AAAAAAH...

BUMBLES BOUNCE!
LITTERING
HOURS
MON-FRI 10AM-10PM
SAT 9AM-10PM
SUNDAY 9AM-7PM
NO PETS, GUNS, SMOKING, RADIO PLAYING.
PARKS DEPT.
TALS

HEY GUYS! I'M GLAD YOU'RE HERE. I WAS WONDERING IF EVERYBODY WAS STIFFING ME!
DON'T THINK WE DIDN'T CONSIDER IT. IT'S COLDER THAN A REPUBLICAN ESKIMO!
HEY, SHERMAN.
HEY, JANICE. YOU LOOK GREAT! I HAVEN'T SEEN YOU SINCE YOU QUIT THE BOOKSTORE.
HOW'S LIFE ON THE OUTSIDE?
OH, PRETTY GOOD. THEY KEEP ME BUSY AT THE BANK AND ALL.
AND LOOK AT YOUR HAIR! HEY, HOW COME DUANE DIDN'T COME?
OH, GOD. DON'T ASK. RIGHT AFTER THE HONEYMOON HE WAS SHIPPED BACK TO FORT ELTON.
I WON'T EVEN SEE HIM FOR CHRISTMAS.
SPEAKING OF WHICH, CHECK OUT THIS CHICK IN THE ELF SUIT.
HUBBA HUBBA!
HI, SWEETIE!
SORRY I'M LATE!
WOW! THAT'S SOME OUTFIT!
YOU LIKE IT? I KNOW YOU LOVE THE CLASSIC SHORT-SKIRT-FISHNET LOOK.
HOW WAS I SUPPOSED TO KNOW IT WAS HIS GIRLFRIEND?

HEY! LOOK EVERYBODY, IT'S ED! HI, ED!
HI EVERYBODY!
EVERYBODY, THIS IS MY COUSIN DAISY.
HELL O.
OH! THE ONE FROM COSTA RICA?
YEAH. I'M AFRAID SHE DOESN'T SPEAK ENGLISH TOO GOOD.
DIG THIS: DAISY'S SUPPOSED TO BE THE BEST FIGURE SKATER IN HER COUNTRY! SHE WAS IN THE '94 OLYMPICS!
WOW! DID SHE WIN ANYTHING?
NAH, SHE MISSED THE BRONZE BY LIKE ONE-MILLIONTH OF A POINT. SHE'S A REAL CELEBRITY BACK HOME, THOUGH.
SHE EVEN MET MADONNA ONCE!
¿ERES LA MEJOR, UH, PANT, PATINADORA SOBRE HIELO DE COSTA RICA?
¿NO ES COMO SER LA MEJOR ALPINISTA DEL DESIERTO SAHARA?
HAHA! PUEDE SER. ¡NO SOMOS MUCHOS!
BIENVENIDA A NUEVA YORK, DAISY. ME LLAMO JAMES.
JAMES! I DIDN'T KNOW YOU SPOKE SUCH GOOD SPANISH!
YOU'LL FIND I'M FULL OF SURPRISES ...
WELL, NOW THAT THE GANG'S ALL HERE, LET'S HIT LA AGUA FRIO, SHALL WE?
I JUST HAVE TO MAKE A QUICK STOP AT THE LADIES ROOM. I'LL CATCH UP!
OH, WAIT, I'LL GO WITH YOU!

HEH HEH.
WHAT? WHAT'S SO FUNNY?
I KNOW YOU'RE GOING TO GET PISSED, BUT... YOU KNOW WHO DOROTHY LOOKS LIKE?
IN THAT OUTFIT AND EVERYTHING?
UM.
HOO BOY, HERE IT COMES. I GIVE UP. WHO?
WELL, REMEMBER THAT OLD "RUDOLPH" CHRISTMAS SPECIAL WITH
HERBIE! HOLY SHIT! HAHA!
HUH? WHAT'RE YOU TALKING ABOUT?
SO... SHERMAN TOLD ME YOU WORKED AT A MAGAZINE. THAT MUST BE GREAT.
YEAH. IT IS.
YEP.
I just thought I'd find a way to fit in...
REMEMBER HERBIE? HE WAS THAT GAY ELF WHO WANTED TO BE A DENTIST?
??OH YEAH! HAHA! "WHY AM I SUCH A MISFIT?"
WOMEN

LAST TIME I TALKED TO SHERMAN HE WAS TRYING TO GET SOME OF HIS WRITING PUBLISHED IN MAGAZINES.
HAS HE HAD ANY LUCK?
WHAT?! DIDN'T HE TELL YOU?
TELL ME WHAT?
THE NEW YORKER BOUGHT ONE OF HIS STORIES! THEY'RE PUBLISHING HIS JOHN LENNON STORY!
WOW! THAT'S FANTASTIC!!
I KNOW! ISN'T IT, THOUGH?!
HAHA. YOU'RE NOT MAD, ARE YOU?
MAD? NO.
THE SCARY PART IS I FIND IT ODDLY AROUSING.
11½, PLEASE.
RULES
WHAT GIVES, JAMES? THEY DIDN'T HAVE YOUR SIZE?
NAH. I DIDN'T EVEN ASK. TOUGH GUYS DON'T SKATE.
HEY, WHAT EVER HAPPENED TO THAT SEVENTEEN YEAR OLD GIRL YOU WERE GOING WITH? THAT CHINESE GIRL?
FIRST OF ALL, SHE JUST TURNED SIXTEEN IN NOVEMBER, SECOND OF ALL SHE WAS JAPANESE.
THIRD OF ALL, WE BROKE UP TWO WEEKS AGO.
JESUS, I'M SORRY. WHAT HAPPENED?

SHIT, SHE DUMPED ME FOR SOME HEROIN DEALER IN HER DRIVER'S ED CLASS. WHAT THE HELL CAN YOU DO? TRA-LA-LA, LIFE GOES ON.
WHOA...
WHAT ABOUT YOU, ED? YOU STILL A SWINGIN' SINGLE?
WHO? ME? OF COURSE.
I'VE GIVEN UP ON TRYING TO GET LAID. I'M DEVOTING ALL OF MY SEXUAL ENERGY TO MY ART.
SOUNDS LIKE WE'RE IN FOR SOME STICKY CANVASES. OUCH!
¿Y TÚ DAISY? SIENDO UNA SEÑORITA TAN BONITA Y FAMOSA DEBES DE TENER UN NOVIO.
¡HA HA! EHH... NO NOS QUEDAMOS EN UN LUGAR POR MUCHO TIEMPO A CAUSA DE LA GIRA.
DAMN, YOU GUYS ARE ALL READY TO GO! CAN YOU WAIT UP WHILE--
JAMES, WAIT A MINUTE. YOU DON'T GOT ANY SKATES. WHAT'S--
I'M NOT--UH, I DON'T REALLY... MY FOOT SORT OF HURTS, SO I JUST--
GET OUTTA HERE! YOU ARE NOT GOING TO BEG ME TO TEACH YOU AND THEN BACK DOWN!

COME ON, TOUGH GUY!
OKAY, OKAY...
Heh Heh.
SHERM, UH, I'M NOT NORMALLY A, LIKE, VIOLENT GUY, BUT IF JAMES KEEPS, UH, HITTING ON MY COUSIN?
I'M GONNA HAVE TO TAKE HIM DOWN!
SO, ARE WE READY TO HIT THE ICE, TWINKLE TOES?
COME ON THEN, DOROTHY HAMILL!
SEE? IT'S EASY! JUST LIKE ROLLER SKATING.
SWELL! BUT I'VE NEVER --
HEY! WATCH IT, ASSHOLE!
FUCK YOU! HAW HAW!

SO, HAVE YOU THOUGHT ABOUT WHAT YOU WANT FOR CHRISTMAS YET?
I SURE HAVE. LET'S TAKE A TRIP! LET'S GO TO EUROPE IN SPRING!
EU-- UH, EUROPE?
COME ON! EUROPE WOULD BE, LIKE, SO GREAT!
YOU KNOW WE CAN'T AFFORD THAT, SA-- DOROTHY.
OKAY, ENGLAND, THEN! WE COULD SEE ABBEY ROAD, ALL THE PALACES AND STUFF! TEA AND KRIMPETS AT KENSINGTON...
IMAGINE ALL THE BOOKS THEY HAVE THAT YOU CAN'T GET HERE ...
I DON'T KNOW...
SO, LIKE WHEN? APRIL? MAY?

I KNOW, BUT WE'VE NEVER GONE ON A TRIP TOGETHER! WE COULD ALWAYS SLAP IT ON OUR CREDIT CARDS!
"OUR CREDIT CARDS?" DID YOU SUCKER ANOTHER POOR BANK INTO GIVING YOU A CREDIT CARD?
I THOUGHT EVERYONE KNEW ABOUT YOU BY NOW.
I'M SERIOUS! YOU DON'T THINK THAT WOULD BE COOL AND ROMANTIC?
PARIS IN THE SPRINGTIME?
WAIT, PARIS? NO WAY.
I DON'T WANT TO RISK GOING ANYWHERE THEY DON'T SPEAK ENGLISH. IT WOULD ONLY BE A MATTER OF TIME BEFORE I GOT LOST AND WOUND UP ENLISTED IN THE FOREIGN LEGION OR SOMETHING.

HAHA! I KNEW I'D GET YOU WITH THAT ONE! YAY!
WELL... LET'S THINK ABOUT IT. BUT DON'T GET YOUR HOPES UP.
SO... DO YOU WANT TO KNOW WHAT I GOT YOU FOR CHRISTMAS?
YOU GOT IT ALREADY?! WHAT IS IT?!
♪ CAN'T TELL YOU!
COME ON! GIVE ME A HINT! IS IT THAT NEW BENCHLEY BIOGRAPHY WE SAW LAST WEEK?
CAN'T TELL YOU, BUD.
IS IT THAT OUT OF PRINT ARNOLD ROTH BOOK I MENTIONED?
CAN'T.
TELL.
YOU.
OOH! WAIT!
THAT BIG HARDCOVER PHOTO BOOK BY THAT PHOTOGRAPHER GUY I SHOWED YOU AT THE STRAND TWO WEEKS AGO? WITH THE GIRL ON THE COVER? HOLDING THOSE TWO THINGS?
HEY, WHAT'S UP WITH THAT GIRL JANET, ANYWAY?
HUH? WHO, JANICE?
YEAH. ON THE WAY TO THE HEAD SHE WAS GRILLING ME WITH QUESTIONS ABOUT YOU.
DOES SHE HAVE LIKE A CRUSH ON YOU OR SOMETHING?
JANICE?! NO WAY! SHE'S MARRIED!

THAT DOESN'T MEAN SHE CAN'T FIND YOU ATTRACTIVE. YOU'RE GOING OUT WITH ME AND I'M SURE YOU LIKE PLENTY OF OTHER GIRLS.
OH NO YOU DON'T. YOU WON'T GET ME IN THAT TRAP A SECOND TIME!
I'VE SEEN THE WAY SHE LOOKS AT YOU...
BESIDES, IF SHE'S MARRIED AND ALL, WHY IS SHE ON A DATE WITH THIS JAMES GUY?
IT'S NOT A "DATE". THEY'RE JUST FRIENDS.
WE ALL USED TO WORK TOGETHER!
I CAN'T BELIEVE YOU THINK JANICE HAS A CRUSH ON ME!
IT'S JUST SO... RIDICULOUS!
HA HA...
"I AM NOT A WRITER AND NOT AN ACTOR," ROBERT BENCHLEY ONCE COMPLAINED TO HIS FRIEND HAROLD ROSS, EDITOR OF THE New Yorker...
YOU.. AHEM.. YOU WANT TO TAKE A REST AND GET SOME COCOA?
OR SOMETHING?

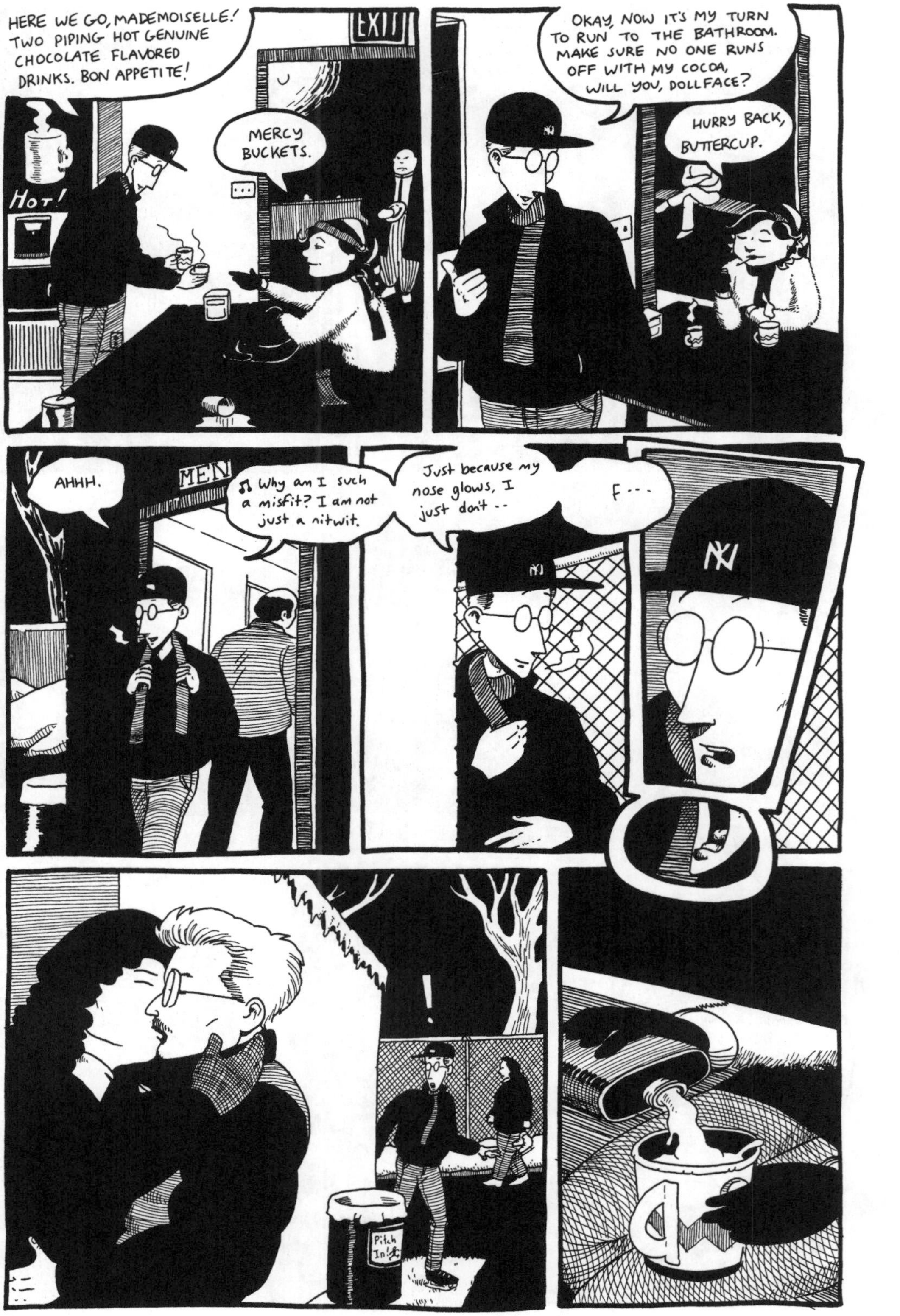
HERE WE GO, MADEMOISELLE! TWO PIPING HOT GENUINE CHOCOLATE FLAVORED DRINKS. BON APPETITE!
EXIT
HOT!
MERCY BUCKETS.
OKAY, NOW IT'S MY TURN TO RUN TO THE BATHROOM. MAKE SURE NO ONE RUNS OFF WITH MY COCOA, WILL YOU, DOLLFACE?
HURRY BACK, BUTTERCUP.
AHHH.
MEN
♫ Why am I such a misfit? I am not just a nitwit.
Just because my nose glows, I just don't --
F---
!
Pitch In!

WHAT?!
TEN CUIDADO... SUAVE...
OWOW OWOW OW!

WHAT ON EARTH HAPPENED TO YOU?
¿EH, HE, EH, FALL DOWN?
I DIDN'T FALL DOWN. SOME HOTSHOT KID KNOCKED ME DOWN. IT'S JUST MY ANKLE.
SHERMAN? SWEETIE WHAT'S WRONG?
HUH?
OH, UH NOTHING. WHY?
YOU LOOK LIKE YOU'VE SEEN A GHOST.
UH, NO. NO. I'M JUST...
ED, WHAT HAPPENED TO YOUR FOOT.
HEY, WHAT, ARE YOU LOSERS TIRED ALREADY? COME ON! LET'S GET BACK OUT THERE!
I CAN'T. I HURT MY ANKLE WHEN THIS KID -- A BUNCH OF KIDS, REALLY -- KNOCKED ME DOWN.
HE FALL.
SAY JAMES, WHAT SAY YOU AND ME GET POOR ED SOME COCOA, HUH?
UHHH... OKAY...
HOLD ON, I'LL COME WITH YO
NO, NO! IT'S OKAY! WE'LL DO IT AND BE RIGHT BACK. IT'S OKAY.

SHIT, THESE THINGS ARE HARD TO WALK AROUND IN!
SO WHERE ARE WE REALLY GOING? THEY SELL COCOA IN THE LITTLE SNACK BA--
JAMES, WHAT THE HELL IS THE MATTER WITH YOU, HUH?
JANICE IS FUCKING MARRIED.
UHH...
YEAH. SO?
I SAW YOU MAKING OUT WITH HER BY THE BATHROOMS.
OH.
Heh Heh...
I CAN'T BELIEVE IT. I NEVER THOUGHT YOU WOULD STOOP THAT LOW. YOU DO--
FUCK YOU, WHAT THE HELL DO YOU MEAN "STOOP --
I NEVER SAID A WORD WHEN YOU CHEATED ON LISA, I DIDN'T SAY ANYTHING WHEN YOU WERE SCREWING WITH THAT HIGH SCHOOL KID...
THAT'S YOUR BUSINESS. WHATEVER.
BUT WHEN YOU'RE WILLING TO FUCK UP JANICE'S MARRIAGE, JUST SO YOU CAN GET SOME NEW--

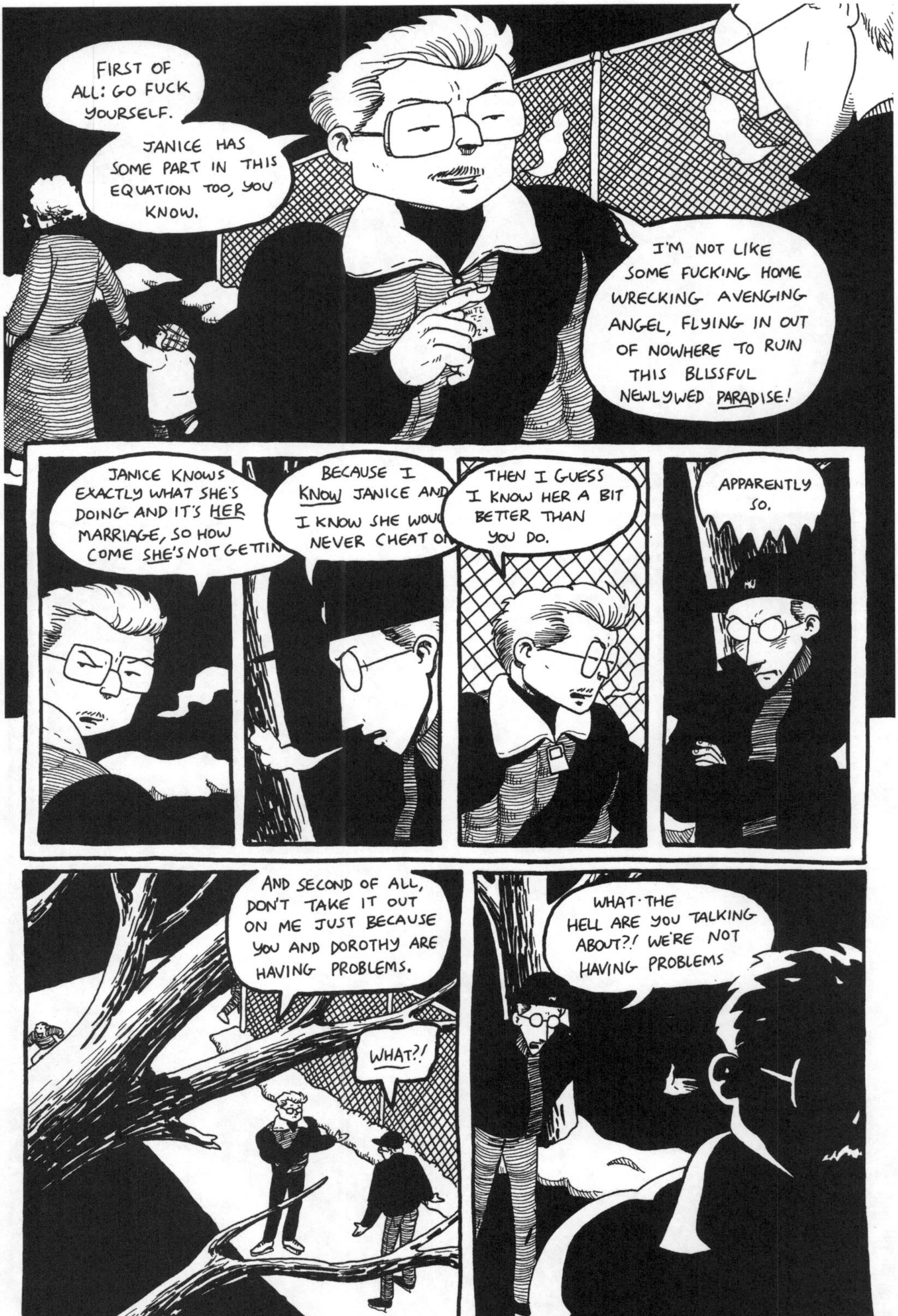
FIRST OF ALL: GO FUCK YOURSELF.
JANICE HAS SOME PART IN THIS EQUATION TOO, YOU KNOW.
I'M NOT LIKE SOME FUCKING HOME WRECKING AVENGING ANGEL, FLYING IN OUT OF NOWHERE TO RUIN THIS BLISSFUL NEWLYWED PARADISE!
JANICE KNOWS EXACTLY WHAT SHE'S DOING AND IT'S HER MARRIAGE, SO HOW COME SHE'S NOT GETTIN
BECAUSE I KNOW JANICE AND I KNOW SHE WOU NEVER CHEAT O
THEN I GUESS I KNOW HER A BIT BETTER THAN YOU DO.
APPARENTLY SO.
AND SECOND OF ALL, DON'T TAKE IT OUT ON ME JUST BECAUSE YOU AND DOROTHY ARE HAVING PROBLEMS.
WHAT?!
WHAT·THE HELL ARE YOU TALKING ABOUT?! WE'RE NOT HAVING PROBLEMS

AHHHH...
ED,
I TALKED TO MY EDITOR ABOUT DOING THAT STORY ABOUT YOUR ARTIST FRIEND...
REALLY? WHAT DID THEY SAY? BECAUSE THIS WEEK HE'S SUPPOSED...
UH... THEY SAID NO.
BUT DON'T WORRY. THREE OF MY IDEAS THAT THEY REJECTED SOME HOW GOT PUBLISHED UNDER ANOTHER WRITER'S MASTHEAD...
FOR SOME REASON.
BUT THAT'S SUPPOSED TO BE ... IT WAS YOUR IDEA!
SHERMAN! WHERE'VE YOU BEEN?

ANHHH...
JUST WALKING AROUND. WHAT'RE YOU DOING OUT HERE BY YOURSELF?
WATCHING EVERYBODY SKATING. THERE'S SOME GOOD PEOPLE OUT THERE.
SO, JANICE, UH...
ARE... HOW'S THINGS WITH YOU AND DUANE? DO--
RATS! I ALMOST FORGOT! CONGRATULATIONS! I HEARD THE GREAT NEWS ABOUT THE NEW YORKER!
WHAT ABOUT IT? THAT I'D BEEN REJECTED YET AGAIN?
REJECTED? WHAT DO YOU MEAN? DOROTHY TOLD ME THAT THEY WERE GOING TO PUBLISH YOUR STORY ON THE ROLLING STONES OR SOME--

DOROTHY TOLD YOU THAT?
SHE THOUGHT I WAS SERIOUS?!
I WAS ONLY JOKING! DIDN'T SHE--
WELL, I'M GLAD YOU CONSIDER MY CAREER ASPIRATIONS A SOURCE OF AMUSEMENT.
I SUPPOSE I DIDN'T REALIZE HOW SENSITIVE YOU WERE ABOUT IT.
SORRY
UH.
I'M GOING BACK ON THE ICE. DO YOU WANT TO COME?
I WANT TO FINISH MY COCOA.
OKAY.

500
⁝SIGH⁝ ED, WOULD DAISY BY ANY CHANCE FEEL LIKE SKATING?
HUH? OH, LET ME ASK.
SHIT!
DAISY, SHERMAN QUIERE SABER SI PAT--
DEATH FURY III
¡SÍ!

I... I SHOULDN'T HAVE DRAGGED YOU OUT HERE. YOU'RE SO MUCH BETTER THAN I AM.
EH... I DON'T SPEAK VERY ENGLISH PLEASE...
OH, RIGHT, RIGHT! I'M SORRY -- PAR DONE!
I'M -- FOR SOME REASON, I FEEL REAL SELF-CONSCIOUS, I'M --
SHHHH....

YEAH, SHE'S PART OF A TOUR THAT'S GOING ALL ACROSS NORTH AMERICA.
I THINK SHE LEAVES FOR TORONTO ON MONDAY.
GOD, I WISH I COULD BE THAT GOOD AT SOMETHING.
HEY, HAVE YOU GUYS SEEN... SHERMAN?
NY
I'M MORE AMAZED AT HIM! I NEVER KNEW HE WAS SUCH A GOOD SKATER!
SHIT!
I THINK IT'S ALL HER. SHE'S GOOD ENOUGH FOR THE TWO OF THEM!

SHERMAN!

YEAH?
WHAT?
WHAT'S THE MATTER?
NOTHING'S THE MATTER, I WAS JUST HOPING I COULD SKATE WITH YOU.

UH, I DON'T -- I GUESS, IF YOU WANT TO.
WELL, DON'T GET SO EXCITED!
I REALIZE I WAS NEVER THE ICE QUEEN OF ECUADOR, AND NEVER ALMOST WON A --
I WANTED TO SKATE WITH YOU BEFORE -- BUT YOU WERE TO BUSY WITH YOUR COCOA.
YEAH, SO -- WHOA! -- SO NOW THAT I'M FINISHED YOU CAN STOP WITH HER AND GO --- WHOAA ---

RUMP!
Uh Oh
OW OW OW...
¿ESTÁS BIEN? ¿QUÉ..
KEEP YOUR FUCKING HANDS OFF OF ME YOU STUPID BITCH!
JESUS, TAKE IT EASY, WOULD YOU? SHE WAS TRYING TO..
I DON'T NEED HER GOD DAMNED HELP AND I DON'T NEED YOURS EITHER FOR THAT MATTER!
¿QUÉ ES SU PROBLEMA?
UH, WAIT, UN MOMENTO.

WHAT THE HELL'S GOTTEN IN TO YOU?! WHY--
ME?
OF COURSE! I FORGOT! I'M ALWAYS THE BAD GUY!
YOU CAN SKATE ALL OVER THE PLACE WITH SOME HONDURAN TRAMP AND IF I GET MAD I'M THE FUCKED UP ONE!
FOR CHRIST'S SAKE! WE WERE SKATING! BESIDES I ASKED YOU
ALWAYS MR. INNOCENT, RIGHT? YOU DO WHATEVER YOU WANT, YOU DON'T HAVE TO WORRY ABOUT WHAT AN
YOU KNOW YOU PICKED A HELL OF TIME TO BRING THIS UP!
CAN WE MAYBE TALK ABOUT THIS WHEN THERE AREN'T FIFTY THOUSAND PEOPLE AROUND?!
NO
NO, WE'RE NOT GONNA DISCUSS IT AT ALL. I'M GOING HOME.
FINE.

SHERMAN, YOU --YOU SHOULD GO AFTER HER.
WHAT?!
NO FUCKING WAY.
WHY SHOULD I GO AFTER HER?! SHE'S THE CUCKOO ONE!
I GUESS I JUST... THOUGHT...
WHAT.. WHAT'S THE MATTER? WHY'D YOU STOP?
I-- I DON'T KNOW! ALL OF A SUDDEN I JUST FELT A WAVE OF--
IT WAS LIKE PURE JOY!
STEPHEN YOU OLD DOG, YOU STILL GOT IT!

WHAT ARE A FEW OF YOUR FAVORITE THINGS?
HALLOWEEN. CATS.
OH! AND FINISHING A DRAWING.
FRANK SINATRA, SLEEPING LATE AND THE TWO MOST BEAUTIFUL WORDS IN THE ENGLISH LANGUAGE: "CHECK ENCLOSED."
PIÑA COLADA, MOJARME EN LA LLUVIA, HACER EL AMOR A LA MEDIANOCHE (SOBRE LAS DUNAS DEL CABO).
THANKS ANDREW R.
ABRAHAM LINCOLN, "BREAKFAST OF CHAMPIONS" BY KURT VONNEGUT, MONTAUK AND JANE PEKAR.
AWWW...
LEMME SEE... "NIGHTSTALKER" #22, THE ONE WITH THE HITLER ROBOT, "A TOUCH OF EVIL" AND LOUIS ARMSTRONG.
S.J. PERELMAN, "SONS OF THE DESERT" ...UH, "WHAT GOES ON" BY THE VELVET UNDERGROUND.
(THE "LIVE 1969" VERSION)
MOONPIES, TYRA BANKS, JERRY SPRINGER AND THE "STAR WARS" TRILOGY.
THANK YOU AND GOOD NIGHT.

QUIET! ♫♪
QUIET!
REAL PEOPLE, REAL CASES. JUDGE JUDY...
POLICE ARE QUESTIONING MAXWELL ABOUT THE BRUTAL MURDERS.
SPEAKING OF BRUTAL MURDERS, HERE'S AL TO TELL US ABOUT SOME BRUTAL WEATHER HEADING OUR WAY. AL?
HE BEATS YOU, INSULTS YOU AND NOW HE'S SLEEPING WITH YOUR SISTER! WHY DO YOU STAY WITH HIM?!
CUZ AH LUV 'IM.
AWWWW...
THE TARGET AREA IS ONLY TWO METERS WIDE. IT'S A SMALL THERMAL EXHAUST PORT, RIGHT BELOW THE MAIN PORT. THE...
JORDAN WILL REMAIN A FACTOR. HE HAS COME TO PLAY, THAT'S FOR SURE. HE'S EIGHT FOR NINE TODAY SO... IT'S UP... AND IT'S GOOD!
PUSH DOWN & TURN
ARE YOU DEPRESSED? TIRED OF LIFE? NEED ANSWERS? HI, I'M KIM "TOOTIE" FIELDS HERE TO TELL YOU ABOUT THE PSYCHIC PSISTERS CONNECTION.

SHREWD
CHRIS FARLEY FRAN DRESCHER
WILLIAM SHAKESPEARE'S THE TEMPEST
BUT MR. FLAVOR, ALL I'M SAYING IS THAT WE SHOULD HAVE A LAWYER GO WITH US. THAT--
FIRST OF ALL, THERE AIN'T NO US: YOU AIN'T GOIN' INTO THIS MEETING.
SECOND OF ALL, I DON'T NEED NO SHARK IN THERE WITH HIS METER RUNNIN'.
I'VE BEEN HANDLING CHUMPS LIKE J.C. FOR A LONG TIME, SEE?
OH YEAH, AND LOOK HOW GREAT THAT TURNED OUT.
RUMBLE
SKREEEEEEEEEEEK
WHAT?
ZIS IZZEELLE DRAINDOO AYETH AVENOO ZTANGLEER OFFTOORS
Bing-Bong!

I'M JUST AFRAID YOU WON'T HOLD OUT FOR WHAT YOU HAVE COMING.
YOU'LL GET ALL INTIMIDATED BY J.C. AND YOU'LL--
WHAT KIND OF AN IDIOT DO YOU TAKE ME FOR, KID? I KNOW! I KNOW!
I AIN'T GONNA BE THE SAME SUCKER TWICE!
OKAY, SO WHAT WOULD YOU SETTLE FOR? WHAT WOULD BE THE LOWEST AMOUNT YOU'D ACCEPT?
THE...?
LEMME SEE NOW... HUH...
$15,000?
FIFTEEN? BUT THE LAST NIGHTSTALKER MOVIE MADE $82 MILLION JUST ON ITS OPENING WEEKEND! YOU SHOULD--
EXCUSE ME, LADIES AND GENTLEMEN!

MY SISTER COOKIE AND I RAN AWAY FROM HOME CUZ MY PARENTS WANTED ME TO ABORT MY BABY, 'KAY?
SO WE'RE GONNA SING A SONG AND YOU GUYS WILL GIVE US SOME MONEY, 'KAY?
INJURED? HURT? CALL 1-800-WESUE4U!
MS CULLOUGH, MS KINNEY MC DONALD & FOLEY ATTORNEYS AT LARGE!
READY?
DID I EVER TELL YOU YOU'RE MY HERO?
LOTTO!
IT'S NOT JUST FOR SUCKERS!
YOU CAN SPEAK GOOD! IT'S EASY! LEARN ENGLISH
DUH DUH DUH THAT I COULD BE
METRO CHIC
I COULD BE
THAN AN E
I'M JUST SAYING YOU SHOULD GET A LAWYER. SOMEONE WHO
LOOK, LET'S JUST DROP IT, OKAY? I W--
OU ARE
VING B
MY WINGS!
NO TALKING!

WELCOME
ZOOM
COMICS
HELLO. MY NAME IS IRVING FLAVOR AND I HAVE AN APPOINTMENT TO SEE J.C. LEBLANC?
GREAT! I'LL TELL HIM YOU'RE HERE, MR. FAVOR!
C'MON! AT LEAST LET ME GO IN WITH YOU!
WHAT THE HELL DO I KEEP TELLING YOU? EN-OWE! I'LL--
IRVING!
J.C.! HOW YA DOIN'? IT'S GREAT TO SEE YOU.
YOU LOOK GREAT, IRV! WHAT'S IT BEEN, TWO YEARS? THREE?
OH, THIS IS MY FRIEND, MR. MAKO.
PLEASED TO MEET YOU, IRV.
HE'LL BE... SITTING IN ON OUR MEETING WHILE WE TRY TO SORT THIS WHOLE MESS OUT, OKAY?
SO... LET'S GO BACK TO MY OFFICE, SHALL WE?
MMMHMMM
UH... I DON'T WANT TO BOTHER YOU, BUT CAN I ASK YOU SOMETHING?
DO YOU ACTUALLY READ ANY OF THE COMICS THEY MAKE HERE?
WELC
Z

ME? NO. I MEAN THEY LOOK LIKE THEY'RE FUN AND EVERYTHING, AND MY LITTLE NEPHEW LOVES THEM.
I GUESS I ALWAYS JUST THINK COMICS ARE FOR KIDS, RIGHT?
YEAH. YOU'RE RIGHT.
KATHLEEN, DID ROSIE COME BY AND GIVE YOU THOSE PROOFS FOR "HELL CAT" #27 YET?
NO, PAULIE. SHE SAID BRAYSHAW WAS STILL WORKING ON THE COLOR.
BRAYSHAW'S DOING IT?! TELL ROSIE TO SEND THAT ASSHOLE TO MY OFFICE.
I'M SICK OF HIS...
...HIS...
?!
ED, YOU COULD DO A LOT WORSE THAN BEING HIS ASSISTANT. GIVE HIM A CALL!
IRVING FLAVOR, HUH?

... RUN IT BY THE NUMBERS BOYS AND I'LL GET IN TOUCH WITH YOU, OKAY?
UH, SURE ... OKAY.
I WANT TO THANK YOU BOTH FOR STOPPING BY.
COME ON, ED. LET'S GET THE HELL OUTTA HERE.
I GOTTA TELL YOU: I'M GOD DAMNED STUMPED. WE'RE IN THIS MEETING, RIGHT?
MAKIN' SMALL TALK AND BULLSHIT AND WHAT NOT AND I'M WAITIN' FOR HIM TO MAKE ME AN OFFER.

SO IN THE MIDDLE OF IT, HE GETS THIS PHONE CALL...
WHAT IS IT, PAULIE? I'M IN THE MIDDLE OF NEGO--
UH-HUH.
REALLY.
THAT IDEA IS... A GOOD ONE DO IT.
OKAY.
THANK YOU. GOOD WORK!
"SO AFTER HE GETS OFF THE PHONE, IT'S BACK TO THE BULLSHIT! HOW'VE I BEEN DOING, WHO'VE I BEEN WORKIN' FOR, EKSETERA."
AND THEN THAT'S IT!
HE SAYS THE DAMN ACCOUNTANTS HAVEN'T COME UP WITH A FIGURE YET BUT WHEN THEY DO, HE'LL CALL ME!
CAN YOU BELIEVE THAT?!
SOMETHIN' FUNNY'S GOIN' ON, ED.
NOW MAYBE I'M GETTIN' PARANOID, BUT I THINK THAT THAT PHONE CALL IS IT...
SOMETHING ABOUT THAT CALL MADE HIM--
ED, WHAT THE HELL'S THE MATTER WITH YOU?!
ZOOM COMICS JUST HIRED ME TO DO A NIGHTSTALKER GRAPHIC NOVEL!
SHIT! I LEFT MY COAT UPSTAIRS!

When Titans Clash!

Just in time for the holiday crunch, Cadbury films has relesed the home video version of "Nightstlker IV", the summer blockbuster which grossed an eye popping *$300 million.* In fact, the success of the latest sequel has made the series the most successfull ~~series~~—financially at least—of all time. Including the sales figures on action figures, bed spreads, halloween costumes, the animated series and literally hundreds of other spin offs would make croesus blush.

The Video Vault ~~in~~ Driggs Avenue in Brooklyn has fifteen copies of the "Nightstalker IV" to rent ~~(two legal and thirteen bootlegs)~~ and they are all out on this Saturday morning. The Vault is typical in this regard, but is very unusual in another: two doors down, up a three story walk up, in a one bedroom apartment which doubles as a studio is an old man with a fantastic secret.

His name is Irving Flavor and half a century ago, he created The Nightstalker.

And then sold him for $55.

ED... PLEASE TELL ME YOU AREN'T SERIOUSLY THINKING ABOUT TAKING THIS JOB!
CAN'T YOU SEE THAT LE BLANC IS JUST TRYING TO DIVIDE YOU GUYS UP?

HE FIGURES THAT WITHOUT YOUR HELP, MR. FLAVOR WILL FOLD LIKE AN ACCORDION!
BUT THIS IS THE CHANCE I'VE BEEN WAITING FOR! MY OWN GRAPHIC NOVEL!
YOU CAN'T HELP MR. FLAVOR AND WORK FOR ZOOM AT THE SAME TIME.
BUT... A GRAPHIC NOVEL!

YOU APPLIED FOR A JOB THERE IN AUGUST AND THEY TURNED YOU DOWN.
WHAT ELSE DO YOU THINK MADE THEM CHANGE THEIR CORPORATE MINDS?
WELL, BECAUSE --
BE -- BECAUSE ...

Irving Flavor was all of sixteen years old when he was first employed by Zoom Comics ans signed a "work-for-hire" contract. It stated that any work he would create during his time with the company—and he would work there for nearly thirty years—would be owned lock, stock and barrel by Simon LeBlanc, publisher of Zoom Comics.

Nevermind that Irving was the first one to come up with the character, or was the first one to write and drwa his adventures. Never mind, in fact, that he was the *only* one to create the stories for the first ten years of Nightstalker's existence. Most of the characteristics of the world's most famous vigilante ("*Justice comes by night!*") are details created by Irving Flavor. Nevermind any of that: Nightstalker is the property of Zoom Comics and a more golden goose would be hard to contemplate.

Ed Velasquez, Irving's assistant on what few art jobs whimper his way, doesn't think that's right. It was Ed who persuaded Irving to try to get

I DON'T IMAGINE MY OPINION COUNTS FOR MUCH, BUT --
I THINK HE SHOULD DO IT.
YOU DO?!
EDDIE, YOU GOTTA MAKE HAY WHILE THE GETTIN'S GOOD.
"WHEN OPPORTUNITY KNOCKS, DON'T KNOCK OPPORTUNITY."
I DON'T WANT YOU MISSIN' A GOOD JOB 'CUZ OF ME.

BUT HE'D BE WORKING FOR THE SAME CORPORATE SWINE WHO ARE RIPPING YOU OFF!
HE WOULD BE ONE OF THOSE CORPORATE SWINE!
BZZZ!
YOU CAN'T SHAKE THE DEVIL'S HAND AND SAY YOU'RE ONLY KIDDING.
YOU BETTER GET THE DOOR.

Zoom Comics to at last give him what he had coming: financial security, a steady job, and at long last, recognition of his hand in the creatin of Nightstalker. Without him, Zoom Comics would've gone out of business decades ago, instead of being the largest publisher of comic books on the planet.

"As soon as I realized that comic books were made up and drawn by real people and not carved in stone by gods or something, I knew that that's what I wanted to do when I grew up" Ed reveals, a smile crossing his face "I was nineteen at the time."

Ironically, it was Zoom Comics itself who recommended that Ed begin his cartooning career as an apprentice to a seasoned pro. An editor there gave him Irving's number and the rest is, with hope, history.

"It's really sad and disgusting. If Mr. Flavor had been a guy who made movies, like George Lucas or somebody, he'd be a multi-trillionaire and retired by now. But in comics, ripping

NOW, LET'S SEE IF I'VE GOT THIS STRAIGHT...
FIRST, YOU TELL ED THAT YOUR EDITOR PASSED ON YOUR IDEA FOR A STORY ON FLAVOR.
NOW, SUDDENLY OUT OF THE BLUE, YOU SHOW UP AND REVEAL THAT NOT ONLY IS THE STORY BACK ON, BUT THEY'VE SENT YOU -- THE ASSISTANT EDITOR ON THE "ENTERTAINMENT LISTINGS" SECTION--
TO COVER IT.
THAT'S RIGHT.
ED, I'D SAY THAT THIS IS YOUR LUCKY DAY!
YEAH!
SO HOW DO YOU WANT TO WORK IT? SHOULD YOU AND MR. FLAVOR GO--
BECAUSE WHILE YOU TWO MIGHT HAVE FALLEN FOR HER LITTLE STORY, I LIVED WITH HER AND I KNOW WHEN SHE'S LYING!!
WHAT THE HELL'RE YOU TALKING ABOUT?!

WHAT WOULD SHE GET OUTTA LYING ABOUT THAT?
WHY THE HELL WOULD SHE LIE ABOUT THAT?
DECEMBER

~~The first thing one notices about Irving Flavor is~~ SURPRISING

The first ~~surpassing~~ thing about Irving Flavor—and there are many—is that he doesn't *look* like a fighter. But when one takes into account that this man has drawn comic books (home of secret identities and bespectacled nerds with superpowers) all his life, it makes perfect, poetic sense. Of course! The person who created a musclebound crime fighter who can deck a mugger with one right hook would be a short, quiet and gentle man.

"I admit, Eddie practically had to twist my ~~god-damned~~ arm to get me to do this" Irving concedes, slightly embarrassed to be the center of so much hoopla. "I didn't want to make ~~no~~ trouble. I just want my fair share."

Despite the fact that he's slowly losing his eyesight and his drawing hand isn't as steady as it used to be, Irving would liked nothing better than to return to the company he helped build and the character he created. ~~"I spent longer on that character than some people get married" he chuckles.~~

"I worked on Nightstalker for ten years" he chuckles "That's longer than most marriages!"

Irving was born and raised in Brooklyn, where he still lives. His

AH! BECAUSE THEN SHE... SHE, UM,
WELL, BECAUSE... IF SHE... UH

COME ON, MR. FLAVOR. WE'LL GET STARTED. I JUST WANT TO ASK YOU SOME QUESTIONS ABOUT...
SURE, SURE.
BOY, YOU REALLY DO HATE HER, DON'T YOU? I THOUGHT--
I DON'T "HATE" HER!
I DON'T HATE ANYBODY! I JUST KNOW SHE'S GOT TO BE LYING!

I GUESS SO... BUT UNTIL WE KNOW FOR SURE, IT COULDN'T HURT TO GIVE HER THE BENEFIT OF THE DOUBT.
HA! FAMOUS LAST WORDS!
YOU WANT SOME TEA OR COFFEE?
DO YOU HAVE ANY COCOA? :GROAN: I SHOULD GET GOING. I'M THIS CLOSE TO BLOWING MY NEXT DEADLINE!
HOW'S SHERMAN HOLDING UP?
WHAT DO YOU MEAN? HOLDING UP WHAT?
YOU DON'T KNOW?!
YOU'LL LOVE THIS: SHERMAN AND DOROTHY GOT INTO A HUGE FIGHT AT THE SKATING RINK!
THEY HAVEN'T SPOKEN TO EACH OTHER SINCE THEN!
I GUESS THEY'RE SORTA LIKE BROKEN UP!

YEAH, SO WE WERE FACING SOME TOUGH TIMES AFTER MY FATHER PASSED AWAY.
I WAS... I GUESS I WAS AROUND EIGHTEEN YEARS OLD, SO I WAS LIKE THE BREADWINNER NOW. IT WAS TOUGH.
CHRIST! EVEN AFTER SELLING MY FATHER'S HALF OF THE SHOP TO MY UNCLE, WE BARELY HAD ENOUGH TO BURY HIM!
GOD BLESS SIMON FOR GIVING ME THE EXTRA WORK! IT WAS

was a great man "used his heart his head and his brain, built zoom up from nothing"—went fishing in westchester—believes murder was a robbery—most of his coworkers from that time dead definitely not working anymore—arthur epstein—len levant—tony gilligan—work dried up for old timers—crowning achievements?—nightstalker 44—"armor hammer and sickle"—teamed up villain admiral armor with josef stalin to try to kill John Wayne—good lesson for kids—fighting nazis in comics promoted patriotism

SO, I COULDN'T GO INTO THE SERVICE CUZ OF MY GOD DAMN EYES AND ALL, BUT I DID SOME WORK WITH THE DRAFT BOARD OVER THERE.
MY BROTHER, ISSAC, THOUGH, WENT TO THE PACIFIC, FOUGHT AT A PLACE CALLED KIRIWINA! GOT HIMSELF A FUCKIN' MEDAL!
KLKLK!KLK
LK!

alot of talk today about comics as "art"—doesn't get it—"half of them don't make any god damned sense"—no one can tell a story clearly—"stories never ran more than ten pages, now you got stories that run for ten issues and nothing fucking happens"— doesn't read much anymore except newspaper—hasn't seen any of the nightstalker movies—was lent a tape but doesn't have vcr—only person who could've played nightstalker—douglas fairbanks—would go back to work for zoom if given chance—doesnt

I DON'T HAVE NO GRUDGE AGAINST J.C. PERSONALLY, YOU UNDERSTAND.
THE SON OF A
UH, SORRY TO INTERRUPT BUT I HAVE TO GET HOME AND DO SOME WORK.
SO I JUST WANTED TO SAY GOOD LUCK WITH THE, ER, "ARTICLE" AND EVERYTHING.

JANE! WAIT A MINUTE!
I...UH, I WAS WONDERING IF YOU COULD DO ME A SMALL.. UH
A SMALL FAVOR.
WHAT.
COULD YOU GIVE THIS TO SHERMAN?
WHEN YOU GET HOME?
WHAT IS IT?
IT'S JUST A ...SORT OF A NOTE.
SURE.

Dear Sherman, By the time you read this, I will be dead. I can't go on
Dear Sherman, I am pregnant with your child.
Dear Sherman, Our plan is working perfectly! Jane doesn't realize our whole "relationship" is nothing but an elaborate plan to drive her insane!!! HaHaHa!

Apology
HOW YA DOIN', PUNK?
WHAT? OH, FINE. I'M FINE.
I'M JUST WATCHING MRS. MEYER TRY TO GET KRIMPET OUT OF MR. KAPLAN'S TREE.
I'M... I'M SORRY I YELLED AT YOU BEFORE, SHERM.
I SHOULDN'T HAVE GOTTEN SO ANGRY.
IT'S OKAY, MOM.
NO, IT'S NOT OKAY.

I KNOW YOU GUYS ARE HAVING A HARD...
IT'S BEEN ROUGH ON ALL OF US, NOT JUST ME.
BUT LATELY, I HAVEN'T...
I JUST SHOULDN'T HAVE YELLED. I'M SORRY.
ARE WE OKAY?
YEAH... WE'RE OKAY.
THANKS, PUNK.
WILL YOU COME IN AND GIVE ME A HAND WITH THE GROCERIES?
OKAY.
UM. DR. ENGEL SAYS THAT I HAVE TO GO BACK IN ON THURSDAY, SO YOU AND JOEY WILL HAVE TO STAY AT AUNT PHINN'S FOR A WHILE.
HUH? WHAT?

SORRY, AM I INTERRUPTING SOMETHING?
NAH.
I WAS JUST THINKING ABOUT THIS ONE TIME MY NEIGHBOR'S CAT GOT STUCK IN A TREE.
WHAT'S UP?
NOTHING. I'M JUST LOOKING FOR SOMETHING TO DISTRACT ME FROM THE FINALS I HAVE TO GRADE.
SO, HAVE YOU, UH, SPOKEN TO DOROTHY YET?
NO.
YOU GUYS REALLY HATE HER, DON'T YOU?
"HATE" HER? NO, THAT'S TOO... WELL, OKAY. JANE DOES HATE HER.
I THINK SHE'S OKAY, THOUGH.
YEAH, THAT'S WHAT I HEAR
SHE AND JANE ARE JUST DIFFERENT KINDS OF PEOPLE, THAT'S ALL.
EVEN YOU HAVE TO ADMIT THAT DOROTHY'S NOT THE EASIEST PERSON TO LIVE WITH.
GROAN
TELL ME ABOUT IT...

SHE'S MOODY, SHE SMOKES TOO MUCH, SHE DRINKS TOO MUCH.
SHE'S MESSY, SHE'S DANGEROUSLY IRRESPONSIBLE. HOW SHE'S MANAGED TO HOLD ONTO THIS JOB I CAN'T IMAGINE.
:SIGH: IT'S ONE OF THOSE THINGS, THOUGH, WHERE THE GOOD PARTS...
YOU KNOW, WHERE YOU'RE JUST WATCHING T.V. TOGETHER OR SOMETHING, AND THE SMELL OF HER HAIR OR THE WAY SHE, I DON'T KNOW, BITES HER PINKY NAIL... OR LYING IN BED, IN THE DARK, LISTENING TO HER BREATHE.
IT'S, I GUESS, THOSE LITTLE BITS THAT DO IT. THEY MAKE YOU FORGIVE THE OTHER PARTS.
YEAH, I...
I KNOW THAT FEELING.
THOSE LITTLE THINGS THAT ONLY YOU NOTICE.
I DON'T WANT TO SOUND GAY OR ANYTHING BUT ...
I GUESS I'M IN LOVE WITH HER.
WHAT?! YOU'RE IN LOVE WITH A GIRL? WHAT ARE YOU, SOME KIND OF HOMO?
HAHA. YOU KNOW WHAT I MEAN. GUYS ARE NEVER SUPPOSED TO SAY THAT KIND OF THING.

HAVE YOU READ THIS NEW ONE? ABOUT THE TEN WORST PRESIDENTS?
HE HAS A SORT, OF "BONUS" CHAPTER ABOUT THE TWO MOST OVER-RATED ONES.
CARE TO GUESS?
STEPHEN, SHE ...UH...
DOROTHY TOLD ME WHAT... ABOUT THAT, UH, INCIDENT THAT HAPPENED.
WHEN SHE LIVED HERE.
HA, WHICH INCIDENT WAS THAT? THEY HAPPENED ABOUT EVERY HOUR WHEN SHE LIVED HERE.
WELL, ahem YOU KNOW, THAT TIME YOU... SHE TOLD ME WHEN YOU...
SLAM
HONEY! I'M HOME!
WE'RE IN HERE!
IN SHERMAN'S ROOM!
SO WAIT A SECOND: WHAT HAPPENED?
I MEAN, IT'S NO BIG DEAL, YOU KNOW.
I JUST THOUGHT ahem WELL, SINCE WE WERE BEING
ahem
I MEAN, IT'S NOT A BIG, UH
A BIG
THING.
STAR SPANGLED MEN

CAN YOU BELIEVE THAT STUPID COW LAND LADY STILL HASN'T SHOVELED THE STOOP?
I SHOULD PURPOSELY FALL AND SUE HER SORRY ASS.!
I HAVEN'T SEEN OR HEARD HER ALL DAY.
AAAH, SHE'S PROBABLY OUT RIDING HER BROOMSTICK OR SOMETHING.
OH YEAH! THAT REMINDS ME: DOROTHY WAS AT MR. FLAVOR'S AND SHE GAVE ME THIS TO GIVE TO YOU.
HUH?
THANKS.
OH, DR. VICTORY CALLED AND SAID IT'S TIME FOR BIG NOSE TO COME IN FOR HIS ANNUAL CHECK-UP.
UH-HUH.
I MADE AN APPOINTMENT FOR NEXT FRIDAY. THAT WAS THE SOONEST THEY COULD DO IT.
YEAH... YOU'RE RIGHT.
BUT THEN I CHANGED MY MIND, CANCELLED THE VET AND CHOPPED BIG NOSE UP AND MADE HIM INTO TACOS.!

WHATEVER YOU...UH, WHATEVER YOU THINK IS BEST, BALLOO.
SO WHAT, UH, WHAT DOES IT SAY?
IF IT'S NOT TOO PERSONAL, SHE MEANS.
HMMM?
OH, IT'S...
IT'S AN APOLOGY.
...ON THE PRESIDENT'S NEW ATTACK ON DRUGS, BUT FIRST WE'LL MEET THE NEWEST STAR IN RAP: 80-YEAR OLD ROXANNE SALVI! NEXT ON CHANNEL Z NEWS!
MAN, LIFE SUCKS!
IF THIS IS THE BEST T.V. CAN DO, I'M GETTING BACK TO WORK.
IT'S JUST NOT FAIR! THEY CAN'T GET BACK TOGETHER!
I ONLY FOUND OUT THIS MORNING THEY BROKE UP! I NEVER GOT A CHANCE TO SAVOR IT!
IF YOU DREAMED OF HAVING THAT PERFECT BIKINI BODY FOR SUMMER...
HEY! ARE YOU HUNGRY? DID YOU SAY YOU MADE TACOS EARLIER?
ROWR?

WHO IS IT?
DELIVERY, MA'AM.
RRRRING!
RRRRING!

≷KLIK!≶ HI, THIS IS DOROTHY LESTRADE AND I'M NOT TAKING ANY CALLS AT THE MOMENT, SO PLEASE LEAVE A MESSAGE AT THE BEEP. THANKS!

ZOOM COMICS AND ITS PARENT COMPANIES HAVE NO COMMENT AT THIS TIME. THANK YOU.

looking back.

"I just want to get what's coming to me" he laments. "I just want my fair share."

Tomorrow he'll go back to work. He managed to snag one of the best paying jobs he's gotten since Ed has come aboard: an illustration for a plumber's union newsletter. "There's no shame in an honest day's work" he comments wistfully. "An honest day's pay for an honest day's work."

Even if that day was over fifty years ago...

≷BEEP!≶ UH, HELLO, THIS IS SUSAN LEBOWSKI CALLING FROM ZOOM COMICS IN REFERENCE TO...

IRVING FLAVOR...

KLIK

WHAT DO YOU WANT FOR X-MAS?
THE SEARS STAR WARS CANTINA PLAYSET.
WITH THE TALL SNAGGLETOOTH.
A CYLON RAIDER AND "THE RETURN OF THE GREAT BRAIN."
SHRINKY DINKS
A SHAUN CASSIDY POSTER AND A CUTE LITTLE PUPPY!
A RED RYDER BB GUN RIFLE WITH A COMPASS IN THE STOCK.
A HUFFY THREE SPEED WITH THE BRAKES ON THE HANDLE BARS.
ZOOM COMICS.
BROWNE'S
BROWN O-O'S

Irving's Christmas

I BETTER CALL THE BOYS AND TELL THEM TO CANCEL CHRISTMAS.
WARN THE PEOPLE! TELL THE PAPERS!
I'M MUCH TOO TIRED FOR CHRISTMAS CAPERS.
WHAT THE HELL ARE YOU LOOKIN' AT?
B-B-BUT SANTA! YOU MUST BE KIDDING!
RRR!
BUT IT WAS TRUE, SANTA WAS TAKING A HOLIDAY AND THE WORLD...

HOW COULD I RESIST A CUTE FACE LIKE THAT!
COME ON! COME ON!
GENTLE BEN!
DID YOU EVER HEAR OF THAT TERRIBLE YEAR,
WAY BEFORE YOU WERE BORN? WHEN SANTA CLAUS TOOK
A HOLIDAY, ON THE NIGHT BEFORE CHRIST
WHAT THE HELL ARE WE WATCHING HERE? PUPPETS?!
WOULD SOON KNOW THAT IT WAS TO BE THE YEAR WITHOUT A SANTA CLAUS!

ED'S CHRISTMAS
'TWAS CHRISTMAS AFTERNOON AND ALL THROUGH THE PLACE WERE DOZENS OF RELATIVES ALL IN MY FACE.
THERE'S MY COUSIN HECTOR, THE STOCK MARKETEER WHO MADE AS MUCH LAST WEEK AS I MADE LAST YEAR.
DRUNK UNCLE EARL ASKS FOR THE THIRD TIME TODAY
"YOU STILL AIN'T GOT A GIRLFRIEND? YOU SURE YOU AIN'T A GAY?"
HERE COMES AUNT CLARA.
YOU KNOW, HECTOR'S A BROKER! HE'D GIVE YOU A JOB!
HOW I WISH I COULD CHOKE HER.
I MENTION MY JOB (WHY I BOTHER I'M NOT SURE) AND HOW I WANT TO DRAW COMICS.
YOU LIKE BEING POOR?

YOU STILL DOING THOSE CARTOONS?
ASKS MY COUSIN, LUIZ.
YOU SHOULD GO WORK FOR DISNEY! DID YOU SEE "HERCULES?"
YOU GOTTA KNOW ABOUT COMPUTERS! IT'S COMPUTERS THEY USE!
DECLARES UNCLE DAVID, AN IMPORTER OF SHOES.
I JUST SMILE AND NOD, EATING PRETZELS AND CRUD.
INSIDE I AM WEEPING THAT THESE DOPES ARE MY BLOOD.
BANG!
I THINK BACK TO WHEN CHRISTMAS WAS ACTUALLY FUN.
STOCKINGS CRAMMED WITH CANDY AND TOYS BY THE TON!
ED
OKAY, SO IT WASN'T ALWAYS GOOD AS ALL THAT, BUT BACK THEN I HAD HOPE AND WASN'T AS FAT.
BUT NOW IT'S JUST ONE MORE DEPRESSING THING IN THE WORLD.
STILL LIVING AT HOME AND CAN'T GET A GIRL.

SURROUNDED BY JOY
I'M AN ISLAND OF GLOOM
SO WHERE ELSE TO GO
BUT THE WOMB OF MY ROOM?
SO I OPEN MY DOOR AND WHAT DO I SPY?
MY TODDLER COUSINS BOTH BARELY THIGH HIGH!
QUICKLY MY MIND RACED TO WHEN I WAS A LAD
TODAY'S CHRISTMAS DAY! HOW CAN THAT BE BAD!
JUST SEEING THEM PLAYING, CONTENT AND HAPPY,
MY COCKLES WERE WARMED AND I FELT MUCH LESS CRAPPY.
UNTIL I NOTICED THAT IN THE HANDS OF THESE BOYS --
IN THE MOUTHS OF THESE BOYS WERE MY "STAR WARS" TOYS!
OH MY GOD! BOBA FETT! HIS LEFT ARM IS TORN OFF!
THERE'S GOVERNOR TARKIN -- NOW NOT SO 'GRAND A MOFF...

BESPIN LUKE'S HAND WAS CHEWED CLEAN OFF!
MY MIND TEETERED TOWARDS INSANITY!
THE IMPERIAL PROBE BASHED TO PIECES!
HOW COULD THEY? OH, THE HUMANITY!!
I STORMED ONTO THE BATTLEFIELD AND GRABBED ONE BY THE COLLAR
GET OUT OR I WILL CUT YOUR THROATS!
I HAD BEEN HEARD TO HOLLER.
MY RAGE DID NOT IMPRESS THEM AS THEY GIGGLED AND THEY FLED.
I STEPPED OVER THE CARNAGE AND CRUMPLED ON MY BED.
THEN MY EYES FELL UPON A HORRIFIC SIGHT!
IT WAS WORSE THAN I HAD FEARED!
THERE WAS MY $125 BANTHA'S HEAD--
BUT IT'S BODY HAS DISAPPEARED...
THE SINGLE BEST PART OF CHRISTMAS (IT'S ALMOST DONE, FORTUNATELY)
IS THAT NEXT CHRISTMAS IS AS FAR AWAY AS CHRISTMAS COULD POSSIBLY BE.
SO NOW THAT YOU'VE HEARD MY HOLIDAY POEM, MERRY CHRISTMAS TO YOU! NOW GO THE HELL HOME!

BEER
5¢
I HOPE IT'S OKAY. I DON'T KNOW MUCH ABOUT JEWELRY, SO...
IT'S MARVELOUS! WOW!
I'LL WEAR IT WHEN WE GO TO YOUR AUNT'S TONIGHT!
HIGH FIDELITY
DOROTHY & SHERMAN'S CHRISTMAS
HAPPY CHRISTMAS.
MMMM, IT IS!
A-A-A-HEM!
WHAT? DID--
OH! RIGHT! NOW I GIVE YOU A PRESENT, RIGHT?

"FOR THAT WE HAVE TO GO BACK TO MY PLACE..."
SIT THERE AND I'LL BE RIGHT BACK!
OOH BOY! THIS SOUNDS SERIOUS! WHAT IS IT? THOSE BOOTS WE SAW ON EIGHTH STREET?
OH MY GOD, YOU'RE SUCH A LITTLE BOY. I'VE GIVING YOU THE PRESENT IN SEVEN SECONDS AND YOU'RE STILL GUESSING!
I KNOW, I KNOW.
HEY, DID YOU CALL YOUR DAD YET?
BATMAN AND ME
YEAH.
HE AND MY WICKED STEPMOTHER ARE GOING TO LAS VEGAS. I PROBABLY WON'T SEE THEM UNTIL FEBRUARY.
OKAY, NOW CLOSE YOUR EYES ...
OKAY. NO PEEKING, NOW...
SHOULD I PUT OUT MY HANDS OR OPEN MY MOUTH OR ANYTHING?
NOPE. JUST SIT STILL AND DON'T MOVE AN INCH...
HMM... WHAT DO HAHAHA! WHAT'RE YOU DOING?!
STOP! HAHA!
CAN YOU GUESS WHAT IT IS?
WHAT THE HELL IS IT? A FEATHER DUSTER OR SOMETHING?
HEH HEH, NO BUT YOU'RE CLOSE.
YAP! YAP!
OOOPS! WELL, THERE'S YOUR HINT! HAHA!
UH...
Hee Hee! OKAY, LOOK!

MERRY CHRISTMAS, BABY!
OH MY GOD!
ISN'T HE A SWEETY-PIE? THEY SAID HIS NAME IS PORKY, BUT WE CAN CHANGE IT.
Heh Heh...
Heh.
WAIT A MINUTE! HERE'S THE BEST PART!
YAP!
TWINS!
YOU GOT ME TWO DOGS?
YOU.. YOU GOT ME ..OOPS!
YAP! YAP!
NO! ONE'S FOR YOU AND THE GIRL ONE'S FOR ME!
YANKS MOVE TO JERSEY
HE'S REALLY GREAT, BUT I DON'T KNOW IF WE --
I DON'T KNOW IF I CAN KEEP HIM RIGHT NOW.
WHAT? WHY NOT?

I DON'T KNOW IF WE'RE ALLOWED TO HAVE A DOG. YOU KNOW HOW MRS. TWEED IS.
PLUS, I HAVE TO CHECK WITH JANE AND STEPHEN.
THEY WOULDN'T LET YOU GET A PET?! IT'S YOUR APARTMENT, TOO!
BESIDES, THEY HAVE A CAT, SO WHY CAN'T --
YAP!
YAP!
EXACTLY! SO I THINK IT WOULD ONLY BE FAIR FOR ME TO CHECK --
:sigh:
HOW ABOUT WE FIGHT ABOUT THIS WHEN WE GET BACK?
I DON'T WANT TO FIGHT ABOUT IT AT ALL!
HOW ABOUT THIS:
YOU ASK STEPHEN AND JANE IF IT'S OKAY. IF IT IS, GREAT.
IF IT'S NOT WE'LL KEEP BOTH OF THEM HERE UNTIL...
UNTIL WHAT?
UNTILLLL... I DON'T KNOW.
BUT I'D RATHER ARGUE ABOUT IT THEN THAN ON CHRIST-MAS EVE.

WOW... I AM TRULY IMPRESSED BY THIS NEW FOUND MATURITY.
HA!
HAPPY CHRISTMAS!
WHAT DO YOU THINK OF THE NAME "WATSON"?
FOR THE DOG I MEAN.
♫ MMM... YOU YA-DUH... MY LOVE....
WHAT KIND OF NUT NAMES A DOG "PORKY"?
LET'S SEE... ASTA? RAFFLES? MUTLEY? BENJI?
WHAT DID YOU NAME THE OTHER ONE? THE GIRL?

ARE YOU OKAY?
ARE YOU MAD ABOUT YOUR DAD NOT COMING?
NO.
I'M NOT... I DIDN'T THINK HE WOULD COME. I JUST THOUGHT I WOULD ASK.
IT WAS STUPID.
EDIS
ROUTE
EXIT

SORA'S CHRISTMAS
DING DONG ♫
DING DONG ♫
NOW, SANTA, I HOPE YOU'RE NOT GOING TO TAKE ANY OF THAT TO HEART.
KNOCK KNOCK!
MRS. TWEED?
ANYBODY HOME?
... TO SNUFF. BESIDES, I'M DUE FOR A HOLIDAY.
I BETTER CALL THE BOYS AND TELL THEM TO CANCEL CHRISTMAS...

mary & cookie's x mas
I'M REALLY SORRY ABOUT THIS YOU GUYS! I AM SO FUCKING SORRY!
BUT MY PARENTS ARE COMING HOME ON THURSDAY FOR HANUKAH AND ALL THAT SHIT AND I'M LIKE NOT SUPPOSED TO HAVE ANYONE OVER!
LAST TIME THEY CAME HOME EARLY ONE TIME AND LIKE FUCKING FREAKED OUT CUZ I LET A BUNCH OF SQUATTER GUYS I MET AT THE SKÄRLET CHYLDE SHOW AT IRVING PLAZA STAY HERE AND THEY FREAKED OUT!
OH MY GOD! THEY -- GOD, YOU WOULDN'T BELIEVE IT!
SO I HAVE TO LIKE CLEAN UP AND ALL THAT SHIT BEFORE THEY GET HOME AND GO APE-SHIT!
I'M REALLY SORRY!
HEY, YOU KNOW WHAT? CALL ME IN LIKE A WEEK AND IF THEY'RE GONE YOU CAN CRASH HERE AGAIN, OKAY?
I'M REALLY SORRY, YOU GUYS!
IT'S OKAY, NYGHT.
YEAH, THANKS, NYGHT.
WELL ...
NOW WHAT?

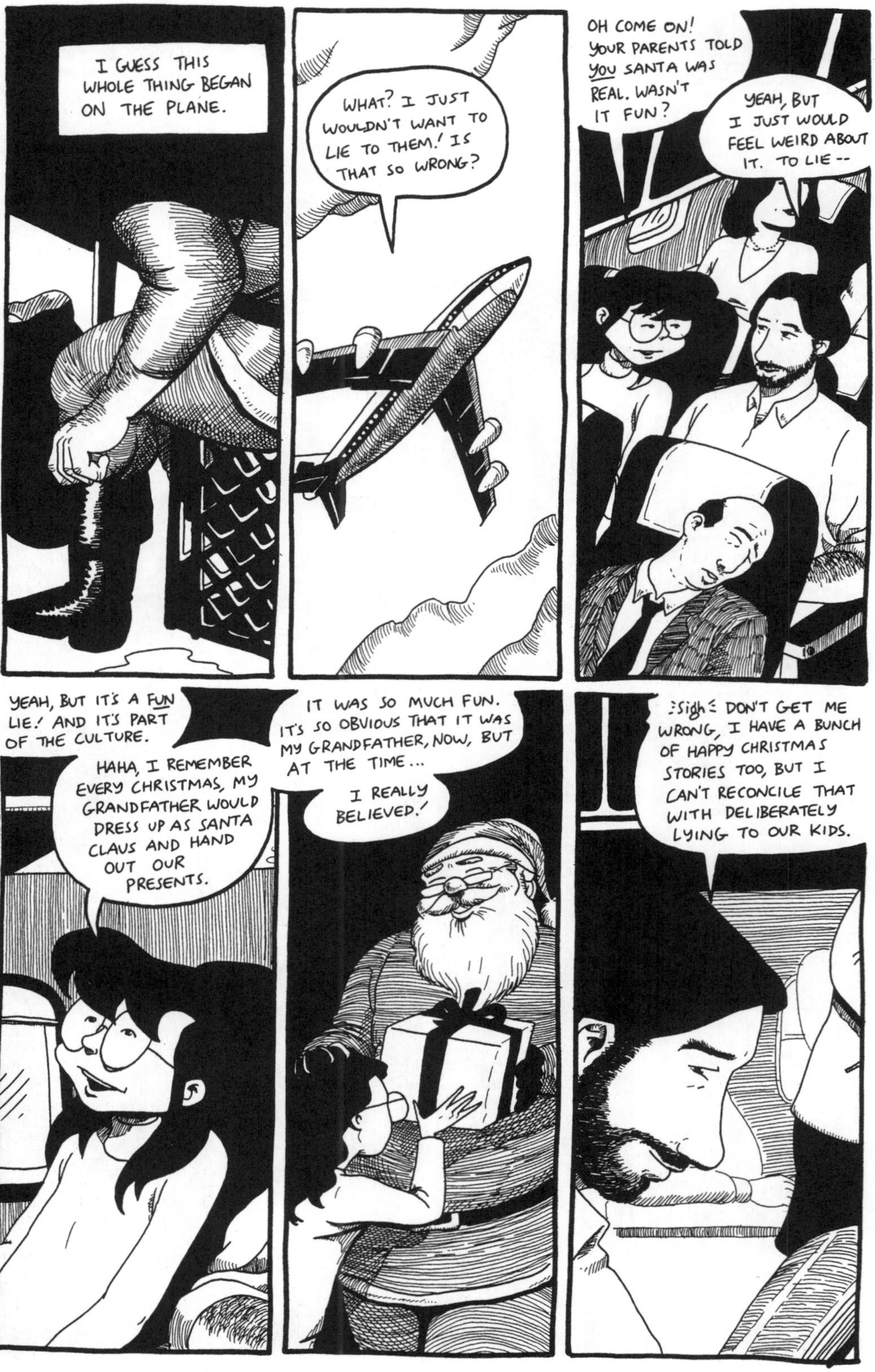
I GUESS THIS WHOLE THING BEGAN ON THE PLANE.
WHAT? I JUST WOULDN'T WANT TO LIE TO THEM! IS THAT SO WRONG?
OH COME ON! YOUR PARENTS TOLD YOU SANTA WAS REAL. WASN'T IT FUN?
YEAH, BUT I JUST WOULD FEEL WEIRD ABOUT IT. TO LIE --
YEAH, BUT IT'S A FUN LIE! AND IT'S PART OF THE CULTURE.
HAHA, I REMEMBER EVERY CHRISTMAS, MY GRANDFATHER WOULD DRESS UP AS SANTA CLAUS AND HAND OUT OUR PRESENTS.
IT WAS SO MUCH FUN. IT'S SO OBVIOUS THAT IT WAS MY GRANDFATHER, NOW, BUT AT THE TIME...
I REALLY BELIEVED!
:sigh: DON'T GET ME WRONG, I HAVE A BUNCH OF HAPPY CHRISTMAS STORIES TOO, BUT I CAN'T RECONCILE THAT WITH DELIBERATELY LYING TO OUR KIDS.

GATE 8
OOH! JANEY! IT'S SO GREAT TO SEE YOU GUYS AGAIN!
HOW WAS YOUR FLIGHT? OKAY?
HAHA! YEAH!
MY LEGS FELL ASLEEP BUT THE REST OF ME WOULDN'T.
THOSE SEATS WERE DESIGNED FOR ANOREXIC DWARVES!
Jane & Stephen's Christmas
HA! YOU DON'T HAVE TO TELL ME!
RICHIE, HOW DO WE GET OUT OF HERE?
UH... THIS WAY!
HOW IS EVERYONE?
ARE WE THE LAST ONES TO GET HERE?
AS ALWAYS.
ACTUALLY, JOYCE JUST GOT IN WITH THE KIDS THIS MORNING.
OH? WAS OL' RACCOON EYES HIS USUAL CHARMING SELF?
WHAT?! MOM DIDN'T TELL YOU?

ONE OF THE COMPLICATIONS OF A LONG TERM RELATIONSHIP IS WHAT TO DO ABOUT HOLIDAYS. VISIT YOUR PARENTS? VISIT HER PARENTS? INVITE THEM ALL TO OUR PLACE?
AS AGREED IN THE GREAT COMPROMISE OF 1993, THIS YEAR JANE AND I FLEW TO OHIO.
IT'S ALWAYS STRANGE WATCHING SOMEONE YOU'RE INTIMATE WITH AROUND THEIR RELATIVES.
I SEE A SIDE OF JANE I DON'T NORMALLY SEE. I CAN'T PIN-POINT HOW, EXACTLY, SHE ACTS DIFFERENTLY. IT'S JUST THIS SORT OF SUBTLE SHIFT FROM JANE-MY-GIRLFRIEND TO JANE-SOMEONE'S-LITTLE-SISTER OR YOUNGEST-DAUGHTER.
AS AN ONLY CHILD OF A DIVORCE WHO GREW UP IN MANHATTAN, MY EXPERIENCES ARE ABOUT AS DIF-FERENT FROM JANE'S AS YOU CAN GET. SHE HAS FOUR SISTERS AND HER PARENTS HAVE BEEN MARRIED FOR FORTY-TWO YEARS.
TO ENTERTAIN MYSELF, I ALSO LOOK AT THESE TRIPS AS AN ANTHROPOLOGICAL EXPEDITION. WHAT WOULD IT BE LIKE TO GROW UP IN THE SUBURBAN MID-WEST?
JANE SAID SHE HATED IT. SHE LEFT THE FIRST CHANCE SHE HAD.
SHE STILL CARES ABOUT HER FAMILY, THOUGH.
I THINK MOST OF THEM ARE OKAY. BUT I'M STILL LOOKING FORWARD TO GETTING HOME.
THREE DAYS TO GO...

BELIEVE ME, JOYCE, YOU'RE BETTER OFF WITH-OUT HIM.
HE'S SCUM. AND THIS LITTLE HAT-CHECK GIRL OR WHATEVER SHE IS?
SHE'S SCUM, TOO. THEY'RE BOTH SCUM. OKAY?
:sniff: I KNOW... BUT THAT DOESN'T MAKE IT ANY EASIER.
HOW'S COURTNEY HANDLING IT?
WE HAVEN'T... SHE DOESN'T KNOW YET.
:sniff:
GREG'S IN HOUSTON ON BUSINESS, SO WE'VE USED IT AS AN EXCUSE.
"IN HOUSTON ON BUSINESS?" ON CHRISTMAS?
I THINK HE JUST KNOWS THAT IF HE DARED SHOW HIS RACCOON-EYED FACE IN THIS HOUSE WE'D RIP HIS BALLS OFF!
HAHAHAHAHAHAHAHAHAHAHAHAHAHA!
POOR COURTNEY... SHE'S SUCH A SWEET KID.
UH, ANY OF THOSE CHRISTMAS COOKIES LEFT?

JANE'S FAMILY ALWAYS REMINDS ME OF A BEEHIVE -- THE WOMEN RUN THE SHOW. JANE'S MOM WOULD BE THE QUEEN, BUT NEXT IN LINE IS KIM, SECOND OLDEST DAUGHTER.
KIM'S ALSO THE MOTHER OF BROOKLYN, THE SPOILED BRAT HOLLERING IN THE NEXT ROOM.
I'VE NOTICED THAT OLDEST KIDS IN FAMILIES TEND TO BE THE NEUROTIC ONES. MAYBE BECAUSE THE PARENTS HAVE TO USE THEM AS A SORT OF "ROUGH DRAFT" FOR THEIR PARENTING SKILLS.
POOR JOYCE'S MARRIAGE HAD BEEN LOSING STEAM FOR A WHILE AND NOW, ONLY A YEAR AFTER SHE HAD "LITTLE JO," HER HUSBAND IS FLYING THE COOP.
LITTLE JO IS NAMED IN HONOR OF JOSIE, THE MIDDLE PEKAR -- NOW ANDERS -- SISTER. I'VE ALWAYS LIKED HER. SHE HAS A... DISARMING QUALITY; REALLY DOWN-TO-EARTH AND APPROACHABLE.
(ACTUALLY, I'VE ALWAYS HAD A SORT OF CRUSH ON HER BUT DON'T TELL JANE -- IT'S NOT IMPORTANT.)
JANE IS THE CLOSEST WITH GERTIE, I GUESS BECAUSE THEY'RE THE CLOSEST IN AGE. I THINK SHE'S THE ONLY ONE JANE TOLD ABOUT MY FUMBLED PROPOSAL LAST SUMMER.
SHE'S BRIGHT ENOUGH TO MAKE ME WONDER WHAT SHE SEES IN THAT GOOFY HUSBAND...
OUT OF ALL THE HUSBANDS, THE ONLY ONE I REALLY LIKE IS ANDREW, JOSIE'S GUY.
HE'S THE MANAGER OF A RECORD STORE IN CHICAGO, BUT HE'S ALSO A CIVIL WAR BUFF, SO WE CAN REALLY GET INTO IT.
BLAH BLAH, BULL RUN, BLAH BLAH, BOSTON CORBETT, BLAH BLAH..
YADDA YADDA SHILOH, YADA YADDA THE "MONITOR" BLAH YADDA!
BUT WHEN IT COMES TO HISTORY, HOWEVER, NO ONE CAN COMPARE TO PROFESSOR HERBERT JOSEPH PEKAR, PHD, CHAIR OF THE HISTORY DEPARTMENT OF OHIO STATE UNIVERSITY AND FATHER OF JANE.

KIDS! WE'RE HOME!
SAY, STEPHEN, DO YOU SUPPOSE YOU COULD HELP ME, UH, UNLOAD SOME THINGS FROM THE CAR?
OH, UH, SURE, PROFESSOR. JUST LET ME GET MY COAT.
HELLO, COURTNEY! DID YOU HAVE A GOOD TIME AT THE MALL?
Hi Aunt Jane!
It was really full with people!
I HOPE YOU STILL GOT TO TELL SANTA WHAT YOU WANTED!
COURTNEY, WHAT'S WRONG?
I DON'T THINK THAT WAS THE REAL SANTA CLAUS.
DID YOU GUYS REMEMBER TO PICK UP THAT SALT SUBSTITUTE?
ALICE...
STEPHEN'S GOING TO HELP ME UNLOAD THE CAR.

I REALLY LIKE AND ADMIRE PROFESSOR PEKAR-- I EVEN LIKE CALLING HIM THAT, AS IF HE'S A CHARACTER FROM "CLUE". HE AND HIS WIFE (WHO'S ALSO A TEACHER) ARE THE ONLY PARENTS I'VE MET WHO REALLY SEEM TO HAVE IT TOGETHER.
IT SOUNDS TERRIBLE, BUT I WISH MY OWN FATHER WAS MORE LIKE HIM.
THESE ARE THE LAST OF THE PRESENTS FOR THE GRAND KIDS.
WILL YOU HELP ME BRING THEM IN TO THE CARPORT?
MY OWN PARENTS JUST SEEM SO... DULL. IF THEY EVER HAD ANY INTELLECTUAL CURIOUSITY, ANY INTEREST IN ANYTHING OTHER THAN TELEVISION OR FOOTBALL SCORES, IT WAS DEAD LONG BEFORE I CAME AROUND.
BUT THE PEKARS... THEY'RE SO VITAL. PASSIONATE.
LOOK AT THE PROFESSOR. HE JUST TURNED SEVENTY, YET HE'S AS CURIOUS ABOUT THE WORLD AS ANYONE I KNOW.
JUST PUT THEM OVER THERE BY THE MOWER.
DID YOU READ MᶜPHERSON'S BOOK ABOUT THE SOUTH DECIDING TO ARM THE SLAVES? HE REALLY--
STEPHEN.
I'M SORRY, BUT I NEED YOUR HELP.

You did these when you were little, too?
YEP. I WAS ABOUT A YEAR OLDER THAN YOU.!
Rrrrar!
CAN I SEE YOUR DRAWINGS, COURTNEY?
THESE ARE TERRIFIC.! YOU'RE A GOOD ARTIST!
um, um, That's our house, like at Christmas time? See, there's mr. kitty and mommy, and dwight and daddy and mommy holding lil' Jo.
look at mine! See?!
it's a t.v. monster wrecking the t.v. with, with power rangers!
Wow!
THIS IS GREAT, DWIGHT!
Mommy Said Daddy won't be here this Christmas cuz of his job with taxes.
Uh, WELL...
I'M SURE NEXT YEAR YOU'LL ALL, Uh, BE TOGETHER, heh...

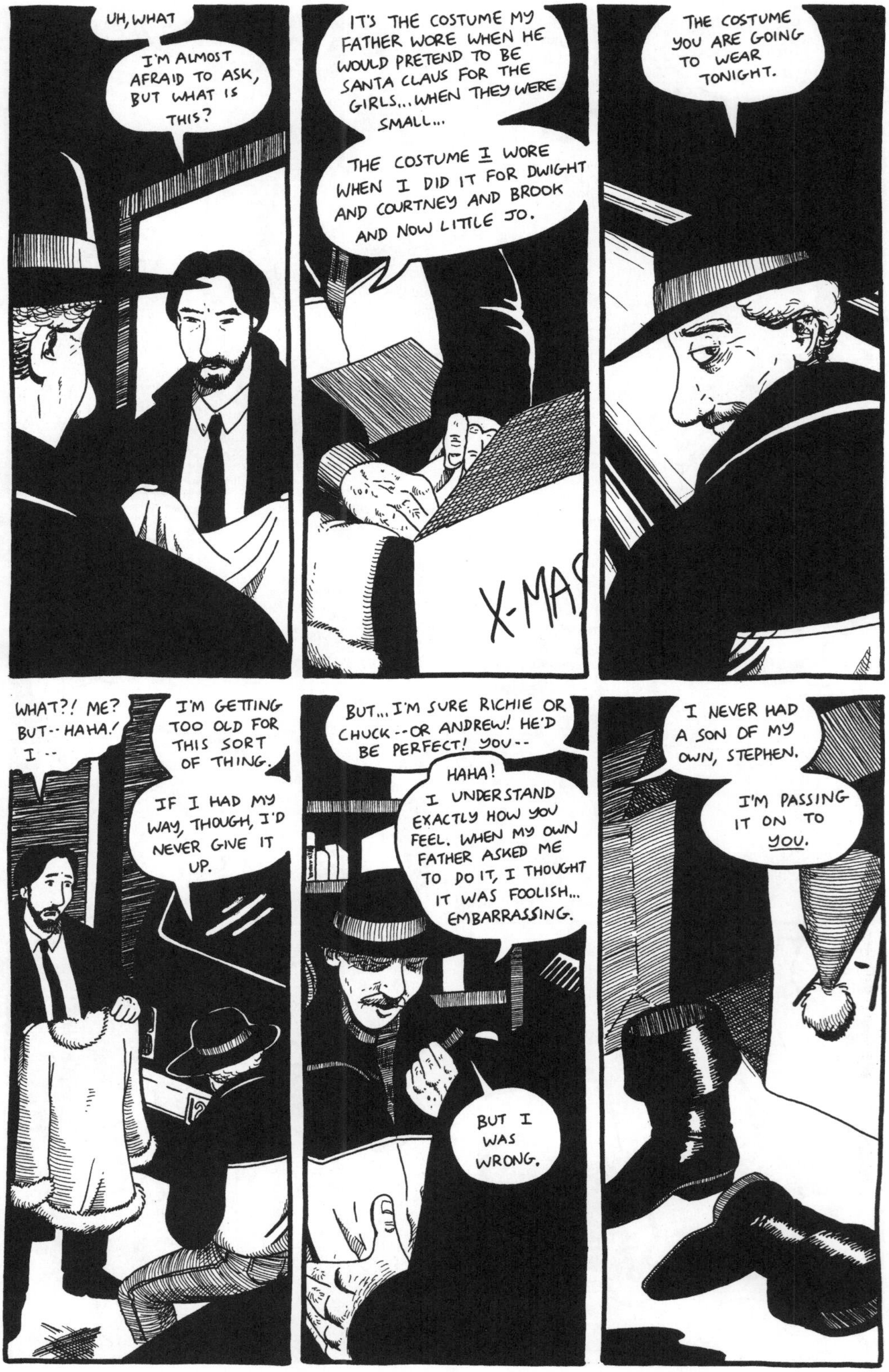
UH, WHAT
I'M ALMOST AFRAID TO ASK, BUT WHAT IS THIS?
IT'S THE COSTUME MY FATHER WORE WHEN HE WOULD PRETEND TO BE SANTA CLAUS FOR THE GIRLS... WHEN THEY WERE SMALL...
THE COSTUME I WORE WHEN I DID IT FOR DWIGHT AND COURTNEY AND BROOK AND NOW LITTLE JO.
X-MAS
THE COSTUME YOU ARE GOING TO WEAR TONIGHT.
WHAT?! ME? BUT-- HAHA! I --
I'M GETTING TOO OLD FOR THIS SORT OF THING.
IF I HAD MY WAY, THOUGH, I'D NEVER GIVE IT UP.
BUT... I'M SURE RICHIE OR CHUCK --OR ANDREW! HE'D BE PERFECT! YOU--
HAHA! I UNDERSTAND EXACTLY HOW YOU FEEL. WHEN MY OWN FATHER ASKED ME TO DO IT, I THOUGHT IT WAS FOOLISH... EMBARRASSING.
BUT I WAS WRONG.
I NEVER HAD A SON OF MY OWN, STEPHEN.
I'M PASSING IT ON TO YOU.

"SO THERE SHE WAS, FAST ASLEEP UNDER THE TREE. IT WAS THE MOST ADORABLE THING I'VE EVER SEEN IN MY LIFE. I WISH I'D TAKEN A PICTURE!"
AWWWW
HA HA!
CUTE!
HEE HEE
HA! HA
HEY, YOU GUYS BETTER WATCH IT! I'VE GOT A LOT OF STORIES I CAN TELL ABOUT EACH OF YOU!
OOOH!
LOOK OUT!
EVERY YEAR! IT WOULDN'T BE CHRISTMAS WITH-OUT DRAGGING UP THE ELSIE STORY!
HAHA! REMEMBER THE FAMOUS CHRISTMAS OF '73? YOU REMEMBER AUNT ELSIE'S, RIIIIGHT, KIM?
Heh, WHAT'S THIS ABOUT? I NEVER HEARD OF THIS!
GOD, IT WAS NO BIG DEAL, CHUCK. WE WERE AT AUNT ELSIE'S CHRISTMAS PARTY AND JOYCE AND I HAD TOO MUCH RUMCAKE!
HAHA! I THINK I WAS AROUND TWELVE, SO YOU MUST'VE BEEN, WHAT? TEN? GOD!
WE HAD TO STOP FIFTY TIMES ON THE WAY HOME SO YOU GUYS COULD THROW UP!
OH, HI, HONEY! COME ON IN, WE'RE ALREADY ON THE RUMCAKE STORY.
IS EVERYTHING ... SET?
ALL SYSTEMS GO.
OH, SHUT UP! YOU WEREN'T EVEN CONCEIVED WHEN THIS HAPPENED!
HAHA!
Mommy, can I have some more juice?
SHHHH! WAIT A SECOND!
DID YOU ALL HEAR SOMETHING? OUTSIDE?

I GIVE THREE DRAMATIC THUMPS AT THE FRONT DOOR. THEN I WAIT, HOLDING A LAUNDRY BAG FULL OF PLASTIC TOYS MADE BY GIRLS IN THE FAR EAST FOR PENNIES.
AS I'M WAITING, A VAN GOES BY AND HONKS ITS HORN AS IT PASSES. WHETHER IT'S IN APPRECIATION OR THEY THINK I'M THE PROFESSOR -- OR A BURGLAR -- I'LL NEVER KNOW.
HO HO HO
I THINK ABOUT THE KIDS AND WHAT I WILL SAY AND DO TO TRICK THEM INTO BELIEVING I'M SANTA. I FEEL ANXIOUS -- EMBARRASSMENT? FEAR THAT THEY WON'T BUY IT?
AT LEAST NEXT YEAR WE'LL BE AT MY FOLK'S HOUSE...
THUMP
THUMP
THUMP
OH MY GOODNESS!
OH, MY GOODNESS! IT'S SANTA CLAUS!!

SHHH!
WAIT A SECOND! DID YOU ALL HEAR SOMETHING? OUTSIDE?
I HEARD IT, MOM!
IT SOUNDED LIKE BELLS -- LIKE SLEIGH BELLS!
THUMP! THUMP!
gasp!
MOMMY, can I go get cookies?
HMMM... THERE'S A BUNCH OF BIG DOGS OUTSIDE! WHO --
OH, WAIT!
THOSE LOOK LIKE NINE REINDEER! WITH A SLEIGH!
SANTA!
where?
Let me see!! I CAN'T see!!
LOOK! RIGHT THERE!
can't see anything! where?!
RIGHT THERE! LOOK!
THAT RED LIGHT IS RUDOLPH'S NOSE!!
oh yeah!
Rudolph!!
Santa!
Eeeeee!!
Rudolph!
OKAY, EVERYBODY JUST CALM DOWN AND --
THUMP! THUMP! THUMP!
I'LL JUST OPEN THE DOOR AND SEE IF --
Santa's Here!!
mommy is it Santa?!
OH MY GOODNESS! IT'S --

SUDDENLY, I AM SANTA CLAUS. I'M NOT A HISTORY TEACHER, I'M NOT ANYONE'S BOYFRIEND OR ALMOST SON-IN-LAW.
I'M FATHER CHRISTMAS.
DWIGHT AND BROOKLYN LOOK AT ME AS IF I'M GOD INCARNATE. AS AN ADULT YOU DON'T REALIZE THAT KIDS BELIEVE IN SANTA, REALLY BELIEVE, THE SAME WAY WE BELIEVE IN CARS OR IN BUILDINGS -- NO QUESTION.
MAGIC IS REAL TO THEM!
I GLANCE OVER AT PROFESSOR PEKAR AND REALIZE HE'S DRAFTED ME INTO A BROTHERHOOD WORDS CANNOT EXPLAIN. I UNDERSTAND, NOW, WHY HE DID IT AND WHY IT MUST'VE BEEN PAINFUL FOR HIM TO GIVE IT UP.
I'M GRATEFUL TO DO IT FOR ONE YEAR, AT LEAST...
THEN I LOOK AT COURTNEY AND IT'S LIKE A SLEDGE-HAMMER TO MY CHEST...
SHE DOESN'T BELIEVE ANY MORE.
IT'S NOT MY PERFORMANCE-- BECAUSE I'M NOT PERFORMING, I AM SANTA CLAUS -- BUT FOR THE FIRST TIME SHE KNOWS THE TRUTH. I FEEL A PANG OF SADNESS... SOMETHING PRECIOUS AND RARE IS GONE FOREVER.

HOHO! YOU'RE WELCOME, BROOKLYN!
OH! WHAT HAVE WE HERE? WHY, IT'S FOR DWIGHT!
COOL! Mom can I open it now?! PLEEEEEASE!
YOU KNOW THE RU ONE TONIGHT, TH REST YOU CAN O TOMORROW.
WOW! THE BRAIN™ WITH SKULL-KRUSHER™ GRIP! COOL!!
MOMMY A TAWKIN SIGGY!
GOOD BOYS AND GIRLS ALWAYS DO AS THEY'RE TOLD, HAHA!
GOD! OUR TO WEREN'T HA AS GOOD AS T TOYS!
I KNO $18.99 FOR A OF PLASTIC!
OOD BYE, COURTNEY! BYE BROOKLYN! GOOD BYE, DWIGHT! SEE YOU NEXT CHRISTMAS!
YE SANTA!
YE!
GOOD BYE, SANTA!

"SOME PEOPLE ARE BORN SANTA CLAUS, SOME WORK ALL THEIR LIVES TO BECOME SANTA CLAUS AND SOME HAVE SANTA CLAUS THRUST UPON THEM."
PROFESSOR PEKAR'S WORDS.
IN TWO MONTHS, FRED, JOSIE AND ANDREW'S SON WILL BE BORN. HE'LL GROW UP TO TEACH BAND AT A HIGH SCHOOL IN MUNSTER, INDIANA.
IN THIRTY-TWO YEARS FRED DONS THE SUIT I WORE TONIGHT AND BECOMES SANTA CLAUS FOR A NEW GENERATION... FOR HIS KIDS AND DWIGHT'S KID AND LIL' JO'S KID...
IN FIVE MONTHS, JOYCE WILL OFFICIALLY DIVORCE GREG.
COURTNEY IS HIT HARDEST BY THE BREAK UP. SHE'LL HAVE AN ESPECIALLY ROUGH ADOLESCENCE. MARRED BY AN EATING DISORDER AND TWO SUICIDE ATTEMPTS. SHE OVERCOMES IT, THOUGH, AND WILL GO ON TO BE A FAMOUS AUTHOR.
AS AN OLD MAN, I'LL SKIM THROUGH HER MEMOIRS AND FIND NO MENTION OF SANTA CLAUS.
AM I RELIEVED OR SAD?
IN THE NEXT FEW YEARS, THE PROFESSOR WILL HAVE TO RETIRE FROM TEACHING AS HIS BODY IS RAVAGED BY CANCER.
HE'LL BEAT IT THE FIRST TIME, BUT SUCCUMB AT THE AGE OF EIGHTY FOUR. WHILE HIS WIFE SITS IN A ROCKER READING TO HIM, HE'LL DIE PEACEFULLY.
SO... WILL I LIE TO MY KIDS? WILL I TELL THEM THAT SANTA CLAUS IS REAL? THAT ONCE A YEAR REINDEER CAN FLY AND IF YOU'RE GOOD AT LEAST SANTA WILL KNOW?

YES
HAVE I EVER HAD AN EROTIC DREAM ABOUT SANDY DUNCAN?
HAVE I EVER GONE TO A NUDE BEACH?
WILL I SHOW UP AGAIN BEFORE THE END OF THIS BOOK?
HAVE I EVER GONE TO A SHRINK?
DID I EVER TRY L.S.D.?
DO I THINK COMICS ARE FOR KIDS--OR AT LEAST EMOTIONALLY RETARDED ADULTS?
WILL I EVER FIND TRUE LOVE?

A ROCK IN A POND

EMS

I... I CAN'T BELIEVE IT. SHE'S-- SHE'S FINALLY GONE. I CAN'T BELIEVE IT!
I DON'T KNOW... I'VE SEEN ENOUGH HORROR MOVIES TO SUSPECT A TRICK.
ANY MINUTE SHE'LL POP UP AND KILL US ALL.
EMS
NO! THIS IS IT! OUR DREAM COME TRUE!
OUT WITH HER ROTTEN WICKEDNESS AND IN WITH A NEW BIRTH OF FREEDOM!
"I BELIEVE IT IS PEACE IN OUR TIME."
HELLO, WHAT'S THIS?
HAS SOMEONE FINALLY DROPPED A HOUSE ON THE WICKED WITCH OF THE SLOPE?
EMS
THE POOR WOMAN'S DEAD! CAN WE SHOW A LITTLE RESPECT PLEASE?
OH, I'M SORRY. I FORGOT HOW CLOSE YOU WERE.
IS SHERMAN HOME?
METRO
YEAH. HE'S INSIDE WITH ED.
THANKS, I'LL GO ON UP. OH! WAIT! HERE: TAKE ONE OF THESE!
YOU KNOW, I REALLY DON'T CARE FOR HER AT ALL.
COME ON, LET'S GET GOING...

I'M ON, LIKE, MY WAY HOME FROM THE BANK AND EVERYTHING, RIGHT? BUT IT'S NOT REALLY MY NEIGHBORHOOD OR ANYTHING. I'M LIKE IN CALIFORNIA OR HAWAII OR SOMEPLACE.
SUDDENLY, THIS GIRL COMES UP TO ME -- SHE LOOKS LIKE THAT CASHIER I'M IN LOVE WITH AT THE KEY FOOD NEAR MY HOUSE -- AND SHE'S ALL FLUSTERED AND EXCITED ABOUT MEETING ME!
SHE'S LIKE CONGRATULATING ME ON WINNING ALL OF THOSE AWARDS FOR MY COMICS AND EVERYTHING AND SHE'S SEEN MY T.V. SHOW AND WANTS TO KNOW WHAT TYRA BANKS AND ANNA NICOLE SMITH ARE REALLY LIKE AND ALL THAT...
THE WHOLE TIME THIS GOING ON I FEEL SOMETHING, LIKE, TUGGING AT MY PANTS
YEAH, I BET YOU DID!
YEAH, RIGHT, SO I LOOK DOWN TO SEE WHAT IS AND
EDDIE... EDDIE! CAN YOU SPARE ME THIRTY PIECES OF SILVER?
cough
SIGGLY NEEDS A NOSE JOB!
AND THAT WAS IT: I WOKE UP IN A COLD SWEAT!
WOW. WHAT DO YOU THINK IT MEANS?
I FELT BAD ABOUT STEALING THE CAMERA. I HADN'T EVEN USED IT YET. I FINALLY...

I THINK IT MEANS YOU GUYS ARE GIVING ME SUCH A GUILT TRIP OVER THIS ZOOM COMICS THING IT'S RUINING MY DREAMS!
COME ON, ED, YOU HAVE TO ADMIT IT WOULD BE REALLY SLEAZY IF YOU TOOK THAT JOB.
IT SOUNDS LIKE A CLICHE, BUT THAT WOULD REALLY BE SELLING OUT.
YOU WANT SOME MORE YOO-HOO?
LOVE ONE.
BUT -- BUT I WOULDN'T BE SELLING OUT! I'D WORK ON THE GRAPHIC NOVEL AND HELP MR. FLAVOR!
COME ON, YOU TOLD ME IT TAKES YOU FOREVER TO DRAW A PAGE. WHEN WOULD YOU HAVE THE TIME?
RING!
MR. FLAVOR WANTS ME TO TAKE THE JOB!
YEAH, WELL HE'S AN IDIOT. WHAT CAN I TELL YOU?
HOLD ON...
BEAT IT, OLD MAN!
OUCH!
OH, EDDIE! giggle!
HEY! WHAT'RE YOU DOING HERE? DIDN'T WE SAY FIVE O'CLOCK?
I KNOW! I KNOW! BUT I HAD TO RUSH OVER AND SHOW YOU SOMETHING!!

OH, HEY, DOROTHY, HOW'RE YOU DOING? I WAS JUST ABOUT TO LEAVE. I --
ED! I'M SO GLAD YOU'RE HERE! HERE: TAKE ONE OF THESE!
ACTUALLY, TAKE ONE TO GIVE TO IRVING AS WELL!
WHY? WHAT IS IT?
PAGE THIRTY TWO...
HEY! LOOK AT THAT! THEY PUBLISHED HER STORY ABOUT ED'S BOSS!
WHAT?! LET ME SEE!!!
"WHEN TITANS CLASH: ZOOM COMICS' BATTLE TO SQUASH IRVING FLAVOR ONCE AND FOR ALL.
BY... DOROTHY... LESTRADE..."

"JUST IN TIME FOR THE HOLIDAY CRUNCH, CADBURY FILMS RELEASED THE HOME VIDEO VERSION OF 'NIGHTSTALKER IV', THE SUMMER BLOCKBUSTER WHICH GROSSED AN EYE POPPING $450 MILLION AT THE --"
GOD ALL-MIGHTY FOR CHRIST'S SAKE JESUS.
SHE WASN'T --
YES, IF YOU COULD TELL PAULIE THAT I SAID "NO DICE" --
YEAH, ED... VELASQUEZ... Q-U-E-Z.
YUP.
THANKS! YEAH, HAPPY NEW YEAR TO YOU, TOO.
I KNOW! I KNOW! ISN'T IT GREAT! THIS IS LIKE THE BIG TIME!
A REAL MAGAZINE!
HOLY FUCKING MOSES AT THE CROSSROADS...
J.C. IS GOING TO BE PISSED FUCKING OFF!
YEAH, COME ON, YOU CAN READ THE WHOLE THING AT LUNCH.
LUNCH?
YEAH. TO SHOW YOUR APPRECIATION YOU'RE BUYING ME LUNCH.
SO PUT YOUR HAIR ON AND LET'S GO!
AWRIGHT, AWRIGHT!
JEEZ! A GUY GETS YOUR NAME IN THE PAPER AND SUDDENLY YOUR HIS RICH UNCLE GOD DAMNED PENNY BAGS BUYING HIM FOOD!

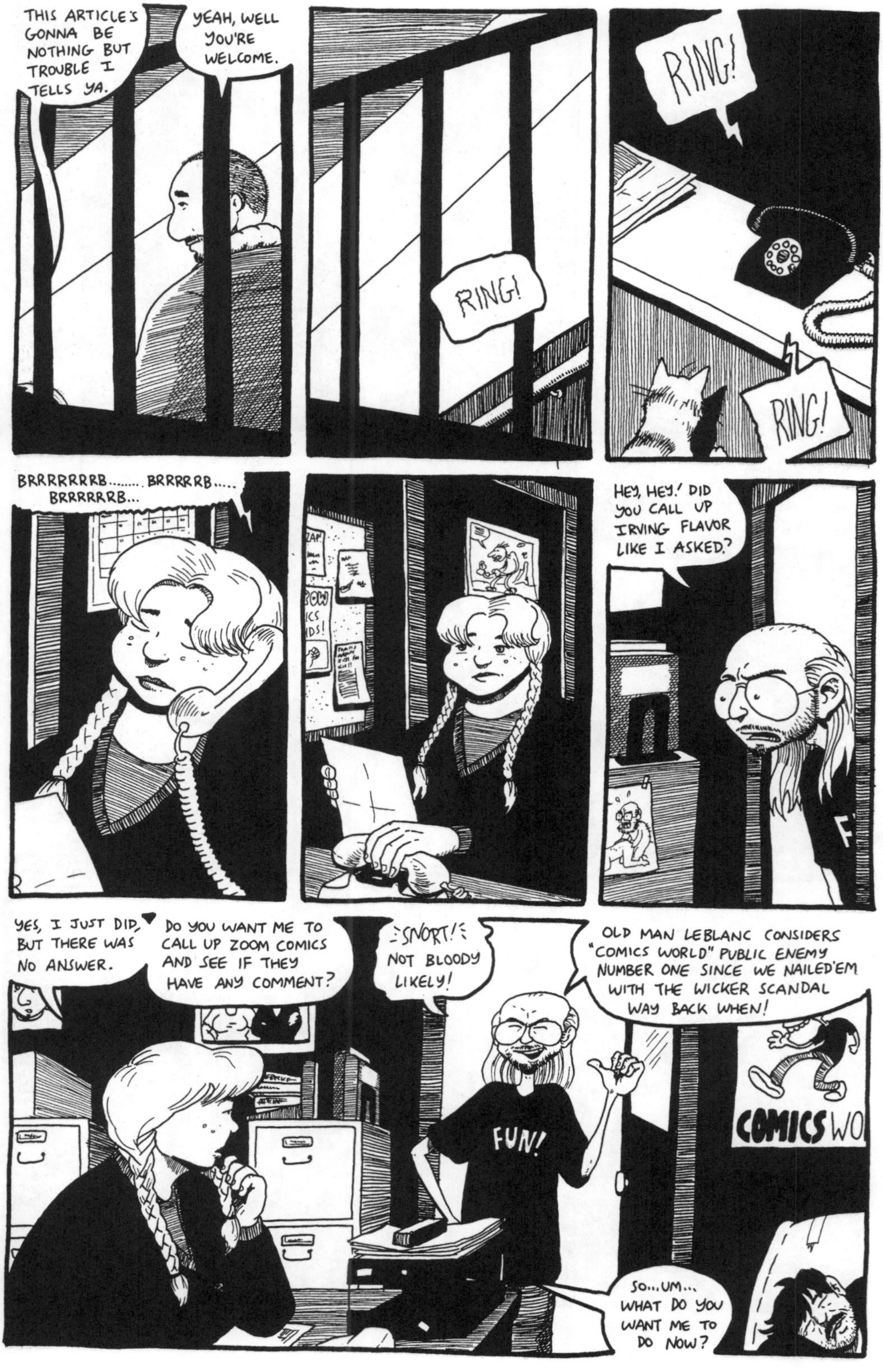

THIS ARTICLE'S GONNA BE NOTHING BUT TROUBLE I TELLS YA.
YEAH, WELL YOU'RE WELCOME.
RING!
RING!
RING!
BRRRRRRRB........ BRRRRRB..... BRRRRRRB...
HEY, HEY! DID YOU CALL UP IRVING FLAVOR LIKE I ASKED?
YES, I JUST DID, BUT THERE WAS NO ANSWER.
DO YOU WANT ME TO CALL UP ZOOM COMICS AND SEE IF THEY HAVE ANY COMMENT?
SNORT! NOT BLOODY LIKELY!
OLD MAN LEBLANC CONSIDERS "COMICS WORLD" PUBLIC ENEMY NUMBER ONE SINCE WE NAILED'EM WITH THE WICKER SCANDAL WAY BACK WHEN!
FUN!
COMICS WO
SO...UM... WHAT DO YOU WANT ME TO DO NOW?

MMMMM...
HEY, GUYS! WHAT DO WE WANT THAT INTERN CHICK TO DO NOW?
HOHO! I CAN THINK OF A FEW THINGS I'D LIKE HER TO "DO!"
HAHA HAHA!
X-FLIES
HeH, YEAH, RIGHT!
HARV, LISTEN! ARCHIE HAS THIS KILLER IDEA FOR HOW TO HANDLE THIS FLAVOR THING! LEBLANC WILL DROP FUCKING D-E-A-FUCKING-D!
FUN!
OH YEAH, HUH? SO WHAT'S THIS?
OKAY, OKAY: YOU KNOW THE BIG COMIC CONVENTION THEY'RE HAVING IN NEWARK THIS YEAR?
X-FLIES
PSSH! THEY MIGHT AS WELL CALL IT THE "LET'S-SUCK-ZOOM-COMICS'-COLLECTIVE-DICK" CONVENTION!
EXACTLY! WELL, THIS YEAR J.C. LEBLANC HIMSELF WILL BE THERE!
COME ON! WE TRIED "OPERATION: SILLY STRING" TWO YEARS AGO AT CHICAGO! THEY JUST THREW US OUT!
"OH, NO, WARREN! WE'VE GOT SOMETHING MORE POTENT THAN MERE SILLY STRING!"
METRO
HOTTEST WRITERS OF GEN-NEXT

...VIVRON EXPECTED TO WIN STUDENT TREASURY, UH, STUDENT TREASURER ONCE AGAIN.
LIZ PARBONI, UNIVERSITY NEWS.
...TOWN COUNCIL HAD NO COMMENT AT PRESS TIME.
LIZ PARBONI, CHANNEL 54 NEWS IN ORANGE COUNTY.
...FUN. BUT ONE THING IS CLEAR: WE ALL LOVE A PARADE!
LIZ PEIRBORNE, NEW YORK NEWS, IN MIDTOWN.
...THE BEAMING STAR AS HE TOOK HOME HIS THIRD OSCAR.
ELIZABETH PEIRBORNE, NATIONAL NEWS, IN HOLLYWOOD.
...SENATOR RAY SAID A TEARFUL FAREWELL AS HE LEFT HIS OFFICE FOR THE LAST AND FINAL TIME.
ELIZABETH PEIRBORNE, LIVE FROM WASHINGTON.
...WITH THE TERRORISTS REMAINS TO BE SEEN.
ELIZABETH PEIRBORNE-SMITH, AT THE WHITE HOUSE.
...ME LATER TONIGHT FOR MY EXCLUSIVE INTERVIEW WITH THE VICE PRESIDENT.
ELIZABETH PEIRBORNE-SMITH, IN WASHINGTON.
...VOWS "THE KILLER WILL BE FOUND." STRONG WORDS...FROM A STRONG MAN.
ELIZABETH PEIRBORNE, CHICAGO NEWS AT 10.
...CLAIMED. BUT OUR HIDDEN CAMERA REVEALED A TALENT A BIT... KINKIER.
I'M ELIZABETH PIERBORNE AND THIS... IS "INSIDE SCOOP!"
INSIDE SCOO

ETRO
GOOD MORNING, ROZ.
GOOD MORNING, MRS. PIERCE.
I NEED YOU TO BOOK ME ON A FLIGHT TO NEW YORK FOR THIS FRIDAY. FIRST CLASS, J.F.K.
TRACK DOWN THE ARTIST MENTIONED IN THIS ARTICLE--IRWIN SOMEBODY--AND ARRANGE AN INTERVIEW FOR FRIDAY NIGHT.
CONTACT SOMEONE AT THIS COMIC BOOK COMPANY AND ASK WHEN WE COULD HAVE AN INTERVIEW FOR THE SHOW.
WHEN THEY SAY "NEVER", CALL RON AND SEND IN AN AMBUSH CREW.
OH, AND TELL DR. CONLEY AND TELL HIM I'LL NEED AN EYE TUCK BEFORE THURSDAY.
CONGRATULATIONS, IRWIN.
SOMEBODY UP HERE LIKES YOU.
Uh...

SHOULD--
SHOULD I KEEP GOING?
UH, WELL SALMON CALLED ABOUT, UH, THE ARTICLE AND WANTED TO KNOW WHAT WE-- HOW HE SHOULD, UH, PRESENT THE STORY IN "COLLECTOR'S WORLD."
AND, UH, LET'S SEE: MR. YTSUMI FROM CAROLCO CALLED. HE WANTED TO TALK WITH YOU ABOUT THE, UM, ARTICLE.
METRO
SAM ROTHSTEIN -- FROM CABURY FILMS?--
HE NEEDS TO SPEAK TO YOU. "URGENT," IT SAYS. IT SEEMS THEY HAVE BEEN GETTING SOME CALLS SINCE THE, AH, ARTICLE CAME, UH, OUT.
:AHEM: AND "INSIDE SCOOP" CALLED. YOU KNOW, THEY DID THAT BIG EXPOSE ON THAT SWEATSHOP WITH THOSE KOREAN GIRLS?
LIFETIME ACHIEVEMENT
J.C. LEBLANC
for his outstanding work in the field in
COMICS
THEY WANT TO KNOW IF YOU HAVE ANY COMMENT ON THE --UH, ANY COMMENT.
AND IT SEEMS THAT FLAVOR'S ASSISTANT WILL NOT BE DOING THE NIGHTSTALKER GRAPHIC
UH
NOVEL

HEY...
WHAT'S WRONG?
HMMM?
WHAT? OH, NOTHING'S WRONG. I JUST--
UH, WOULD IT BE OKAY WITH YOU IF... WE DIDN'T HAVE SEX TONIGHT?
I DON'T KNOW, I'M JUST NOT IN THE MOOD, OR--
WHAT'S THE MATTER? ARE YOU MAD AT ME OR SOMETHING? WHAT DID--
NO, NO, NO. IT DOESN'T HAVE ANYTHING TO DO WITH YOU. I'M JUST--
SIGH
I DON'T KNOW.
WELL, IF YOU CHANGE YOUR MIND, DO LET ME KNOW.
DID YOU ASK JANE ABOUT BRINGING FIDO HOME YET? IT'S BEEN ALMOST A MONTH.
SORRY. I KEEP FORGETTING.
ONE OF MY STUPID NEIGHBORS COMPLAINED TO ME ABOUT ALL THE BARKING AGAIN. WHAT DOES SHE WANT ME TO DO?

OH! HEY, DID YOU EVER HEAR FROM THAT BEATLES FAN MAGAZINE IN ENGLAND? ABOUT PUBLISHING YOUR STORY?
YEAH. THEY TURNED IT DOWN. OF COURSE.
AHHH, THOSE DUMB FUCKS. DON'T LET IT DISCOURAGE YOU, SWEETIE.
DID YOU DO ANY MORE WORK ON THAT STORY YOU WERE DOING? ABOUT THAT WEIRD NEIGHBOR YOU HAD AS A KID?
NO, I HAVEN'T BEEN ABLE TO WRITE FOR AWHILE.
YOU KNOW WHAT YOU SHOULD DO? SET ASIDE A CERTAIN TIME OF DAY -- LIKE AN HOUR, TWO HOURS -- TO DO NOTHING BUT WRITE.
UH-HUH.
OR EVEN BETTER: FORCE YOURSELF TO WRITE AT LEAST FOUR OR FIVE PAGES A DAY, RAIN OR SHINE, NO MATTER WHAT. ONE OF MY OLD TEACHERS SAID THAT.
YEAH. I SHOULD.
I THINK THE PROBLEM WITH MOST ASPIRING WRITERS IS THAT THEY SPEND TOO MUCH TIME ASPIRING AND NOT ENOUGH TIME WRITING!

SOME AUTHOR SAID THAT THE WAY TO BE A GREAT WRITER IS TO WRITE 10,000 PAGES. BY PAGE 10,001, YOU'RE A GOOD WRITER.
MMM.
ACTUALLY, I FEEL PRETTY TIRED. WOULD YOU MIND SHUTTING OFF THE LIGHT AND WE GO TO SLEEP?
OKAY.
I GUESS NOT.
GOOD NIGHT.
'NIGHT.

VE!
Pain
WHAT CAN I SAY? I'M CERTAINLY TORN. ON ONE HAND, IT'S GREAT FOR MR. FLAVOR...
AN ARTICLE IN A BIG MAG LIKE "METRO CHIC" CAN ONLY HELP.
STANDARDS
DOUBLE CROS
BUT ON THE OTHER HAND IT'S KILLING YOU THAT DOROTHY HAS DONE WELL!
BUT... SHE...
YOU MAKE IT SOUND SO CALLOUS!
SPARE CHANGE FOR A VEGGIE BURGER?
SPLINTER

SPARE SOME CHANGE FOR A BAGEL, MA'AM?
COULD YOU SPARE A DIME FOR A SALAD, DUDE?
ARE WE SUPPOSED TO FEEL BAD FOR YOU OR SOMETHING?
HUH? COULD YOU SPARE--
POOR LITTLE RICH GIRL! BOO FUCKING HOO!
THIS SHIT HELL CITY ALREADY HAS ENOUGH REAL HOMELESS WITHOUT "SLACKER" ASSHOLES LIKE YOU BOTHERING US!
YOU FUCKING DANCE HALL TRENDIES WITH YOUR GOD DAMNED NOSE RINGS AND DICK RINGS AND TATTOOS!
FUCK YOU, ASSHOLE, I DON'T--
SPARE ME! YOU'RE SO FUCKING HIP AND COOL BUT A SOON AS YOU GET BORED WITH YOUR ANARCHY AND SQUATTING YOU'LL GO BACK TO FUCKING MOMMY AND DADDY IN CONNECTICUT, BRAGGING TO ALL YOUR KNOCKED UP FRIENDS ABOUT HOW YOU WERE SUCH A REBEL!
LISTEN, FAT ASS, YOU DON'T EVEN KNOW HOW--
I GOT TWO WORDS FOR YOU, YOU SPOILED BITCH:
GET A FUCKING JOB!
YEAH, WELL WHY DON'T YOU JUST FUCKING EAT ME!
WHAT'S GOING ON, MARL?

CRAPPY BAND LIVE!
AHHH, HE'S JUST SOME ASSHOLE.
WHERE THE HELL HAVE YOU BEEN?
OPEN
NOWHERE. I-- I HAD TO GO UPTOWN FOR SOME SHIT IS ALL.
WHAT FOR YOU DIDN'T TELL ME?
I COULDA CAME WITH YOU. WHAT? IS IT SOME KIND OF FUCKIN'...
SECRET...
OH, FUCK YOU!!
MARL, I CALLED MY MA AND SHE... I ⁝sniff⁝ I CAN'T DO IT ANYMORE! I HAVE TO GO
SHUT UP, OKAY? JUST SHUT THE FUCK UP!!
⁝sniff⁝ PLEASE, MAR, IT'S JUST.. COME WITH ME, HUH? YOU-- YOU CAN GO BACK HOME WITH ME AND--AND--

WHY?! SO YOU'RE DAD CAN BEAT THE CRAP OUTTA BOTH OF US?
BULLSHIT!
MY--MY MA SAID--
YOU SUCK! JUST GET THE HELL AWAY FROM ME, OKAY?!
MAR--PLEASE! I DON'T WANT IT TO
LIKE THIS! DON'T
AT ME...
GO BACK HOME TO YOUR FUCKING MOMMY, YOU SPOILED LITTLE BITCH!! HAVE A NICE LIFE!
THIS IS THE 4:15 GRAYLINE BUS TO WASHINGTON D.C. MAKING STOPS AT NEWARK, ELIZABETH, RAHWAY--

NEW JERSEY
LIVE!
MICKEY DEE
LIVE!

"JEALOUS?!" OF COURSE I'M NOT JEALOUS.
I'M HAPPY HER ARTICLE WAS PUBLISHED --FOR THE BOTH OF YOU.
374
COME ON, SHERMAN. I KNOW YOU TOO WELL.
PART OF YOU HATES IT! PART OF YOU IS PISSED THAT YOU'RE NOT PUBLISHED...
OH, OF COURSE I DON'T DENY THAT I --
RECYCLE!
...BUT YOUR GIRLFRIEND IS! ADMIT IT!
HOUSE OF TWEED
THAT'S JUST... UH
HELLO
UH, HI.
WOW, WHO WAS THAT?
DOES SHE LIVE HERE?

YOU KNOW, I'M NOT SURE. MAYBE SHE'S THE NEW TENANT MOVING INTO THAT PUNK ROCK GRRRL'S APARTMENT.
SHE'S GONE, THAT GIRL? SHIT.
HEY, GUYS. WHAT'S HAPPENING NOW?
OH! TELL SHERMAN!
STEPHEN'S BEEN REGALING ME WITH HIS SAUCY ADVENTURES OF HIS LIFE AS A SWINGING BACHELOR!
OH, COME ON! I WAS HARDLY "REGALING!"
SHE SEEMS TO HAVE THIS UNHEALTHY OBSESSION WITH HOW MANY WOMEN I'VE SLEPT WITH BEFORE WE STARTED GOING OUT...
GO AHEAD! TELL THEM HOW MANY.
SIGH
FORTY SEVEN.
WOW...
DOES THAT, UH, DOES THAT BOTHER YOU, JANE?
WHEN I WAS YOUNGER, I...
AND I AM OLDER THAN YOU GUYS.
IT DOESN'T BOTHER ME AS LONG AS THE, UH, BUCK STOPS HERE.
SO... WHAT ABOUT YOU GUYS?
ME? UH... I DON'T KNOW. FIVE? SIX?
I HAVE TO GO TO THE BATHROOM...

WE REALLY NEED TO GET ED A GIRLFRIEND.
HOW LONG HAS IT BEEN FOR HIM?
WHAT, SINCE HE, UH, HAD A GIRLFRIEND? MMMM...
I'M NOT SURE.
YOU SHOULD HOOK HIM UP WITH THAT CUTE GIRL FROM YOUR PUBLISHER'S.
WHAT WAS HER NAME? WITH THE RED HAIR? CLOUDY? CLOUD?
WHO, SKY?
NAH. I'M PRETTY SURE SHE ONLY DATES WYMMYN.
YOU THINK SHE'S CUTE? WOULD SHE HAVE BEEN NUMBER FORTY EIGHT?
MY OLD GIRLFRIEND SALLY USED TO DABBLE IN--
JEEZ! THAT REMINDS ME!
UH, SOMEONE GAVE ME A DOG FOR CHRISTMAS AND I WAS WONDERING IF, WELL, YOU GUYS WOULDN'T MIND IF I BROUGHT IT HOME.
"SOMEONE?"
WOW, WHAT KIND OF DOG IS IT?
ONE OF THOSE LITTLE ONES. A GORKY OR A SHIT-ZOO OR SOMETHING.
BELIEVE ME, I CERTAINLY DIDN'T WANT A DOG AND I DON'T KNOW IF IT'S FAIR TO PUT THIS ON YOU GUYS, SO IF YOU SAY "NO" I'LL CERTAINLY UNDERSTAND. NO HARD FEELINGS OR ANYTHING.
I DON'T MIND. I LIKE DOGS. WHAT'S ITS NAME?
WELL, WAIT. WHAT ABOUT BIG NOSE?

HOWSABOUT THIS: YOU BRING HOME THIS MYSTERY DOG AND IF BIG NOSE AND IT GET ALONG --AFTER A FEW WEEKS-- THE DOG STAYS.
THAT SEEMS FAIR ENOUGH.
BUT REALLY: IF FOR ANY REASON YOU AREN'T SATISFIED, TELL ME AND I'LL TAKE IT BACK, NO QUESTIONS ASKED.
WHAT ARE YOU BRINGING HOME? A DOG OR A SET OF ENCYCLOPEDIAS?
OH YEAH: SOME IDIOT COMES INTO THE STORE TODAY AND WANTS TO KNOW IF WE HAVE ANY BOOKS ON ADDING AND SUBTRACTING MONEY.
YOU KNOW, LIKE HOW MUCH IS $3.45 PLUS $7.93?
SO I SAY "KID'S WORKBOOKS ARE IN THE NEXT ROOM ON THE LEFT"
SO HE SAYS "IT'S NOT FOR KIDS. IT'S FOR ADULTS."
SO I'M THINKING: IF YOU'RE AN ADULT AND YOU DON'T KNOW HOW TO ADD AND SUBTRACT MONEY, YOU PROBABLY SHOULDN'T
BZZZZ!
OH! THAT'S PROBABLY THE FOOD WE ORDERED! HOLD ON, I'LL BE RIGHT BACK!
BZZZ!
COMING! I'M COMING!
FORTY SEVEN? WHEN THE HELL DID YOU SLEEP?
WHAT CAN I TELL YOU, MY LAD?

SORRY ABOUT THE -- OH.
UM, CAN I HELP YOU?
YES. ARE YOU MRS. GAEDEL? I'M LOOKING FOR YOUR HUSBAND.
MY--? OH, STEPHEN? SURE, COME ON IN.
HELLO?
HELLO, I'M OLGA FITZHUGH.
UH, I'M SORRY, BUT I CAN'T --
MY MOTHER IS... OR WAS SORA TWEED, YOUR LANDLADY?
OH, RIGHT, RIGHT. UH, MY CONDOLENCES ABOUT... YOU HAVE MY DEEPEST --
OH, PLEASE, IT'S OKAY. I'M AWARE THAT SHE WAS A MISERABLE OLD BAT AND YOU'RE PROBABLY AS HAPPY TO HAVE HER OUT OF YOUR LIFE AS I AM.
I'VE COME BY TO TELL YOU, MR. GAEDEL, THAT MY MOTHER LEFT THIS BUILDING TO ME IN HER WILL.
OH! WELL, THAT'S ... UH...
THIS SUMMER, I PLAN ON SELLING THIS BUILDING TO THE CAROLCO COMPANY.
THIS MEANS I WILL NOT BE RENEWING YOUR LEASE.

YOU HAVE UNTIL THE END OF FEBRUARY AND I'M THROWING YOU OUT.
YOU TOLD THEM I'M A VIRGIN, DIDN'T YOU?!

WHAT WILL YOUR AUTO-BIOGRAPHY BE CALLED?
"ME JANE."
"SHERMAN DAVIES: A LIFE."
"YES I CAN (IF FRANK SINATRA SAYS IT'S OKAY)"
Heh Heh.
"KING OF SELF-ABUSE."
"HOW I LEARNED TO STOP WORRYING AND HATE EVERYBODY'S STUPID GOD DAMNED GUTS."
"STRANGE BREW: MY LIFE ON THE ROAD WITH RICK MORANIS."
WHO THE HELL WOULD WANT TO READ MY AUTO-BIOGRAPHY?
JUST PLAY ALONG
OKAY, OKAY. UHH... "CREATOR! THE HARD PATH TO GLORY FOR THE FATHER OF THE NIGHTSTALKER."

HEY, WAIT! YOU'RE THAT GUY WHO TALKED TO ME FOR THAT THING YOU GUYS DID.
WHAT WAS IT? PUFFIN?
STAGE ONE: OPENING GAMBIT!!
PUPKIN, ARCHIE PUPKIN III.! AND THIS, IRVING, IS MY EDITOR AND, ONE WOULD HOPE, FRIEND, HARVEY HITCHCOCK!
HEY, GOOD TO MEET YOU, IRVING.
YEAH.
SO WHAT'S THIS ABOUT, ANYHOW?
AS YOU KNOW, IRVING, THE EDITORS OF "COMICS WORLD" HAVE BEEN BEHIND YOU 150% IN YOUR FIGHT FOR THE NIGHTSTALKER!
AND THAT'S WHEN IT CAME TO US: GRANO-SEQUON!
THIS YEAR WE'LL --
GRANOLA WHAT?

UHHHHHHHH
SURELY YOU'RE FAMILIAR WITH GRANO-SEQUON, IRVING!
THE TREMENDOUS GRAPHIC NOVEL AND SEQUENTIAL ARTS CONVENTION, HELD EVERY YEAR AT THE NEWARK SHERATON HOTEL?
WHERE THEY PRESENT THE COVETED "GOOGLE" AWARDS FOR EXCELLENCE IN THE COMICS FIELD?
OH, COME NOW! SURELY YOU'VE BEEN! WHY, ANYONE WHO'S ASSOCIATED WITH COMIC BOOKS OR DREAMS OF SO BEING ATTENDS GRANO-SEQUON! IT IS THE ONE WEEKEND A YEAR WHEN A UNITED INDUSTRY SHOUTS:
WE MATTER, DAMMIT!
THEY DO, HUH?
YEAH, BUT IT'S ALSO A WEEKEND FOR THE INDUSTRY TO KISS THE ASS OF ZOOM COMIC'S CORPORATE BEHIND!
PRECISELY! BUT THIS YEAR, WE'RE GOING TO HAV
ARCH! WOULD YOU LET ME FINISH, FOR CHRIST'S SAKE?!
sorry.
DAMN! ANYWAY, THIS YEAR WE'RE GOING TO SHOW EVERYONE THAT LEBLANC CAN'T GET AWAY WITH THIS BULLSHIT!

YES! AND WE DON'T JUST MEAN YOUR BATTLE OVER THE NIGHT-STALKER! WHY, HAVE YOU READ THE LATEST ISSUE OF "A.T.A.C.* FORCE?" NINJA'S NEW COSTUME IS ATROCIOUS!
* AMERICAN TEAM AGAINST CRIME --Ed.
THE WAY IT MAKES HER --
UH...
I'M SORRY.
I'LL--
SORRY.
ANYWAY, SO WE WERE HOPING THAT THIS YEAR WE COULD GET YOU TO COME TO GRAND-SEQUON.
ME? WHAT FOR?
WHAT WE WANT TO DO IS HAVE YOU SHOW UP AND THE "COMICS WORLD"
BZZZZ!
HILDY! WHAT THE DEVIL ARE YOU DOING UP HERE? WE TOLD YOU TO STAY WITH THE CAR!
YOU GO STAY WITH THE CAR! THE HEATER DOESN'T WORK AND IT'S FREEZING OUT!
BUT-BUT-BUT! BUT MY CAR! IT WON'T LAST FIVE MINUTES IN THIS CRIME RIDDEN NEIGHBORHOOD!
IF YOU'RE REALLY WORRIED, YOU'RE WELCOME TO GO DOWN AND --
HARVEY! WOU TELL HER TO G WITH THE CAR SHUT UP? I
CAN I PLEASE TELL IRVING OUR SECRET PLAN WITHOUT ANYMORE FUCKING INTERRUPTIONS?!?

MR. LEBLANC! MR. LEBLANC! WHAT DO YOU SAY TO CRITICS WHO SAY ZOOM COMICS IS BUILT ON THE BONES OF A POOR OLD MAN WHO--
I'M SORRY BOYS. IF YOU WANT AN INTERVIEW, YOU'LL HAVE TO CALL MY OFFICE DURING REGULAR BUSINESS HOURS. I'D BE HAPPY TO ANSWER ANY OF YOUR QUESTIONS WHEN--
IS IT RIGHT THAT YOU LIVE IN A MILLION DOLLAR HOME IN CONNECTICUT WHILE IRWIN FLAVOR LIVES IN A SQUALID--
I -- I DON'T LIVE IN A --
SPUTTER
I SUPPOSE THAT WHERE IRVING FLAVOR LIVES IS HIS OWN CONCERN. COME ON, FELLAS, PLEASE. I'M JUST ON MY WAY HOME HERE. COME ON, HUH?
MR. LEBLANC, HOW MUCH MONEY DID NIGHTSTALKER MAKE FOR ZOOM COMICS AND ITS STOCKHOLDERS? HOW MUCH DID YOU, PERSONALLY, EARN FROM IRWIN--
TOMORROW! CALL MARGIE KREIDER AND SHE'LL SET SOMETHING UP!
BYE!

GOD DAMN IT...
OH, MY POOR LITTLE LAMBY CHOP...
FIRST THING TOMORROW, CALL MAKO AND TELL HIM I NEED TO SEE HIM ABOUT FLAVOR.
WE'RE GOING TO END THIS NOW.
SIEB
OKAY, SO STAGE ONE OF OPERATION: ANNIHILATE IS NOW COMPLETE!
WE CAN BEGIN PREPARATIONS FOR THE FINALE OF OUR LITTLE DRAMA:
STAGE TWO: THE FINAL BATTLE!

IN THE COMPANY OF GUYS
WOW! SO WHAT ARE YOU GUYS GOING TO DO? LOOK FOR A NEW PLACE SOMEWHERE?
:sigh: I DON'T KNOW.
AND I'M NO MENTAL SHAPE TO HANDLE A BIG MELODRAMATIC CRISIS LIKE THIS.
I'VE BEEN SO DEPRESSED LATELY.
YEAH? WHAT'S WRONG? ARE YOU STILL JEALOUS ABOUT DOROTHY GETTING PUBLISHED AND NOT YOU?
I'M NOT -- I DON'T KNOW. BETWEEN MY CRAPPY DEAD END JOB AND A CONSTANT STREAM OF REJECTION LETTERS AND NOW THIS EVICTION THING...
I JUST FEEL ONE OF MY TURNS COMING ON.
(DOES THIS GIRL BREAK YOUR HEART OR WHAT?)
WELL, IT DOESN'T SOUND LIKE SOMETHING SEVEN RUM AND COKES COULDN'T HELP.
SO COME ON! ARE YOU READY TO ROCK?!
Heh Heh, OKAY, OKAY, LET'S --
I SAID ARE YOU READY TO ROCK?!

OKAY! OKAY! I'M READY TO ROCK! SHEESH!
JUST LET ME PAY FOR THIS.
HA HA!
BRAIN WASHING
SO WHAT'S THAT?
OH, IT'S THIS NOVEL "COUGHING SPELL" BY CYNTHIA GRUNVELT. IT'S ABOUT THIS TWENTYSOMETHING WHO FINDS OUT THAT HER BOYFRIEND HAS A A WHOLE WEIRD PREVIOUS LIFE.
IT GOT GOOD REVIEWS. CAN YOU BELIEVE THE AUTHOR'S ONLY TWENTY SEVEN? HOO BOY.
SPEAKING OF PUBLISHED PEOPLE, WHAT DID DOROTHY SAY ABOUT YOUR APARTMENT SITUATION?
UGH, DON'T REMIND ME...
"WE WERE IN WASHIN
PARK, WALKIN
DOGS. SO S
SAYS "LO
THE CHIN
LOOK AT IT THIS WAY: THE CHINESE WORD FOR "CRISIS" IS THE SAME AS IT IS FOR "OPPORTUNITY!"
YOU KNOW, THAT'S EXACTLY THE KIND OF CLICHED PLATITUDE I DON'T NEED TO HEAR. WHAT'S NEXT?
A POSTER OF A KITTEN SAYING "HANG IN THERE, BABY?"
WELL, FUCK YOU, THEN. I'M JUST TRYING TO MAKE YOU FEEL BETTER.
FIDO! LULU!
GET AWAY FROM THAT STROLLER!!
SO WOULD YOU LIGHTEN UP ALREADY? GOD, YOU'RE GETTING A NEW APARTMENT, NOT GOING IN FOR CHEMO!
YEAH, WELL, IT'S EASY FOR YOU TO SAY.

IT IS EASY FOR ME TO SAY, BECAUSE YOU KNOW HOW MANY TIMES I'VE BEEN KICKED OUT OF APARTMENTS?
I GIVE UP. HOW MANY TIMES?
UMMMMM...
BALTI... SECOND AVE... CLARK..
FIVE TIMES!
I LIVED IN SAN FRANCISCO FOR LIKE TWO MONTHS BEFORE MY LOVABLE ROOMMATES ASKED ME TO LEAVE.
THERE WAS TWICE IN BALTIMORE, RIGHT OUT OF SCHOOL.
I HAD A BRIEF STINT IN CHICAGO UNTIL MY BUILDING WAS CONDEMNED.
CONDEMNED
AND TWO TIMES IN NEW YORK -- ONCE BY MY COUSIN AND ONCE BY YOUR PALS STEPHEN AND JANE, SO...
POLICE LINE
NOT CROSS
THAT'S SIX TIMES! SIX!
AND I'M JUST TALKING ABOUT APARTMENTS, NOW, NOT DORMITORIES OR OTHER SCHOOL HOUSINGS!
WOW! SIX TIMES. IS THAT TRUE?
AH, WHO THE HELL KNOWS.
OH, WAIT, I HAVE THE SEVENTEEN CENTS.
SO THEN WHAT HAPPENED NEXT?
WELL, SOME GUY COMES OVER AND STARTS HOLLERING ABOUT DOROTHY NOT HAVING THE DOGS ON LEASHES.
I GUESS ONE OF THEM TRIED TO BITE HIS DUMB KID OR SOMETHING.
MATTHEW'S BOOKS
MATTHEW'S BOOKS
I WAS GLAD SOMETHING CAME UP TO CHANGE THE SUBJECT.

YOU KNOW WHAT MY PROBLEM IS? MY PROBLEM IS I DON'T MEET ENOUGH WOMEN.
AMEN, BROTHER!
NO, REALLY. I HAVE TWO JOBS: ONE WITH A CRANKY OLD GUY,
THE OTHER IS AT A HARDWARE STORE WITH MY FATHER! I'M NEVER IN SITUATIONS WHERE I CAN SOCIALIZE WITH CHICKS!
AS BAD AS MATTHEW'S MAY BE, AT LEAST YOU GET TO MINGLE WITH GIRLS OF THE, UH, FEMALE PERSUASION.
IT'S A DOUBLE EDGED SWORD, OLD CHUM. TEMPTATION ABOUNDS...
ARE YOU STILL FIXATED ON THAT PUERTO RICAN GIRL?
HER, THAT BLONDE GIRL WHO'S IN CHARGE OF THE SCIENCE SECTION, THIS NEW GIRL AT SPECIAL ORDERS... I GOT A MILLION OF 'EM...
HAHA... THE OTHER DAY I'M AT WORK, RIGHT? AND I'M HELPING THIS GIRL, SUSAN, PUT SOME BOOKS AWAY. SO SHE'S UP ON THIS LADDER...
UH OH!
SO SHE'S UP ON THIS LADDER, PUTTING SOME BOOKS UP ON THE HIGHER SHELF, AND HER SHIRT SORT OF... RIDES UP. IT DIDN'T REALLY REVEAL MUCH, JUST LIKE TWO INCHES OF HER STOMACH.
NOTHING YOU COULDN'T SEE A MILLION GIRLS SHOWING OFF IN THE SUMMER... BUT THAT CUTE BELLY BUTTON WILL HAUNT ME 'TIL MY GRAVE.

HAHA! YEAH, IT'S THAT, I DON'T KNOW, FORBIDDEN-NESS THAT MAKES IT SO GREAT.
A FEW YEARS AGO, I WAS TAKING THIS ART CLASS WHERE WE'D SPEND, LIKE, SIX HOURS DRAWING FROM A NUDE MODEL.
DURING THE BREAKS, SHE'D WALK AROUND AND LOOK AT EVERYONE'S STUFF.
SHE LIKED MY PICTURES, AND WE STARTED TALKING AND ALL THAT. (SHE MADE IT CLEAR FROM THE START THAT SHE HAD SOME DUMB BOYFRIEND, SO I WAS ABLE TO RELAX).
"ANYHOW, AFTER CLASS WE WOUND UP TAKING THE SAME BUS HOME. IT WAS PRETTY CROWDED...
YEAH, SO WHAT HE REALLY WANTS TO DO IS PLAY GUITAR, BUT FOR NOW HE'S--
!!!
I TOLD HIM "FOLLOW YOUR DREAM. BUT DO
YOU JUST SPENT SIX HOURS LOOKING AT ME TOTALLY NAKED BUT YOU STILL WANT TO LOOK DOWN MY SHIRT?!
Uhhhhh... HehHeh...
HAHAHA! THAT'S A GREAT STORY! I CAN'T BELIEVE SHE BUSTED YOU LIKE THAT!
BUT SHE WAS RIGHT!
HA HA HA!
I GUESS GUYS JUST CAN'T HELP IT. IF THERE'S CLEAVAGE, YOU JUST HAVE TO-- LOOK.
I THINK IT'S A HORMONAL THING -- THE MALE VERSION OF P.M.S.
SHIT!
I HOPE WE CAN GET A TABLE. FUCKING COLLEGE KIDS!
199
Chalmun's BAR

THE FUNNY THING IS, YOU COULD BE MARRIED TO THE MOST BEAUTIFUL LEGGY SUPERMODEL ON EARTH AND HAVE GREAT SEX WITH HER FIFTEEN TIMES A DAY BUT WHEN YOU WALK DOWN THE STREET, YOUR EYES ARE STILL GOING TO WANDER.
NYU
I DON'T KNOW... IF I WAS HAVING SEX FIFTEEN TIMES A DAY I DON'T THINK I COULD WALK DOWN THE STREET.
WHAT ABOUT-- OKAY, DO YOU THINK YOUR GIRLFRIEND ACTS THE SAME WAY?
WHEN SHE GOES OUT WITH HER FEMALE FRIENDS DOES SHE PISS AND MOAN ABOUT LUSTING AFTER GUYS?
440
HMMMM...
JOHNSON
TH THE BLITZ
AND IT'S GOOD! LANCE CATCHES IT ON THE TEN
TOUCHDOWN!!
THIS
YOU KNOW, NOW THAT YOU MENTION IT, I DON'T THINK DOROTHY HAS ANY FEMALE FRIENDS.
MEN
BUT, YEAH, I'M SURE THEY'RE JUST AS BAD AS WE ARE.
WELL, OKAY NOT AS BAD...
HEHHEH. HEY LISTEN, WAS DOROTHY --
CAN I ASK YOU A PERSONAL QUESTION?
UH,OH. JAMES ISN'T EVEN HERE YET AND ALREADY WITH THE PERSONAL QUESTIONS? GO AHEAD AND AXE.

WAS DOROTHY RIGHT TO GET MAD ABOUT YOU SKATING WITH MY COUSIN THAT TIME? YOU KNOW, DID...
WHAT?! NO.
WELL... MAYBE.
I MEAN THERE WAS A CERTAIN... THRILL WHEN WE WERE SKATING, EVEN THOUGH WE COULDN'T TALK TO EACH OTHER...
(ACTUALLY, IT WAS PROBABLY BECAUSE WE COULDN'T TALK TO EACH OTHER)
BUT IT WAS JUST A PASSING THING. CERTAINLY NOTHING SHE HAD THE RIGHT TO FLIP OUT OVER. SHE SAYS--
HEY, GUYS, SORRY I'M LATE!
JESUS, JAMES! WHAT THE HELL HAPPENED TO YOUR FACE?!
OW!
WHAT, THIS OLD THING? AHH, IT'S NO BIG DEAL. ACTUALLY, IT'S KIND OF FUNNY. YOU'LL ESPECIALLY LIKE IT, SHERM.
WELL, LAY IT ON ME, DUDE!
"IT SEEMS THAT DUANE -- JANICE'S HUSBAND -- GOT A LITTLE R&R OR WHATEVER AND DECIDED TO COME HOME AND SURPRISE HIS BLUSHING YOUNG BRIDE."
"IT WAS AROUND THIS TIME THAT I STARTED TO LAUGH, LIKE REALLY HARD. IT WAS SUCH A CLICHÉ SITUATION. HOW COULDN'T YOU LAUGH?"
"HE PICKS ME UP, THREATENING TO KICK MY ASS, ETC, ETC, WHILE JANICE IS SCREAMING FOR HIM TO CALM DOWN, ETC, ETC "IT'S NOT WHAT IT LOOKS LIKE", ETC."

SO THAT'S WHEN HE KICKED THE CRAP OUT OF YOU?
OH NO!
WELL...
HE DIDN'T REALLY BEAT ME UP.
HE JUST SORT OF THREW ME DOWN THE STAIRS A LITTLE.
I DON'T KNOW ABOUT YOU GUYS, BUT FALLING DOWN A FLIGHT OF STAIRS ISN'T NEARLY AS MUCH FUN AS IT WAS WHEN YOU WERE A KID.
YOWCH!
IT'S A GOOD THING I HAD MOST OF MY CLOTHES. AS IT WAS I HAD TO LEAVE MY GLASSES THERE.
SO WHAT HAPPENED AFTER YOU, UH, LEFT? BETWEEN JANICE AND DUANE?
HUH?
I DON'T KNOW. I WASN'T EXACTLY GOING TO POP ON IN FOR TEA TO CATCH UP ON OLD TIMES.
THEY PROBABLY HAD A FIGHT OR SOMETHING, I DON'T KNOW.
BUT YOU DIDN'T CALL HER AND SEE IF --
....
WELL, I GUESS YOU GOT WHAT YOU HAD COMING, EH?
I DON'T KNOW... YOU'RE PROBABLY RIGHT. BUT YOU KNOW WHAT?
LOSING MY GLASSES, TAKING THAT TUMBLE, THE HUMILIATION OF TRYING TO HAIL A TAXI IN MY BRIEFS...
IF I COULD DO IT ALL OVER AGAIN?
I WOULDN'T CHANGE A THING.
Sigh
I GUESS I'LL GET THIS ROUND. WHAT'LL IT BE?

Sigh
IT JUST MAKES ME SAD TO KNOW I'LL NEVER GET TO HAVE SEX WITH TWO GIRLS AT THE SAME TIME.
WHAT MAKES YOU SAY THAT? YOU'RE STILL A YOUNG GUY WITH A FEW YEARS LEFT.
COME ON, AT THIS POINT I'D BE AMAZED TO HAVE SEX WITH A GIRL IN THE SAME ROOM, LET ALONE TWO GIRLS AT ONCE. NO WAY.
JESUS! HAVE SOME SELF-ESTEEM, YOU ASSHOLE!
LOOK AROUND! THERE'S PLENTY OF CUTE SINGLE GIRLS HERE! THE LAW OF AVERAGES SAYS ONE OF THEM WILL SLEEP WITH YOU.
YOU'VE GOT STATISTICS ON YOUR SIDE!
I KNOW, I KNOW, BUT... I'M NOT GOOD IN THESE KIND OF SITUATIONS! I HAVE TO KNOW A GIRL FOR A LONG TIME BEFORE I MAKE A MOVE.
I KNEW MY ONLY GIRLFRIEND, OCEANA, FOR LIKE THREE YEARS BEFORE I LET HER KNOW I WAS MADLY IN LOVE WITH HER.
HE HAS TO WEAR'EM DOWN.
"OLD IRON THIGHS"
BESIDES, I KNOW NONE OF THESE GIRLS WOULD HAVE SEX WITH ME.
I KNOW WHAT TIME IT IS. I KNOW I'M NO TOM CRUISE.

GODDAMMIT, SHERMAN! WE HAVE A MISSION TONIGHT: WE HAVE TO GET THIS BOY LAID! BY SUN UP!
IN FACT, LET'S ALL GET FUCKIN' LAID! COME ON!
HehHeh... WELL, YOU BOYS GO ON AHEAD WITHOUT ME. I'M AFRAID I FORGOT MY DICK IN DOROTHY'S PURSE.
AAAAH, YOU BIG PUSSY!
WHAT ABOUT YOU, ED? ARE YOU WITH ME IN THAT WE SHOULD GET OUR WICKS DIPPED TONIGHT? HUH?
UH, I DON'T THINK ..
COME ON, EDDIE!!
YOU WANT TO BREAK SOME HEARTS TONIGHT? YOU WANT TO GET THE OLD PIPES CLEANED? YOUR OIL CHANGED?
I WOU I CA
A BIT OF THE OLD IN-OUT-IN-OUT? TAKE 'ER FOR A TEST DRIVE? PUT THE "ED" IN "BED SPORTS?"
BULLSEYE SOME WOMP RATS? GIVE SOME GAL THE GREAT PUMPKIN? SHOCK THE MONKEY? VIOLATE YOUR PAROLE?
PUT YOUR PENIS IN A GIRL'S VAGINA?
YEAH!
SMACK!

DO LESBIANS FIND THE SAME WOMEN ATTRACTIVE THAT MEN FIND ATTRACTIVE?
PERSONALLY, I CAN'T BELIEVE MORE WOMEN AREN'T LESBIANS. HAVE YOU LOOKED AT GUYS?
I MEAN, CHECK OUT THESE WINNERS. THEIR WHOLE LIVES REVOLVE AROUND WHICH OVERPAID STEROID ADDLED FREAKS ARE BETTER AT PLAYING CHILDREN'S GAMES.
BEER, VIOLENCE AND FARTING. IF I WAS A WOMAN I'D HAVE TO PASS ON THAT ONE.
YEAH... I'MGONNA BE A LESBIAN TOO.
SHIT, YOU GUYS ARE FUCKING PATHETIC!
YOU'RE NOT FOOLING ANYONE, YOU'RE NOT. JUST CUZ YOU GOT PICKED ON BY THE WRESTLING TEAM IN HIGH SCHOOL YOU'RE MR. AND MRS. SENSITIVE SOULS!
BUT YOU KNOW IF YOU COULD'VE SWITCHED PLACES WITH, LIKE, "REFRIGERATOR" PERRY OR SOME ASSHOLE YOU WOULD'VE DONE IT IN SEVEN SECONDS!
BUD
SO, WHAT? I SECRETLY YEARN TO BE SOME CRO-MAGNON PITUITARY CASE WITH THE BRAINS OF A DUST BUSTER SO I--
ALL I'M SAYING IS THAT IF SOMEONE OFFERED YOU MILLIONS OF DOLLARS TO DO BEER COMMERCIALS, KICK A FOOTBALL AROUND ONCE A WEEK AND SLEEP WITH PILES OF SUPERMODELS, YOU WOULD DO IT.
PLUS IT'S YOUR TURN TO BUY.
AND DON'T DENY IT, CUZ YOU'RE A LYING DOG.

SO THIS GUY WALKS INTO A BAR AND SITTING NEXT TO THE BARTENDER IS THIS GORILLA, RIGHT?
I REALLY LIKED "THE WISHBONES" BETTER. IT WAS LIKE AN AMERICAN "HIGH FIDELITY."
WHENEVER I'D SEE HER I'D GET THAT ACHEY FEELING IN MY CHEST.
THE BEST "PLANET OF THE APES" MOVIE HAS TO BE "CONQUEST" -- WELL, EXCEPT FOR THE ORIGINAL, OF COURSE.
"WATCH." HE PICKS UP A BAT AND STARTS, LIKE, WHACKING THE GORILLA.
OH, OF COURSE!
SO THIS STUPID CUSTOMER ASKS ME IF I WORK HERE...
A BLOW JOB.
"YOU HAVE FAILED ME FOR THE LAST... TIME, ADMIRAL." IT'S THAT SLIGHT PAUSE THAT MAKES THE LINE...
SO HE TELLS US THAT HE'S DONE IT WITH FORTY SEVEN DIFFERENT WOMEN! CAN YOU
SAYS "DO YOU WANT TO TRY?" AND THE GUY SAYS "SURE, BUT DON'T HIT ME SO HARD!"
HAHAHA!
NO WAY. HE'S LIKE AN ENGLISH TEACHER OR SOMETHING, RIGHT?
HEY, I THOUGHT YOU WERE SUPPOSED TO BE GETTING US LAID?
YEAH.
FORGET IT.
SUCKED.
GREAT SOME DONKEY'S HAVING SEX BUT I'M NOT.
YEAH, I WISH!
WE'RE DOOMED
THIS ROUND ON ME, FELLAS.
HAHAHA! HAHA!

YOU'D PICK "YER BLUES" OVER "DEAR PRUDENCE?"
YOU'RE CUCKOO, MAN!
I MEAN, I WOULD RATHER HAVE "CRY BABY CRY" OVER "YER BLUES."
THAT'S CUZ YER A BIG SISSY. "YER BLUES" IS, LIKE, ONE OF LENNON'S BEST SONGS!
HEY
YOU GUYS...
WHAT'S THE WORST THING YOU'VE EVER DONE?
I WENT TO A ROD STEWART CONCERT WHEN I WAS FIFTEEN.
WAS THAT THE ONE WHERE HE COLLAPSED ON STAGE?
NO, NO. I MEAN SOMETHING YOU'VE DONE THAT, I DON'T KNOW, YOU'RE ASHAMED OF OR WISH YOU DIDN'T DO. YOU KNOW?
HMMM. LET ME THINK.
WHAT ABOUT YOU? YOU GO FIRST.
WELL... I'M NOT SURE IF IT'S THE WORST THING...
BUT IT'S DEFINITELY IN THE TOP FIVE.

"WHEN I WAS LITTLE -- LIKE TEN OR NINE -- I WENT TO MY OLD COUSIN DONNA'S WEDDING. HER FATHER, MY GREAT UNCLE JOE WAS A REAL ASSHOLE. HE HATED KIDS, AND FOR SOME REASON HE SINGLED ME OUT FOR EXTRA CRUELTY."
"THE WEIRDEST THING ABOUT HIM WAS THAT EVEN THOUGH HE WAS LIKE IN HIS MID-FIFTIES, HE WAS AS INCONTINENT AS AN EIGHTY YEAR OLD. HE WOULD GO TO THE BATHROOM LITERALLY EVERY HALF AN HOUR."
UH-OH. I'VE GOT A BAD FEELING ABOUT THIS.
"YEAH, WELL, JUST BEFORE THE WEDDING WAS ABOUT TO START, HE STARTS PICKING ON ME. HE'S CALLING ME A FAT LITTLE FAGGOT, STUFF LIKE THAT. I WAS JUST A LITTLE KID, SO I RUN TO THE BATHROOM BECAUSE I DIDN'T WANT TO CRY IN FRONT OF EVERYBODY."
YOU WERE GOING TO START CRYING?
HE WAS RIGHT! YOU WERE A FAT LITTLE FAGGOT!
STILL, HE DIDN'T HAVE TO BE MEAN ABOUT IT!
"SO I'M IN THE MEN'S ROOM OF THE CHURCH, ALL SOBBY AND STUFF, WHEN MY MIND HATCHES A WICKED SCHEME!"

CLICK
SO IT'S THE LAST FEW MINUTES BEFORE THE CEREMONY AND, AS I EXPECTED, UNCLE JOE GOES TO MAKE ONE LAST PIT STOP. BUT--
HUH? WHO'S IN THERE?
HEY, LEMME IN, BUDDY! IT'S AN EMERGENCY!
I HAD LOCKED THE DOOR BEHIND ME ON MY WAY OUT. SOMEONE RAN TO TRY AND FIND THE JANITOR WHO HAD A KEY...
HEY! OPEN THIS GODDAMED DOOR WILL YA?
BUT FOR MY UNCLE JOE
LET ME IN THE MOTHER
KKIN' CAN
MMIT!
TIME HAD
RUN OUT

Heh Heh... OH MY GOD. I GUESS HE DIDN'T WEAR DEPENDS™, HUH?
SHIT, MAN! YOU SHOULDN'T FEEL BAD ABOUT THAT! YOU SAID HE WAS A DICK, RIGHT?
I KNOW... BUT I GUESS I FEEL BAD FOR MY COUSIN. IT SORT OF RUINED THE WHOLE WEDDING.
SHE JUST GOT DIVORCED (THAT'S WHAT REMINDED ME) AND I CAN'T HELP BUT FEEL THAT I'M SOMEHOW RESPONSIBLE...
WELL... I THINK MINE'S WORSE THAN THAT...
WHEN I WAS AROUND FIFTEEN, I STARTED GOING OUT WITH THIS GIRL...
ROMY VANGILDER. GOD, SHE WAS A CUTIE. WE WOULD JUST FOOL AROUND, THOUGH. WE NEVER HAD SEX, BUT MY BALLS ACHED EVERY NIGHT.
LED ZEPPLIN
MY BEST FRIEND WAS MY NEXT DOOR NEIGHBOR, GARY CARBONE. HE WAS THE ONLY ONE OF US OLD ENOUGH TO DRIVE, SO THAT SPRING WE WOULD ALL DRIVE AROUND IN HIS DAD'S CAR.
CAN YOU SEE WHERE THIS IS GOING?
ANYWAY, ONE DAY I WENT OVER TO GARY'S HOUSE...
SKULL
OZZY
♫ WE'RE GONNA ROCK DOWN TO ELECTRIC AVENUE!

I WAS JUST ABOUT TO RING THE DOORBELL WHEN SOMETHING IN THE WINDOW CAUGHT MY EYE...
INSTEAD OF BARGING IN OR RUNNING HOME, I WALKED DOWN THE ROAD. THE ROAD I KNEW HE'D DRIVE DOWN WHEN HE TOOK ROMY BACK TO HER HOUSE.
THEN I WAITED.
I SAT IN THE BUSHES -- FOR AN HOUR? SIX HOURS? TWENTY YEARS? -- CONTEMPLATING WHAT I'D SEEN, GETTING MORE AND MORE PISSED OFF. FINALLY, I SAW HIS DAD'S CAR COMING DOWN THE ROAD. I COULD FEEL MY HEART BEATING IN MY THROAT...

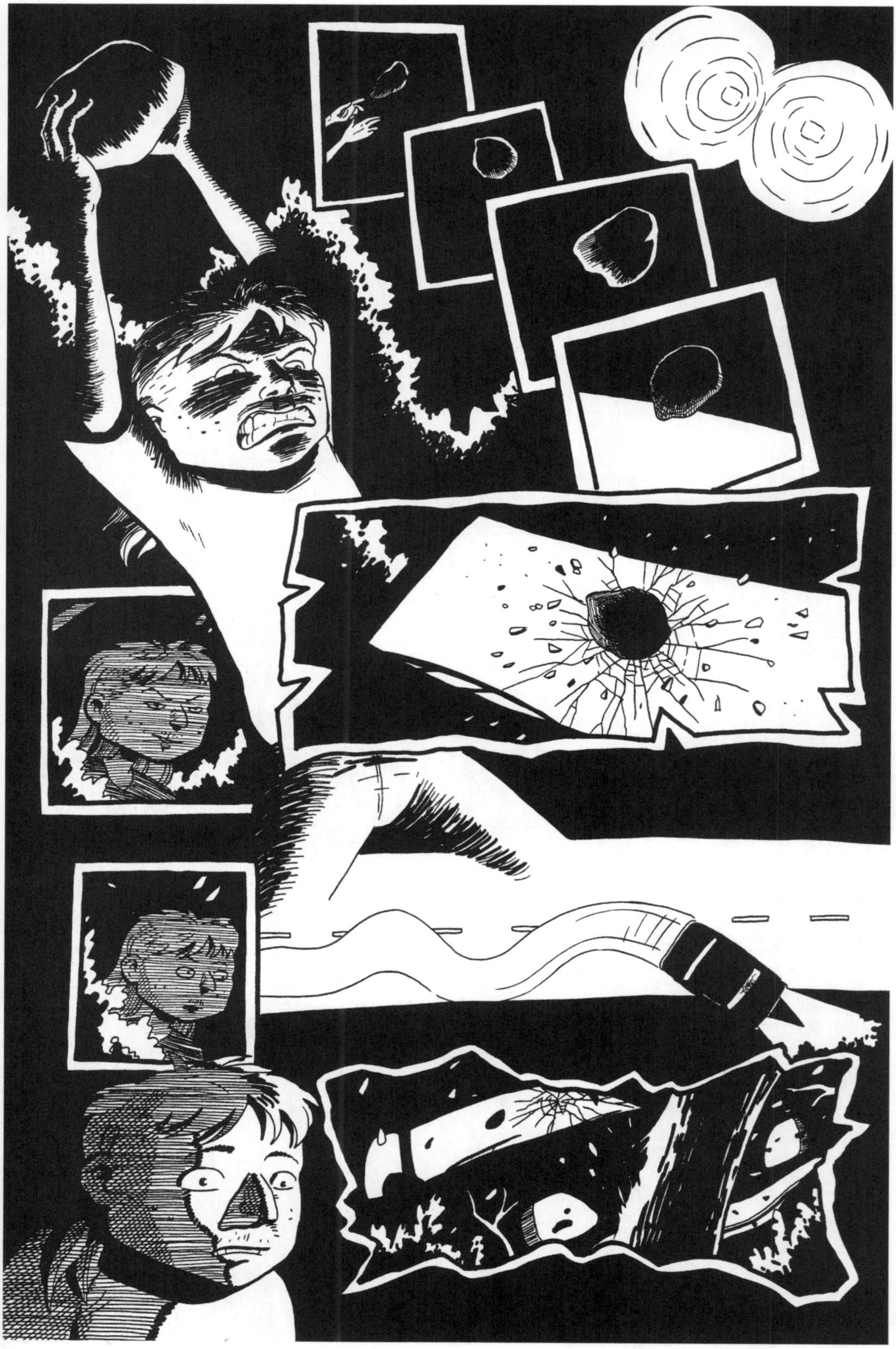

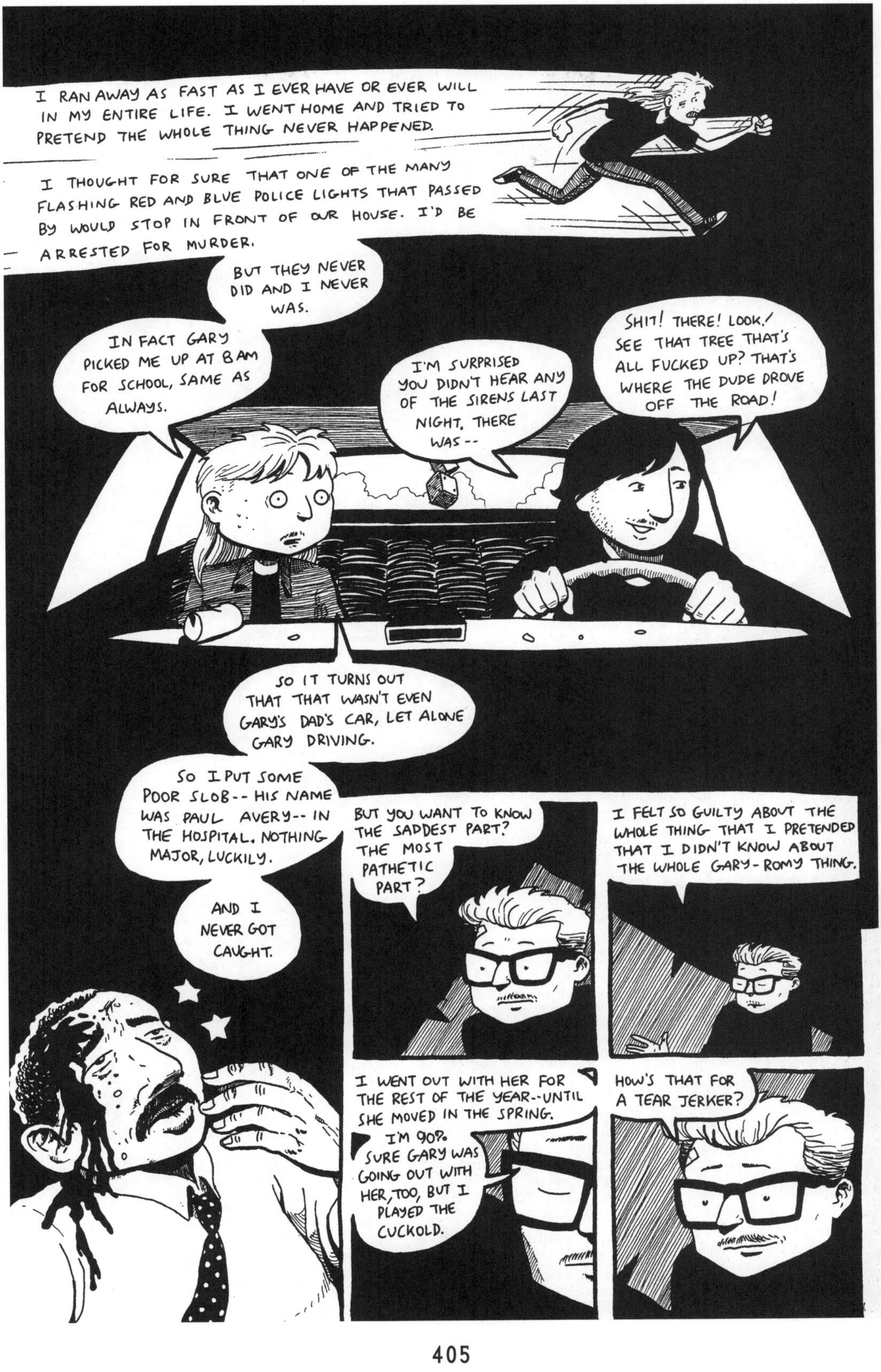
I RAN AWAY AS FAST AS I EVER HAVE OR EVER WILL IN MY ENTIRE LIFE. I WENT HOME AND TRIED TO PRETEND THE WHOLE THING NEVER HAPPENED.
I THOUGHT FOR SURE THAT ONE OF THE MANY FLASHING RED AND BLUE POLICE LIGHTS THAT PASSED BY WOULD STOP IN FRONT OF OUR HOUSE. I'D BE ARRESTED FOR MURDER.
BUT THEY NEVER DID AND I NEVER WAS.
IN FACT GARY PICKED ME UP AT 8 AM FOR SCHOOL, SAME AS ALWAYS.
I'M SURPRISED YOU DIDN'T HEAR ANY OF THE SIRENS LAST NIGHT. THERE WAS--
SHIT! THERE! LOOK! SEE THAT TREE THAT'S ALL FUCKED UP? THAT'S WHERE THE DUDE DROVE OFF THE ROAD!
SO IT TURNS OUT THAT THAT WASN'T EVEN GARY'S DAD'S CAR, LET ALONE GARY DRIVING.
SO I PUT SOME POOR SLOB-- HIS NAME WAS PAUL AVERY-- IN THE HOSPITAL. NOTHING MAJOR, LUCKILY.
AND I NEVER GOT CAUGHT.
BUT YOU WANT TO KNOW THE SADDEST PART? THE MOST PATHETIC PART?
I FELT SO GUILTY ABOUT THE WHOLE THING THAT I PRETENDED THAT I DIDN'T KNOW ABOUT THE WHOLE GARY-ROMY THING.
I WENT OUT WITH HER FOR THE REST OF THE YEAR--UNTIL SHE MOVED IN THE SPRING.
I'M 90% SURE GARY WAS GOING OUT WITH HER, TOO, BUT I PLAYED THE CUCKOLD.
HOW'S THAT FOR A TEAR JERKER?

I CAN BEAT THAT.
WHEN I WAS FOURTEEN MY BEST FRIEND WAS DOUG RUBENSTEIN.
THAT SUMMER, HE AND HIS FAMILY WERE GOING TO FLORIDA ON VACATION AND THEY ASKED ME IF I WANTED TO GO AS WELL.
MY MOTHER HAD BEEN SICK FOR A WHILE, SO MONEY WAS TIGHT.
I ARGUED THAT WE ONLY HAD TO PAY FOR THE AIR FARE -- DOUG'S PARENTS WOULD COVER THE REST.
"I'M SURE THEY WOULD, BUT IT WOULD BE AN IMPOSITION. THEY --"
BUT I WAS RELENTLESS. I BEGGED. I WAS EXTRA NICE. I WAS MEAN. I POUTED. I HINTED SUBTLY.
FINALLY SHE GAVE IN. I COULD GO!
IT WAS MY FIRST TRIP ON AN AIRPLANE AND WHAT COULD BE BETTER THAN A TRIP TO FLORIDA WITH YOUR BEST FRIEND?
WE DIDN'T SPEND MUCH TIME WITH HIS FAMILY. AT NIGHT WE'D ROAM THE DINERS AND ARCADES, HANGING OUT AND OGLING GIRLS.
WE WERE TWO NERDS SURGING WITH HORMONES AND NOWHERE TO CHANNEL THEM BUT INTO "BERSERK" AND "DIG DUG."
IT WAS THEN THAT I MET ALLISON.
IT'S FUNNY HOW YOU GET TO KNOW PEOPLE FASTER ON VACATION THAN YOU DO IN REAL LIFE.

RAIDERS LOST ARK
EVERY NIGHT, ALLISON, ME, DOUG AND ALLISON'S OLDER SISTER WOULD MEET AT BANISZEWSKI'S ARCADE AND FUN HOUSE...
AND WIND UP MAKING OUT IN THE BACK OF JOHN'S DRIVE-IN DINER.
THE FIRST TIME WE KISSED, "WHEN DOVES CRY" WAS ON THE RADIO AND THE SMELL OF GREASY FRENCH FRIES HUNG IN THE AIR.
WE IMAGINED A WHOLE ELABORATE FUTURE WITH EACH OTHER, WITH THE KIND OF EXCITEMENT TEENAGERS CAN HAVE BUT ADULTS HAVE LOST.
I STILL GET CHILLS REMEMBERING THE FIRST TIME SHE LET ME TOUCH HER CHEST -- OVER THE SHIRT, OF COURSE.
I CAN ALSO VIVIDLY RECALL THE NIGHT I DROPPED HER OFF AT HER PARENTS' HOTEL. I WALKED BACK ALONE, ALONG THE BEACH...
WHEN I GOT BACK TO THE ROOM, MRS. RUBENSTEIN SAID THAT MY AUNT PHIN CALLED AND TO CALL HER BACK TONIGHT.
MY MOTHER HAD DIED THAT AFTERNOON.
THE NEXT DAY I HAD MY SECOND TRIP ON AN AIRPLANE -- BACK HOME TO NEW JERSEY.
THE WHOLE WAY BACK, I THOUGHT ABOUT HOW I HAD WANTED TO GO ON THAT TRIP MORE THAN ANYTHING IN THE WORLD.

I SUPPOSE WE RESPECT EACH OTHER TOO MUCH.
We don't respect... anyone.
OH, MRS. PARKER. SUPPOSE IT DIDN'T WORK?
Suppose it did.
I DON'T KNOW, IT'S A LOT EASIER TO TAKE DISAPPOINTMENT WHEN YOU'RE YOUNG AND ALL DUMB AND DON'T
BZZZZ!
BZZZ!
HUH? WHOOIZIT, LULU?
BZZZ! BZZZ!
YAP! YAP!
I'M COMIN', I'M COMIN'!
HI. I'M...
ZIT OGAY IF I STAY HERE TONIGHT?
SORRY.
OH SWEETIE...

YEAH, SO MY GRANDFATHER LIVED HERE FOR, LIKE, TWENTY YEARS. WHEN HE HAD HIS STROKE LAST YEAR, MY FOLKS SHIPPED HIM OFF TO ARIZONA.
THEY LET ME HAVE THIS PLACE, BUT I'M NOT READY TO LEAVE THE CITY YET.
YOU CAN USE WHATEVER FURNITURE YOU'D LIKE, JUST PUT THE REST IN THE BASEMENT.
THERE'S A FIREPLACE...
THE END
YOU'D HAVE TO GET A CAR, OF COURSE, AND CABLE, IF YOU WANT ANY T.V. AT ALL.
BUT OVERALL, IT'S A NICE LITTLE PLACE, REASONABLE RENT...
YOU COULD MOVE IN AS SOON AS WE HAMMER OUT A LEASE!

WE'LL TAKE IT!

THAT LAZY BUM NICHOLAS CALLED OUT SICK SO I'LL NEED YOU IN THE SHOP TODAY. COME ON.
BUT... I'M OFF TODAY. I HAVE TO DRAW.
STAR WARS
MA? WHAT-- WHAT ARE YOU DOING?! IT'S 4:30 IN THE MORNING!
I'M DOING A LOAD OF LAUNDRY. DO YOU HAVE ANY WHITES?
EDUARDO!
TURN THAT MUSIC DOWN!
HEY! I GOTTA USE THE TOILET! WHAT'RE YOU DOING IN THERE?
OPEN UP!
OKAY! OKAY! I'LL BE OUT IN A SECOND DAD!
MMBLE GRMBLERAZZA FRAZZIN
WORKING CLASS HERO
HEY, ED. HOW'S IT GO--UT!
HEY! YOU KNOW WHAT? WHY DON'T YOU AND ME GET AN APARTMENT, HUH? HUH?!

YEAH, IT'S GOOD TO SEE YOU, TOO.
I CAN'T STAND IT ANYMORE! MY PARENTS ARE DRIVING ME INSANE!
SO HOW ABOUT IT, OLD BUDDY, OLD PAL? IF JANE AND STEPHEN CUT YOU LOOSE THEN YOU AND ME WILL GET A PLACE TOGETHER, RIGHT?
NOE FIE
WHAT? YOU AND ME? HA HA... COME ON, ED, IT'S ... YOU...
ACTUALLY, THAT'S NOT A BAD IDEA... HOW MUCH RENT COULD YOU PAY?
I'D HAVE TO PAY RENT?
WHA--?! OF COURSE YOU'D HAVE TO PAY RENT! I'M NOT GOING TO--
HAHA! RELAX, TOUGH GUY! I'M JUST KIDDING.
I'LL HAVE TO CHECK WITH MY ACCOUNTANT TO SEE WHAT I CAN AFFORD.
BUT WE HAVE A DEAL?
DONE AND DONE!

UNCLE A
COMIC GA
OF FUN AND
AH! HERE IT IS...
ISN'T "COLLECTOR'S WORLD" THE ONE THAT DID THE EDITORIAL CONDEMNING FLAVOR ABOUT THE NIGHTSTALKER THING? I THOUGHT YOU WEREN'T GOING TO BUY IT.
SEX
ACTION
ZOOM
NAUGHTY HEROINE
HOTH ECHO BASE
I'M NOT! I'M JUST SKIMMING THE NEWS SECTION IN THE STORE.
SINCE IT'S A WEEKLY PAPER IT HAS MORE UP-TO-DATE --
WHAT TH--?!
Collector's World
$2.50 (U.S.) $13.95 (CAN)
Volume 9, Issue 5
This Issue:
What's New?-pg 4
The Pain-pg7
Dr Physician-pg7
Brayshaw's Bookshelf-pg8
Comics Critic-pg34
Dracula Chronicles-pg35
Professor Panels-pg37
Gutter Snipe-pg39
Men in Tights-pg40
Thor vs Hulk-pg 43
Eggiest!-pg47
Turn me on, Deadman-pg50
Classified-pg52
Dream Big Dreams-pg55
Noe Fie-pg57
Young Tim's Advice to the LoveLorn-pg56
Kolor Komik Kickoff-pg59
TK421-pg65
Subliminal Sexual Message-pg69
Comics Crap-pg78
Antarctic Blast-pg79
Jerry Langford-pg80
Who Reads This Junk?!-pg82
Irving Flavor to Attend GraNoSequon
It was announced that golden age legend and creator of The Nightstalker Irving Flavor, would be a guest at this year's Graphic Novel and Sequential art Convention at the Newark Sheraton this February.
Comics 1942. He has remained out of the spotlight since his retirement and this will be his first convention in eight years.
He will be attending as a guest of another comics magazine who will be giving him a "lifetime achievement award" at a ceremony on the second day of the con.
For more information about the convention, call (516) 922-9463 or go to http://members.aol.com/BOPalex
Golden Age Artist Irving Flavor
Flavor recently became a figure of controversy as he has begun a crusade to win the rights to The Nighstalker, who he created for Zoom
Comics' Best Year: Record Number of Shops Open, Sales Climb as Never Before
The comics industry has boomed, according to Wall Street, with an unprecedented eight comics publishers entering the Forbes 500 for the first time.
"It's just incredible" raves store owner Kristen Siebecker. "Who would've guessed comics sales would go from the toilet to, well, what ever the opposite of a toilet would be!"
Shop owner Larry Vivron is also happy. "Fuck yeah! I (Story continued on page 7)
Nut Tony Consiglio
Consiglio "Double Crosses" Another Publisher
Comics genius Tony Consiglio has broken his contract with Zoom Comics, making them the fifth publisher he has worked with in just two years. "Tony's a nut!" claims Top Shelf publisher Chris Staros "But I love him"
JUSTICE IS BACK!
ZOOM COMICS

HMMM... FROM ALL YOU'VE SAID I ALWAYS PICTURED HIM OLDER.
WHAT? OH, THAT MUST BE SOME FILE PHOTO OF HIM. BELIEVE ME, HE'S ANCIENT.
BUT WHY DIDN'T HE TELL ME ABOUT THIS CONVENTION?
CROSSS!
STINKY
BOOSK
BAD GIRL
WIGGLY READER
IGBB
St Elsewh
CRACKLE YEAH?
IT'S ME, MR. FLAVOR. BUZZ ME IN.
CLICK CLICK!
BZZ!
FINALLY!
OOPS! SORRY!
EXCUSE ME.
EDDIE!

MR. FLAVOR, WHO WAS THAT WHO JUST LEFT?
HIM? AH, HE WAS JUST SOME GUY. HE WANTED TO SELL ME SOME INSURANCE OR A JEHOVAH'S WITNESS OR SOME CRAP.
HUH...
ANYWAY, WHAT'S ALL THIS ABOUT YOU GOING TO THIS CONVENTION? WHY DIDN'T YOU TELL ME?
WELL I'M SORRY I DIDN'T CHECK WITH YOU, "MA!!"
FOR YOUR INFORMATION, SMART GUY, THE EDITOR GUYS FROM "COMICS WORLD" WANT ME TO GO SO THEY CAN GIVE ME THEIR LIFETIME ACHIEVEMENT PRIZE!
IT'S A VERY MAJOR AWARD!
REALLY? WOW, THIS COULD REALLY HELP YOUR CASE!
HELP MY--?
OH, YEAH, SURE. MY CASE.
HAHA! WHAT A GREAT IDEA! ZOOM PRACTICALLY RUNS THAT CONVENTION! IT WOULD REALLY STICK IT TO THEM!
UH, YEAH, YEAH!
HEH HEH!
I DON'T KNOW, BUT I FEEL LIKE THINGS ARE GONNA BREAK SOON!
FIRST THE "COMICS WORLD" ARTICLE, THEN THE "METRO CHIC" THING, NOW THIS CONVENTION!

HEY, I'M GONNA CALL "COMICS WORLD" AND GET MORE INFO, OKAY?
HUH? OH, SURE, SURE. RIGHT.
I GOTTA USE THE CAN ANYHOW.
MICS SUCK
"COMICS WORLD, YOUR GUIDE TO THE WORLD OF COMICS."
CAN I HELP YOU?
YES, THIS IS ED VELASQUEZ. I'M CALLING ON BEHALF--
OH MY GOD! ED?
UH.... YYYEEAH?
YOU'RE IRVING FLAVOR'S ASSISTANT, RIGHT? THIS IS HILDY!
HIL--? OH YEAH! HOW, UH, HOW YOU DOING?
OH, FINE. YOU KNOW: HANGING IN. HOW ABOUT YOU?
YEAH, YEAH... OKAY... HEH!
IT'S GREAT NEWS ABOUT MR. FLAVOR GETTING THAT AWARD, RIGHT?
YEAH! GREAT NEWS!
UH... YOU'LL PROBABLY GO TO THE CONVENTION, RIGHT? TO SEE HIM GET IT.
YEAH, I GUESS SO! HEH!
GREAT!
I GUESS WE'LL BE SEEING EACH OTHER, THEN!
UH, SEEING EACH OTHER AT THE CON, I MEAN!!
SURE! OKAY, THEN!
ALRIGHT! HEH HEH!
HEH... UH.
OKAY, THEN! I'LL SEE YOU!
ALRIGHT! BYE, ED!
BYE!
BYE!

SHE MUST THINK I'M A FUCKING IDIOT.
HE MUST THINK I'M SO DESPERATE.
SO? WHAT'D THEY SAY?
WHAT DID WHO SAY ABOUT WHAT?
OH! RIGHT, THE CONVENTION! UH, YEAH.
IT'S...
THEY...
I'LL CALL BACK LATER. UH. TODAY.
GREAT. ANYWAY, I WANTED TO SHOW YOU SOMETHING.
LOOK AT THIS, WOULD YA?
UH... WHAT'S THIS FOR?
THEY'RE MY NEWEST CHARACTERS: METEON AND THE COMET KID!

WHAT'S THIS FOR? ANOTHER CEREAL BOX? OR A MEXICAN TOY COMPANY?
NAH! THEY'RE MY NEW CHARACTERS! I WAS STRUCK BY A GOD DAMNED BOLT OF INSPIRATION THE OTHER DAY!
I FIGURE INSTEAD OF BELLY-ACHIN' ABOUT THE NIGHTSTALKER ALL THE TIME I SHOULD COME UP WITH A NEW CHARACTER.
METEON!
HMM... THAT'S NOT A BAD IDEA, ACTUALLY. WITH ALL THE PUBLICITY YOU'VE BEEN GETTING, SOMEONE'S BOUND TO PICK IT UP!
ONLY...
"ONLY?" WHAT? WHAT "ONLY?!"
WELL...
HE'S SORT OF, UH, OLD FASHIONED.
WHAT?!
UH, SUPER HEROES HAVE SORT OF CHANGED. NO ONE HAS TEEN-AGE SIDE KICKS ANYMORE.
AND HIS SHOES LOOK A LITTLE WIMPY.
WHAT ARE YOU TALKING ABOUT?! A BUNCH OF 'EM WEAR THOSE KIND OF SHOES!
ALL I'M SAYING IS HE COULD BE MORE, LIKE, MODERN. GRITTIER, MORE... REALISTIC.
WAIT A SECOND...

WHAT ABOUT SOMETHING MORE LIKE THIS?
WHAT?! ED, HE'S SUPPOSED TO BE THE DAMN GOOD GUY!
AND WHO THE HELL IS SHE?! THEY'D NEVER LET YOU GET AWAY WITH AN OUTFIT LIKE THAT!
THAT'S WHAT COSMIC KID SHOULD
COMET KID.
...COMET KID SHOULD LOOK LIKE, I THINK.
AND YOU CAN GET AWAY WITH AN OUTFIT LIKE THAT NOWADAYS.
(PEOPLE SORT OF EXPECT IT, ACTUALLY.)
WELLLL...
I GUESS I COULD USE SOME OF YOUR SUGGESTIONS.
I DO LIKE THE SPIKES.
WELL, WHATEVER. I'M JUST TRYING TO HELP OUT.
ANATOMY

ED, I WANT TO... UH...
WHAT I'M TRYIN' TO SAY IS ... YOU'VE BEEN... UH.
YOU DO GOOD WORK, ED.
YOU'RE A GOOD ARTIST.
THANK YOU, MR. FLAVOR.
SO WHAT DO YOU SAY WE GET TO WORK?

WHAT WILL YOU ASK GOD?
CAN I SEE SOME DINOSAURS?
UH...
MASTURBATION ISN'T REALLY LIKE A SIN, IS IT?
CAN YOU TELL ME WHERE MY SISTER IS?
WHY?
HOW COULD YOU INVENT BUSTER KEATON, AFTER-NOON NAPS AND "THE FOUR SEASONS" BUT ALSO PAULY SHORE, HEMORRHOIDS AND ANTIETAM?
HOW DO YOU SLEEP AT NIGHT?
FORGIVE ME.

Love is Here to Stay

"Do you work here?" Every time Grant heard the question at his job, he wanted to run an awl into his ear—or the customer's ear, either would do. But he knew he never would. He'd continue to be the same spineless, aimless jellyfish of a bookstore clerk he always was (and always would be), who would rather complain about life than do something to cha

Old Nick, the sea captain, was a rough, tough, son of a bitch his mother had asserted, shortly before he fed her entrails to the crocodiles he kept below decks. If only she had listened to reason, Nick thought as he breathed in the salty air nibbling a cuticle, and told me where Captain Ghoti had buried his t

"I Quit!!" Grant hollered so loud the veins on his neck bulged with fury.

"B-b-b-but you can't!" his stupid puny boss stammered. "I know we've treated you shabbily in the past but without you, who will handle the stupid customers with all their stupid questions about their stupid fucking god damned books? Who will help the stupid fucking shit piss asshole mother fu

Dear Editors,

I never believed the letters in your magazine until I met Nina, the model who moved in to my building last fall.

"Can I borrow a cup of sugar?" she purred, licking her full, ruby red lips. Under her pleated plaid skirt and tantalizingly unbuttoned white blouse I recognized her curvy physique from magazine ads. As my hand kneaded her firm, dusky buttocks, I couldn't help noticing she wasn't wearing kni

RING!
DAMMIT!

YELLO?
SHERMAN? OH SWEETIE! I'VE BEEN TRYING TO CALL YOU SINCE--
BZZZZ!
OH, WAIT, DOROTHY, SOMEONE'S RINGING THE DOORBELL. LET ME JUST
SWEETIE-- I'M IN THE EMERGENCY ROOM...
WHAT?! OH MY GOD! WHAT'S WRONG?!
Sniff
I-- I WAS CROSSING 59th STREET AND SORT ...OT HIT BY ...BUS...
BZZZZ!
WHAT? WHAT HAPPENED? YOU GOT HIT BY A BUS?!
ARE YOU OKAY?! HOW--
...NOT MY FAULT....
I-- I DON'T KNOW... I'M A BIT DIZZY AND I, UH, I CAN'T REALLY MOVE MY LEGS...
JESUS! WHAT DID THE DOCTORS SA...? IS IT--
ST. VINCENTS, AT THE CORNER OF 14th AND 7th. PLEASE HURRY...
NO, NO! THE DOORBELL IS-- LISTEN: WHICH HOSPITAL ARE YOU--
GRRRR!
BZZZZ! BZZZZ!
BZZZZZZZZZZZZZZZZ!
GODDAMN IT! I'LL BE RIGHT THERE!
OKAY! OKAY! WHAT THE HELL'S THE BIG--
UH... ARE YOU TALKING TO ME?

CAN SHERMAN COME OUT AND PLAY?
Y--
THE BUS?
LOOK! I GOT ONE OF THOSE CELL PHONES!
SO THAT WAS YOU RINGING THE BELL THE WHOLE TIME?!
HAHAHAHA! I WISH I'D BROUGHT A CAMERA SO YOU COULD'VE SEEN YOUR FACE!
WELL, I'M GLAD YOU FIND MY PANICKING CONCERN SUCH A SCREAM!
YOU SHOULD HAVE DETECTED IT WAS A PRANK:
ST. VINCENTS IS ON SEVENTH AND TWELFTH!
WHEN AND HOW DID YOU GET A CELL PHONE ANYWAY? YOU KNOW THEY CAUSE BRAIN CANCER?

PUT YOUR SHOES ON AND I'LL TELL YOU ALL ABOUT IT ON THE WAY.
WH-- ON THE WAY WHERE? ST. VINCENT'S? MOUNT SINAI? THE MORGUE?
IT'S A SURPRISE, SUGAR CAKES, SO COME ON AND GET DRESSED!
OH, YAY. ANOTHER SURPRISE.
WHAT, DID YOU KILL SOME BODY? YOU HAVE HERPES? LONG LOST TWIN?
YES, YES AND YES! NOW HURRY UP!
SO I GET THIS MESSAGE AT MY VOICEMAIL AT WORK, OKAY? YOU'LL NEVER GUESS WHO IT WAS!
UMMM... YOKO ONO?
F
Ma
ELIZABETH PIERBORNE! FROM "INSIDE SCOOP!"
CAN YOU BELIEVE IT?!
SHE READ MY ARTICLE AND WANTS TO DO A STORY ABOUT IRVING FOR THE SHOW!
AND THE BEST PART IS THEY WANT TO INTER-VIEW ME FOR A PART OF IT!
ISN'T THAT MARVELOUS?!

YOU'D GET TO BE ON TELEVISION? WOW! THAT'S GREAT! SO WHEN'S IT --
SEE, THAT'S THE CATCH! THEY WON'T DO IT WITHO AND HE
THIZDOPIZ GARROLGODDENZ!
THIS IS US!
HMM. CARROLL GARDENS? GIVE ME A HINT!
ALL IN GOOD TIME, MY PRECIOUS, ALL IN GOOD TIME!
SO THEY GAVE YOU MONEY TO BE ON THE SHOW AND YOU ALREADY BLEW IT ON A CANCER CAUSING PHONE?
EXACTLY!
EXCEPT THEY HAVEN'T ACTUALLY GIVEN ME ANY MONEY YET.
SOUNDS LOGICAL TO ME.
SO WAIT: WHAT WAS I --?
OH YEAH! SO THEY MIGHT NOT DO THE STORY BECAUSE IRVING AND FRED ARE, LIKE, STALLING!
WHO, ED? THAT'S WEIRD. I IMAGINE ED WOULD JUMP AT THE CHANCE TO BE ON T.V.
I KNOW!! WHO WOULDN'T?!
SO NEXT TIME YOU TALK TO HIM, TELL HIM TO GET HIS ASS IN GEAR.
THIS COULD BE THE BREAK ALL OF US HAVE BEEN -- OH!
HERE WE ARE!

YOU KNOW MY BIRTHDAY ISN'T UNTIL MARCH, RIGHT?
:CRACKLE: YEAH?
HI, IT'S DOROTHY!
THIS DOESN'T HAVE TO DO WITH AMWAY DOES IT?
:CRACKLE: WHO?
DOROTHY.
I CALLED BEFORE ABOUT YOU-KNOW-WHAT-FOR-YOU-KNOW-WHO?
OKAY!
SO? SO? DO YOU HAVE ANY GUESSES?
YOU'D THINK I'D KNOW BY NOW NOT TO EVEN INDULGE YOU IN THESE SCHEMES.
B
HA! YOU'LL THANK ME LATER, SUGAR PIE!
??
OKAY NOW: DON'T STARE AT HIS ANKLE, AND WHATEVER HAPPENS...
DON'T MENTION THE WAR!!
HEY! SORRY I DIDN'T BUZZ YOU IN AT FIRST, BUT THIS IS NEW YORK, RIGHT?
WELL, BROOKLYN, BUT CLOSE ENOUGH, RIGHT?
SHERMAN, THIS IS RON, HE USED TO WORK IN METRO-CHIC'S ART DEPARTMENT!
UH... HI.
OKEY DOKE. SO COME ON IN, HAVE A LOOK AROUND.

DOROTHY TOLD ME ABOUT YOU NEEDING A NEW CRIB IN LIGHT OF YOUR EVICTION.
VU
AHHH! SO THAT'S WHAT THIS IS ALL ABOUT!
IT'S THE PERFECT PLACE FOR YOU, SWEETIE! LOOK AROUND!
THIS IS THE KITCHEN. I WAS IN HERE MAKING HOT COCOA WHEN MY GIRLFRIEND FRANCI TOLD ME SHE WAS DUMPING ME.
THE LIVING ROOM. FRANCI AND I ARGUED WHETHER OR NOT WE SHOULD GET CABLE...
THIS USED TO BE FRANCI'S DARK-ROOM. IT'S EMPTY NOW. ITS WARM, RED GLOW REPLACED BY THE STARK GLARE OF A FLORESCENT BULB.
AND FINALLY, THE MASTER BED ROOM... WHERE...
WHERE WE...
SO WHAT DO YOU THINK?

IT SEEMS LIKE A GREAT PLACE, ROB.
SO WHAT WOULD THE DAMAGE BE? WHAT KIND OF RENT WOULD I PAY?
UH... WELL, THE RENT FOR THE WHOLE PLACE IS $800, WHICH ISN'T TOO BAD FOR THIS NEIGHBORHOOD.
HMM, SO I'D BE PAYING $400? I GUESS I COULD SWING THAT.
WHATEVER, DUDE. HOWEVER YOU WANT TO WORK IT.
THE UTILITIES AREN'T INCLUDED AND IF YOU--
WAIT... UH, SHOULDN'T WE JUST SPLIT THE WHOLE THING FIFTY-FIFTY? I'LL PAY $400 AND YOU PAY $400?
UNLESS YOU HAD...UH...
WH..?
OHHHH!
NO, NO! YOU THINK I'M LOOKING FOR A ROOMMATE! NO!
NOW THAT I LOST MY JOB I CAN'T PAY EVEN HALF THE RENT.
I'M MOVING OUT, DUDE!
OH, OKAY. BUT I COULD NEVER AFFORD THIS PLACE ON MY OWN.
OOOH, YOU'RE RIGHT SWEETIE YOU PROBABLY COULDN'T...

BUT WE COULD.

UHHHHHHH...
WHAT DID YOU JUST SAY?

C'MON, SWEETIE! FOR REAL!
BUT WE...
Uh
MAYBE WE SH--
DOROTHY, I DON'T KNOW IF..
!
WAIT A MINUTE! I CAN'T! I TOLD ED THAT HE AND I WOULD GET A PLACE TOGETHER!
W--
What?
YEAH, YESTERDAY HE WAS TELLING ME HOW MUCH HE HATED HIS PARENTS AND HE PROPOSED WE LOOK FOR A PLACE TOGETHER.
I SAID YES.
Oh.
Okay.
UM, THANKS, RON. I'M SORRY IF WE WASTED YOUR TIME.
OH, HEH, IT'S OKAY.
YEAH, THANKS, RON.
DUDE!

DON'T FUCK THIS ONE UP!
DOROTHY, ARE YOU ALL RIGHT?
WHAT'S WRONG?
SNIFF
WHAT? NOTHING.
READY TO GO? DO YOU WANT TO GET SOMETHING TO EAT?
UH. SURE, I GUESS. BUT..
GREAT!
I THOUGHT I SAW A NICE DINER NEAR THE SUBWAY STATION.
UH, SHOULDN'T WE TALK ABOUT WHAT WENT ON BACK THERE?
WHAT'S TO TALK ABOUT? YOU'RE MOVING IN WITH ED, RIGHT?
YEAH, BUT..
WE'VE NEVER EVEN DISCUSSED YOU AND I LIVING WITH EACH OTHER! I WAS CAUGHT OFF GUARD.

AND I WAS CAUGHT OFF GUARD THAT YOU'D MAKE PLANS FOR NEW LIVING ARRANGEMENTS AND NOT EVEN MENTION IT TO ME!
SO I GUESS WE'RE EVEN.
I WAS GOING TO TELL YOU BUT YOU THREW ME OFF WITH THAT WHOLE PHONE PRANK!
OH, OKAY. WELL, I GUESS THAT'S THAT.
MENU
I NEVER EVEN--
IF I HAD THOUGHT THAT YOU WERE THINKING OF US MOVING IN TOGETHER OF COURSE I WOULD'VE TALKED ABOUT IT WITH YOU.
OKAY.
I THINK IT WILL BE GOOD FOR ED, TOO. HE'S 23 AND HE'S NEVER LIVED AWAY FROM HOME.
YOU'RE RIGHT!
WELL, TALK TO ME ABOUT IT! DON'T JUST GET MAD AND BE--
I'M NOT MAD.

Another satellite
NEXT!
SHERMAN!
boiling frog no. 3
HEY, JOLIE. YOU DON'T WORK TODAY. DID YOU JUST COME BY TO GET YOUR CHECK?
YEAH. I WAS ON MY WAY TO CLASS AND THOUGHT I'D SWING BY.
YOU HEAR THE BIG NEWS?
NAME?
DAVIES, SHERMAN.
PAYROLL
I'VE BEEN WORKING HERE FOR 800 YEARS AND THEY STILL DON'T KNOW MY NAME.
SO WHAT'S UP?
THEY FINALLY FOUND A NEW MANAGER TO REPLACE NELLIE!
HERE YOU GO: ONE, TWO HUNDRED, AND TWENTY, FORTY, SIXTY, EIGHTY SEVEN...
AND TWENTY NINE CENTS.
Whew! GOVERNMENT DO TAKE A BITE, DON'T SHE?
I HAVEN'T SEEN HIM YET. THEY SAY HE HAS A LISP.
WAIT! HERE'S YOUR JACKET, "SHERMAN."
JACKET? WHAT'S THIS FOR?
NEW POLICY.
ALL CLERKS AT MATTHEW'S MUST NOW WEAR JACKETS.
HEH HEHHEHHEHHEH.
NEXT!

:SIGH:
Hello! I'm SHARMAN How Can I Service You? MATTHEWS
EXCUSE ME... DO YOU WORK HERE?
YEAH, CAN I HELP YOU?
UH, MY NAME IS CAPRICE?
TODAY'S MY FIRST DAY, AND THEY TOLD ME YOU'RE SUPPOSED TO SHOW ME AROUND?
OH, OKAY! I'M SHERMAN, BY THE WAY. I GUESS WE'LL START WITH THE COMPUTER SYSTEM.
OH! AND... WELCOME TO HELL!
HEH!
...SO IF YOU WANT TO SEE HOW MANY WE HAVE IN STOCK, HIT "J".
LUNCH SCHEDULE
FUCK YOU ALL!
OKAY, WAIT, LET ME TRY ONE. UM... DAVID EDDIE... "CHUMP CHANGE."
OKAY: NOW HIT "RETURN" AND THE NUMBER.
THAT'S A GREAT BOOK. DID YOU READ IT?
OH, SURE! IN FACT, MY BOYFRIEND AND I WENT TO SEE HIM DO A READING AT STEINBECK AND SON!

THAT'S RIGHT! I REMEMBER READING ABOUT THAT!
REALLY?
UH, THAT HE WAS DOING A READING, I MEAN. NOT THAT YOU WENT TO IT, OBVIOUSLY!
HA HA!
HEH
SO
UM
WHAT DO WE DO NOW?
HMM?
OH! RIGHT! UH... CUSTOMERS, I GUESS.
YOU'LL FIND THAT THE BEST WAY TO RELATE TO THE CUSTOMERS IS TO THINK OF THEM AS RETARDED CRO-MAGNONS.
AH, YES: "BOOBUS AMERICANUS." I USED TO WORK AT THE MAIN BRANCH OF THE LIBRARY SO I THINK I'LL GET THE HANG OF IT.
REALLY? THE ONE WITH THE LIONS AND EVERYTHING? WOW! DID YOU WORK IN THE BIG READ--
EXCUSE ME, YOU WORK HERE, CHIEF?
YES. CAN I HELP YOU, SIR?
YEAH, I'M LOOKIN' FOR A TEX BOOK. FOR A CLASS.
"ADVANCED ECONOMICS"
OKAY. DO YOU KNOW THE AUTHOR'S NAME?
IT'S FOR A CLASS. HUNTER COLLEGE.

DO YOU KNOW WHO WROTE THE BOOK?
?! WHAT DO YOU MEAN? IT DON'T SAY. IT'S A TEX BOOK: NO ONE WROTE IT.
COME ON, BIG GUY!
OKAY, WELL GO LOOK IT UP. WAIT RIGHT HERE.
YEAH!
SO I TYPE IN "ADVANCED ECONOMICS" AND HIT THE . .
NAH. WE MUST HAVE 900 BOOKS CALLED "ADVANCED ECONOMICS" AND SINCE BRANIAC-5 THERE DOESN'T KNOW THE AUTHOR WE DON'T KNOW WHICH ONE HE WANTS.
OH... UH, SO WHAT DO WE DO?
WE PUTTER AROUND BACK HERE FOR A FEW MINUTES AND THEN WE TELL HIM IT'S SOLD OUT.
SO, CAPRICE, DO YOU GO TO SCHOOL OR . . ?
I'M A FRESHMAN AT N.Y.U. I'M GOING FOR FILM. IT WAS EITHER THAT OR ENGLISH.
REALLY? I WAS AN ENGLISH MAJOR AT HUNTER!
I WANT TO BE A WRITER.
THAT'S COOL! HAVE YOU HAD ANY OF YOUR STUFF PUBLISHED?
UM.
NO, SIR. I'M AFRAID WE'RE SOLD OUT OF "ADVANCED ECONOMICS." CHECK BACK IN, LIKE, SIX WEEKS.
AHHH, 'ATS AWRIGHT. I'LL DROP THE CLASS.

WOW! YOU'VE BEEN WORKING HERE FOR FOUR YEARS?
I KNOW, I KNOW, PATHETIC ISN'T IT? WHAT CAN I DO?
YOU CAN QUIT!
BELIEVE IT OR NOT, THERE WAS A TIME I ACTUALLY LIKED THIS JOB.
I USED TO ACTUALLY NOT DREAD COMING IN.
I LIKED THE BOOKS, NATURALLY, BUT I ALSO USED TO LIKE MOST OF MY CO-WORKERS.
IT SUDDENLY HIT ME THE OTHER DAY THAT I'VE BEEN HERE THE LONGEST OF ALL THE CLERKS!
ALL THE PEOPLE WHO WERE HERE WHEN I STARTED ARE GONE.
HAVE YOU EVER QUIT A JOB BEFORE?
IT'S A GREAT FEELING!
IT'S AS IF YOU'VE SOMEHOW BROKEN THE RULES OF PHYSICS. WHAT SEEMED IMPOSSIBLE IS NOW REAL!
YOU FEEL LIKE YOU'RE THE MASTER OF YOUR OWN DESTINY.
WHICH YOU ARE!
YEAH, THAT'S GREAT BUT YOU STILL GOTTA PAY RENT SO YOU HAVE TO GET A NEW JOB.
OF COURSE, BUT AT LEAST YOU'VE PROVEN TO YOURSELF THAT YOU ARE IN CHARGE OF YOUR LIFE, NOT SOME, UH, MANAGER?
DO WE HAVE ANY MORE "PORTABLE WILDES"
HEH... WELL, IF YOU STILL --
NEVERMIND.

WHAT? WHAT WERE YOU GOING TO SAY?
I WAS JUST GOING TO SAY LET'S SEE IF YOU STILL BELIEVE THAT ONCE YOU FINISH SCHOOL.
ANGRY YOUTH
WELL, MAYBE I WON'T BUT THAT DOESN'T MEAN I'M NOT RIGHT.
I'M GETTING MORE WILDE.
EXCUSE ME?
SIGH
YES, SIR. CAN I HELP YOU?
IS THAT THE TONE YOU USE WITH ALL THE CUSTOMERS?!
NO, I JUST... YOU...
WHAT IS IT YOU NEED? ARE YOU LOOKING FOR A BOOK OR--
MY NAME'S ARTIE VALLENTINE. I'M YOUR NEW MANAGER, UH...
SHARMAN.
HEH... A-ACTUALLY, IT'S, UH, SHERMAN. SEE, THEY MISSP--
SHERMAN? SHERMAN.
LET'S GO INTO MY NEW OFFICE, OKAY SHERMAN?
UM OKAY.

AS YOU KNOW, THEY HIRED ME SO I COULD BRING SOME ORDER TO THIS LITTLE FUN FACTORY.
HUH.
YOU'RE THE SINGLE HIGHEST PAID CLERK ON STAFF. CAN YOU TELL ME WHY?
Uh. WHY? I GUESS IT'S BECAUSE I'VE BEEN HERE THE--
SURE, SURE.
LET'S CUT OUT THE, HUH, CRAP, OKAY? SHERMAN?
I DON'T LIKE YOU.
UH...BUT, BUT YOU ONLY MET ME A--
I'VE BEEN IN RETAIL FOR TWENTY-SEVEN YEARS, PAL. I'VE SEEN YOUR TYPE POP UP AGAIN AND AGAIN, LIKE A BAAAAAD FUCKIN' PENNY.
SMART GUYS
JERKS.
COMPANIES HIRE, HUH, GUYS LIKE ME TO CLEAR OUT GUYS LIKE YOU.

DEAD
WOOD.
YOU GET ME?
UHH, SO DOES THIS MEAN... AM I FIRED OR--
HAHA! FUCK YOU! YOU WISH YOU WERE FIRED!
NO. YOU'RE WARNED, MY FRIEND.
GIANTS
NO MORE BAD ATTITUDE.
NO MORE LATENESSES.
NO MORE EXCUSES!
UH, YES.
YES.
GOOD!
G
GI
IS THERE SOMETHING ELSE I CAN DO FOR YOU, BIG GUY, OR, HUH, DO YOU NEED A SPECIAL GOLD PLATED INVITATION TO GET BACK TO WORK?
UH, WELL, I-- I, UH DIDN'T KNOW IF YOU WERE FINISHED OR IF--
HERE'S A TIP, GUY: WHEN SOUND STOPS COMING OUT OF MY MOUTH, I'M "FINISHED" AND YOU GO BACK TO WORK!
ARE WE CLEAR? YOU WANT THAT IN FUCKIN' NOTARIZED MEMO FORM?

YOU WORK HERE, RIGHT? WHERE DO YOU SELL CHILDREN'S BOOKS ON TAPE?
DO YOU WORK HERE? WHO DO I TALK TO ABOUT GETTING MY MANUSCRIPT PUBLISHED?
LAST NIGHT, RIGHT? I PICKED OUT SOME BOOKS I WANTED TO GET BUT I DIDN'T HAVE ANY MONEY, RIGHT? SO I HID THEM ON A SHELF BUT NOW IT LOOKS LIKE SOMEONE PUT THEM AWAY SO CAN YOU TELL ME WHERE I CAN FIND THEM?
YOU DO WORK HERE, RIGHT?
SEE YOU TOMORROW!
YEP.
SHERMAN?
SHIT!
HI, DAD.

YOU KNOW, YOU'VE GOT A LOT OF GUTS COMING HERE AFTER WHAT YOU PULLED.
NOW THAT THE COAST IS CLEAR YOU FIGURE YOU CAN JUST WALTZ BACK IN?
HOW DARE YOU JUDGE ME?
NO MATTER WHAT HAPPENS, PHIN, THEY'RE STILL MY BOYS!
IT'S MY RIGHT TO--
THAT'S FUNNY, THEY DIDN'T SEEM TO BE YOUR "BOYS" WHEN THEIR MOTHER WAS SICK!
HOW COME YOU DIDN'T COME SEE YOUR "BOYS" THEN, GREG?
I'LL TELL YOU WHY: YOU WERE TOO BUSY WITH YOUR OWN BULLSHIT!!
I'M NOT OBLIGATED TO TOLERATE THIS!
YOU HAVE NO POWER OVER ME.
I'M GOING TO COME BACK WHEN YOU'RE ACTING LIKE A RATIONAL PERSON!
YOU COME BACK WHEN YOU'RE READY TO TELL SHERMAN AND JOE YOU'RE SORRY!
I HAVE NOTHING TO BE SORRY FOR!!
YOU PATHETIC SON OF A BITCH!!

HAHA! WELL, IT'S GOOD TO SEE YOU, TOO!
NO, NO, I JUST MEAN YOU...
I DIDN'T EXPECT TO BUMP INTO YOU.
WELL, IT IS GOOD TO SEE YOU. YOU LOOK GREAT!
UH, SO WHAT ARE YOU DOING HERE?
IS THERE SOMETHING WRONG?
BOOK EI
NO, NOTHING'S WRONG! I WAS JUST PASSING THROUGH TOWN AND WANTED TO GET TOGETHER WITH MY BOYS.
YOU, UH, YOU CALLED JOE?
YEAH. HE--
HE SAID HE HAS TO WORK LATE AT THE SHOP.
SO DO YOU WANT TO GET A DRINK OR A BITE TO EAT? IT'S ON ME!
A DRINK SOUNDS GREAT.

Return of the Daddy

HEYYYY! SHE'S A LOOKER!
YEAH. SHE WORKS AT "METRO-CHIC." IN FACT SHE JUST HAD HER FIRST ARTICLE PUBLISHED RECENTLY.
A WRITER!
YOU KNOW NEXT YEAR I ACTUALLY GET TO RETIRE AND I'VE THOUGHT ABOUT TRYING MY HAND AT WRITING.
POETRY, AND SUCH.
WOW, YOU'RE RETIRING?
HOW LONG HAVE YOU BEEN WORKING THERE?
PHHHHEW... NEXT YEAR IT WILL BE THIRTY YEARS! ACTUALLY I WAS ABOUT YOUR AGE WHEN I FIRST STARTED! YOU'RE, WHAT? 25?
23.
THAT'S RIGHT.
I REMEMBER I'D BEEN WORKING THERE A YEAR WHEN I FIRST MET YOUR MOTHER.
SHE'D JUST STARTED IN THEIR PUBLICITY DEPARTMENT, FRESH OUT OF SCHOOL. THE FIRST TIME WE MET--
DO YOU KNOW THIS STORY?
SHE HAD INK ALL OVER HER HANDS FROM TRYING TO USE THIS, UH, LIKE, MIMEOGRAPH.

SO, HAVE YOU TALKED TO YOUR AUNT PHIN LATELY? WHAT'S SHE UP TO?
WE WENT TO SEE HER AROUND CHRISTMAS. SHE'S DOING OKAY.
SHE'S GOING TO HOLLAND THIS SUMMER.
GOD. I--
YOU KNOW? I HAVEN'T SEEN HER SINCE YOUR GRANDFATHER'S FUNERAL. FIVE YEARS AGO!
UH, YEAH I THINK I RECALL HER MENTIONING THAT.
HAVE YOU SEEN OUR WAITRESS?
HA! I'M SURE SHE DID MENTION IT!
YOUR AUNT CAN BE A VERY... DOMINEERING WOMAN.
I CAN'T IMAGINE WHAT HORRIBLE THINGS SHE TOLD YOU BOYS ABOUT ME.
UH, YEAH, WELL, I GUESS I WOULDN'T CALL YOU HER FAVORITE PERSON ON EARTH
HEH...
NO.
WHEN WE WERE GROWING UP, SHE WAS VERY ABUSIVE WITH ME. ALWAYS PUTTING ME DOWN.
BELITTLING ME.
I THINK SHE USED--WHEN YOUR MOTHER AND I SEPERATED, THAT WAS YOUR AUNT'S EXCUSE FOR THE ... ANGER SHE'S ALWAYS FELT.
SHE'S--
SHE'S A VERY UNHAPPY WOMAN.

JOANNE? WE'RE BACK! WOO-EE, YOU SHOULD'VE SEEN HOW PACKED IT WAS! EVERY SLOB FROM HERE TO TRENTON --
? OH MY GOD, WHAT'S WRONG? DID DR. ENGEL CALL OR --
NO... GREG.
HE'S..
HE'S IN PITTSBURGH.
HE SAID HE'S NOT COMING BACK.
WHAT?! WHAT DID--
MOM! LOOK WHAT WE FOUND DOWN AT THE SHORE!
ITS A HORSEFLY CRAB!
LET ME SHOW HER, DICKWEED!
GUYS, UM, YOUR MOM'S NOT FEELING WELL, SO WHY DON'T YOU SHOW HER LATER, OKAY?
AND JOEY, DON'T SAY "DICKWEED."
SORRY, AUNT PHIN.

PART OF MY PROBLEM --AND I THINK YOU'LL FIND IT'S PART OF YOURS AS WELL--
IS THAT I CONSTANTLY FOUND MYSELF DOING THINGS TO PLEASE OTHER PEOPLE, BUT NEGLECTING MY OWN NEEDS.
BUT IT'S NOT AN EASY THING TO DO.
WE LIVE IN A SOCIETY WHICH MAKES US FEEL GUILTY FOR DOING WHAT MAKES US FEEL GOOD.
WE FEEL THAT WE DON'T DESERVE IT.
I DISCOVERED THAT I CAN LIVE MY LIFE THEY WAY I WANT TO! THAT I HAVE THE RIGHT TO SAY "NO."
I CAN TELL YOU THIS: SHE'LL PROBABLY BECOME UPSET... ANGRY, CRYING.
TAKE THIS SITUATION WITH YOU GIRLFRIEND, DOROTHY. (DOROTHY, RIGHT?) IF YOU FEEL THAT YOU DON'T WANT TO LIVE WITH HER, FOR WHATEVER REASON, SAY "NO."
I MEAN, ESPECIALLY WITH A BIG DECISION LIKE THAT.
AND SHE HAS A RIGHT TO HER FEELINGS BUT THAT IS EXACTLY WHAT THEY ARE: HER FEELINGS.
YOU CAN'T MAKE PEOPLE ANGRY--OR SAD, OR HAPPY OR WHATEVER --ONLY THEY HAVE THAT POWER.
WE ALL CONTROL OUR EMOTIONAL LIVES, SHERMAN.
YOU CAN'T BE RESPONSIBLE FOR THE WAY OTHER PEOPLE FEEL
JUST YOURSELF.
AND ONCE YOU BREAK OUT OF THAT TERRIBLE PATTERN...
THE PATTERN THAT SAYS "OTHER PEOPLE'S NEEDS ARE MORE IMORTANT THAN MY OWN. MY WISHES DON'T COUNT!"
ONCE YOU FREE YOURSELF FROM THAT EMOTIONAL QUICKSAND...
YOU'LL FIND YOURSELF A WHOLE LOT HAPPIER.
DAD...
WHY DID YOU COME HERE?

I WANT TO THANK YOU GUYS FOR COMING. I--
I KNOW WE'VE HAD SOME ROUGH PATCHES IN THE PAST AND IT'S BEEN ... WELL, WAY TOO LONG SINCE WE'VE BEEN ALL TOGETHER, BUT I'M HOPING...
WELL, I'M HOPING THIS CAN BE A NEW START.
I KNOW I'VE MISSED OUT ON ALOT SINCE, UH, SINCE THE SEPARATION, BUT...
I'M FEELING THAT WE CAN START THE HEALING PROCESS AND BECOME A FAMILY AGAIN.
I'VE... STARTED THIS PROCESS IN MY OWN LIFE, STARTING...
...
I'D LIKE YOU ALL TO MEET MARA. WE MET IN MY GROUP.
HELLO! HEH.
I SUPPOSE THE BIG NEWS IS THAT THIS SPRING, MARA AND I ARE--
WE'RE GETTING MARRIED!
HAHA!
I KNOW! IT'S A SHOCK, BUT WE'RE HOPING YOU'LL SUPPORT US IN OUR--
UH... DAD?
I NEVER WANT TO SEE YOU AGAIN UNTIL YOUR FUNERAL.

YOU'RE MY SON! Heh! I...
:Sigh: MARA IS DIVORCING ME.
OH, I'M, UH SORRY.
IT'S ALL BEEN VERY... UPSETTING. SHE BECAME...
I MET THIS WOMAN AT A WORK-SHOP I WAS PROCTORING. HER NAME WAS ELOISE.
SHE WAS A VERY WARM, A VERY GIVING, WONDERFUL WOMAN.
WELL...
WHEN MARA FOUND OUT THE ELOISE AND I WERE HAVING A RELATION-SHIP SHE BECAME VERY ANGRY.
SHE DIDN'T UNDERSTAND THA THE RELATIONSH WE HAD WASN'T
WAIT A MINUTE: YOU CHEATED ON HER?
:UHHHEM: NOW YOU SEE, IT WASN'T THAT OF... OUR RELAT WASN'T BASED
DID YOU HAVE SEXUAL RELATIONS WITH THIS WOMAN WHO WAS NOT YOUR WIFE?
OKAY, OKAY, IF YOU WANT A STARK, BLACK AND WHITE ANSWER, THEN YES. WE DID MAKE LOVE, OKAY?
BUT MARA DOESN'T SEE THAT ALL OF US NEED TO EXPRESS OUR--
I CANNOT BELIEVE WHAT I'M HEARING!

"MARA NEEDS TO UNDERSTAND..."
"MARA GOT UPSET!"
YOU MAKE IT SOUND AS IF SHE'S THE ONE TO BLAME FOR YOU CHEATING ON HE
NO ONE IS TO "BLAME." WE ALL HAVE TO LOOK INTO OUR--
NO! WRONG! YOU ARE TO BLAME! YOU CHEATED ON YOUR WIFE!
GOD! CAN'T YOU EVEN ADMIT THAT WHAT YOU DID WAS WRONG?!
(WOULD YOU PLEASE LOWER YOUR VOICE?!)
LABELING SOME... IT DOESN'T DO ANY GOOD LABELING THINGS AS "RIGHT" OR "WRONG" WHEN IT COMES TO OUR EMOTIONS. WHAT WE DID IS--
JESUS! YOU'LL USE ANY, UH, UH, UH, COCKAMAMIE, SELF-HELP BULLSHIT PRETZEL RATIONALE TO GET OUT OF ADMITTING THAT YOU JUST PLAIN FUCKED UP!
AIT JUST A MINUTE! HOW DARE..
YOUR PROBLEM ISN'T THAT YOU NEVER TAKE YOUR OWN FEELINGS INTO ACCOUNT! YOUR PROBLEM IS YOU DO NOTHING BUT TAKE YOUR OWN FEELINGS INTO ACCOUNT!
YOU'RE LIKE A BULL IN A, UH, CHINA STORE! YOU RUN AROUND DOING WHATEVER YOU WANT AND WHEN SOMETHING BREAKS, IT'S NOT YOUR FAULT!
"THE CHINA SHOULD'VE BEEN MORE CAREFUL!"
YOU HAVE NO RIGHT TO TALK TO ME LIKE THIS.
WHAT DO YOU KNOW ABOUT MARRIAGE?
YOU CAN'T EVEN--

I KNOW YOU DON'T LEAVE.
-UHHHEM- I'M GOING TO LEAVE. THIS IS EMBARRASSING. I THOUGHT WE COULD SIT AND DISCUSS THIS LIKE ADUL YOU'RE ACT IRRATION
NO SPITTING GAMBLING
WHAT WOULD YOU KNOW ABOUT BEING AN ADULT? YOU'VE NEVER TAKEN RESPONSIBILITY FOR ANYTHING IN YOUR LIFE!
YOU KNOW... AS YOU GET OLDER YOU'RE GOING TO FIND THAT YOU'LL BE LESS AND LESS HARSH IN YOUR JUDGEMENTS OF OTHERS. WE --
WELL, MAYBE I WON'T BUT THAT DOESN'T MEAN WHAT YOU DID WASN'T WRONG.
I'LL SEND YOUR REGARDS TO JOE!

DAD?
DELI
MUSIC
DELI DELI
UH OH...

WHAT WAS YOUR WORST JOB EVER?
I WAS THE ASSISTANT MANAGER OF A PATTY PALACE MY SENIOR YEAR OF HIGH SCHOOL.
NEXT!
JANE
ONE SUMMER I WORKED AS A LANDSCAPER.
(YOU THOUGHT I WAS GOING TO SAY THE BOOK STORE, RIGHT?)
FOR ONE DAY I WAS A BUSBOY AT A GOURMET DELI.
UMMM... MY JOB AT "A&J'S PIERCING SHACK" WAS PRETTY BORING.
THIS WAS IN ROCHESTER, MINNESOTA, SO YOU CAN IMAGINE.
BABY SITTER.
I WOULD HAVE TO SAY MY BABYSITTING JOB.
ONE TIME I WAS AN ASSISTANT TO THIS OLD CARTOONIST GUY WHO DID NOTHING BUT ABUSE ME.
I REMEMBER ONE TIME THEY MADE ME PENCIL A WHOLE ISSUE OF "CRIME CRACKERS" IN --
HEYYYY! WAIT A MINUTE!

TWENTY BUCKS, THEN?
UM... ARE... YOU'RE NOT A, UH, LIKE A COP, RIGHT?
FAREWELL
ME? HAHAHA! NO, I'M NOT A COP. COME ON, MY PLACE IS RIGHT AROUND THE CORNER.
UM... OKAY.
COLD NIGHT, HUH?
I GUESS.
OKAY! HERE WE ARE. RIGHT UP THESE STEPS... FOURTH DOOR... HOME SWEET HOME!
SO... WHAT DO YOU WANT, BABY?
WHOA! HEH, HEH! YOU IN A HURRY? JUST HOLD ON A SEC ... YOU WANT SOME COKE?
SURE
SNIFFFFFF--AHHHHHH--
SNIFFFFF--
SNIFSNIFF--OKAY, OKAY, NOW STAND RIGHT THERE, OKAY? NOW JUST TURN AROUND.. OKAY...
WHAT DO YOU WANT, BABY? TELL ME WHAT--
YEAH, JUST... OKAY, OKAY... DO YOU LIKE THAT?
WAIT, WHAT'RE--

HUH...HUH.... TELL ME YOU LIKE IT...
WHAT THE FUCK?! GET OFF--
NGH!
LET GO--- AACHHH! CHOKE!
YOU BITCH!!
ACCHCH COUGH COUGH
AHH
GASP
COUGH
NNGAHHHHHH!
AHH AHH AHH

SO, WAS LIKE DEREK MAD WHEN YOU TOLD HIM YOU WERE STILL GOING?
NEWS
YEAH, BUT WHO CARES? I WAS INVITED, SO I'M GONNA GO. IF HE DOESN'T WANT ME TO THAT'S HIS OWN PROBLEM! HMM... THIS WAY, I THINK.
Twilight Dance
MAYBE HE'S RIGHT, THOUGH. I MEAN YOU HAVE TO ADMIT COMING ALL THE WAY OUT TO BROOKLYN FOR A GOING AWAY PARTY FOR SOME PEOPLE YOU NEVER MET IS PRETTY WEIRD, CAPRICE.
SHERMAN SAID IT WAS JUST AN EXCUSE TO HAVE A PARTY. A LOT OF PEOPLE DON'T KNOW THEM.
UM. WILL ANYONE WE KNOW BE THERE? FROM LIKE SCHOOL?
HE DID SAY HE INVITED A FEW PEOPLE FROM THE BOOKSTORE.
GREAT! SO I WON'T KNOW ANYONE!
READY?
BZZZ!
TWEED
YEAH?
UM, HI, WE'RE HERE FOR THE PARTY? WE'RE FRIENDS OF SHERMAN'S?
OH! OKAY! I'M STEPHEN. COME ON IN, LADIES!

MAKE YOURSELF AT HOME. DRINKS ARE IN THE KITCHEN!
He gives me
(whatcha need?)
got? I need it all so badly!
I FIND
LACK OF
DISTURBING
AND LADY WAS
RAZY! SHE WOULD
YELL WHENEVER
WALKED DOWN
WOW!
HE IS
CUTIE!
YET WHEN THEY CALLED MR. FLAVOR ABOUT AN INTERVIEW FOR THEIR SHOW HE TURNED THEM DOWN!
WHAT?! WHY?!
WHY WON'T THEY REWIND?!
Our House! In the middle
GOOD BYE
CATTON
Whew! IT'S HOT IN HERE! OH, SHERMAN, THIS IS MY ROOM-MATE LEIA. LEIA: SHERMAN.
HI! HEH HEH!
NICE TO MEET YOU, LEIA! GLAD YOU GUYS COULD SHOW.
OH! HERE, LET ME SHOW YOU THE COAT ROOM.
JUST THROW THEM ON MY BED WITH THE REST.
THIS IS YOUR ROOM? WOW, WHAT A COOL CEILING!
IS THERE ANYONE ELSE FROM THE STORE HERE?

ALMOST FINISHED HER GOLDMAN BOOK, RIGHT? THAT'S
HAV BOYFR
So Whyyy Do you sit there and Crrry? And Whyyy... Don't you moan and sigh? ♫
ONNIE AND MARIE?
CAPRICE! HEY! GLAD YOU COULD MAKE IT!
♫ Won't you take me to... Funk-KAY town!
SO THIS GORILLA IS BEHIND THE BAR, RIGHT?
YEAH, FROM WHAT I SAW IT LOOKS LIKE A CUTE LITTLE HOUSE. ALMOST LIKE A FARM!
REALLY WANT QUIT THE BOOK STORE. THIS NEW MANAGER'S AWFUL!
PAIN! WHEN WILL IT END?!
ONE OF MY TRADEMARKED CHANGES OF HEART...
VEGATAR
I'M WRITING MY NEXT ESSAY ON THE INHERENT SEXISM IN NATURE.
JANE & STEVEN!!
HMMM? OH, YEAH! JANICE IS HERE, AND... WAIT, I GUESS SHE WAS BEFORE YOUR TIME. CLARISSA! SHE'S HERE. JOLIE SAID SHE'D COME BY.
UM... IS THERE LIKE A BATHROOM?
SURE. COME ON, I'LL SHOW YOU.
I HOPE YOU DIDN'T HAVE ANY TROUBLE FINDING US...

YEAH, OF COURSE PART OF ME WILL MISS THE CITY, BUT...
I DON'T KNOW, AFTER SEVEN YEARS IN THIS PEE-PEE SOAKED HECK HOLE WE'RE READY FOR A BREAK, Y'KNOW?
YOU KNOW WHAT THEY SAY: ONCE YOU MOVE OUT OF NEW YORK YOU NEVER MOVE BACK...
SO WHAT'S STEPHEN GOING TO DO ABOUT TEACHING? IS HE GOING TO COMMUTE FROM SANITARIA SPRINGS? THAT'S SOME DRIVE!
WELL, HE ONLY HAS CLASSES THREE DAYS A WEEK, SO HE'S WORKED OUT A DEAL TO STAY AT CATTON'S DURING THE SCHOOL WEEK.
STEPHEN'S ALREADY TALKED TO A NEARBY STATE SCHOOL ABOUT TEACHING THERE.
"PLUS HE'S FINALLY GOING TO START HIS T.R. BIOGRAPHY..."
T.R.? CHRIST, STEVE, THE LAST THING THE WORLD NEEDS IS ANOTHER TEDDY ROOSEVELT BIO!
OH! WHO SHOULD I DO, CATTON? YOUR PRECIOUS, POMPOUS JOHN ADAMS? PUH-LEASE!
OH, YEAH, THAT'S RIGHT! ADAMS ONLY MASTERMINDED THE AMERICAN FUCKING REVOLUTION! HE NEVER SHOT A RHINO OR WAGGLED HIS BIG STICK IN COLUMBIA'S FACE!
YEAH! AND HE NEVER WON THE NOBEL PEACE PRIZE, EITHER!
THE FACT THAT THE MOST WAR HUNGRY PRESIDENT UNTIL KENNEDY WON THE PRIZE F... PEACE IS LUDIC...
FELLAS! FELLAS!
NEITHER OF YOUR ALSO-RANS CAN COMPARE WITH THE MOST OVERLOOKED POLITICAL GENIUS OF THIS CENTURY:
UM... IS THIS WHERE THE BEER IS?

WILLIAM
HOWARD
TAFT.
HAHAHAHAHA! HAHAHAHA! HAHAHA! TAFT! GOOD ONE. HA! HA!
?
I'M SORRY, DID YOU SAY YOU NEEDED A BEER?
HEY, DOROTHY, THIS IS CAPRICE. SHE'S NEW AT THE BOOKSTORE.
HELLO. PLEASED TO MEET YOU.
HELLO, HEH.
I'M GOING TO THE KITCHEN FOR SOME DRINKS. CAN I GET YOU A REFILL?
SURE. SCREWDRIVER, EASY ON THE JUICE.
UM, I'LL JUST HAVE A BEER.
SO... SOME PARTY, HUH?
AC/DC
MMM HMM.
SO... DID YOU WORK WITH SHERMAN AT THE BOOKSTORE?
IT SEEMS LIKE HALF THE PEOPLE HERE WORKED AT MATTHEWS.
NO, ACTUALLY SHERMAN'S SORT OF MY BOYFRIEND.
?
REALLY? WOW, HE ... I DIDN'T KNOW HE HAD A GIRLFRIEND.

REALly.
SO HE'S NEVER MENTIONED ME. AT ALL.
UM. NO...
YEAH, SO ELIZABETH PIERBORNE HERSELF IS GOING TO DO THE STORY.!
"INSIDE SCOOP" IS COMING TO GRAND-SEQUON TO FILM MR. FLAVOR GETTING HIS BIG AWARD!
WOW, THAT SOUNDS LIKE FUN. I SHOULD TALK HERA INTO PAYING FOR ME TO GO TO THAT CONVENTION.
YOU KNOW, TO PROMOTE MY BOOK AND EVERYTHING.
THAT'S RIGHT! I HEARD YOU FINALLY FINISHED YOUR EMMA GOLDBERG BOOK! CONGRATULATIONS!
UH, YEAH. IT'S SUPPOSED TO HIT THE SHOPS NEXT MONTH.
THAT REMINDS ME: SHERMAN TOLD ME YOU GUYS ARE GETTING A PLACE TOGETHER.
YEAH, WE'VE LOOKED AT A FEW PLACES SO FAR.
BUT THE ONLY PLACES WE CAN AFFORD ARE EITHER RAT INFESTED SHOE-BOXES OR LIKE A SIX HOUR TRAIN RIDE FROM MANHATTAN...
OR BOTH.
SHERMAN TOLD ME THAT DOROTHY TOOK THE NEWS PRETTY HARD. APPARENTLY, SHE THOUGHT THEY WERE GOING TO LIVE TOGETHER.
REALLY? HUH...HE NEVER TOLD ME THAT. I HOPE I'M NOT MAKING ANY TROUBLE.
OH, PLEASE! THE TROUBLE WOULD BE IF HE DID MOVE IN WITH HER! YOU'RE DOING HIM A FAVOR.
UH! YOU'LL HAVE TO EXCUSE ME, ED, I HAVE TO MINGLE.

He's got a million doll
He's got a 37-year ol
HERE YOU GO: I BROUGHT YOU A BEER. A BEER, M'DEAR!
HEE! HEE!
OH! THANKS, LEIA. UH... YOU SEEM TO HAVE GOTTEN A HEAD START ON ME, HEH.
HEE HEE!
I WAS DOING SHOTS WITH THESE GUYS IN THE KITCHEN!
SHER-MAN! SHER-MAN! SHER-MAN! SHER-MAN!
YAY!!
WHOO! EAH!
JEEPERS! OKAY YOU GUYS, REALLY. I HAVE TO GET BACK!
THE LADIES ARE EXPECTING THEIR DRINKS!
AWWWW! WHI-KISH!
HEY, IS THAT GIRL WITH THE, UH, TANK TOP THE ONE YOU WERE TELLING ME ABOUT?
YUP. HELP ME BRING THESE IN, WOULD YA? YEAH, SO THAT'S HER. SHE...
AH, NEVER MIND.
AFTER ALL THESE YEARS, I KNOW EXACTLY WHAT THAT "NEVER MIND" MEANS.

♪ Let My Love open the door.. to your heart
HERE YOU GO! I HOPE YOU DON'T MIND IF IT'S -- HEY, WHERE DID DOROTHY GO?
THANKS... UM, I DON'T KNOW, REALLY. SHE JUST SORT OF...LEFT.
I DON'T KNOW WHAT I SAID.
OOH! I LOVE THIS SONG!!
UM... WHAT SHOULD I DO WITH DOROTHY'S DRINK?
OH! ED, THIS IS CAPRICE AND ... I'M SORRY, WHAT WAS IT?
LEIA! MY NAME IS LEIA!
IT'S GREAT TO MEET YOU, ED.
♥ SHERMAN TELLS ME YOU GUYS ARE GOING TO BE ROOMMATES.
GULP GULP GULP GULP GULP
UM...
SO, CAPRICE, I THOUGHT YOU WERE BRINGING YOUR BOYFRIEND?
HM? OH, HIM. WE... DEREK AND I ARE IN THE MIDDLE OF THIS BIG FIG
LEIA!
LEIA...
I WANT TO DANCE WITH YOU IN THE WORST WAY.

HeeHee! OKAY!
I... I CAN'T BELIEVE IT!
I KNOW! SHE TOLD ME SHE HATED GUYS WITH SHAVED HEADS!
NO, NO! IT'S... I'VE KNOWN ED FOR LIKE 2,000 YEARS AND I'VE NEVER SEEN HIM EVEN ASK A GIRL FOR THE TIME LET ALONE A DANCE!
HAS THE WORLD GONE UPSIDE DOWN?!
WELLLLL...
SOMETIMES THE WORLD NEEDS A GOOD SHAKE-UP.
HAHA! YOU'RE A GREAT DANCER!
REALLY?! THANKS!
YOU'RE NOT SO BAD YOURSELF ...LEIA.

I suppose that you're going to stay all night...
KIND OF LIKE
I'M TRYING TO STEAL THE COPIER FROM OUR OFFICE
WHEN ARE YOU GOING
SO
THEY WERE PLAYING AT
The Roof! The Roof is on fire!
THIS
WHAT?
I WAS JUST GETTING OFF THE SUBWAY WHEN I PUKED MY GUTS OUT!
1981?
HE'S A HOTTIE, NO ARGUMENT.
Y'KNOW, EVERYONE GOES ON AND ON ABOUT "GOODFELLAS" BUT I LIKED "CASINO" BETTER.
NO WAY!
YEAH, HE GOT ME "THE PLANETS" BY... FINNEY? FINLEY? IT WAS GOOD!
HAIR!
OVER!
SOME PARTY ALL RIGHT!
THE CITY.
KIKER'S BRAIN WAVES?
HER
I'M GONNA GET ANOTHER ROUND.
I'M GOING TO MISS THIS KITTY.

DOROTHY? WHAT'S GOING ON? WHAT'RE YOU, UH,
DOING?
NOTHING.
I...
I WANT TO APOLOGIZE FOR ALL THE HEADACHES I'VE CAUSED YOU AND JANE THIS WHOLE TIME.
I HOPE YOU GUYS ENJOY YOUR NEW LIFE IN SARATOGA SPRINGS AND I WISH YOU THE BEST OF LUCK.
IT'S SANITARIA SPRINGS.
BUT THANKS.
HOW COME YOU'RE NOT OUT WITH EVERYONE ELSE? I WAS ON MY WAY TO GET A DRINK. WANNA COME?
NAH. I'M ALL SET.
WANT SOME?
ISKY
hiskey
YEECH IT'S BEEN AWHILE SINCE I'VE DRANK AND NOW I REMEMBER WHY...

IT'S FUNNY. THIS PLACE SEEMS SO EMPTY.
YEAH. WE TOOK MOST OF OUR STUFF UP ALREADY.
"GOODBYE, CITY LIFE!"
HEY, LET ME BUM ONE OF THOSE OFF OF YOU, HUH?
REALLY?! SINCE WHEN DOES JANE LET YOU SMOKE?
AHHH, SHE DOESN'T.
ACTUALLY, I QUIT A LONG TIME AGO--IN COLLEGE-- BUT WHENEVER I DRINK THE URGE COMES BACK.
YEAH. SHERMAN KEEPS HOUNDING ME TO QUIT. HE'S PROBABLY RIGHT BUT... YOU KNOW.
WELL, HE IS RIGHT. IT'S A FILTHY HABIT.
MMM! LEMME SEE IF I CAN STILL...
VERY EXCELLENT! LET ME SHOW YOU MY FAVORITE. EVEN SHERMAN LIKES THIS ONE...
COUGHCOUGH
HEM
YOU GET THE IDEA.

YEAH.
DOES, UH.
DOES SHERMAN EVER, LIKE... TALK ABOUT ME?
WHAT DO YOU MEAN? LIKE BAD STUFF BEHIND YOUR BACK? NO.
NO, NO, I DON'T MEAN THAT. MORE LIKE...
WAIT: WHY? DOES HE SAY BAD STUFF ABOUT ME? UGH! DO I EVEN WANT TO KNOW?!
NO. NO! I MEAN, IT'S LIKE, Y'KNOW EVERYONE COMPLAINS ABOUT THEIR LIKE GIRL-FRIENDS. Y'KNOW, FROM TIME TO TIME.
YOU KNOW...
WHAT... WHAT KIND OF THINGS DOES HE SAY? WHEN HE... COMPLAINS.?
UM... WELL... I DON'T KNOW IF I SHOULD...
UM...
HE DOESN'T REALLY SAY...
UH... I HEARD ABOUT THE WHOLE, UH, APARTMENT THING.
SORRY IT DIDN'T WORK OUT.

THE SCENE WHERE EMMA IS ADDRESSING THE UNION SQUARE CROWD WAS FANTASTIC!
HeeHee! THANKS.
SIGGLY CHIP?
SIGGLY CHIPS
YEAH, THOSE CROWD SCENES TOOK FOREVER. BUT I WOULD AMUSE MYSELF PUTTING MY FRIENDS IN...
I'M SURE YOU'D RECOGNIZE A FEW F--
OH, HEY.
RIGHT. WHAT'S ALL THIS THEN?
AH, NOTHIN'. WE WERE JUST... TALKING ABOUT SOME THINGS.
Sniff!

HAHA! SO SHE SAYS "THINK YOU VEDDY MOCK!" AND PUTS THE BOOK DOWN!
HAHAHA! MAN! HEHHEH!
It's no use. He sees her. He starts to shake and cough.
HEY.
HEY! WHAT?
HOW COME YOU NEVER TOLD ME ABOUT DOROTHY?
HUH? WHAT DO YOU MEAN? DIDN'T I?
WELL, I, UH GUESS SHE NEVER CAME UP.
HUH.
HEY!
STEPHEN WANTS TO TALK TO YOU. IT SEEMS BEATRICE IS HAVING SOME KIND OF COLLAPSE.
OH, GOD. WHERE IS SHE? WHAT'S WRONG?
YOU GOT ME. STEPHEN'S TALKING TO HER AND NEXT THING SHE STARTS BAWLING.
SHE'S IN MY STUDIO.

CLAP CLAP CLAP CLAP CLAP CLAP CLAP
HEH HEH! THAT WAS FUN!
YEAH! I SHOULD DO THIS MORE OFTEN!
UM... I'M GONNA GO GET A DRINK! I'LL BE RIGHT BACK!
OH, I THINK I SEE CAPRICE CALLING ME OVER! EXCUSE ME!
I KNOW THIS MAY COME AS A SHOCK, BUT I THINK SHE MAY HAVE BEEN DRINKING! Heh Heh.
Y'KNOW, I BET THAT'S WHAT YOU'LL MISS THE MOST, RIGHT?
THESE GREAT OPPORTUNITIES TO MAKE, UH, WITTY, DEMEANING REMARKS ABOUT SOMEONE I LOVE?
BUT... SHE...
SORRY.

OH MY GOD! DOROTHY! IS SHE OKAY?!
UM, YEAH. IT LOOKS LIKE IT HIT HER ALL AT ONCE WHEN SHE TRIED TO STAND UP.
'M SO SORRY!
SNIFF
THANKS, STEPHEN. SORRY ABOUT THE MESS!
WOULDN'T BE A PARTY WITHOUT A FEW SURPRISES, RIGHT? DON'T WORRY ABOUT IT.
HELP ME PICK OUT A NEW SHIRT, HUH?
ARE YOU OKAY, SWEETIE?
YEAH, 'M OGAY. I JUS' GOT UP TOO FAST...
SNIFF
OH, I'M SO SORRY, SWEETIE!
IT'S OKAY. COME ON, LET'S LAY DOWN SOMEWHERE, OKAY? COME ON...
I'M... I'M NOT GONNA DRING... I'M NOT DRINGIN' ANYMORE, 'KAY?
SHHH, IT'S OKAY. DON'T WORRY ABOUT THAT NOW. COME ON...
AN', AN', I'M NOT GONNA BE A SLOB ANYMORE AN' I'LL BE NICE'N'CLEAN!
RILLY!
JUST STAY WITH ME.

HMM?
OKAY, LET'S JUST GET IN AND LAY YOU DOWN. I'LL JUST --
??
!
UMMM... HEH.
HOW'S IT GOING?
WH..?
OH MY GOD.
OH! JAMES! HERE'S THAT DARN CONTACT!
FOUND IT!
WELL, THAT'S A RELIEF! COME ON, LET'S MOVE IT ALONG.
JESUS! ON MY BED NO LESS!
SHITSHITSHIT SHITSHITSHIT
HeeHee! SORRY, BUDDY!
LET ME JUST MOVE THE COATS.
HOW MUCH DID YOU DRINK ANYWAY?
THINK YOU CAN GET YOUR SHOES OFF?
HehHeh... IF YOU CAN STOP THE BED FROM SPINNING..
I LOVE YOU, SWEETIE.
I LOVE YOU, TOO. SO YOUR SHOES WILL BE RIGHT HERE BY THE BED OKAY?

WAIT WAIT WAITWAIT! WHERE'RE YOU GOIN'?
UM... I WAS GOING BACK TO THE PARTY.
LAY DOWN FOR A SPELL AND--
OHHHH! NO! STAY! STAY HERE WITH ME...
C'MON! I'LL FEEL BETTER'N A LIDDLE BIT. JUS' LAY DOWN WITH ME F'R...
COME ON! C'MERE...
SO JANE SAID YOU WERE PRETTY UPSET. WHAT'S THE MATTER?
PSSSH!
JANE CAN KISS MY FINE, FAT ASS!
HEH HEH... I
I JUS' DRANG TOO MUCH 'TSALL.
SOME PARTY. YOU SHOULD SEE ED! HE--
HEY! WHAT WAS ZAT STORY YOU TOL' ME? Y'KNOW?
THE ONE WHERE Y' STOLED YER COUSINS DOLL?
WHO, DR. IMPULSE?
HE WAS NO "DOLL."

NOT ONLY WAS HE THE COOLEST ACTION FIGURE IN A DECADE FULL OF COOL ACTION FIGURES, HE WAS THE ONLY ONE I NEEDED TO COMPLETE MY "SATURNAUTS" COLLECTION...
COME ON! I'LL TRADE YOU BIOTRON
AND MY COLONIAL VIPER
AND MY SET OF YANKEE CARDS!
AND MY COUSIN ANDY WAS THE ONLY ONE OF US WHO HAD ONE.
NO WAY!
NO WAY, MAN.
BESIDES, YOU TOLD ME YOU'RE MISSING RON GUIDRY!
BEEP BEEP YA ASS!
IT DROVE ME CRAZY BECAUSE HE DIDN'T EVEN CARE ABOUT DR. IMPULSE! HE LET HIS DOG CHEW ON IT, HE ALMOST RAN OVER IT WITH A LAWN MOWER-- HE'D LEAVE HIM LAYING AROUND ANYWHERE!
ONE OF THESE DAYS HE WAS GOING TO--
?
I FOUND HIM (DR. IMPULSE, NOT ANDY) LAYING IN THE BACK YARD. ANDY AND MY BROTHER WERE OFF PLAYING IN THE STREET OR SOMETHING...
I HID HIM ON A LEDGE IN THE SEWER. I'D GET HIM OUT RIGHT BEFORE MY MOM PICKED US UP.
IT WAS THE PERFECT CRIME.
IT WAS A STUPID PLAN. HOW WOULD I EXPLAIN WHERE I SUDDENLY GOT THIS RARE ACTION FIGURE?
HOW DID IT GET ALL CHEWED UP
I DIDN'T TH
SNFFFX

ZZZZZ
WHOA, ED! TAKE IT EASY. YOU'RE GOING TO MAKE YOUR FLESH WEAK.
YOU WERE REALLY CUTTING THE RUG WITH THAT FRIEND OF CAPRICE'S. HOW'S THAT GOING?
WELL-- URP
AS LONG AS I KEEP DRINKING I'M OKAY. BUT... UH...
AS SOON AS I START THINKING CLEARLY IT HITS ME THAT I'M, UH, TALKING TO A CUTE GIRL WITH BIG BREASTS, AN' I ...UH...
I LIKE FREEZE UP.
AW, COME ON, ED!
JUST BE YOURSELF AND SHE'LL FIND YOU CHARMING.
WHERE'D THEY GO, ANYWAY?
I'M HAVING A GOOD TIME, Y'KNOW.
I DON'T KNOW. WE'LL SEE WHAT HAPPENS.
I THINK HE, LIKE, LIKES YOU.
I DON'T KNOW.
HE'S GOT A GIRLFRIEND, LEE.

I KNOW. ISN'T IT EXCITING? THE FORBIDDEN?
COLLEGE IS SO COOL!
PLUS DEREK AND I HAVE BEEN LIKE FIGHTING ALL THE TIME. IT'S REALLY...
Sigh
PART OF ME THINKS I CAME TO THIS PARTY HOPING SOMETHING WOULD HAPPEN SO I WOULD BE PUSHED INTO...
Y'KNOW, SO THINGS BETWEEN US WOULD...
OH! HEY, LADIES! ED SAID YOU WERE OUT HERE. MIND IF WE JOIN YOU?
SURE, COME ON OUT. HEY, CAN YOU BRING US SOME BEERS?
HERE YOU GO!
Whew! THIS COLD AIR FEELS GOOD OUT HERE.
THANKS.
UMMMM...
ACTUALLY, IT'S A BIT TOO NIPPY FOR ME OUT HERE. I'LL MEET YOU INSIDE CAPRICE.
CAN YOU HELP ME IN, ED?
OH, OKAY.
I'LL SEE YOU LATER, LEE.

SO, LEIA, DO YOU WANT TO DANCE AGAIN?
I GUESS SO. DANCING'S FUN.
BOTTOMS UP!
Heh Heh...

:SIGH: COME ON, WE SHOULD GET BACK TO THIS THING BEFORE WE'RE MISSED.
MMMMM... OKAY.
Whew.! I NEEDED THAT, THOUGH.
LOTHES
SO WHAT WAS DOROTHY SO UPSET ABOUT ANYHOW?
AH, YOU KNOW. I GUESS HER AND SHERMAN ARE HAVING A ROUGH PATCH, HUN.
THE USUAL RELATIONSHIP INSECURITIES. PLUS, I THINK SHE WAS MORE UPSET ABOUT THE APARTMENT THING THAN SHE LET ON.
GREAT.! NOW THAT WE'RE MOVING AWAY, THEY BREAK UP.! CAN YOU HAND ME THAT HAIR THING?
HAHA. YOU KNOW, FOR ALL OF YOUR COMPLAINING, I THINK YOU'RE SECRETLY GOING TO MISS HAVING HER AROUND.
UMMER CLOTHES
HEHHEH...
HAHA HA.!
HEH.
NOOOOOOO WAY.

UMMM... CAN WE LIKE SLIDE DOWN A LITTLE?
Some of them are "Davids" but most of us are "Daves"...
STINKY ALE

WHAT ABOUT YOU? DID YOU GO?
THE PROM? JESUS, I HAVEN'T THOUGHT ABOUT THAT IN YEARS.
BUT, UH, YEAH. I WENT TO MY PROM.
HMM. IS THERE A TALE BEHIND THE NOTE OF BITTERNESS I HEAR?
CONFESS IT, PAL!
STOP! GO BACK! DON'T EVEN CONSIDER IT!
WHAT? CONSIDER WHAT?
WELL, THERE'S NO STORY, REALLY. WHICH I GUESS IS THE PROBLEM. MY GIRLFRIEND AT THE TIME WAS... WELL, CATHOLIC.
Very Catholic
IF YOU, UH, CATCH MY, LIKE DRIFT...
HEE HEE! OH, POOR BABY! HOW LONG DID YOU TWO GO OUT?
UMM... ABOUT THREE YEARS OR SO.
YOU KNOW.
THREE YEARS?! SO WAIT: DID SHE EVER CAVE IN? DID YOU GUYS EVER, LIKE, UH, CONSUMATE YOUR, UH...
NOPE. PATHETIC, ISN'T IT? BELIEVE ME, I TRIED BUT SHE WAS "SAVING HERSELF."
I THINK IT'S KIND OF SWEET! THAT YOU CARED ENOUGH FOR HER TO WAIT THREE YEARS.
HAHA! I DON'T THINK I COULD'VE DONE IT!
KISSING THIS GIRL.

SO... YOU HINTED THAT THERE WAS A STORY ABOUT YOUR PROM?
SOMETHING SPICY, I HOPE? HEH HEH.
LET'S SAY THAT MY DATE, ERIK, WASN'T NEARLY AS... PATIENT AS YOU WERE.
BUT THAT ISN'T THE FUN PART, THOUGH.
I DON'T KNOW...
I GET THE FEELING SHE WANTS ME TO KISS HER.
NO WAY.
WHAT ABOUT DOROTHY?
WO OF US... ALONE OUT HERE. IT'S PERFECT.
I WONDER WHAT IT WOULD FEEL LIKE? IT'S BEEN SO LONG SINCE I'VE KISSED A GIRL WHO DIDN'T SMOKE.
AT THE TIME OF THE 'ROM, I'D JUST BROKEN IP WITH THIS GUY, JERRY, VHO WAS LIKE A YEAR OLDER.
HE DIDN'T HANDLE IT VERY WELL. I HAD TO GET, LIKE, A RESTRAINING ORDER AGAINST HIM!
HE WAS LIKE A TOTAL PSYCHO. HE WOULD CALL UP MY HOUSE AND, LIKE, THREATEN ME AND MY PARENTS AND SHIT LIKE THAT. I MEAN HE WAS REALLY CRAZY.
WOW.
JUST ONE TIME.
DO IT, ASSHOLE!
SHE MADE A POINT OF TELLING ME SHE WAS BREAKING UP WITH HER BOYFRIEND.
WENT OUT OF HER WAY TO TELL ME!
HAT ABOUT YOUR GIRLFRIEND?
CAME TO THIS PARTY WITHOUT HIM.
NE LITTLE PECK.
VEN KNOW HOW UT WITH HIM IG AS I DID. REALLY MEAN.
ANYWAY, SO I GO TO THE PROM WITH THIS GUY ERIK. EVERYTHING'S GOING GREAT. WE'RE AT THE RAMADA AND DANCING AND ALL.
SUDDENLY, I SEE JERRY COME IN TO THE, LIKE, HALL!
UH HUH.
DIDN'T I READ THAT WHEN A WOMAN FIDDLES WITH HER HAIR IT MEANS SHE'S INTERESTED?
BOY, I'M A REAL CLASS ACT, HUH? MY GIRLFRIEND IS PASSED OUT, SICK IN MY BED AND THE FIRST THING I DO IS MAKE A PASS AT SOME GIRL.
SHEER-FUCKING-CLASS.

SO AFTER THAT, ERIK WAS A LITTLE RATTLED, BUT WE ALL JUST WENT ON WITH THE NIGHT.
OKAY, SO AT OUR TABLE WAS THIS GIRL JOANIE, WHO WAS ERIK'S FRIEND'S DATE. SO SHE WAS REALLY FREAKED OUT!
SO BY THAT TIME WE WERE ALL REALLY, LIKE, WASTED. SO WE PILED INTO THE LIMO TO GO TO DENNY'S.
WOW! SO WHAT DID YOU DO? JEEZ!
OKAY! OKAY! I WON'T DO ANYTHING.
STILL...
WOULDN'T IT FEEL NICE?
THINKING MUCH AND JUST DO IT!
SEVENTH ONE.
I CAN'T
WARM LIPS. I WONDER HOW SHE'S GOING TO KISS.
OPEN HER MOUTH...
TONGUE...
I'LL BET SHE'S A GREAT KISSER.
A VIRGIN? IT DOESN'T
WHOA! WAIT A SECOND! WE'RE TALKING A KISS HERE! LET'S NOT GET CRAZY!!
WE WOULD JUST HAVE THAT ONE KISS, THEN I WOULD STOP! I SWEAR!
"CAPRICE... I--I CAN'T DO THIS!"
HEROIN!
DOROTHY WOULD NEVER EVEN KNOW!
I'D KNOW.
OF CONTROL!
TAKE ADVANTAGE OF IT!
CROWDED PARTY! OF COURSE SHE'LL FIND OUT!
FUCK NOT?! LET ME DO SOMETHING CRAZY FOR ONCE!
ACT ON IMPULSE INSTEAD OF USING YOUR FUCKING HEAD ALL THE TIME!
TAKE HER!
JUST LEAN OVER AND PRESS YOUR LIPS TO HERS...
THEN MOVE TO HER CHEEK...
THEN DOWN HER NECK... TO HER SHOULDERS...
HOW WOULD YOU FEEL IF DOROTHY DID THE SAME THING?!
WHERE DO I SIGN UP?
HAVE ANOTHER
YOU CAN JUSTIFY THIS ALL YOU WANT: IT'S A BETRAYAL.
THAT'S WHAT JUDAS
IT'S JUST ONE KISS!

OH BOY, I'M SORRY! BORING YOU WITH THIS LONG BORING STORY ABOUT MY STUPID PROM!
WHEN I GET DRUNK I TEND TO, LIKE, RAMBLE.
NO, NO! IT WAS A GREAT STORY! SOUNDS LIKE YOUR PROM WAS WAY MORE EXCITING THAN MINE.
ARE YOU REALLY DRUNK? YOU DON'T SEEM LIKE IT.
HEE HEE! MAYBE IT DOESN'T SHOW ON THE OUTSIDE...
BUT ON THE INSIDE I'M ALL A FLUTTER.
HOW... WHAT ABOUT YOU?
HEHHEH..... I GUESS I'M A LITTLE BUZZED...
YOU LOVE DOROT
ONE KISS
"CAPRICE...WAIT. I CAN'T DO THIS."
"WE CAN'T DO THIS."
DO I
LOOK AT HER SHOULDERS. THEY'RE ALL GOOSE BUMPY.
SOFT...FLESHY SHOULDERS...
TOP. STOP!
WHOA
THAT'S YOUR CUE!
BATTLESTATIONS! ALL HANDS BRACE FOR IMPACT!!
LUCK SEVE
I BETTER HURRY THIS UP... IT'S GETTING COLD OUT HERE.
SEIZE DAY!
DON'T KNOW IT FEELS WARM TO ME...
DO IT! DO
DO IT!
THIS IS IT!
DON'T! IT'LL BE A SHORT TERM THRILL FOR A LONG-TERM HEARTACHE!!
"SOMETIMES THE WORLD NEEDS A GOOD SHAKE-UP."
YOU THINK THIS IS COLD WAIT UNTIL YOU SEE DOROTHY
I FELT THAT DOWN TO MY TOES!
ONE YOU'RE WITH...

I'm happy Standing on my feet of clay...
LUCKY
SHE'LL BE THE SEVENTH GIRL I'VE KISSED.
WAIT, SEVEN OR EIGHT?
SOFT... FLESHY
DO IT!
OH, OKAY! STEPHEN CAN HAVE SEX WITH FORTY-NINE GIRLS AND YOU'RE WORRIED ABOUT KISSING YOUR SEVENTH?
FIRST OF ALL,
WITH THIS!
EIGHTH
HOLD ON: SALLY, ANNE. VICKY. CHRISSY...
DON'T FORGET DOROTHY
OOH! VICKY WAS A GOOD ONE!
FOR GOD'S SAKE
AND KISS HER!
DO IT!
OH YEAH! SHE WAS A
THE ONE WITH THE GLASSES? BROWN HAIR?
WHICH ONE WAS ANNE?
DOROTHY. UM... LISA?... LAURA!
HMM...
THAT'S SIX
OKAY, SO CAPRICE WILL BE NUMBER SEVEN.
IT! IT'S NOT TOO LATE TO TURN BACK!
HERE GOES NOTHING.

AREN!
WAIT! KAREN!
FROM SCHOOL
SO CAPRICE ILL BE EIGHT.
SHE'S NUMBER SEVEN!
HAT'S RIGHT! ORGOT ABOUT HER!
EASY TO SEE WHY...
I CAN'T BELIEVE ING THIS.!!
OH YEAH!
OKAY! NOW! MAKE YOUR MOVE!
UH... EXCUSE ME, WHERE'S THAT HAND GOING?
SHE WANTS ME TO KISS HER! CAN SENSE IT!
HAND?
WHAT? NOTHING!
NOWHERE! IT'S A HARMLESS GESTURE OF AFFECTION!
ALL SYSTEMS GO!
THIS IS WRONG! MOVE HAND!
STOP! S STOP! STO
WHAT IF SHE DOESN'T WANT ME TO? I'M MAKING AN ASS OUT OF MYSELF!
IF SHE DIDN'T NT YOU TO SHE'D ELL YOU TO MOVE YOUR HAND!
ROCK AND UCKING ROLL!
LESHY BUTTOCKS...
"CAPRICE WE CAN'T DO THIS! I... YOU'RE REALLY ATTRACTIVE AND ALL..."
HERE WE GO!
"AND I WOULD LOVE TO TAKE YOU RIGHT HERE AND ALL..."

YAHOO!
HERE GOES...
SORRY....
JESUS EFFIN CHR
NUMBER EIGHT!
"CAPRICE, WAIT! I... I CAN'T!
SHIT! THIS IS WRONG!
MY HEART'S EATING IN MY THROAT...
ONE KISS!
SO EXCITING!
FIVE UTES?
SIX MONTHS?
EVEN GES!
HOW LONG HAVE WE BEEN SITTING LIKE THIS
STOP!! PULL BACK!!
OOSE BUMPS...
THIS IS SCARY...
OR AM I ANING IN?
IS SH TREMBLING OR IS IT ME?
HOLY SHIT!
"CAPRICE, WAIT! I... I CAN'T DO THIS!"
UT! HERE WE GO!
OH BOY!
SHE'S LEANING IN...
WHAT ABOUT DOROTHY?!
DO THIS YOU'LL JUST AS BAD R FATHER
NOT A DREAM AT AN ALTERNATE EALITY!
"AND I WOULD LOVE TO RUB MY DOWN ALL BODY...
BREATHE, DAMMI
YOU'RE A GUY! GUY'S CHEAT!
IT'S HUMAN NATURE!
SHIT, I'M REALLY DOING THIS, AREN'T I?
DAMN RIGHT YOU ARE!!
WOULD YOU STOP ACTING LIKE A FAGGOT AND JUST KISS HER ALREADY?!
NO, IT'S ASSHOLE NATURE.
DO IT
THIS SO EXCITIN

♫ Woke up, fell out of bed, dragged a comb ac
WHAT'S WRONG?
HeeHee! I'VE NEVER KISSED A GUY WITH A MUSTACHE. IT'S SO TICKLEY!
I'M REALLY GLAD CAPRICE TALKED ME INTO COMING TO THIS PARTY!
I HOPE SHE'S HAVING FUN.
SO, DO YOU LIKE GO TO SCHOOL?
WHO, ME? NO, I, UH...AHEM GRADUATED ALL
UH
ALREADY.
THAT'S COOL. WHAT DID YOU MAJOR IN?
I'M PROBABLY GONNA PICK
PSYCH.
OR LAW. PSYCH OR LAW.
REALLY? I GUESS... THAT'S GOOD. IT...
SAY, DO YOU WANT ANOTHER DRINK? I'LL GET ONE FOR EACH OF US! I'LL BE BACK IN A SECOND!
♫ one banana, two banana three banana four....
ED.
ED, ED, ED, ED! THAT I SHOULD LIVE TO SEE THE DAY MY BOY ED BECOMES A MAN...!
UH, THANKS, JAMES, BUT I DON'T THINK IT'S GONNA HAPPEN.
"NOT GONNA--?!" ED, YOU GUYS WERE GOING AT IT LIKE AN ENDANGERED SPECIES OUT THERE!
THIS GIRL'S READY TO TAKE A LETTER AND YOU ARE THE MAN WITH THE DICTAPHONE, MY FRIEND!

I DON'T KNOW. I THINK I NEED A DRINK.
EVERYTIME I TALK TO HER I FEEL LIKE I'M GOING TO THROW UP.
SIGH
SO DON'T TALK TO HER!
SHIT, ED, YOU GOTTA RELAX! SHE SEEMS TO LIKE YOU SO DON'T WORRY, JUST GO WITH THE FLOW!
WHAT'RE YOU DRINKING, BIG GUY?
WHISKEY. STRAIGHT. OH, UH, AND A SCREWDRIVER FOR HER, PLEASE.
COMIN' RIGHT UP, CHIEF.
YEAH, YOU'RE DOING FINE. THE TRICK IS TO HAVE GOOD SELF-ESTEEM. WHEN YOU'RE FOOLING AROUND WITH THIS GIRL, TELL YOURSELF SHE DOESN'T DESERVE YOU.
SHE SHOULD BE HONORED YOU EVEN LOOK AT HER STUCK UP ASS!
UH. SHE SHOULD?
OF COURSE!
GIRLS... WOMEN ARE LIKE BEES: THEY CAN SMELL FEAR. IF YOU GO INTO ANY SO-CALLED ROMANTIC SITUATION WITH ANYTHING LESS THAN 100% SENSE OF CONFIDENCE...
IF YOU GO IN THINKING "OH, OH, I'M FAT AND I HAVE A BIG NOSE AND, OH, MY DICK IS TOO SMALL. SHE MIGHT NOT LIKE ME" THAN YOU WON'T LAST TWO MINUTES!
BUT! IF YOU GO IN THERE, READY TO GO, TELLING YOURSELF: "I CAN NAIL THIS GIRL IF I WANT!"
"SHE YEARNS FOR ME."
"MAYBE I'LL GIVE HER A THRILL AND GIVE HER A TASTE OF ED."
"MAYBE I'LL DO HER."
"UNLESS, MAYBE, THERE'S A HALF-WAY DECENT EPISODE OF, SAY, "THE ROCKFORD FILES" ON, IN WHICH CASE THIS BITCH CAN HIT THE FUCKING ROAD."
"SORRY, MISSY."
PYRAMID

IF THIS IS YOUR ATTITUDE?
YOU'LL HAVE HER EATING OUT OF THE PALM OF YOUR HAND, BOSS!
NOW GET BACK THERE AND SHOW'ER WHAT YOU GOT.!!
THANKS, JAMES!
ROCKFORD FILES! ROCKFORD FILES! ROCKFORD FILES!
UH, EVERYBODY? CAN I HAVE YOUR ATTENTION?
OKAY, SO THIS MAY BE THE SCOTCH TALKING, BUT AT THIS JUNCTURE, I'D LIKE YOU ALL TO JOIN ME IN A TOAST.
STEPHEN, OLD BEAN, WHILE I CONFESS I'M GOING TO MISS OUR SEEMINGLY ENDLESS DEBATES--
ABOUT THE FOUNDING FATHERS, THE ROLE OF WOMEN DURING THE CIVIL WAR, THE, THE MANLINESS OF TEDDY ROOSEVELT--
I WANT TO TAKE THIS TIME TO WISH YOU AND JANE THE BEST OF LUCK ON YOUR NEW COUNTRY ESTATE.
"YOU ARE, AND ALWAYS SHALL BE, MY FRIEND."
LNU
CLAP! CLAP! CLAP! CLAP! CLAP! CLAP! CLAP!

HAHA..(HE KNOWS I HATE IT WHEN HE CALLS HIM "TEDDY")
UM, ANYWAY, I GUESS THIS IS AS GOOD A TIME AS ANY TO THANK YOU ALL FOR COMING TO OUR LITTLE FAREWELL SHINDIG.
I'M, UH, GLAD YOU COULD ALL COME AND, UH...
WE'LL BOTH MISS ALL OF YOU VERY MUCH.
SO... THANK YOU ALL AGAIN FOR YOUR FRIENDSHIP AND SUPPORT OVER THE YEARS.
YOU'RE... YOU'RE A SWELL BUNCH OF FOLKS.
THERE YOU ARE! I WAS STARTING TO THINK YOU WERE GONNA LIKE STAND ME UP.
HEH, NO. SOMEBODY JUST STARTED TALKING TO ME IN THE KITCHEN. HERE'S YOUR DRINK!
THANKS! SO WHEN DID... ?!
UM, IS THERE LIKE ORANGE JUICE IN THIS?
UHHH... IT'S A SCREWDRIVER, SO PROBABLY.
OH, I SHOULD'VE TOLD YOU: I'M LIKE ALLERGIC TO IT.

OH, OKAY... WELL I GUESS WE CAN TRADE.
(I SORT OF DRANK HALF OF MINE...)
REALLY? YOU DON'T MIND? THANKS.
YOU'RE SUCH A NICE GUY.
GEE, THANKS.
ROCKFORD FILES! ROCKFORD FILES!
DO I LOOK LIKE SOMEONE FAMOUS TO YOU? EVERY TIME I RIDE THE SUBWAY, I FEEL LIKE PEOPLE ARE STARING AT ME.
REALLY?
I TOLD MY ROOMMATE THAT AND CAN YOU BELIEVE HE SAID THAT WAS CONCEITED?
THAT'S WEIRD.
SO... DO YOU WANNA DANCE AGAIN OR SOMETHING?
SURE, DANCING'S GOOD... FOR STARTERS.
CHEERS, BABY DOLL!
Hee Hee!
I KNOW! I DIDN'T SAY I LOOKED LIKE A BEAUTIFUL PERSON! I JUST THINK PEOPLE ARE CONFUSING ME WITH SOMEONE ELSE.
SO COME ON, STUDLY, LETS GO!
HEH HEH, OKAY! OKAY! JUST LET ME...
JUST LET ME.....
?!
YOU KNOW, LIKE ... MADONNA OR SOMEBODY.

JUST LET ME FINISH.. FIN GULP!
UM, WHAT'S THE MATTER? ARE YOU OKAY?
LEIA... I THINK...
SOMEBODY
PUT SOMETHING
SOMEBODY PUT SOMETHING IN MY DRI---
OH, ED, ED, ED, NO!
HAVE YOU EVER HEARD OF SYLVIA PLATH? SHE'S A POET.
UH, YEAH, THAT'S GREAT! YOU'LL HAVE TO EXCUSE ME, EVELYN!
EVELyn! IT'S EVELyn!
HEY! LOOKS LIKE YOUR FRIEND'S GIVING YOU SOME TROUBLE.
OH MY GOD! I DON'T KNOW WHAT HAPPENED! WE WERE GONNA DANCE...
IT'S OKAY. HE PROBABLY JUST DRANK TOO MUCH. HELP ME GET HIM OVER HERE...

MMMMM....
WAIT!
WHAT? WHAT'S THE MATTER?!
SHERMAN, WE... WE SHOULDN'T DO THIS. I CAN'T.
BUT--!
WHAT DO YOU MEAN? WE'RE NOT... WE...
YOU'RE RIGHT.
YOU'RE PROBABLY RIGHT.
WE SHOULDN'T.

I DON'T... I'M SORRY.
NO, THERE'S NOTHING TO BE SORRY ABOUT.
IT WAS JUST... A THING. IT DOESN'T MATTER.
DON'T FEEL BAD.
UM... SORRY WE DID IT OR SORRY WE STOPPED?
HAHA! I...
IT'S GETTING COLD. WE SHOULD GET BACK IN.
I GUESS YOU'RE RIGHT.
SO... WHAT DO WE...UH, DO?
MAYBE LIKE YOU SAID: IT WAS JUST, LIKE, A THING.
NO BIG DEAL.
RIGHT?

RIGHT.
YOU KNOW, IT ONLY JUST OCCURRED TO ME: I'M FINALLY GOING TO HAVE TO GET A DRIVER'S LICENSE!
THAT'S RIGHT! CITY MOUSE HAS NEVER DRIVEN!
YEAH, JANE'S GOING TO START TEACHING ME AS SOON AS WE GET--
HELLO, WHAT'S THIS?
HE SORT OF PASSED OUT. WE DIDN'T KNOW WHERE ELSE TO PUT HIM.
HMMM. EVERYONE'S GOING TO NEED THEIR COATS. CAN WE MAYBE MOVE HIM TO THE FLOOR?
WE COULD JUST GET THE COATS OUT FROM UNDER HIM.
SHIT! HE'S DROOLING ON MY SCARF!
LET'S GET THESE--OH MY GOD! YOU'RE BACK!
YEAH. YOU, LIKE, READY TO SPLIT? IT'S LATE.
OH MY GOD! ED!
WHAT HAPPENED?
SO WHAT HAPPENED? ARE YOU SURE YOU WANT TO GO? WE COULD STAY IF YOU WANT.
NAH. SHERMAN CALLED A CAR SERVICE. THEY'LL BE HERE IN A FEW MINUTES.

WELL, THANKS FOR COMING. I HOPE YOU HAD AN OKAY TIME.
YEAH, IT WAS FUN!
HEH HEH, I HOPE HIS PASSING OUT DIDN'T R--
JAMES! WHEN YOU BROUGHT ED IN HERE WAS DOROTHY HERE? ON THE BED?
NO, BUT WE HAVEN'T GOTTEN TO THE BOTTOM OF THE COATS YET. MAYBE--
JESUS! SHIT! FUCK!
I'LL BE RIGHT BACK!
WAIT, WHAT'S THE --?
UM... THERE'S SOME CAR WAITING OUT-SIDE DOWNSTAIRS.
THAT'LL BE FOR US. READY?
ONE SECOND!
BYE, JED.
THANKS FOR COMING, LADIES!
GOOD LUCK AT YOUR NEW PAD.
TELL SHERMAN I SAID GOOD-BYE AND I'LL SEE HIM AT WORK.

♫ CUZ THERE'S A MAN IN YA, GNAWING YA, TEARING YA INTO TWO...
I THINK IT'S A GREAT IDEA, JANEY! JUST LET US KNOW WHAT TO DO ON OUR END.
TERRIFIC! IT'S A REALLY BIG CONVENTION SO
JANE!
SORRY! SORRY! BUT, UH, HAVE YOU SEEN DOROTHY?
UMM, NOT LATELY. SHE LEFT LIKE TWENTY MINUTES AGO.
OH, THIS IS HERA, MY PUB--
TWENTY--?! DID SHE SEEM, Y'KNOW, LIKE SHE, UH, WAS, LIKE, UPSET OR... BETRAYED...
or anything?
?!?
NNNNNNOOOO. I MEAN, NOT VISIBLY BETRAYED.
WHY? WHAT'S--
SHERMAN?
THIS IS A MANHATTAN BOUND "F" TRAIN STAND CLEAR A THE CLOSING DOORS!!

SHE SAW
SHE KNOWS.
RELAX IT'S NO BIG DE
I FUCKED UP. I THINK I FUCKED UP.
IT WAS JUST RMLESS KISS!
KNOWS
SHE SAW
"WHAT? I DIDN'T KISS HER. SHE TRIED TO KISS ME!"
MAYBE SHE DIDN'T SEE.
MAYBE S LEFT BEFORE WE...
"WHAT GIRL? WHAT'RE YOU TALKING ABOUT? YOU MUST'VE BEEN DRUNK."
AGAIN.
IF SHE HAD SEEN IT SHE WOULD'VE BUSTED ME RIGHT THERE!
"I'M SORRY. I MADE A MISTAKE."
SHE WOU BUSTED YOUR HEAD OPEN RIGHT THERE.
SHE KNOWS
THE MISTAKE WAS NOT FUCKING HER BRAINS OUT!
IF SHE DIDN'T SEE... SHOULD I TELL?
NO!
NO!
THROW MYSELF AT HER MERCY.
NIGHTMARE
DENY. DENY. DENY.
HONE BEST PO
"DOROTHY... I HAVE TO TELL YOU...
"IT WAS JUST A... THING."
"I DON'T K WHAT CAME OVER ME."
I CAN'T BELIEVE I DID IT.
"IT MEAN NOTHING."
IT DI FEEL GOO
"SOMETIMES THE WORLD COULD USE A GOOD SHAKE UP."
DID IT MEAN NOTHING?
YEAH... A MINUTE OF FUN AND NOW I FEEL LIKE SHIT.
GOOD. THAT'S WHAT YOU GET.
I'M AN ASSHOLE
I'M A PRICK.
A BASTARD.
WHAT YOU ARE IS A PUSSY! BIG DEAL! YOU KISSED SOME GIRL!
SWIN
LIAR
JERK...
WO TIMER
DICK
HEATER
NOW YOU'RE READY TO HAND HER YOUR BALLS ON A PLATTER!
WHAT KIND OF MAN ARE YOU?!
DON'T DO NYTHING RASH... E HOW SHE ACTS.
I FUCKED UP.
LIKE CHESS!
ON'T CONFESS UNLESS YOU THINK SHE KNOWS!

TO WHAT DO I OWE THIS NOCTURNAL PLEASURE?
SORRY IF I WOKE YOU UP, WHEN I SAW THAT YOU LEFT I JUST, UH...
YEAH, I DIDN'T FEEL SO HOT SO I LEFT. WHEN I WOKE UP YOU WERE GONE.
YEAH, WELL, HEHHEH... SO, UM, HOW DO YOU FEEL... NOW?

ED
WAKEY WAKEY...
GROAN WHAT'S UH GOING ON?
IT'S SATURDAY MORNING. YOU'RE IN SHERMAN'S BED (DON'T WORRY, HE'S NOT IN IT RIGHT NOW).
YOU CAN STAY IF YOU WANT, BUT STEPHEN AND I ARE SPLITTING.
SHIT. MY MOM'S GONNA KILL ME. I GOTTA GET GOING.
LIKE I SAID, STAY AS LONG AS YOU WANT. THERE'S JUICE IN THE 'FRIDGE.
SO I GUESS WE'LL SEE --
WAIT! UM... BEFORE YOU GO, CAN I ASK YOU A SORT OF, UH, PERSONAL QUESTION?
HEH... SURE, ED. SHOOT.
LAST NIGHT, DID YOU SEE ME SORT OF DANCING WITH THAT GIRL, LEIA?
SORT OF DANCING AND SORT OF FEROCIOUSLY NECKING, YEAH. WHY?
HEH HEH...
SEE, I REMEMBER THAT PART, BUT IT ALL GETS A LITTLE..HAZY AFTER THAT. I...
I DON'T KNOW IF I DREAMT IT, OR IF IT....
BUT, DO YOU KNOW IF WE -- SHE AND I -- UM, DID WE...
Y'KNOW...

LIKE, DO... IT?
NO.
"NO."
"NO, ED, YOU DIDN'T."
JUST SAY "NO."
"SORRY, CHIE
"YES, ED. YOU DID."
WHAT?! YOU CAN'T TELL HIM THAT!!
WHY NOT?
BECAUSE IT'S A LIE! WHATTAYA MEAN "WHY NOT?"
THIS IS A SIMPLE WAY TO MAKE A NICE GUY VERY HAPPY.
THINK OF IT AS A GOING AWAY PRESENT.
LOOK AT HIM. HOW CA I BREAK THA HEART?
THINK OF IT AS A LIE!
"NO, I'M SORRY, ED. YOU DIDN'T."
YOU CAN'T TELL A WHITE LIE ABOUT HOW YOU LOSE YOUR VIRGINITY!
"YOU ROCKED HER WORLD!"
YOU KNOW HOW HUNG UP HE IS ABOUT IT.
IT WILL PROBAB BOOST HIS SELF ESTEEM.
"YEAH, E YOU DID
WHAT HAPPE WHEN/IF HE T TO THAT GIRL A
HE'LL BE HUMILATED WHEN HE LEARNS THE TRUTH!
"SORR
"NO, ED."
"UM... I DON'T THINK SO."
"I DON' KNOW, ED."
UM... WAS I GOOD?
YES.

GOODBYE, ED.
HMMM?
OH, YEAH. BYE, JANE.
MEOW
MEOW
READY?
MEOW.
UM.
YEAH.
MOO V·IT

WHAT WOULD YOU LOOK LIKE AS THE OPPOSITE SEX?

"HOLD UP: AREN'T YOU THAT RICH DUDE WHO, LIKE PAID FOR MY OPERATION."
"YEAH, YOU BUSTED ME!"
OKAY, TRY NOW.
YOU SHOULD DO IT NOW.
COME ON.
OKAY. READY? ONE... TWO..... THREENOW!
NOW!
NOW!
NNNNNNNOW!
NOW!
REALLY, NOW. COME ON, CAPRICE.
READY? DO IT.

Kiss Off

OKAY! OKAY! I'M CALLING ALREADY!!
I HOPE YOU'RE LIKE HAPPY WHEN I MAKE A FOOL OUT OF MYSELF!
"SO... I GUESS YOU CAN, LIKE, SEE, NOW, HUH."
"I GUESS I CAN."
"AWESOME. LET'S PARTY!"
WHAT THE HECK ARE YOU.. OH!
HELLO, IF YOU'RE CALLING FOR STEPHEN GAEDEL OR JANE PEKAR THEY HAVE MOVED FAR AWAY AND CAN BE REACHED
DAMN! HE'S NOT THERE. THE MACHINE GOT IT.
LEAVE A MESSAGE THIS TIME!

IF YOU'RE CALLING FOR SHERMAN DAVIES, LEAVE A MESSAGE AND, GOD WILLING, I'LL GET BACK TO YOU.
BEEP!
UM... HEY, SHERMAN, THIS IS CAPRICE FROM THE BOOKSTORE AND I... UH, JUST WANTED TO SEE IF YOU'RE, LIKE, OKAY AND EVERYTHING SINCE YOU HAVEN'T BEEN TO WORK FOR A FEW DAYS AND MAYBE YOU'RE SICK OR WHATEVER... SO...
UM, ANYWAY, YOU CAN CALL ME OR HOPEFULLY I'LL SEE YOU AT WORK ON...
UH... MONDAY.
UM... OKAY. BYE.
CLICK
NIN

NEXT!
SHEKATON
COMIC BO KS
FEB 24-26
UH, I'M TOMMY NICOHAY. I PLAYED JAWA #7 IN "EMPIRE STRIKES BACK."
OF COURSE! OH, IT IS A THRILL TO FINALLY LURE YOU TO GRANO-SEQUON!
WE'RE ALL FANS OF YOUR GIANT BODY OF WORK! HUGE FANS!
UM. THANKS.
ZOOM
--Part One--
GRANO-SEQUON!
NO, THANK YOU, MR. NICOHAY! ANYWAY, YOU'LL BE AT TABLE #1138, IN THE MADISON ROOM.
YOU'LL BE NEXT TO IVY SANCHEZ, THE PENTHOUSE PET AND TONY MALLETTE WHO PLAYED ENSIGN WILDE ON "STAR TREK."
Sigh
THANK YOU.
WOW! JAWA #7!
NEXT!
NEXT, PLEASE!

MY NAME IS IRVING FLAVOR AND THIS IS MY ASSISTANT, ED VELASQUEZ.
AH! MR. FLAVOR! I'M SO PLEASED THAT WE COULD FINALLY LURE YOU TO GRAND-SEQUON! IT IS INDEED AN HONOR!
LET ME SEE... OH, YOU'RE AT THE "COMICS WORLD" BOOTH. TABLE #5450 IN THE McKINLEY ROOM.
WOW! THERE'S A LOT OF FAMOUS PEOPLE HERE. ROBBIE GARR IS THE GUEST OF HONOR!
GRANDSEQUON
EXIT
ROBBIE GARR?!
YEAH. HE'S THE HOTTEST ARTIST THIS MONTH. I'M SURPRISED YOU'VE NEVER HEARD OF HIM.
HE'S LIKE ONE OF THE RICHEST
WORK...
OH, I HEARD OF HIM ALRIGHT. ROBBIE GARR USED TO BE MY GOD DAMNED ASSISTANT!
WHAT? REALLY?
AND LET ME TELL YOU SOMETHING: HE COULDN'T DRAW FLIES WITH HONEY! THAT COCK SUCKER WAS ONE OF THE WORST GUYS THEY SENT ME! THAT NO-TALENT SCHMUCK!
SO WHAT DOES MR. T-SQUARE DO THAT THEY PAY HIM SO MUCH?
GEMSTONE
GRANDSEQUON
SPECIAL GUEST
ROBBIE GARR
PLUS:

IRVING! WE WERE STARTING TO WORRY!
:ERF: HOW'S THIS? IS IT STILL CROOKED?
NO... PERFECT.
RIPPING NEW A-HOLES SINCE
SO WHERE SHOULD I PUT MY STUFF? I BROUGHT SOME ART.
TERRIFIC! ARCHIE! CLEAR SOME OF THAT CRAP OFF THE TABLE!
ZOOM SUCKS DICKS!
OH! HEY! HOW'S IT GOING?
OH, IT'S GOING OKAY. WE'RE LIKE SETTING UP AND ALL THAT.
DID YOU LIKE GET A HAIRCUT OR LOSE WEIGHT OR SOMETHING?
YOU LOOK DIFFERENT, BUT I CAN'T... MMM.
REALLY? GOOD DIFFERENT OR BAD DIFFERENT? HAHA.
NO! NO! YOU LOOK GOOD!
DID YOU GROW A BEARD OR...
NO, IT LOOKS GOOD.
YOU LOOK GOOD, TOO, HILDY.
ORLD
1986"
SO, BESIDES THE AWARD CEREMONY, WE'VE ALSO SIGNED YOU UP FOR A DISCUSSION PANEL:
"GOLDEN AGE: MYTH OR LEGEND."
THIS IS YOUR WEEKEND, MR. FLAVOR! WHEN THE COMMUNITY OF COMICDOM WILL EMBRACE YOU TO ITS BOSOMS WITH OPEN ARMS!!
YOU BET!

FWOOSH!
NO SMOKING
FINALLY! I WAS STARTING TO WORRY. ARE WE CHECKED IN TO THE HOTEL?

HUH? OH, YEAH. ROOM 1213. I ALREADY BROUGHT OUR STUFF UP.
OH! I WANTED TO BRING MY COAT AND STUFF UP. WHY DIDN'T YOU ASK ME!
AND BEFORE I FORGET: YOUR PRESS BADGE.
UH... WHO'S "RANDY B. WOODCOCK?"
YOU. MY FAITHFUL ASSISTANT. UNLESS YOU FEEL LIKE SHELLING OUT THE $17 ADMISSION FEE. COME ON, RANDY, THEY'RE OPENING UP.
OKAY. KEEP YOUR EYES OUT FOR VERISIMILITUDE!
PATHFINDER?
ACCORDING TO MY CALCULATIONS, THEY SHOULD BE THIS-A-WAY.
Sniff! Sniff! WHAT IS THAT?
PRICED AS MARKED

OKAY, YOU IDIOTS!
HERE'S YOUR CHANCE TO MEET A LIVING LEGEND!!
ZOOM SUCKS DICKS!
UM. OKAY: IN THE LAST ISSUE, ADMIRAL ARMOR SAYS HE HASN'T SEEN THE NIGHT-STALKER SINCE THEY FOUGHT IN THE SEWER OF MAZE CITY IN #318, RIGHT?
HE DID, HUH?
BUT WAIT! THAT'S NOT RIGHT! IN "ZOOM ACTION TEAM UP" #119, NIGHT-STALKER AND LIGHTNING ROD TEAMED UP AGAINST HIM!
MAYBE HE FORGOT. HA HEH...
ORIGINAL ART
HE "FORGOT?" BUT NIGHTSTALKER DESTROYED HIS TELEMATRIX ZERO CONVERTER! HE COULDN'T JUST "FORGET" THAT! HE WOULDN'T!!
COME ON! THAT'S FUCKIN' BULLSHIT, MAN!
LOBO
FUCKIN' BULLSHIT!
WHICH TABLE IS DAVE NORGSTROMME AT?
WHAT DO YOU THINK ABOUT THEM CASTING JAMES VAN DER BEEK AS MOONBOY IN THE NEXT MOVIE? ISN'T THAT JUST WRONG?
"WIZARD" NAILED IT: NICHOLAS BRENDAN IS MOONBOY!
SPACE GHOST
I TOTALLY SUPPORT YOU IN YOUR FIGHT WITH ZOOM, MAN!
THANKS, MAN!
HEY! WILL YOU SIGN THIS LIMITED EDITION HARDCOVER REPRINT OF "NIGHT-STALKER" #1?
NIGHTSTALKER
DO YOU HAVE CHANGE FOR A FIFTY?
I WANT TO GET LOU FERRIGNO'S AUTOGRAPH!
Cable 3:16
WHAT DO YOU THINK OF ZOOM FINALLY SHOWING MOON BOY AND NIGHTSTALKER FINALLY DOING IT?
I MEAN, COME ON! THEY'VE BEEN "BUDDIES" FOR LIKE 50 YEARS!
PRESS

WHAT?! WHEN DID--?!
OH! HEY, GUYS! GOOD TO SEE YOU!
MR. FLAVOR, YOU REMEMBER DOROTHY FROM THAT MAGAZINE? AND THIS IS MY FRIEND, SHERMAN.
HELLO, SIR.
IRVING, I'M WORKING ON A FOLLOW-UP PIECE AND I WAS HOPING WE COULD TALK SOME MORE.
MMMM... I DON'T KNOW. I THINK I SAID EV--
YOU--- GULP! YOU'RE THE JOURNALIST WHO DID THE ARTICLE ON MR. FLAVOR?
FOR...FOR..."METRO CHIC?"
WOW.
ZOOM SUCKS DICKS!
I WAS PLANNING ON INTERVIEWING SOME PEOPLE HERE ABOUT MR. FLAVOR. COULD I ASK YOU GUYS A FEW--
YES!
SAVE US!
WHILE YOU GUYS DO THIS, ED AND I ARE GOING TO LOOK AROUND, OKAY?
SURE, SWEETIE.
FINALLY! WE CAN LET THE WORLD KNOW THAT COMICS AREN'T JUST FOR KIDS!
"RIPPING NEW A-HOLES IN COMICS SINCE 1986!"
ZOOM SUCKS DICKS!
SO? WHAT DO YOU THINK? WEIRD, WILD STUFF, HUH?
I FEEL LIKE I'VE ENTERED THE LOWEST CIRCLE OF POP CULTURE HELL.

ON THE WAY IN I SAW HALF OF THE CAST OF "THE BUGALOOS." I HAD FORGOTTEN THAT SHOW EVEN EXISTED!
YEAH. THESE THINGS ARE SORT OF LIKE THE ELEPHANT GRAVEYARDS OF SHOW BUSINESS.
YOU KNOW WHO'S HERE? THE KID IN THE COWBOY SUIT FROM "JIMMY JUMBLE'S CANDY FACTORY."
HE'S LIKE FORTY NOW AND WANTS PEOPLE TO PAY HIM $10 FOR HIS AUTO-GRAPH.
THE FUNNY PART IS THAT SINCE HE'S SO OLD YOU CAN'T EVEN RECOGNIZE HIM AS THE COW-BOY KID. HE COULD BE ANYONE!
DIDN'T YOU PAY $25 FOR ARTOO-DETOO'S AUTO-GRAPH?
YOU MEAN MR. KENNY BAKER? THAT'S TOTALLY DIFFERENT.
IT CAME WITH A CERTIFICATE OF AUTHENTICITY!
HEY, SPEAKING OF RIP OFFS, DID YOU CALL THAT GIRL ABOUT THAT APARTMENT IN ASTORIA?
SHIT!
NO, I'M SORRY. I COMPLETELY FORGOT. SHIT, I'M SORRY.
I DON'T CARE, BUT DON'T YOU HAVE TO MOVE OUT IN A WEEK OR SO?
YOU SHOULD GET GOING.
:Sigh: I KNOW. I SHOULD. I'VE JUST BEEN SO... DISTRACTED.
REALLY? WHAT'S WRONG?
OH YEAH! I FORGOT TO TELL YOU: THAT GIRL CAPRICE? I SORT OF FOOLED AROUND WITH HER AT THE PARTY.
HUH! THAT'S A CORKER ALRIGHT!

SO WAIT: WHAT MAKES YOU THINK DOROTHY SAW YOU GUYS AGAIN?
I... I CAN'T QUITE PINPOINT IT. EVERY NOW AND AGAIN SHE'LL USE A SPECIFIC PHRASE OR HINT AT SOME-THING...
MAYBE I'M JUST BEING TOO PARANOID.
MAYBE IT'S MY OWN GUILT AND I'M READING TOO MUCH INTO IT.
WHAT A MESS.
WOW... I DON'T KNOW WHAT TO TELL YOU, SHERMAN.
IF SHE DOESN'T KNOW AND YOU CONFESS THEN YOU'VE PUT YOURSELF IN THE DOG HOUSE FOR NOTHING.
BUT, IF SHE DOES KNOW, AND YOU DON'T TELL, HOW CAN SHE EVER TRUST A LYING, CHEATING DOG LIKE YOU AGAIN?
JEEZ! THANKS! IT WAS A FEW KISSES!
OR... WAIT:
DOES SHE THINK YOU KNOW SHE KNOWS OR NOT? OR DOES SHE THINK SHE'S THE ONLY ONE WHO KNOWS THAT SHE KNOWS?
OKAY, I GUESS OUR FIRST PRIORITY: DO YOU STILL WANT TO GO OUT WITH HER OR IS THIS JUST A WAY FOR YOU TO BR--
WHAT? NO! OF COURSE I STILL WANT TO GO OUT WITH HER.
I KNOW THAT'S YOUR GUT REACTION, BUT SEARCH YOUR FEELINGS. LET'S FACE IT: PART OF YOU REALLY WANTED TO BE WITH CAPRICE ON THE FIRE ESCAPE.

I LOVE HER.
DOROTHY? OR THIS NEW G--
DOROTHY! FORGET ABOUT CAPRICE!!
OKAY! OKAY! DON'T YELL AT ME. I'M NOT THE ONE WHO CHEATED ON--
"CHEATED!" WHY DO YOU HAVE TO KEEP USING THAT WORD?! IT MEANT NOTHING, OKAY?! SHIT!
SO TELL ME WHAT I SHOULD DO.
YOU...
YOU SHOULD TELL HER.
BUT..! REALLY? WHAT IF SHE DOESN'T KNOW? I'LL--
YOU'RE LIKE THE GUY IN THAT STORY WHO ALWAYS HEARS THE HEARTBEAT OF THE GUY HE KILLED.
ALL THIS GUILT IS GOING TO GIVE YOU AN ULCER.
Y'KNOW, EXPLAIN TO HER THAT IT DIDN'T MEAN ANYTHING. A MOMENTARY LAPSE OF REASON.
HOPEFULLY, SHE'LL GET IT.
EITHER WAY, YOU CAN AT LEAST SLEEP WITH A... CLEANER CON-SCIENCE.
UH, MR. FLAVOR IS ON THIS DISCUSSION PANEL. DO YOU WANT TO COME?
UM... NO.

OKAY. I'M GONNA GO THEN.
SORRY I COULDN'T BE MORE OF A HELP.
THANKS, ED.
YOU KNOW YOU'RE A PIG?
I SAID "YOU WANT ANOTHER DRINK?"
SIR?
UH.
SURE.
AND YES, I KNOW.
MIGHT I ADD WHAT AN HONOR IT IS TO HAVE YOU HERE?
YEAH, SO WHEN'S THIS WING DING SUPPOSED TO START? I NEED LUNCH.
OH... UH, WELL, I GUESS TOMMY CAN GET SOME PRETZELS FROM THE --
"PRETZELS?" IT'S SUCH A BIG HONOR THAT YOU'RE GIVING ME GOD DAMNED PRETZELS?
!
ER... I'M AFRAID WE... WOULD YOU LIKE MY HAM SANDWICH? MY WIFE --
CHRIST ON A CRUTCH! IS THAT YOU, IRV?

NESTOR? SHIT, CHUCK, YOU LOOK TERRIBLE!
WHERE THE HELL HAVE YOU BEEN YOU SON OF A GUN?
TOMMY! GO IN MY BAG AND GET MY SANDWICH!
HEH HEH... I'VE BEEN LIVING WITH MY DAUGHTER SINCE I GOT TOO SICK TO WORK. ARIZONA'S OKAY.
I... UH...
I HEARD ABOUT WHAT YOU'RE DOING. ABOUT J.C. AND THE NIGHTSTALKER.
OH. YEAH, WELL. IT'S MOSTLY MY ASSISTANT'S IDEA. I DIDN'T RE WANT TO--
STICK IT TO 'EM, IRV!
YOU THINK IF J.C. GETS SICK THEY'RE GONNA LET HIM GO? WILL HE BE ARGUING WITH SOME CLERK ABOUT A MEDICAID CLAIM?
FUCK NO! HE'S SET FOR LIFE THANKS TO US!
IT'S OUR CHARACTERS! OUR, OUR, OUR STORIES! OUR ARTWORK! WITHOUT US, HE'D BE SELLING CHEAP SUITS TO SCHMUCKS ON LONG ISLAND! YOU GOTTA SHOW HIM! SHOW HIM COUGH! SHOW HIM! COUGH
HE CAN'T COUGH CAN'T JUST COUGHCOUGH COUGH COUGH!!
UH, DAD? ARE YOU OKAY?
COUGH COUGH YEAH, HONEY. JUST A LITTLE TOO EXCITED.
I'M OKAY. HEM
HEY, YOU KNOW WHO ELSE WAS SUPPOSED TO BE ON THIS, UH, DISCUSSION THING? (YOU'LL LOVE THIS)
ABIE RONKO!
WHAT?! YER SHITTIN' ME! I SWORE IF I EVER SAW THAT COCK SUCKER I'D--

RELAX, IRV.! RELAX. ABE CAN'T MAKE IT. HE'S DEAD.
YOU'RE... NO KIDDING?
NOPE. PANCREATIC PERITONITIS.
HAHAHAHAHA HAHAHA! THE POOR SON OF A BITCH.!
HAHAHAHAHAHA! HACOUGHCOUGHCOUGH! HEM I KNEW YOU'D LIKE THAT.
DAMN, IT'S GOOD TO SEE YOU AGAIN, CHUCK.!
YEAH! THERE AIN'T MANY OF US, UH, "GOLDEN-AGERS" LEFT ANYMORE.
Sigh CHRIST, IRV, LOOK AT US. WHAT THE HELL HAPPENED?
WHERE DID IT ALL GO?

AND THIS YEAR'S WINNER FOR BEST COSTUME -- MALE, IS...
DANNY RAXENBERG!
"ENSIGN SHOT WITH PHASER!"
I'D LIKE TO THANK EVERYONE FOR COMING AND REMIND YOU THAT IN FIVE MINUTES, THE "GOLDEN AGE: MYTH OR LEGEND" DISCUSSION PANEL WILL BEGIN IN THE COOLIDGE ROOM.
CLAP! CLAP! CLAP! CLAP! CLAP! CLAP! CLAP! CLAP!
PRETTY WEIRD STUFF, HUH?
HMM? OH! HI!
YEAH, BUT IT'S PRETTY COOL, RIGHT?
IF I HAD KNOWN THERE WAS GOING TO BE A CONTEST I WOULD'VE COOKED SOMETHING UP. Y'KNOW?
ARE YOU GOING TO MR. FLAVOR'S DISCUSSION THINGY?
I WAS JUST ON MY WAY NOW.
SO WOULD YOU HAVE REALLY MADE A COSTUME?
SURE! DON'T YOU THINK IT LOOKS LIKE FUN? DON'T YOU EVER DRESS UP FOR HALLOWEEN?
IN THE TWO YEARS I'VE BEEN HERE -- IN NEW YORK, I MEAN -- I'VE ALWAYS DRESSED UP FOR THE HALLOWEEN PARADE.
REALLY? WHAT AS?
UM... FIRST AS WILMA FLINTSTONE,
THEN AS A WOMAN FALLING OUT OF A BUILDING.

WOW. I HAVEN'T WORN A HALLOWEEN COSTUME SINCE AROUND... THIRD GRADE?
WELL, THIS YEAR YOU SHOULD! EVERYBODY SHOULD! EVERYONE SHOULD STOP WORRYING ABOUT WHAT'S HIP OR COOL AND JUST HAVE FUN AND RELAX!
SPEAKING OF FUN, HOW ARE THINGS AT THE MAGAZINE? I THOUGHT YOU SAID YOU WERE QUITTING?
OH!
PLEASE DON'T MENTION ANYTHING TO HARVEY AND ARCHIE, BUT...
This is going to be my last assignment with them!
I got another job!
REALLY? WELL, CONGRATULATIONS!
WAIT, SO I GUESS WITH YOU QUITTING THE BUSINESS OUR, UH, PATHS WILL NO LONGER...
WE WON'T BE SEEING EACH OTHER ANYMORE, I GUESS.
WELL... IT DOESN'T HAVE TO MEAN THAT.
Y'KNOW.
Heh Heh... I GUESS YOU'RE...
HILDY! HILDY! OVER HERE!
WHERE THE HELL'VE YOU BEEN?
ZOOM SUCKS DICKS!
SO... I'LL SEE YOU LATER?
SEE YOU LATER...

...SO THEY NEVER FOUND OUT WHO IT WAS THAT KILLED 'EM. I GUESS WE'LL NEVER FIND OUT.
FASCINATING! I THINK WE HAVE TIME FOR ONE MORE QUESTION... MISS?
OH, UH...
"MR. FLAVOR HOW IMPORTANT HAS 'COMICS WORLD' BEEN TO YOUR CAVES?"
"CAUSE"
"YOUR CAUSE?"
UH, WELL, YOU GUYS'VE BEEN A BIG HELP GE ME--
BOOO! "COMICS WORLD" SUCKS!!
WHO SAID THAT? HUH?
WHERE'S SECURITY?
SIDDOWN YA HIPPY SNOB!
UM...CAN WE ALL CALM DOWN?
Heh Heh...
YOU HEARD HIM, ASSHOLE! SIDDOWN!
ROBBIE RULES!
YOU... YOU FUCKING CAVEMEN! YOU WO KNOW SEC ART IF IT--
YOU SUCK!!
HA! HA!
GO WRITE A REVIEW OF SOME BLACK AND WHITE COMIC NO ONE READS!!
ROBBIE GARR RULES!
HA!
HAHAHAHA!
"COMICS WORLD" SUCKS, CHIEF!
ROBBIE! ROB-BIE! ROB-BIE!
HA! HA!
DICK!
LOSER!
They'll pay! They'll pay! Fools! Little bastards!!
THIS IS AMAZING. THAT PEOPLE CAN GET THIS WORKED UP OVER COMIC BOOKS?
YEAH. "COMICS WORLD" ISN'T TOO POPULAR WITH THESE CAPES-N-TIGHTS BOYS.

ATTENTION CONVENTIONEERS! AT 4:00pm, WE WILL BE HAVING OUR POKEMON CONTEST IN THE BUCHANAN ROOM!
SMAC
?
WUT ARE YOU LOO AT?
BOP
HEY, WHAT'S, UH, WHAT'S THIS LINE FOR?
YOU CAN GET YOUR PICTURE TAKEN WITH SUSAN BOYLE. SHE--
REALLY?! FROM "SOLAR PATROL?!"
AH! I SEE FROM YOUR REACTION THAT YOU'RE FAMILIAR WITH HER, AH, BODY OF WORK?
ARE YOU KIDDING? I HAD A HUGE CRUSH ON HER WHEN I WAS TWELVE!
HAHA! YOU AND EVERY OTHER RED BLOODED MALE IN THE WORLD!
DIDN'T YOU JUST HATE THAT BASTARD COMMANDER NIXTAQ?
YEAH! HOW COULD A CUTIE LIKE HER GO FOR A DORK LIKE HIM?
DO YOU REMEMBER THAT ONE EPISODE WHERE THEY GOT STRANDED ON THAT BLUE ASTEROID?
AH! "ESCAPE FROM THE COMET BEAST" FROM THE THIRD SEASON!
THAT'S WHEN SUSAN'S... TALENTS BECAME MORE PRONOUNCED, HMM?
HAHAHA! I MUST'VE MASTURBATED TO THAT EPISODE 200 TIMES!
PRESS
NEXT, PLEASE!
HELLO! I'M A BIG FAN OF YOU, SUSAN!
OH, THANK YOU! THAT'S GREAT!

NEXT, PLEASE!
HEH... I'M SURE YOU'VE HEARD THIS A MILLION TIMES, BUT I HAD A MAD CRUSH ON YOU WHEN I WAS TWELVE!
HAHA...
OH, THANK YOU, THAT'S SO SWEET?
WOULD YOU LIKE TO TAKE A PICTURE? IT'S ONLY $10.
YOU--YOU MEAN WE'RE STUCK ON THIS ASTEROID ... FOREVER, YOU AND I?
SURE. WHY NOT!
YOU MUST MEET A LOT OF WEIRD GUYS AT THESE COMIC SHOWS, I BET!
HAHA! I DO MEET SOME CHARACTERS, BUT THEY'RE MOSTLY HARMLESS.
OKAY, SAY "NIKTAQ."
IF YOUR BOYFRIEND, LIKE, CHEATED ON YOU WOULD YOU WANT TO KNOW?
'CUSE ME?

WHAT-- FUCK! WHAT IS THIS NOW? WHO ARE YOU TO SAY SUCH THINKS?
YOU PRICK!! YOU GOD DAMNED SON OF A BITCH! I KNEW IT!
"BUSINESS TRIP" MY FUCKING ASS!!
HehHeh... WAIT I DID
IT DIDN'T MEAN NOTHINK! WE-- I WAS DRUNK, YOU KNOW? IT WAS AN ACCIDENT!
WHO IS IT?! THAT FUCKING BITCH FROM "BATTLESTAR GALACTICA?"
OR VERUCA SALT?!
SHERMAN!
WOW! WHAT WAS THAT ABOUT?
I, UH, I THINK I MIGHT'VE RUINED SUSAN BOYLE'S LOVE LIFE.
LT. VENUS FROM "SOLAR PATROL?!" WOW! WHAT HAPPENED?
IT'S FUNNY. I WAS GETTING MY PICTURE TAKEN WITH HER WHEN I ASKED
HER
if...
uh...
IF SHE, LIKE, UH... IF...
IF SHE GETS, LIKE, HIT ON, ALOT, AT THESE SHOWS.
Heh...
ARE YOU KIDDING? I'M SURE HALF OF THESE GUYS WOULD GIVE THEIR LEFT NUT FOR A STAB AT LT. VENUS!
I DON'T KNOW... I GET THE SENSE THAT MOST OF THESE GUYS ARE, LIKE, SCARED OF WOMEN.
I MEAN, I'VE NOTICED A BUNCH OF GUYS STARING AT MY CHEST, BUT NO ONE'S EVEN ASKED ME FOR THE TIME, LET ALONE MY NUMBER.

SO I GUESS THINGS ARE CLOSING UP AROUND HERE, HUH?
YOU GUYS WANT TO GET SOME DINNER?
SOUNDS GOOD.
MR. FLAVOR AND I SAID WE'D GO OUT WITH THE "COMICS WORLD" GUYS. YOU CAN EAT WITH US IF YOU WANT.
Stin
I DON'T KNOW. I THINK I'VE HAD ALL THE COMICS I CAN TOLERATE IN A 24-HOUR PERIOD.
OKAY, MAYBE WE'LL SEE EACH OTHER LATER. HEY! THEY'RE HAVING A "PLANET OF THE APES" MARATHON LATER!
SHOULD I CALL YOU FOR "CONQUEST?"
UMMMM.... I DON'T KNOW, ED. I THINK WE'LL MAKE IT AN EARLY NIGHT.
Y'KNOW?
PRESS
GOOD LUCK.
THOSE IGNORANT LITTLE PHILISTINES WITH THEIR SU HERO BULLSH SHOW THEM! THOSE--
HEY, UH, HOLD UP, OKAY? I GOTTA STOP IN THE HEAD.
THE WHAT?! OH, OKAY.
HEY, WHY DON'T YOU AND YOUR ASSISTANT JUST COME TO OUR ROOM WHEN YOU'RE READY, OKAY? ROOM 1030.
GOTCHA
DICKS!

DID
DID I... DO THE RIGHT THING?

I'M NOT SO HIGH-CLASS THAT I CAN AVOID LOOKING AT REALITY. I CAN'T AFFORD TO BE... ALOOF. YOU COME TO ME WITH A HELL OF A PROBLEM AND THEN YOU GET HIGHHANDED ON ME.
...KNOW. PLAYING HARDBALL WAS NEVER YOUR GAME. YOU NEVER LIKED TO GET YOUR HANDS DIRTY
"I KISSED THAT GIRL."
HAVE A ONFESSION TO MAKE."
SO
"LAST WEEK AT THE PARTY... I KISSED THIS GIRL."
"DOROTHY... I FEEL HORRIBLE. I DON'T KNOW WHAT TO..."
I'M SORRY."
"I DON' KNOW HOW TO TELL YOU THIS, BUT..."
BEER
DON'T TELL HER.

DID YOU SAY SOMETHING?
WHAT? NO!
NO.
MAYBE IT WOULD HELP IF YOU TALKED TO SOMEBODY, I MEAN, LIKE, LIKE A THERAPIST OR SOMETH--
DON'T TRICK ME, JUDAH!
IS THE FOOD HERE YET?
NO.
CHRIST! I'M SHAKING!
I BROUGHT YOUR BIRTHDAY PRESENT.
SNIFF
I KNOW HOW MUCH YOU LI--
--DID I CALL YOU?
HAHA, GOSH! I DON'T EVEN REMEMBER WHAT IT WAS.
WELL, DO YOU MEAN WORM?
NO, THAT--
--TAINMENT TONIGHT, ANT--
--EXT--
--SOFT "EL"--
--K--

TELL US SOMETHING YOU'VE NEVER TOLD ANYONE.
I THINK MY FATHER CHEATED ON MY MOTHER.
I HAD A, UH, HOMOSEXUAL, UH, EXPERIENCE IN COLLEGE.
ANNNND I SORT OF LIKED IT.
SEX IS BORING.
WHEN I WAS A JUNIOR IN HIGH SCHOOL I ATTEMPTED SUICIDE WITH SLEEPING PILLS.
GIRLS WITH HAIRY ARMPITS TURN ME ON.
WHEN I WAS A KID I WAS TERRIFIED OF "BIG BIRD."
I RAN OVER A DOG.

CON-
QUEST
THEY ALL DIED WITHIN A FEW MONTHS.
EIGHT YEARS AGO, EVERY DOG AND CAT IN THE WORLD ... IT WAS LIKE A PLAGUE.
THE DISEASE THAT KILLED THEM WAS A MYSTERIOUS VIRUS BROUGHT BACK FROM OUTER SPACE BY ONE OF THE ASTRONAUTS.
BELOVED PET
1971-1991
DIDN'T THE DISEASE AFFECT HUMANS?
"NO, NO, WE WERE IMMUNE."
NO, NO. WE WERE IMMUNE AND SO, IT WAS DISCOVERED, WERE SIMIANS, EVEN THE SMALLEST ONES.
THAT'S HOW IT BEGAN.
HUMANS WANTING LITTLE BLAH BLAH BLAHS TO REPLACE BLAH BLAH BLAH.
BLAH BLAH BLAH BLAH. BLAH BLAH BLAHS. BLAH BLAH
BLAHBLAH.
BLAHBLAH BLAHBLAH.

...AND PLAN FOR THE INEVITABLE DAY OF MAN'S DOWNFALL!
THE DAY WHEN HE FINALLY AND SELF-DESTRUCTIVELY TURNS HIS WEAPONS AGAINST HIS OWN KIND: THE DAY OF THE WRITING IN THE SKY!
WHEN YOUR CITIES LIE BURIED UNDER RADIOACTIVE RUBBLE, WHEN THE SEA IS A DEAD SEA AND THE LAND IS A WASTELAND AND OUT OF WHICH I WILL LEAD MY PEOPLE OUT OF THEIR CAPTIVITY!
AND WE SHALL BUILD OUR OWN CITIES IN WHICH THERE WILL BE NO PLACE FOR HUMANS EXCEPT TO SERVE OUR ENDS! AND WE SHALL FOUND OUR OWN ARMIES! OUR OWN RELIGION! OUR OWN DYNASTIES!!
AND THAT DAY IS UPON YOU NOW!
YOU ARE WITNESS TO THE BIRTH OF THE PLANET OF THE APES!

YEAH!
FUCKING DIRECTOR'S CUT KICKS ASS, MAN!
I DON'T KNOW, I PREFER THE NOTE OF HOPE AND TOLERANCE IN THE ORIGINAL ENDING.
AH, C'MON, ARCH, DON'T BE A SAP! THOSE BASTARD HUMANS GOT WHAT THEY HAD COMING TO 'EM.
WE'RE STAYING FOR "BATTLE" RIGHT?
I KNOW IT'S THE WEAKEST ENTRY IN THE CANON, BUT IT'S GOT SOME COOL GORILLA VIOLENCE IN IT.
AHH... I DON'T KNOW. MAYBE I SHOULD HELP MR. FLAVOR UP TO OUR ROOM.
MM? WH-- IS IT FINALLY OVER?
I SUPPOSE I'LL GO TOO. I'M A BIT TIRED MYSELF.
SO YOU LIKED THAT MOVIE, EDDIE? CHRIST, I MIGHT'VE WELL STAYED IN BROOKLYN!
Heh.. Heh..
ED, SOMETIME I'D LIKE TO SEE THAT STORY YOU MENTIONED AT DINNER.

SURE. I BROUGHT IT WITH ME TO THE CON SO I CAN SHOW IT TO YOU TOMORROW.
OH. OKAY!
OH, WAIT! WHY DON'T I SHOW IT TO YOU NOW?
OKAY!
WHOA, IF YOU GUYS WANNA SOCIALIZE ALL NIGHT, THAT'S YOUR OWN BUSINESS BUT DO IT SOMEPLACE ELSE.
I NEED MY BEAUTY REST, OKAY?
ALRIGHT, ALRIGHT.
HOW ABOUT WE GO TO YOUR ROOM? HARVEY AND ARCHIE ARE AT THE MOVIE, SO.--
281 F
UMMM... HEY, WHY DON'T WE MEET IN THE LOBBY DOWN-STAIRS?
OH, UH, OKAY.
HAWHAW HAWHAW!
MR. BIGSHOT! YOU THOUGHT YOU WERE GETTIN' IN THAT GAL'S PANTS, RIGHT?
I GUESS SHE SHOWED YOU WHAT FOR, HUH?
WHAT? I DON'T KNOW WHAT YOU'RE TALKING ABOUT. GO TO BED.

SO... WHAT PART ARE YOU UP TO?
HMM? OH: THE PART WHERE... WHAT'S HER NAME? ARYSA?... WHERE ARYSA FINDS OUT XENON'S BEEN KILLED.
OH, OKAY.
ARE YOU LIKE THIRSTY OR SOMETHING? SHOULD I GET YOU, LIKE, A SODA?
NO, THANKS. I'M OKAY. THANKS.
HEH.
WHAT WAS THAT? WHICH PART WAS THAT?
I JUST NOTICED THIS GUY IN THE BACKGROUND. HE LOOKS LIKE ELVIS.
OH YEAH! Heh.
DO YOU WANT SOMETHING FROM, LIKE, THE VENDING MACHINE? YOU KNOW, LIKE A SNACK?
ED! I CAN'T READ IF YOU'RE GOING TO KEEP INTERRUPTING EVERY TEN SECONDS!
OH, I'M SORRY. I GUESS I'M JUST, I DON'T KNOW, NERVOUS.

OKAY, YOU KNOW WHAT? MAYBE I'LL WAIT AND READ IT TOMORROW?
GOD ONLY KNOWS I'LL NEED SOMETHING TO OCCUPY MYSELF SITTING AT THE TABLE.
YEAH. MAYBE THAT'S FOR THE BEST. I CAN'T STAND WATCHING PEOPLE READ MY STUFF.
SO.... WHAT DO YOU WANT TO DO NOW?
HMMMM...
WOW, SO YOU'VE LIVED WITH YOUR PARENTS YOUR WHOLE LIFE?
YEAH. I GUESS IT'S SORT OF SAD, HUH?
MY PARENTS ARE FROM COSTA RICA, AND THERE KIDS LIVE WITH THEIR PARENTS UNTIL THEY'RE MARRIED AND ALL.
SO IT MUST BE SORT OF EXCITING ...AND SCARY, HUH? THE IDEA OF MOVING OUT?
YEAH, BUT I'LL STILL BE IN THE CITY, SO IT'S NOT LIKE I WON'T EVER SEE THEM.
BUT, YEAH. I'M REALLY LOOKING FORWARD TO IT.
HOW LONG HAVE YOU GUYS KNOWN EACH OTHER?
MY PARENTS? SINCE I WAS A LITTLE KID.
NO! I MEAN YOU AND YOUR FRIEND, UH... SHERMAN?
HIM? OH, WE'VE KNOWN EACH OTHER SINCE COLLEGE.
"YEAH. THAT WAS... MAN, FIVE YEARS AGO. OUR HISTORY TEACHER MADE US COLLABORATE ON A PAPER."
"OF COURSE, I KNEW NOTHING ABOUT HARRY F. TRUMAN SO HE DID MOST OF THE WORK."

HIS GIRLFRIEND IS SUPPOSEDLY REALLY MAD ABOUT THE WHOLE THING. APPARENTLY SHE THOUGHT HE WAS GOING TO MOVE IN WITH HER.
MY GOODNESS, THAT'S NOT GOOD. WAS SHE THAT SHORT GIRL WITH THE BROWN HAIR?
YEAH. DOROTHY. SHE'S... I WOULD NEVER TELL HIM THIS, BUT I'M NOT... I THINK SHE'S, UH, TROUBLE.
REALLY? WHY?
UMMM... I CAN'T REALLY SAY. THERE'S JUST SOMETHING ABOUT HER THAT I... DON'T TRUST. OR SOMETHING.
SHE DRINKS ALOT. AND EVER SINCE THEY'VE BEEN TOGETHER, SHERMAN HAS
DO YOU THINK MAYBE YOU MIGHT BE JEALOUS? YOU KNOW, THAT YOU TWO WERE SUCH GOOD FRIENDS AND ALL, AND NOW SHE'S, LIKE, MUSCLING IN?
HMMM... I GUESS I COULD BE. I GUESS IT REALLY DOESN'T MATTER MUCH SINCE THEY-- HE-- UM, NEVERMIND.
WAIT! WHAT? WHAT WERE YOU GOING TO SAY?
UHHH, NOTHING. I SHOULDN'T BE
COME ON! TELL ME. PLEEEEASE?
HEH. LISTEN TO YOU! YOU'RE HUNGRIER FOR A BIT OF GOSSIP ABOUT TWO STRANGERS THAN YOU WERE FOR THE ICE CREAM!
SIGH
I KNOW. I HAVE A VOYEURISTIC PERSONALITY. MY OWN LIFE IS SO BORING THAT I LIVE VICARIOUSLY THROUGH OTHERS. HEH, NOW WHO'S THE PATHETIC ONE, HUH?
COME ON. IT CAN'T BE THAT BAD.
TRUST ME. I HAVE NO LIFE, ED.
LET ME ASK YOU ONE QUESTION: WHAT'S THE WORST THING YOU'VE EVER DONE?
HELLO! I'M VIOLA

HAHA! ENT TO COLLEGE!
WAIT, LIKE, WHAT DO YOU MEAN? LIKE, SOMETHING--
YOU--WHAT DO YOU MEAN? I DON'T REALLY--I DON'T KNOW.
WHAT WAS YOURS? WHAT WAS YOUR WORST THING?
I'LL TELL YOU, BUT, AHHH...YOU BETTER FINISH YOUR ICE CREAM FIRST.
(ESPECIALLY THE CHOCOLATE.)
OH MY GOD! YOUR COUSIN MUST'VE BEEN MORTIFIED! THAT IS SO DISGUSTING! HA HA!
YEAH, MORTIFIED AND THEN DIVORCED. HEH, I GUESS THIS ISN'T TYPICAL FIRST DATE CONVERSATION, HUH? OLD GUYS CRAPPING THEIR PANTS?
NO...IT'S BETTER. THAT'S FUNNY.
SO, COME ON. QUID PRO QUO AND ALL THAT. WHAT'S YOUR WORST THING?
UMM...ASK ME AGAIN LATER.
OOOH, SOUNDS SPICY! WHAT DID--OKAY, OKAY. LATER.
SO WHAT DO WE DO NOW? ARE YOU TIRED OR DO YOU WANT TO CALL IT A NIGHT OR..?
HMMMM I DON'T KNOW. WE COULD WALK AROUND AND SEE WHAT'S--
OKAY! SOUNDS LIKE A PLAN!

So did you go to art school or--?
No, actually I majored in business. My dad had aspirations that I would become this, I don't know, business guy. They, my parents, they really aren't interested in my cartooning stuff at all.
Oh, that's really too bad.
Yeah, well. So what about you?
I, uh, was a psych major at Ohio State. I didn't graduate, though. I left after my sophomore year and came to New York. It would be nice to finish up school some time.
You still could. How old are you?
22. What about you? How old are you?
24. I was born on Halloween.
Wow, that's cool. Wait, you were born on Halloween and you don't get dressed up? That's a lowdown, dirty shame! Haha. I was born in August, so the sucky part was, remember, like, in elementary school when kids would get to have a party in school and bring in cupcakes and treats and whatever? Since I was born in August I never got to do that.
My cousin Julia was born on Christmas Eve. She really hated that because everyone, y'know, gave her, like, one lump gift for Christmas and her birthday. She always got gypped.
My friend Christine back home was born on December 29 and you know what she would do? Her and her family would celebrate her half-birthday--on June 29. That way, you see, she wouldn't have to compete with Christmas and all that.
Huh. Well, I guess that's one way to do it, I guess.

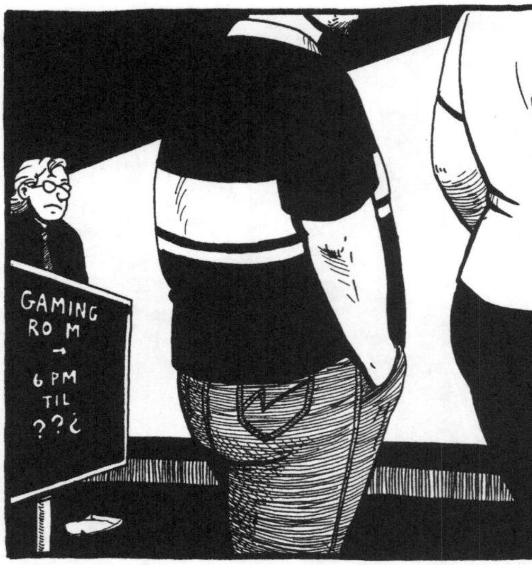
GAMING
RO M
6 PM
TIL
??¿

Oh, look. Have you ever played one of those card games? Like Magic or any of those?
Uhh...I bought the Star Wars one at a garage sale but it was way too complicated. I couldn't get past the basic rules. Why? Have you? Do you want to--?
No, no. I've never played one. I was just curious. I used to play Dungeons and Dragons when I was younger, though.
Really?! Wow. I thought only, y'know...I just never would've picked you out as, uh...
My older brothers were really into it. It was fun, though. I've always been a fan of fantasy novels and that sort of thing, so it was fun. Have you ever read Jordan Robert's books? Or the *Dragon Dreamers* series?
Ummm. No. Pretty much the only thing I read is comics.
Really?
More or less.
You don't read, like, novels or anything? You know, like, fiction?
Not really.
Like Stephen King?
No.
I should lend you my copy of *Argon's Fury*. I think you would like it.
Okay. When did you--Oh my God. Look over by the bar! Wait, don't look--okay, wait: See that, uh, midget? Over by the bar?
Ummm.... yeeeeeaaaah?
He played a Jawa in Star Wars!
He did? Wow. You recognize him?
Yeah, I--well, no not from the movie. I saw him registering for the con. I mean, obviously I wouldn't recognize him from the movie, since you can't really, y'know, see their faces.
Do you want to go talk to him and get his autograph or something?
Huh? No. Nah, I'm sure he gets people coming up to him all the time and everything. He's probably sick of it.
It looks like he's getting along pretty well with that woman. Do you think she knows that he was in Star Wars and everything? Haha, Do you think she's like a groupie or something?
Yeah, probably. You could probably milk a role like that for a long time. That woman...I could swear I've seen her before.
I wonder what it would be like to go out with a midget.
Hahahaha! That's funny.
What's so funny about that?
I don't know. Would you go out with a midget? Have you ever gone out with one? Is that the worst thing you've ever done?
Haha, no. A midget lived in my dorm but she was a girl, so...but I guess I would go out with a midget, if he was cute and nice.
Hmmm. I don't know. It would take some getting used to, I guess. I wonder if she hit on him or he hit on her?
He probably hit on her. You know those movie stars with their big egos and all.

YOU DON'T HAVE A DRIVER'S LICENSE? HOW ODD
THAT'S FUNNY
HARVEY
...PLAYED FIELD HOCKEY IN MY JUNIOR YEAR...
YOU?
... THIS CRAZY ROOM
...STARTED READING COMICS WHEN I WAS NINE YEARS OLD...
HAHA
COMICS WORLD
...COUSIN WON A BRONZE MEDA SKATING...
...NANCY DREW...
...GRAP NOVEL
SPANISH
EALLY? HER AME WAS "OCEANA?" O COOL!
MOVIE SCHEDULE
YFRIEND MATT OKE UP WITH ME...
IDAHO
BEEN TO ONDON, PARIS...
COSTA RIC
TWO CATS...
...FLAVOR CAN BE A REAL PA IN THE ASS...
...SO DRUNK...
"STAR RAIDERS
...NEW JOB AT TH ENTRAL PARK ZOO! ISN'T THA COOL
...SAW STRIKES B 27 TIMES
...MY PARENTS GOT DIVORCE WHEN I WAS SIXTEEN...
I LOVE WINTER SOMETIMES.
ED...

WHEN...
THE WORST THING I'VE EVER DONE?
gh School
Marlys Kierkegaard
Kristenson
JUST, LIKE, SIX MONTHS AFTER MY DAD... AFTER MY PARENTS GOT, Y'KNOW, DIVORCED MY MOM REMARRIED.
RICHARD.
HE WAS... HE WAS HORRIBLE. HE DRANK A LOT AND WAS MEAN TO MY MOM. AND US. HE WAS ... REALLY, UM, ABUSIVE.
Kier
Y'KNOW?
MY BROTHERS, THEY PRETTY MUCH WERE OFF AT COLLEGE BY THAT TIME... AS FAR AWAY AS THEY COULD GET.
THAT LEFT JUST ME AND MY LITTLE SISTER -- SHE'S FIVE YEARS YOUNGER -- THAT LEFT US ALONE WITH HIM.
FOR TWO YEARS.
WE REALLY HATED HIM. WHEN... Heh, WHEN WE WERE ALONE WE'D MAKE UP DIFFERENT WAYS TO, Y'KNOW, KILL HIM. JUST FOR...
I MEAN, WE WEREN'T GOING TO REALLY DO IT.

WHEN I GOT ACCEPTED INTO COLLEGE I WAS SO EXCITED! I COULDN'T WAIT TO GO, TO GET THE HECK OUT OF THERE.
I... IT WAS SO SELFISH. SUCH A... SELF-CENTERED, STUPID --
WHAT WAS I THINKING?!
I LEFT HER THERE ALONE WITH HIM.
HOW... HOW COULD I BE SO STUPID, Y'KNOW?
AND THEN...
AND THEN SHE WAS GONE.
Good Bye
I FOUND OUT WHEN I GOT A POSTCARD FROM NEW YORK CITY AT SCHOOL.
MY MOM TOLD ME THAT SHE'D DONE IT A COUPLE OF TIMES BEFORE, BUT NEVER THAT FAR
OR FOR THIS LONG.
I CAME TO NEW YORK TRYING TO -- HOPING TO FIND HER, Y'KNOW? BUT... IT'S BEEN OVER A YEAR.
Good Bye
I NEVER SHOULD'VE GONE...
NEVER LEFT HER ALONE THERE.

IT'S NOT... YOU SHOULDN'T BLAME YOURSELF.
IT'S NOT YOUR FAULT.
TON
HEHHEH... NOT EXACTLY TYPICAL FIRST DATE MATERIAL, HUH?
NO... ARE YOU GOING TO BE OKAY?
YES.

SWEETIE!
COME ON! I BROUGHT A SHIP!
THANK HEAVENS! I THOUGHT WE'D BE STUCK ALONE ON THIS ASTEROID FOREVER!
LET'S GO!
I CAN'T BELIEVE SHE'S SAVING YOU WHILE YOU'RE SAVING HER!
pant
WELL, WE'RE ALL RESPONSIBLE FOR OUR pant OWN HAPPINESS.
I.. I.. pant pant
ARE YOU OKAY, SWEETIE?
NNN!

I SAID "ARE YOU OKAY, SWEETIE?"
YOU--
OH... I GUESS I MUST'VE DOZED OFF.
THE FOOD SHOULD BE HERE ANY MINUTE.
OKAY.
THE TESTS HAVE COME BACK POSITIVE --SKITTLES HAS FELINE HIV. LORETTA IS DEVISTATED.
GULP!
HMMM?
DR. FLOTTAGE RECOMMENDS THAT THE CAT UNDERGO
UM.
HEM
DO--

DO
DO YOU REMEMBER THAT GIRL CAPRICE? FROM THE
UM
BOOKSTORE?
SKITTLES IS TAKEN IN FOR ANOTHER BATTERY OF TESTS WHILE LORETTA CONSIDERS HER OPTIONS.
TCH! POOR KITTY!
NO, WHO--
OH! YOU MEAN THAT LITTLE FAT GIRL WITH THE VOICE WHO I MET AT THE PARTY?
WHAT ABOUT HER?
WELL, I WOULDN'T SAY SHE W--
YEAH, OKAY, HER.
SOOO... OKAY. YOU REMEMBER HER, RIGHT?
MEANWHILE, IN THE RECOVERY ROOM, SCRAPS FEELS AS GOOD AS NEW!
YEAH, I THINK WE'VE ESTABLISHED THAT. WHAT--
UM...
DO YOU WANT ME TO WAIT 'TIL THIS IS OVER?
IF YOU WANT TO WATCH --
ABBEY WILL NEED TO BRING HIM IN FOR SOME PHYSICAL THERAPY, BUT FOR NOW, HE CAN GO HOME
FAMILY.
NO, GO AHEAD.
I'M... I'M LISTENING.
"WE WERE REALLY AFRAID SCRAPS WAS A GONER!"
"WE'RE JUST SO GLAD HE'S OKAY
OH! GOOD BOY!

Pok!
HEY, WAIT. I WANTED TO SEE THE END OF THAT.
THAT WAS THE END, RIGHT? SCRAPS WAS OKAY AND THEY ALL WENT HOME HAPPY, THE END, RIGHT?
YEAH, BUT THERE WERE TWO OTHER STORIES. THERE WAS THE CAT WHO--
I--GAH!! I WANTED TO TALK TO YOU ABOUT SOMETHING, OKAY?
WELL... IT CAN'T WAIT LIKE FIVE MORE MINUTES OR... IT'S ALMOST OVER.
NO, IT CAN'T WAIT "LIKE FIVE MINUTES" OKAY?
GOD!!
FINE, OKAY? SO WHAT'S SO IMPORTANT?
WELL.
I...
POK!
...SKITTLES DOWN. THE DOCTOR...
WHILE YOU'RE GATHERING YOUR THOUGHTS...

POK!
OH MY GOD! WHAT THE FUCK IS YOUR PROBLEM?
MY PROBLEM IS THAT I'M TRYING TO GODDAMN TELL YOU SOMETHING AND YOU KEEP--
YEAH, WELL, MAYBE IT HASN'T OCCURRED TO YOU THAT I MIGHT NOT BE IN THE MOOD TO HEAR WHAT YOU HAVE TO SAY.?
WHAT? WHAT DOES THAT MEAN?
WHAT IS IT YOU THINK I'M GOING TO--
OH NO! IF YOU FEEL LIKE TALKING, GO RIGHT AHEAD! COME ON!
IF YOU THINK I'M GOING TO SAY IT FOR YOU THINK AGAIN!
WELL, COME ON! WHAT WERE YOU GOING TO TELL ME, SWEETIE? HUH?
I'M MISSING THE END OF THAT CAT STORY SO YOU BETTER FUCKING TELL ME WHAT'S ON YOUR MIND.
WELL? WH--
OKAY! OKAY!
I KISSED CAPRICE, OKAY?!
GOD DAMN IT!

THERE! I SAID IT!
ARE YOU HAP--

I...
IT WAS...
I KNEW IT.
YOU.. Y-YOU DID?
OF COURSE!! I'M NOT FUCKING STUPID, Y'KNOW?!
:sniff:
I HATE TO BREAK IT TO YOU, BIG GUY, BUT YOU'RE NOT THE FIRST ASSHOLE TO FUCKING DUMP ME, OKAY?!
:sniff:
AFTER AWHILE YOU..

BUT... BUT I'M NOT DUMPING YOU.
DOROTHY, I DON'T WANT TO... YOU KNOW.
I LOVE --
OH, OF COURSE! I GUESS IF YOU WANTED TO DUMP ME YOU WOULD'VE GONE AHEAD AND GONE ALL THE WAY AND FUCKED HER, RIGHT?
OH! LUCKY ME! IT WAS A MEASLEY KISS!
IT WAS ONLY A KISS!!
IT WAS A STUPID MISTAKE, OKAY??
I'M SORRY!
JEEZ!
WHA--?! I CAN'T FUCKING BELIEVE YOU!! HOW DARE YOU?! YOU'RE GETTING PISSY WITH ME LIKE THIS IS MY FAULT!!
LIKE I'M BEING A BITCH FOR GETTING MAD YOU FUCKING CHEATED ON ME!!
THAT'S PROBABLY BECAUSE YOU SHOULDN'T --
YOU'RE BLOWING THIS WHOLE STUPID THING OUT OF PROPORTION!
IT. WAS. NOTHING!
OH, RIGHT, AND I'M SURE YOU WOULD BE---
IF I TOLD YOU I FOOLED AROUND WITH RON FROM WORK, BUT DON'T WORRY! "IT WAS NOTHING!"
I'M SURE YOU'D REACT--
WE DIDN'T "FOOL AROUND!" I TOLD YOU IT WAS ONE KISS! SH
KNOCK KNOCK
ROOM SERVICE.

CAN YOU JUST LEAVE IT AT THE DOOR? WE'LL PICK--
UM... TERRIBLY SORRY, SIR, BUT YOU HAVE TO SIGN FOR IT.
SIR.
WE'RE-- SIGH WE'RE SORT OF IN THE MIDDLE OF--
OH, FOR CHRIST'S SAKE! WILL YOU JUST GET THE FUCKING FOOD?!
I'M STARVING!
OVER THERE, I GUESS.
I'M SORRY TO BOTHER YOU, SIR, BUT HOTEL POLICY DICTATES THAT ANY MEALS DELIVERED MUST HAVE A SIG--
YEAH, YEAH.
$228(!) x .15 = UMM...
OKAY, HERE YOU GO.
VERY GOOD, SIR. BON APETIT!
MERCI, GARCON.
WOW. ARE YOU SURE THIS WILL BE ENOUGH?
WELL, I FIGURE SINCE "METRO-CHIC" IS PICKING UP THE TAB AND ALL...
sniff
CHEERS.

OH, TRISH, SOMETIMES I WISH I HAD YOUR LIFE: HUSBAND, KIDS, CARPOOL..
Oh, I May "have it all" but sometimes I wonder what my life Might've been like if I'd actually tried to write a novel.
I'M SURE IT WOULD'VE BEEN GOOD.
Well, maybe I will write
POK!

CLIK!
Y'KNOW... :SNIFF:
I ALMOST WISH YOU HADN'T EVEN TOLD ME
WELL.
I'M, UH, BEGINNING TO QUESTION THE WISDOM OF THAT DECISION MYSELF.
SO
WHAT DO WE DO NOW?
I GIVE UP:
WHAT DO WE DO NOW?
I GUESS IT'S UP TO YOU.
WELL...
I MEAN...
LIKE I SAID
I DON'T WANT US TO BREAK UP.
I LOVE YOU AND WHAT I DID WAS... WRONG. IT WAS A MISTAKE.
I... DEEPLY REGRET IT AND AM ... I CANNOT CONVEY HOW SORRY I AM.
BUT...
I DON'T WANT US TO BREAK UP, BUT I COULD UNDERSTAND THAT YOU MIGHT... FEEL...
YOU, UM,
I WOULD UNDERSTAND IF YOU...
I DON'T WANT US TO BREAK UP, EITHER.
BUUUUUUT....?

BUT NOTHING. I... I JUST NEED SOME TIME TO... RUMINATE OVER ALL OF THIS.
FAIR ENOUGH.
UM.
WELL, AS LONG AS YOU'RE RUMINATING, THERE'S SOMETHING ELSE I WANT TO...
:ahem:
EVER SINCE THIS WHOLE THING... THIS IS GOING TO SOUND ODD OR, UH, FUNNY BUT IN A WAY I'M ALMOST GLAD THIS WHOLE THING, UH... HAPPENED.
HOLD ON, HOLD ON. LET ME FINISH:
THE, UHHH, REASON I'M SORT OF GLAD IS THAT IT'S MADE ME, I DON'T KNOW, LIKE RE-EXAMINE OUR RELATIONSHIP AND SORT OUT HOW I...
YOU KNOW, HOW I FEEL ABOUT YOU AND US...
AND, UH,
IT MADE ME REALIZE THAT I DON'T WANT ANYONE ELSE. I WANT YOU.
I LOVE YOU. I DO LOVE YOU.

AAAAAND... I'VE BEEN THINKING ABOUT WHAT YOU SAID AWHILE AGO FOR, UH, A FEW WEEKS. SO...
IF YOU DID DECIDE THAT YOU... WE SHOULD... Y'KNOW, THAT YOU COULD FORGIVE ME, THEN....
MAYBE WE COULD MOVE IN TOGETHER.

·OMEN·

¡NO!
CHRIST, EDDIE! I JUST HAD THE WEIRDEST DREAM!
WHAT THE HELL TIME IS--
WILSON ROOM →
POLK ROOM →
NIXON ROOM ←
I'VE BEEN WAITING FOR YOU, MR. FLAVOR.
WE MEET AGAIN AT LAST...

GUYS, THIS IS IRVING FLAVOR. HE TAUGHT ME EVERYTHING HE KNOWS ABOUT COMICS.
IT WAS THE MOST FASCINATING TWENTY-MINUTES OF MY LIFE.
HAWHAW!
I'LL BE DAMNED! LITTLE BOBBIE GARR! HOW YA DOIN'? I HEAR YOU'VE BECOME QUITE A, UH, SUPERSTAR, HUH?
IT COULDN'T HAVE HAPPENED TO A SWELLER GUY.
THANKS, MR. FLAVOR! MAYBE YOU ALSO HEARD THAT I'VE MADE MORE MONEY DRAWING NIGHTSTALKER THAN YOU MADE IN YOUR ENTIRE CAREER, HM?
WHOA! SHIT! HAHA!
(WELL, I MEAN EXCEPT FOR THOSE PORNO COMICS YOU DREW IN THE FIFTIES. I'M SURE THAT WAS A LUCRATIVE GIG.)
YOU UNTALENTED LITTLE PRI--
I ALSO HEARD THAT NOW THAT YOUR HANDS ARE TOO SHAKY TO DRAW A STRAIGHT LINE WITH A RULER YOU'RE CRYING THAT J.C. RIPPED YOU OFF.
"OOOOH! I'M POOR AND MADE A STUPID DECISION SO NOW I WANT A FREE RIDE! BOOHOO!"
HAHA! SHIT, DUDE!
WHOA! HAHA!
YEAH AND YOUR JOKES AREN'T AS FUNNY AS YOUR GOD DAMNED ANATOMY, ROBBIE. MAYBE YOU --
YEAH, MAYBE I SHOULD GET TO MY TABLE WHERE MY FANS ARE LINED UP TO PAY FOR MY AUTOGRAPH, RIGHT?
ENJOY THE CON, IRVING!

YIGO!
DOUBLE CROSS
MORNING...
♫ HILDY... HILDY...
MMM..
HEM MORNING... I GUESS WE SORTA DOZED OFF, HUH?
I GUESS IF WE HAD KNOWN THE COUCHES WERE THIS NICE WE COULD'VE SAVED SOME MONEY AND SKIPPED GETTING ROOMS.
Heh...
UM.
SORRY I KEPT YOU UP ALL NIGHT.

DON'T BE SORRY, I HAD A GOOD TIME.
SOOOO... I SUPPOSE WE SHOULD GET CLEANED UP, HUH?
YEAH. WE'VE GOT A BIG DAY AHEAD OF US.
I SHOULD SEE HOW MR. FLAVOR --
HEY! YOU GUYS ARE UP EARLY. I TRIED CALLING YOUR ROOM BUT THERE WAS NO--
OH, WAIT. I HOPE I'M NOT INTERRUPTING ANYTHING. SHOULD--
PRESS
NAH, WE WERE JUST GOING TO GO TO OUR ROOMS TO FRESHEN UP. OH, YOU REMEMBER HILDY RIGHT?
OH, SURE, FROM, UH, "COMICS, UM, MAGAZINE," RIGHT?
I WAS JUST GOING TO GET A BITE. YOU WANT TO JOIN ME FOR SOME BREAKFAST?
OH, YOU BASTARD, YOU KNOW MY WEAKSPOT! SOUNDS GOOD. WHAT ABOUT YOU?
NO, YOU GUYS GO AHEAD. I'LL SEE YOU AT THE SHOW.
OH, OKAY. WAIT: UH, SHERMAN I'LL BE RIGHT BACK IN A SEC, OKAY?
OKAY. LET'S RUSTLE US UP SOME GRUB!

BOY, GET A LOAD OF YOU! EVER SINCE THAT PARTY YOU'VE BECOME A REGULAR DON JOO-AN!
MY FRIEND, WHAT CAN I TELL YOU?
I TRADED IN MY VIRGINITY FOR A STRONG, ALMOST HYPNOTIC POWER OVER THE WOMEN.
SIGH
YEEEEEUP.
WELL... YOU WEREN'T THE ONLY ONE WHO WAS UP ALL NIGHT.
YOU...
WHAT DID SHE, UH.
SAY?
HEM
WELL.
OF COURSE SHE WAS ANGRY AND EVERYTHING AT FIRST, BUT I FINALLY CONVINCED HER THAT I WAS SORRY, AND THAT IT WAS WRONG AND THAT IT DIDN'T MEAN ANYTHING.
DID IT?
WHICH IT DIDN'T
SO, UM, THEN WE TALKED ABOUT WHAT WE WOULD DO NEXT. Y'KNOW, DO WE BREAK UP, DO WE TRY TO WORK IT OUT, LIKE THAT.
SOOOO...
WELL, WE PRETTY MUCH AGREED TO STICK TOGETHER. SO, UH...
TO SORT OF, Y'KNOW, SWEETEN THE DEAL, I SAID THAT SHE AND I SHOULD, UH,..
WELL, LIKE,
MOVE IN TOGETHER.

I'M... I FELT LIKE I HAD TO, ED, AS A SHOW OF GOOD FAITH OR WHATEVER. TO SHOW HER...
I FEEL TERRIBLE ABOUT LEAVING YOU IN THE LURCH THIS WAY, BUT IT WAS...
I HAD TO DO IT, YOU KNOW?
DON'T BE-- COME ON, YOU'LL STILL BE ABLE TO MOVE OUT OF YOUR PARENTS' PLACE! BETWEEN FLAVOR AND YOUR DAD'S STORE YOU CAN PROBABLY AFFORD A NICE STUDIO.
IN QUEENS, AT LEAST.
OH! COME ON! I FEEL BAD ENOUGH AS IT IS! WOULD YOU SAY SOMETHING ALREADY!
YOU'RE KILLING ME HERE!
I THINK YOU'RE MAKING A BIG MISTAKE.

I THINK YOU'RE ONLY DOING THIS BECAUSE YOU FEEL GUILTY ABOUT KISSING THAT GIRL CLARICE. I DON'T THINK YOU --
BUT THAT'S NOT WHY I'M DOING IT.!
(AND HER NAME WAS CAPRICE)
I'M DOING IT BECAUSE THIS WHOLE THING HAS MADE ME REALIZE THAT I DON'T WANT TO LOSE HER. DOROTHY.
I DON'T KNOW... IT'S SUCH A BIG DECISION, THOUGH. WOULDN'T IT BE BETTER IF YOU GUYS WAITED A BIT?
'TIL THINGS, YOU KNOW, CALMED DOWN A SPELL?
YOU DON'T WANT TO MAKE A DECISION BASED --
NO, NO, I'VE BEEN THINKING ABOUT IT FOR A LONG TIME, EVER SINCE SHE BROUGHT IT UP LAST MONTH. THE THING WITH THIS GIRL JUST SORT OF CONFIRMED -- SOLIDIFIED -- MY THINKING.
I KNOW YOU'RE MAD BECAUSE YOUR PLANS FOR MOVING OUT ARE DELAYED, BUT THIS IS SOMETHING...
IT SOUNDS HOKEY, BUT IT'S PART OF LIFE, YOU KNOW?
YOU MEET SOMEONE, YOU GET TO KNOW THEM, YOU "FALL IN LOVE" AND YOU START, Y'KNOW, BUILDING A LIFE TOGETHER.
NO, I'VE THOUGHT ABOUT IT AND IT'S THE RIGHT THING TO DO.
I LOVE HER.
MMMOKAY.
YOU DON'T SOUND TERRIBLY CONVINCED.
YOU SHOULDN'T FEEL LIKE YOU NEED TO CONVINCE ME OF ANYTHING.
BUT I JUST HOPE YOU'RE NOT MAKING A DECISION YOU MIGHT... REGRET.
NOW, OF COURSE I'M DISAPPOINTED I'LL BE STUCK WITH MY FOLKS A LITTLE LONGER, BUT IT WILL WORK OUT.

Sigh
WELL, I APPRECIATE YOUR HONESTY... AND YOUR CONCERN. BUT...
SO, IN ANY CASE, WE'RE STILL "COOL", RIGHT? I DON'T WANT TO GET TOO, UH, CORNY ABOUT IT...
BUT WE'RE STILL FRIENDS, RIGHT?
WELLLLLLL...
PAY FOR MY BREAKFAST AND MAYBE IT'S A DEAL.
DONE AND DONE, OLD BUDDY, OLD PAL.
I GOTTA GET UPSTAIRS. WE'LL SEE YOU AT THE SHOW. FLAVOR'S BIG DAY AND ALL!
YOU GOT IT, PUNK! ONE O'CLOCK IN THE HAYES ROOM!
SEE YA LATER.
Shit.

YOU READY, SWEETIE?
"ZOOM COMICS MAKES BILLIONS OFF OF THIS GUY AND THEY CAN'T THROW A FEW BUCKS HIS WAY? THAT'S... THAT'S JUST NOT RIGHT."
UHHHH... YEP.
"UH... I DON'T KNOW, MAN. NIGHT-STALKER'S COOL AND SHIT, BUT I LOOKED AT THIS GUY FAVOR'S STUFF AND... I DON'T KNOW, MAN, IT SORT OF SUCKED. IT... REAL OLD SCHOOL."
ED FOR CRYIN' OUT LOUD, WILL YOU GET THE LEAD OUT?
YEAH, OK.
YOU'RE GONNA MAKE ME LATE FOR MY OWN AWARD!
"I THINK IT'S TERRIBLE WHAT THEY, LIKE, DID TO HIM, RIGHT? THE NIGHTSTALKER HE'S, Y'KNOW, LIKE, AN IDOL, LIKE, AN ICON? IT'S JUST NOT RIGHT."
HUBUB
...COMICS WORLD...
...I HEARD
...NEAR MINT
...ZOOM COMICS...
...FLAVOR...
DAHLIA...
WANTS HIM DEAD...
"NOT ONLY SHOULD THEY GIVE THAT FLAVOR MONEY, THEY SHOULD GIVE BACK ALL THE MONEY THEY MADE ON 'NIGHTSTALKER IV' 'CUZ THAT MOVIE FUCKING SUCKED."
OKAY, KIDS. SHOWTIME.

TKO
THANK YOU ALL FOR COMING.
FIRST OF ALL, WHILE I CERTAINLY DON'T AGREE WITH EVERYTHING "COMICS WORLD" HAS TO SAY...
HAHAHAHAHA HAHA HA HA HA HA
COMICS WORLD
I'M GLAD WE CAN ALL SET ASIDE OUR DIFFERENCES TO HONOR A GENUINE... LEGEND IN COMICS HISTORY ON THIS DAY.
WHILE IT IS AN UNFORTUNATE CIRCUMSTANCE THAT BROUGHT IRVING FLAVOR BACK INTO THE PUBLIC EYE --
HIS BRUTAL RAPE AT THE HANDS OF J.C. LEBLANC AND ZOOM COMICS --
IT IS FORTUNATE THAT WE'RE GIVEN THIS OPPORTUNITY TO THANK THIS CREATOR FOR HIS CONTRIBUTION TO OUR CULTURE...
OUR COMMUNITY.

TOO MANY OF HIS CONTEMPORARIES HAVE VANISHED INTO THAT DARK NIGHT ALL BUT FORGOTTEN BY THE INDUSTRY BUILT ON THEIR BACKS
ON THEIR SWEAT, ON THEIR TEARS.
PRETTY GOOD TURNOUT, HUH?
I'LL SAY! I NEVER REALIZED THAT MR. FLAVOR HAD BECOME SUCH A PUBLIC CAUSE.
OF COURSE, HAVING BRUCE KNIGHT AS EMCEE DOESN'T HURT.
HIS WORK ON NIGHTSTALKER BACK IN THE '80s REALLY REVIVED THE FRANCHISE.
WHEN IRVING FLAVOR MET SIMON LEBLANC IN 1940, HE WAS JUST SIXTEEN YEARS OLD. THE SON OF A TAILOR, HE SPENT HOURS DOODLING AT...
YOU MUST BE SORT OF PROUD. ALL THE WORK YOU TWO DID TO GET THIS FAR.
HMMM. YEAH. Y'KNOW, I GUESS I AM A LITTLE PROUD. I'M ALMOST STARTING TO BELIEVE THIS WHOLE THING MIGHT WORK.
WE MAY ACTUALLY WIN THIS THING!
...AND THE AMERICAN DREAM ITSELF.
NOW WE CAN ONLY HOPE THAT JUSTICE IS ON HIS SIDE, HOPE THAT ZOOM WILL DO THE HONORABLE THING.
THANK YOU.
CLAP! C
AP! CLA
! CLAP!
CLAP! C
OKAY: NOW, TO PRESENT IRVING WITH HIS LIFE-TIME ACHIEVEMENT AWARD IS THE EDITOR AND PUB-LISHER OF "COMICS WORLD"
HARVEY HITCHCOCK!
COMICS WORLD

CLAP CLAP CLAP
COMICS WORLD
UM, THANK YOU, BRUCE.
BEFORE WE GET TO OUR GUEST OF HONOR, I'D LIKE TO MENTION -- I'D LIKE TO SAY HOW, UH, PROUD AND HAPPY I AM.
HAPPY THAT IT WAS "COMICS WORLD" THAT BROUGHT IRVING FLAVOR IN TO THE PUBLIC EYE.'
COMICS
BUT... I GUESS THAT'S THE WAY ITS ALWAYS BEEN, HASN'T IT?
FIRST WITH REGGIE WICKER... THEN WITH JONAS SOLSON...
"COMICS WORLD" BREAKS THE STORY, AND THEN EVERYONE JUMPS ON THE BANDWAGON.
PEOPLE LOOOOVE TO GIVE US SHIT BUT, PARDON MY FRENCH, BUT IF IT WASN'T FOR US,
COUGH
:LOSER:
HA HA HA HA HA
COMICS WORLD
IF IT WASN'T FOR US, WHERE WOULD YOU HEAR ABOUT STUFF LIKE THAT?
WHAT, FROM "COLLECTOR'S WORLD?!" OPEN YOUR EYES!
COUGH
:PENIS:
HA HA HA HA HA HA HA HA HA HA HA
COUGH! COUGH!
HA HA HA HA
SO MAYBE, JUST MAYBE, IRVING FLAVOR ISN'T THE ONLY ONE DUE A LITTLE RESPECT FROM THIS SHITHOLE INDUSTRY?!
COUGH
:DICK:
COUGH
ANUS
COUGH!
:LOSER!

YOU... YOU CRETINS WOULDN'T... HUH? WHAT?
NO! I HAVE TO-- BUT-- BUT-- THEY--
OKAY! OKAY! FINE! Ahem
AND NOW, LADIES AND GENTLEMEN, IT IS MY... PLEASURE TO PRESENT "COMICS WORLD'S" LIFETIME ACHIEVEMENT AWARD TO OUR GUEST OF HONOR. PLEASE GIVE A WARM WELCOME...
TO MR. IRVING FLAVOR.
CLAP CLAP CLAP CLAP CLAP! CLAP
CLAP! CLAP! CLAP! CLAP! CLAP!
CLAP! CLAP! CLAP! CLAP! CLAP!
CRAP!
CLAP! CLAP!
COMICS WORLD

UH, THANKS, FELLAS.
THANK YOU, EVERYBODY.
UH...
COMICS WORLD
LIKE THAT GUY BEFORE SAID, I'VE BEEN IN THIS BUSINESS FOR OVER FIFTY YEARS, AND IT'S, UH, NICE TO KNOW IT WASN'T ALL FOR NOTHING, Y'KNOW?
REALLY NICE.
EXIT
NOW, BEFORE I GO ON THERE'S SOMEONE I'D LIKE TO BRING UP ON THE STAGE WITH ME.
I'M SURE HE DOESN'T NEED NO INTRODUCTION AND YOU ALL KNOW WHO HE IS SO...
LET'S BRING HIM UP.
EX
NO WAY!

CLAP!CLAP!
CLAP!CLAP!CLAP!CLAP!
CLAP!CLAP!CLAP!
CLAP!CLAP!

HAHA! THANK YOU FOR THAT TUMULTUOUS WELCOME, O FAITHFUL ZOOMBIES!
WHOOOO!
YEAHHH
WOOOOO
ZOOM
I AM HAPPY THAT IRV LET ME JOIN HIM TODAY BECAUSE I HAVE A BIG ANNOUNCEMENT TO MAKE AND WHAT BETTER PLACE TO MAKE IT THAN HERE?
COMICS WORLD
I HAVE HERE IN MY HAND A DOCUMENT WHICH WILL END THE... TERRIBLE MISUNDERSTANDING BETWEEN ZOOM COMICS AND ONE OF ITS MOST CHERISHED FOUNDING FATHERS.
I WON'T GO INTO ALL THE LEGAL MUMBO-JUMBO
(I HAD TO HIRE A TEAM OF LAWYERS JUST TO TRANSLATE THE DARN THING!)
BUT I WILL BOIL IT DOWN TO THREE SIMPLE WORDS.
WE WERE WRONG.
NOW, THE LAWYERS HAVE TOLD ME THAT FOR A BUNCH OF BORING, TECHNICAL REASONS, THEY CANNOT GIVE IRV HERE LEGAL OWNERSHIP OF THE NIGHTSTALKER.
BUT I FELT THAT WE HAD TO GIVE HIM SOMETHING. WE ALL OWED HIM SOMETHING, RIGHT?
COMICS WORLD

BUT WHAT IRVING TOLD ME WAS VERY REVEALING: HE TOLD ME THAT WHAT HE WANTED...
MORE THAN ANYTHING...
WAS TO WORK.
WHO CAN BLAME HIM? HE MISSED THE HUSTLE AND BUSTLE OF THIS CRAZY BUSINESS OF OURS. HE MISSED THE FAN MAIL, THE DEADLINES, THE... THRILL OF CREATION.
OF BEING AN ARTIST.
I'M ASHAMED TO SAY THAT I UNDERESTIMATED THIS MAN.
COMIC WORLD
ED, WHAT'S GOING ON?
DO YOU KNOW ANYTHING ABOUT THIS?
WHAT? NO! I CAN'T--
WHY DIDN'T HE TELL ME?!
SO TODAY, IN FRONT OF YOU ALL, I'M GIVEN THE RARE CHANCE TO CORRECT A GRAVE ERROR.
IRV, THIS CONTRACT NOT ONLY GIVES YOU A LUMP SUM PAYMENT AS A TOKEN OF OUR ESTEEM FOR GIVING US THE NIGHTSTALKER...
IT ALSO, AFTER A TEN YEAR HIATUS, WELCOMES IRVING FLAVOR BACK INTO ZOOM'S GALAXY OF TALENT!
SO?
WHAT DO YOU SAY?

J.C... IT'S
IT'S GOOD TO BE BACK!
CLAP! CLAP! CLAP! CLAP!
(OKAY, BRING 'EM OUT!)
LADIES AND GENTLEMEN...!
LADIES AND GENTLEMEN, I WANT YOU TO TAKE A LOOK AT IRVING FLAVOR'S NEWEST CREATIONS!
LOOK FOR THEM THIS SUMMER IN A BRAND NEW SERIES FROM ZOOM COMICS!

CLAP! CLAP! CLAP! CLAP! CLAP! CLAP! CLAP! CRAP! CLAP!
LADIES AND GENTLEMEN, WE GIVE YOU METEOR AND THE COMET KID!
IRV... THE COMICS COMMUNITY SAYS "WELCOME HOME."
WOW! I CAN'T BELIEVE ALL THIS. ED, YOU REALLY DIDN'T KNOW ANY--
ED?
ED?
CLAP! CLAP! CLAP!

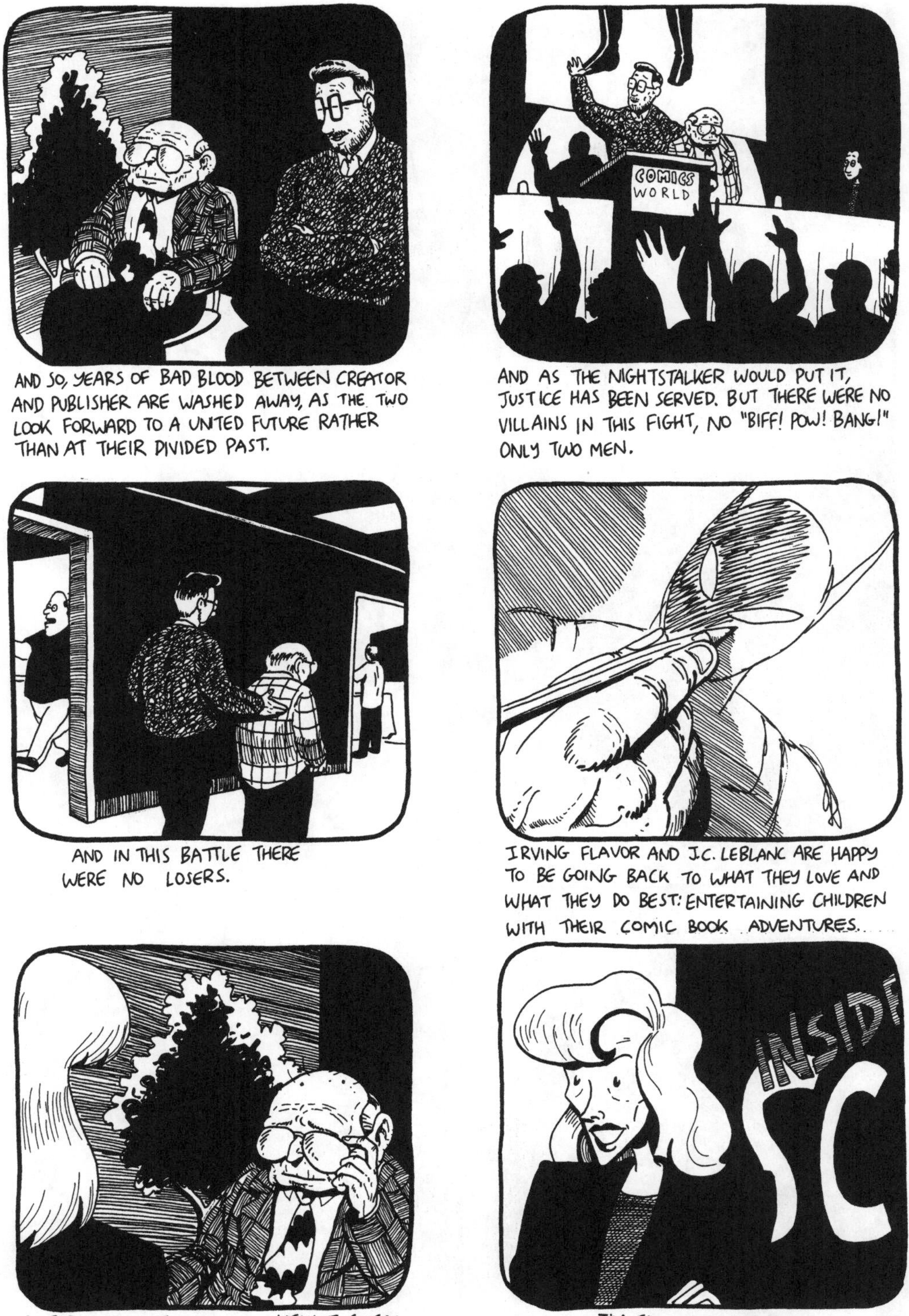
AND SO, YEARS OF BAD BLOOD BETWEEN CREATOR AND PUBLISHER ARE WASHED AWAY, AS THE TWO LOOK FORWARD TO A UNITED FUTURE RATHER THAN AT THEIR DIVIDED PAST.
COMICS WORLD
AND AS THE NIGHTSTALKER WOULD PUT IT, JUSTICE HAS BEEN SERVED. BUT THERE WERE NO VILLAINS IN THIS FIGHT, NO "BIFF! POW! BANG!" ONLY TWO MEN.
AND IN THIS BATTLE THERE WERE NO LOSERS.
IRVING FLAVOR AND J.C. LEBLANC ARE HAPPY TO BE GOING BACK TO WHAT THEY LOVE AND WHAT THEY DO BEST: ENTERTAINING CHILDREN WITH THEIR COMIC BOOK ADVENTURES...
SO FOR ONCE, LIFE IS LIKE A COMIC BOOK, RIGHT? A HAPPY ENDING?
YEAH, I GUESS IT IS.
INSIDE SC
I'M ELIZABETH PIERBORNE, AND THAT... WAS THE INSIDE SCOOP.

GAME OVER
ED, FOR CHRIST'S SAKE, WHERE YA BEEN? COME ON, THEY WANNA TALK TO YOU FOR THAT T.V. SHOW.!
MR. FLAVOR, I QUIT.
QUIT? WHAT DO MEAN YOU--
I CAN'T BELIEVE YOU DIDN'T -- HOW COULD YOU NOT TELL ME ABOUT ALL THAT?!
WHAT ARE--WHAT, THAT STUFF WITH J.C.? I...
THAT WAS BETWEEN HIM AND ME, OKAY?
I DIDN'T THINK THAT I NEEDED YOUR GODDAMNED APPROVAL IF I WAS GOING TO...

HOW LONG AGO DID YOU SET ALL OF THIS STUFF UP?
SHIT! WHEN YOU SHOWED ME THOSE METEON AND THE COSMIC KID SKETCHES THE DEAL WAS ALREADY DONE WASN'T IT?
FOR CHRIST'S SAKE, ED! I DID THIS FOR THE BOTH OF US! NOW THAT WE'RE BACK IN ACTION WE'LL BE MAKING REAL MONEY! GOOD MONEY!
WHAT DID --
SHIT, I'M ALMOST AFRAID TO ASK...
J.C. MENTIONED A LUMP PAYMENT FOR THE NIGHTSTALKER, DIDN'T HE?
HOW, UH...
HOW MUCH, UH...
WAS IT?
I'M NOT-- THE CONRACT SAYS I CAN'T DISCUSS THE SETTLEMENT WI--
HOW
MUCH?
GODAMMIT, ED, THE IMPORTANT THING IS WE CAN GO BACK TO WORK! NO MORE CEREAL BOXES OR --
$48,000.
NOW, I DON'T WANNA HEAR A DAMNED WORD--

THEY
ED, I COULDA GOT NOTHING!
OKAY, SEE, I KNOW HOW YOU GOT THIS COCKAMAMIE IDEA THAT WE COULDA GOT TEN BILLION DOLLARS FROM THEM OR SOMETHING, BUT WE ALSO COULDA GOT JACK SHIT!
LET'S FACE IT, I DIDN'T HAVE A LEGAL LEG TO STAND ON.
I'M SURE THAT'S JUST WHAT J.C. LEBLANC TOLD YOU, HUH?
THEY PROBABLY SPENT $48,000 ON CATERING THE LAST MOVIE! YOU SHOULD'VE AT --
WOULD YOU PLEASE NOT TALK ABOUT THINGS YOU DON'T KNOW ANYTHING ABOUT?
THE MOVIE STUFF IS ENTIRELY A SEPARATE CONCERN FROM THE COMIC BOOK SIDE OF THINGS! ZOOM COMICS DOESN'T HAVE NOTHING TO DO WITH THAT END OF IT!
SEE, THIS IS EXACTLY WHY I DIDN'T WANT TO TELL YOU ABOUT IT. I KNEW YOU'D GET ALL, UH, ALL DIFFICULT.
I GUESS AS LONG AS YOU'RE SATISFIED THAT'S ALL THAT REALLY MATTERS.
THAT'S RIGHT, CHIEF, AND I AM 100%, NO QUESTIONED ASKED SATISFIED, OKAY?
NOW, COME ON, THOSE T.V. PEOPLE ARE WAITING FOR YOU DOWNSTAIRS.

I TOLD YOU I'M NOT GOING.
I CAN'T KEEP WORKI FOR YOU AF
COME ON, EDDIE! THIS IS A ONCE IN A LIFETIME OPPORTUNITY! THIS IS THE TICKET INTO THE BUSINESS YOU'VE BEEN WAITING FOR ALL YOUR LIFE!
HAHA! AND BESIDES, WHO ELSE CAN I GET THAT WILL WORK SO CHEAP!
I'M SURE YOUR PAL J.C. CAN HELP YOU FIND A NEW ASSISTANT, MR. FLAVOR.
ESPECIALLY NOW THAT YOU'VE GOT THAT BIG $48,000, Y'KNOW?
YOU KNOW WHAT YOU CAN DO, MR. BIGSHOT?! YOU CAN GO FUCK YOURSELF, THAT'S WHAT!!
AFTER ALL I'VE DID FOR YOU!! AFTER ALL WE·· THAT YOU CAN TREAT ME WITH SUCH, UH, UH·UH·CONTEMPT
YOU?! I'M THE WHO SH
WALK A·GODAMN·WAY! THROW AWAY EVERYTHING I'VE FUCKING WORKED FOR, YOU, YOU INGRATE!!

ANDANDAND LEMME TELL YOU THIS, CHIEF: ONCE YOU REALIZE YOU AIN'T GONNA MAKE IT ON YOUR OWN, DON'T COME CRAWLING BACK TO ME, GOT IT?
CUZ I'LL SPIT RIGHT IN YOUR GODDAMN FACE, YOU UNGRATEFUL LITTLE PRICK!
YOU GUYS ARE ALL THE SAME, WITH--
1213
1215
I CAN'T BELIEVE IT... HE STOLE OUR P.R. COUP RIGHT OUT FROM UNDER US... I CAN'T BELIEVE IT...
HERO
KRISTEN
CAT
MAN-BABY!
DOUBLE

HAYES
EXIT
GAMING ROOM
AHH! MY FRIEND! YOU ARE LOOKING FOR A RIDE, YES, MY FRIEND?
SURE. WHY NOT?
HAHA! YES! OKAY, YES, I WILL TAKE YOU VERY MUCH! OKAY! HAHA!
ED!
ED! WAIT!

WHERE ARE YOU GOING?
UH... HOME, I GUESS.
IT'S BEEN--
I CAN'T STAY HERE ANYMORE.
OH, OKAY. UMM...
CAN I COME WITH YOU?

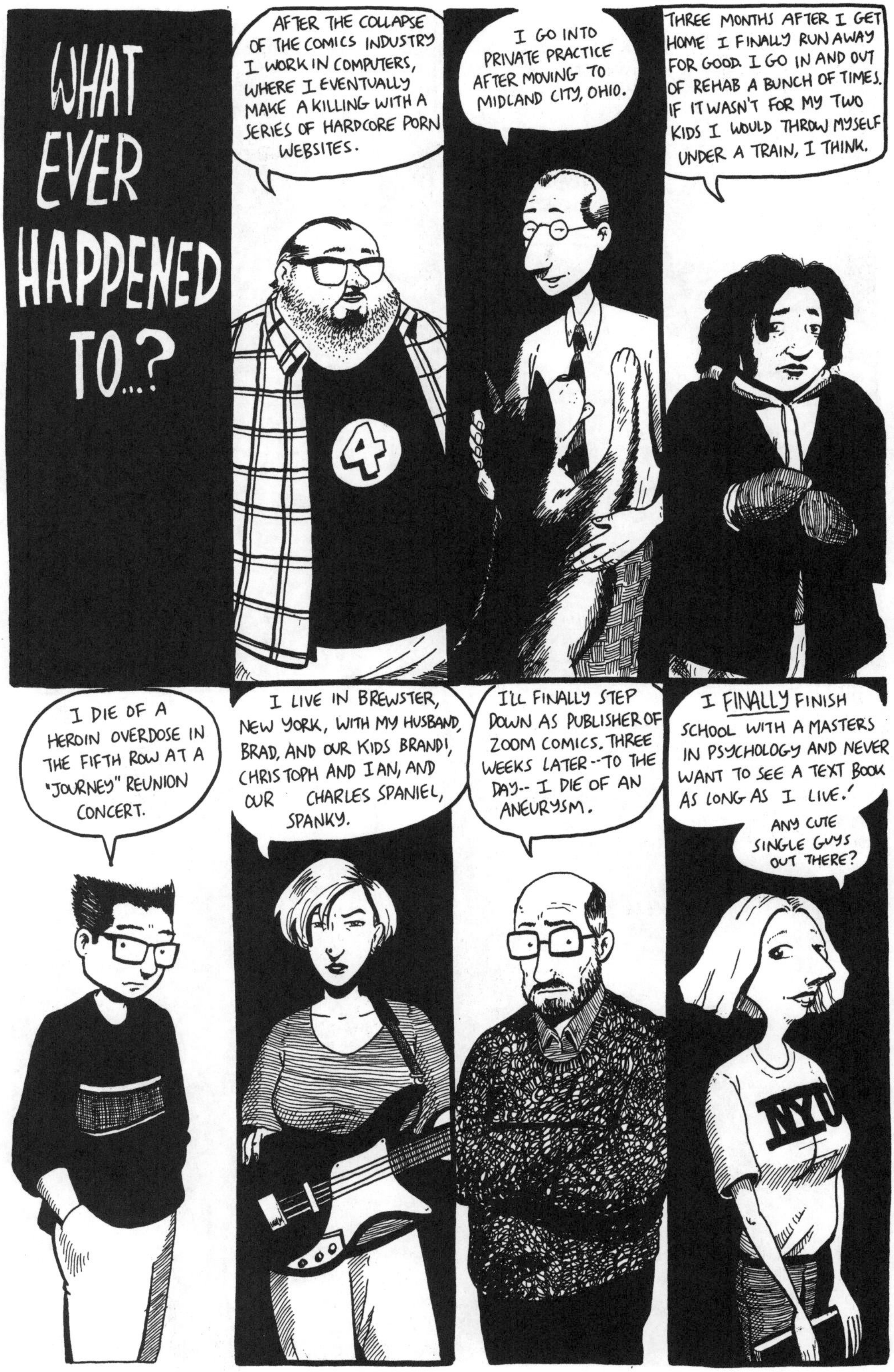
WHAT EVER HAPPENED TO...?
AFTER THE COLLAPSE OF THE COMICS INDUSTRY I WORK IN COMPUTERS, WHERE I EVENTUALLY MAKE A KILLING WITH A SERIES OF HARDCORE PORN WEBSITES.
I GO INTO PRIVATE PRACTICE AFTER MOVING TO MIDLAND CITY, OHIO.
THREE MONTHS AFTER I GET HOME I FINALLY RUN AWAY FOR GOOD. I GO IN AND OUT OF REHAB A BUNCH OF TIMES. IF IT WASN'T FOR MY TWO KIDS I WOULD THROW MYSELF UNDER A TRAIN, I THINK.
I DIE OF A HEROIN OVERDOSE IN THE FIFTH ROW AT A "JOURNEY" REUNION CONCERT.
I LIVE IN BREWSTER, NEW YORK, WITH MY HUSBAND, BRAD, AND OUR KIDS BRANDI, CHRISTOPH AND IAN, AND OUR CHARLES SPANIEL, SPANKY.
I'LL FINALLY STEP DOWN AS PUBLISHER OF ZOOM COMICS. THREE WEEKS LATER--TO THE DAY-- I DIE OF AN ANEURYSM.
I FINALLY FINISH SCHOOL WITH A MASTERS IN PSYCHOLOGY AND NEVER WANT TO SEE A TEXT BOOK AS LONG AS I LIVE.
ANY CUTE SINGLE GUYS OUT THERE?
4
NYU

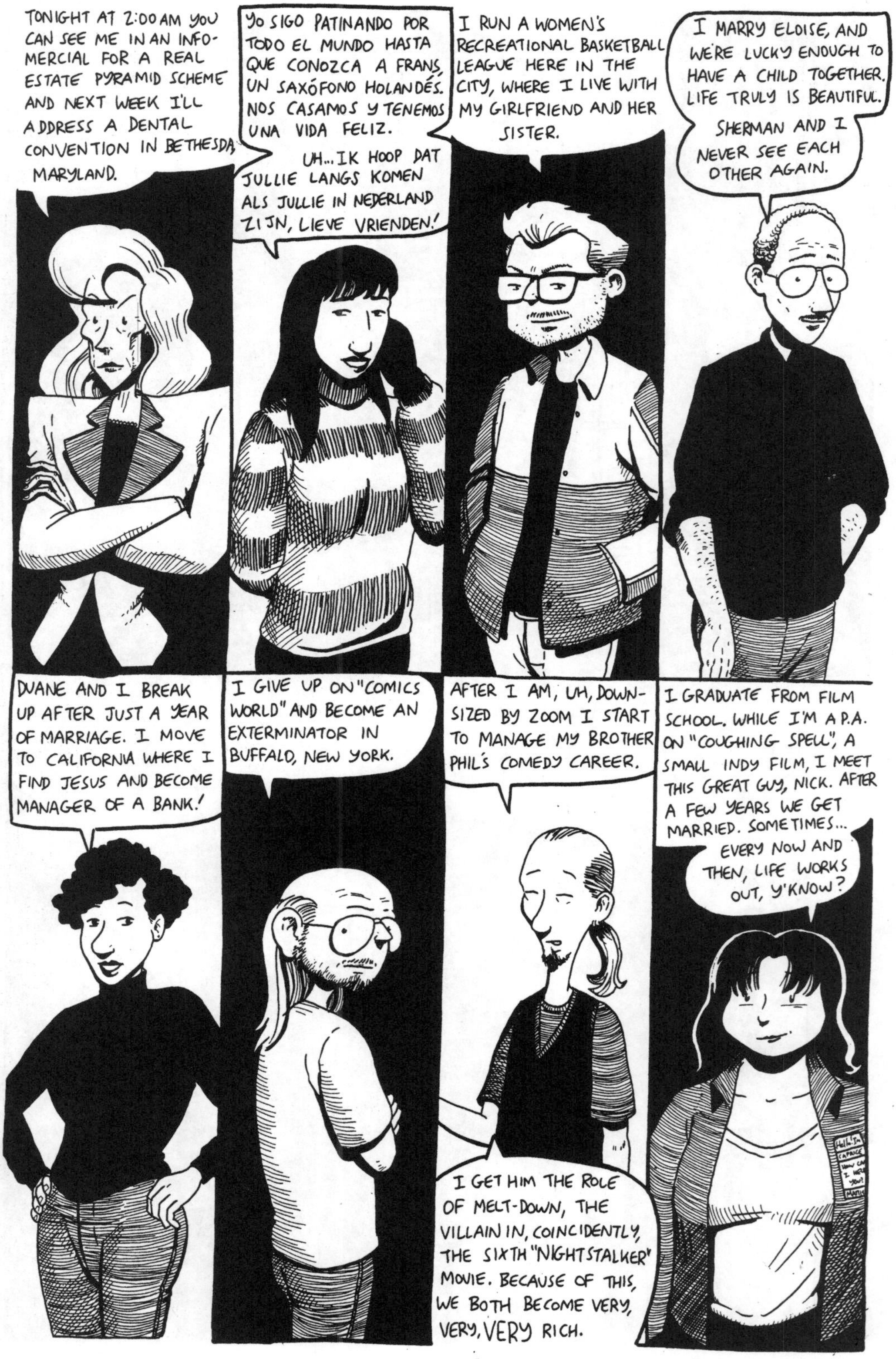
TONIGHT AT 2:00AM YOU CAN SEE ME IN AN INFO-MERCIAL FOR A REAL ESTATE PYRAMID SCHEME AND NEXT WEEK I'LL ADDRESS A DENTAL CONVENTION IN BETHESDA MARYLAND.
YO SIGO PATINANDO POR TODO EL MUNDO HASTA QUE CONOZCA A FRANS, UN SAXÓFONO HOLANDÉS. NOS CASAMOS Y TENEMOS UNA VIDA FELIZ.
UH... IK HOOP DAT JULLIE LANGS KOMEN ALS JULLIE IN NEDERLAND ZIJN, LIEVE VRIENDEN!
I RUN A WOMEN'S RECREATIONAL BASKETBALL LEAGUE HERE IN THE CITY, WHERE I LIVE WITH MY GIRLFRIEND AND HER SISTER.
I MARRY ELOISE, AND WE'RE LUCKY ENOUGH TO HAVE A CHILD TOGETHER. LIFE TRULY IS BEAUTIFUL.
SHERMAN AND I NEVER SEE EACH OTHER AGAIN.
DUANE AND I BREAK UP AFTER JUST A YEAR OF MARRIAGE. I MOVE TO CALIFORNIA WHERE I FIND JESUS AND BECOME MANAGER OF A BANK!
I GIVE UP ON "COMICS WORLD" AND BECOME AN EXTERMINATOR IN BUFFALO, NEW YORK.
AFTER I AM, UH, DOWN-SIZED BY ZOOM I START TO MANAGE MY BROTHER PHIL'S COMEDY CAREER.
I GET HIM THE ROLE OF MELT-DOWN, THE VILLAIN IN, COINCIDENTLY, THE SIXTH "NIGHTSTALKER" MOVIE. BECAUSE OF THIS, WE BOTH BECOME VERY, VERY, VERY RICH.
I GRADUATE FROM FILM SCHOOL. WHILE I'M A P.A. ON "COUGHING SPELL", A SMALL INDY FILM, I MEET THIS GREAT GUY, NICK. AFTER A FEW YEARS WE GET MARRIED. SOMETIMES...
EVERY NOW AND THEN, LIFE WORKS OUT, Y'KNOW?

EPILOGUE

IT WAS ABOUT FOUR YEARS AGO THAT IRVING FLAVOR WENT TO THAT BIG BULLPEN IN THE SKY.

I READ ABOUT IT AT SOME COMICS RELATED WEBSITE AND FIGURED I'D OWED HIM THIS MUCH.

IT WAS... WEIRD.

THERE WERE ONLY SIX OTHER MOURNERS THERE AT THE FUNERAL. NO ONE SPOKE TO ONE ANOTHER, SO I WAS FREE TO CONCOCT IDENTITIES FOR THEM.

HIS LAST IN A LONG LINE OF ASSISTANTS? A FAN?

HIS LAST EDITOR? SOME LOW LEVEL BUREAUCRAT FROM "ZOOM COMICS" WHO DREW THE SHORT STRAW AT THE OFFICE?

HIS NURSE? HIS NEIGHBOR? A DISTANT RELATIVE? I NEVER DID KNOW MUCH ABOUT HIS FAMILY.

THE LAST TIME I SAW HIM WAS AT A COMIC CONVENTION IN COLUMBUS, OHIO. I DIDN'T SAY ANYTHING AND IF HE SAW ME HE DIDN'T LET ON.

I SHOULD'VE SAID SOMETHING. IF I HAD KNOWN WHAT HE'D DONE...

EXIT

Star Raiders

I'VE BEEN THINKING ABOUT FLAVOR A LOT LATELY, ABOUT THE WHOLE TIME. IT WAS PROBABLY SPURRED ON BY THE NICE SURPRISE I GOT WHEN I DID THAT SIGNING AT "UNCLE AL'S COMIC GALAXY OF FUN, CARDS, VIDEO GAMES AND COLLECTABLES."

I COULDN'T BELIEVE IT WHEN I SAW HER!

"WOULD YOU SIGN THIS, MR. VELASQUEZ? I'M YOUR BIGGEST FAN IN THE WORLD!"

Star Raiders

I'D SEEN JANE AND STEPHEN A FEW TIMES AFTER THEY MOVED UPSTATE. I KNOW I SAW THEM WHEN KIRBY WAS BORN, BUT BY NOW IT HAD BEEN--

I WAS GOING TO SAY "TWO" BUT NOW I REALIZE IT'D BEEN CLOSER TO FIVE YEARS SINCE I'D SEEN THEM. FIVE YEARS!

PEOPLE ALWAYS SAY "TIME FLIES" AND ALL THAT BUT IT'S NOT UNTIL YOU HIT A CERTAIN AGE THAT IT BECOMES TRUE-- REALLY TRUE. YOU'RE LIVING YOUR LIFE AS IF NOTHING'S WRONG AND ALL OF A SUDDEN YOU REALIZE THAT "PURPLE RAIN" CAME OUT FIFTEEN YEARS AGO AND TEEN-AGERS SCARE YOU.

IF YOU THINK I'M FULL OF CRAP... MORE POWER TO YOU! SAVOR THIS MOMENT.

X-FOOLS
X-CRAP
X-SHIT
Star Raider

ANYWAY, JANE LOOKED TERRIFIC.

AFTER THE SIGNING, THE THREE OF US WENT OUT TO EAT (JANE WAS WITH HER... COUSIN? NIECE? I FORGET. IT DOESN'T MATTER BECAUSE SHE DIDN'T SAY A WORD THE WHOLE TIME).

SO ANYWAY, AFTER JANE AND STEPHEN HAD MOVED, HE GOT A JOB TEACHING AT ONE OF THE NEARBY S.U.N.Y. COLLEGES AND FINALLY GOT TO WORK ON HIS THEODORE ROOSEVELT BIOGRAPHY.

JANE'S EMMA GOLDMAN BIO WAS POPULAR ENOUGH FOR HER TO START ANOTHER CARTOON BIO, THIS TIME ABOUT A WRITER CALLED MARY McCARTHY.

SO THINGS WERE GOING PRETTY WELL. THEY LOVED LIFE IN THE COUNTRY, AND STARTED MAKING ARRANGEMENTS TO BUY THE HOUSE OFF OF CATTON. THEY WOULD MAKE THE LEAP FROM RENTERS TO OWNERS.

THEN... TROUBLE.

I DON'T KNOW ALL THE DETAILS, BUT SUFFICE TO SAY THEY WENT THROUGH WHAT'S POLITELY KNOWN AS A "ROUGH PATCH."

RED EMMA
A CARTOON BIOGRAPHY

THEY'D BEEN TOGETHER FOR ABOUT SEVEN OR EIGHT YEARS BY THEN. WHAT DO YOU DO?

IN THE MOVIES AND ON T.V. NO DOUBT SOMETHING DRAMATIC WOULD HAPPEN WHICH WOULD MAKE THEM REALIZE HOW MUCH THEY CARED ABOUT EACH OTHER AND TRUE LOVE CONQUERS ALL AND THEY'D EMBRACE AND SMILE, KNOWING THAT EVERY-THING WOULD GO BACK TO NORMAL AS THE CREDITS ROLL AND A VOICE TELLS YOU WHAT'S COMING UP ON THE EVENING NEWS.

BUT, OF COURSE, MOVIES AND T.V. (AND BOOKS) LIE. THAT DIDN'T HAPPEN.

THERE WAS NO BIG DRAMATIC EVENT. JUST A LOT OF TALKING AND HARD WORK.

THEY WERE NEVER "BACK TO NORMAL" AFTER THAT ROUGH YEAR OR SO, BUT JANE SAYS THAT IN MANY WAYS THEY'RE BETTER. "THE WAY THAT WHEN A BROKEN BONE MENDS ITSELF IT'S STRONGER THAN BEFORE."

TWO YEARS AGO JANE FINALLY SAID YES, AND THEY GOT MARRIED IN A SMALL CEREMONY IN BERMUDA.

THEY'RE EXPECTING THEIR DAUGHTER, GWENDOLYN, NEXT MONTH.

I GUESS IT WAS INEVITABLE THAT SHERMAN CAME UP.

HE AND DOROTHY MOVED IN TOGETHER LIKE THEY PLANNED. AFTER THAT... I'M NOT SURE WHAT HAPPENED.

I GUESS BETWEEN HIM AND DOROTHY AND ME AND HILDY IT WAS NATURAL THAT WE DRIFTED APART.

AT FIRST WE MADE AN EFFORT. A FEW TIMES A MONTH WE'D GET TOGETHER FOR SOME DRINKS -- BOYS' NIGHT OUT. AFTER AWHILE, THOUGH, ALL HE WOULD DO IS COMPLAIN, ABOUT HIS JOB, ABOUT HIS WRITING (OR LACK THEREOF) BUT MOSTLY ABOUT DOROTHY.

I SAW HER A FEW TIMES OVER THE YEARS, ON THE RARE AND AWKWARD DOUBLE DATES WE TRIED. MY IMPRESSION IS THAT SHE WAS AS UNHAPPY AS HE WAS.

HER CAREER HAD BEEN GOING WELL FOR AWHILE, AND SHE GOT A PRIMO JOB WRITING FOR A NATIONAL MAGAZINE OR SOMESUCH, WHEN SHE JUST SORT OF... STALLED OUT.

NOT ONLY DID SHE LOSE THE NATIONAL GIG, SHE HAD TROUBLE GETTING ANY WRITING JOBS.

CATCH 22
JOSEPH HELLER
ROD STEWAR
My Biggest Hits Vol I

AS FOR SHERMAN'S WRITING...

THE GOOD NEWS IS THAT HE FINALLY GOT OUT OF THE BOOKSTORE. WHEN THE GIANT CHAIN STORES STARTED POPPING UP ON EVERY CORNER, A DINOSAUR LIKE MATTHEW'S BOOK EMPORIUM JUST COULDN'T COMPETE. I THINK THEY TURNED IT INTO A GAP... OR WAS IT A STARBUCKS?

SHERMAN, NATURALLY, GOT A NEW JOB: HE BECAME A CLERK AT THAT BIG "MUSICCZAR" SUPERSTORE THEY OPENED IN UNION SQUARE.

AT FIRST I LIKED THE IDEA, SINCE IT MEANT I COULD GET HIS DISCOUNT TO BUY MOVIES AND JUNK BUT THE FUNNY THING: I NEVER TOOK HIM UP ON IT.

MOST FRIENDSHIPS, IF THEY END AT ALL, END NOT BY EARTHQUAKE, BUT BY EROSION.

YOUR TIME TOGETHER, WHICH YOU USED TO TAKE FOR GRANTED, BECOMES SOMETHING YOU NEED TO SCHEDULE.

SLOWLY YOU'RE AWARE THAT THE EASY INTIMACY YOU SHARED GOT LOST SOMEWHERE.

YOU TALK MORE AND MORE ABOUT THE PAST.

ONCE SHERMAN BECAME AN ASSISTANT MANAGER AND STARTED WORKING FIFTY PLUS HOURS A WEEK... THAT WAS MORE OR LESS THE END OF IT.

THE END OF US.

JANE, NATURALLY, BLAMES ALL OF SHERMAN'S TROUBLES ON HER, BUT AS MUCH AS I'M NOT EXACTLY CO-CHAIR OF THE DOROTHY LESTRADE FAN CLUB, IT ISN'T FAIR TO LAY IT ALL ON HER FEET.

SHERMAN'S A BIG BOY AND COULD WALK OUT ANYTIME HE WANTS TO. BUT FOR ALL HIS COMPLAINING, I GUESS HE REALLY DOESN'T WANT TO.

WE INVITED HIM TO THE WEDDING BUT THEY COULDN'T MAKE IT.

THANKS TO MY HUGE FAMILY, HILDY AND I HAD A PRETTY BIG WEDDING (WELL, NOT LIKE A KENNEDY WEDDING OR ANYTHING, BUT BIGGER THAN YOU'D EXPECT MY WEDDING TO BE ANYWAY).

WE'D BEEN LIVING TOGETHER FOR TWO YEARS BY THEN, SO IT WASN'T THAT BIG OF A DEAL.

THE BIG DEAL ARRIVED SIX MONTHS LATER: THE ARRIVAL OF THE FRUIT OF OUR LOINS, THE LITTLE BUNDLE OF JOY:

KIRBY ROSE VELASQUEZ.

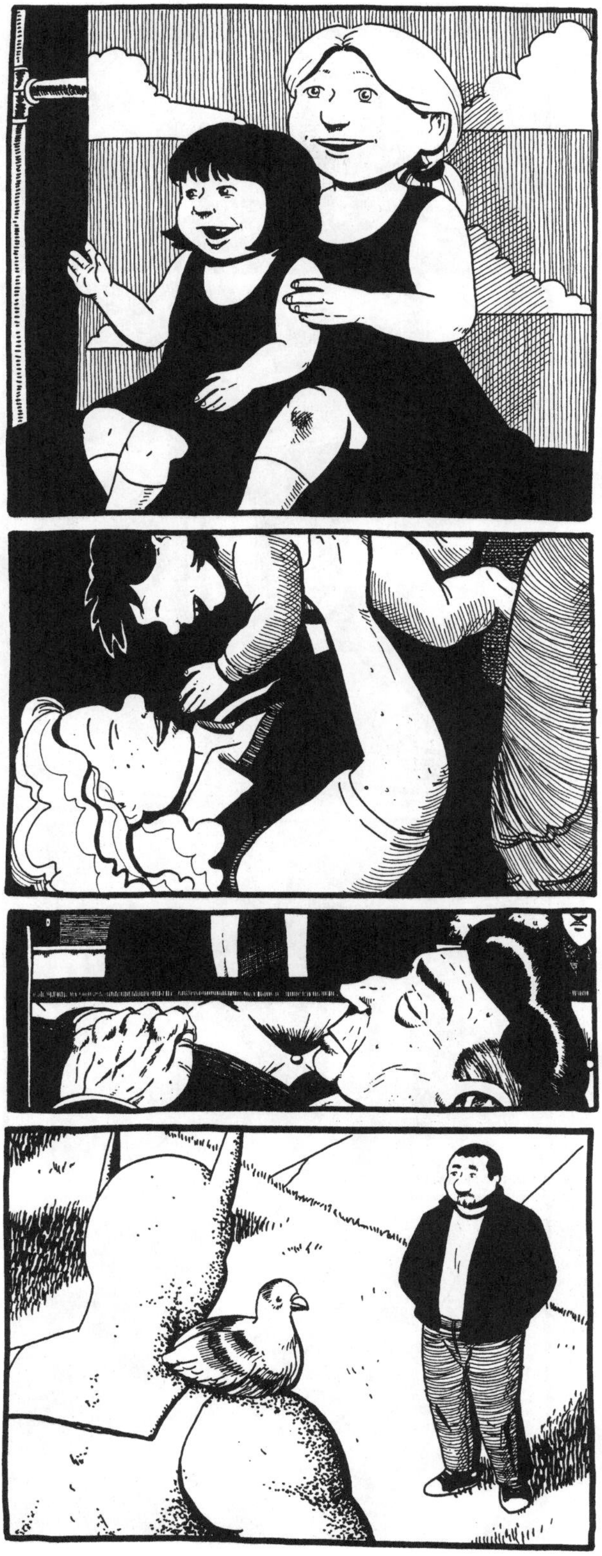

SHE'S FOUR YEARS OLD NOW AND HER YOUNGER SISTER, MARLYS, JUST TURNED TWO.

I KNOW. CAN YOU BELIEVE SUCH THINGS?

I COULD GO ON AND ON ABOUT HOW CRAZY I AM ABOUT THEM, AND HOW EVEN THOUGH I WASN'T SURE I WANTED KIDS YET THESE TWO GIRLS HAVE ENRICHED MY LIFE IN WAYS I NEVER EVEN IMAGINED. YOU SHOULD SEE THEM! THE WAY MARLYS WILL..

LIKE I SAID, I COULD GO ON AND ON BUT I WON'T BECAUSE UNLIKE MOST PARENTS, I REALIZE THAT NOTHING IS AS BORING AS HEARING ABOUT HOW GREAT AND TERRIFIC SOMEONE ELSE'S KIDS ARE.

OF COURSE MY KIDS ARE THE GREATEST AND MOST TERRIFICEST, BUT I'LL LET IT DROP.

YEAH, SEEING JANE MADE ME THINK ABOUT THE OLD DAYS AND ESPECIALLY THAT POOR, WONDERFUL BASTARD, IRVING FLAVOR.

IRONICALLY, HE ALWAYS HATED THE "TROUBLEMAKERS" WHO ROCKED THE BOAT OF THE COMICS INDUSTRY. BUT IT WAS BECAUSE OF THEM THAT CONTRACTS LIKE THE ONE HE SIGNED IN 1944 ARE PRETTY MUCH EXTINCT IN THE INDUSTRY.

METEON

So when he gave J.C. LeBlanc Meteon and the Comet Kid they became the property of Zoom Comics, but Flavor still got a piece of the action. It was a small percentage, but it was a royalty nonetheless.

Anytime they made a Meteon comic book or bed spread or tooth brush or candy bar or action figure or video game or Saturday morning cartoon or whatever, anywhere on Earth, Mr. Flavor would get a cut, til the day he died.

After he died, said cut is to be transferred to, and paid to, Mr. Ed Velasquez "as a payment of thanks for his six months of loyal service as my assistant."

It wasn't a huge sum. Let's face it, Meteon isn't a household name. But it helped us pay a few bills and get set up for Kirby.

We were happy at this unexpected little windfall.

Until...

ZOOM COMICS WAS FACING SOME FINANCIAL HARD TIMES, SO IT STARTED LEASING OUT SOME OF ITS CHARACTERS TO PROFESSIONAL WRESTLING. THEY DIDN'T WANT TO LEND OUT ANY OF THEIR BIG GUNS AT FIRST, SO GUESS WHO WAS AMONG THE FIRST BATCH OF HEROES TO COME TO LIFE IN THE RING?

THE "WRESTLING MONEY" TURNED THE QUARTERLY ZOOM ROYALTY CHECKS FROM A FEW EXTRA VIDEO RENTALS AND MOON-PIES INTO A TRULY LIFE ALTERING CHUNK OF CHANGE.

I'M SURE THERE'S SOME KIND OF IRONY OR POETIC JUSTICE OR WHAT HAVE YOU TO THE FACT THAT I'M USING MONEY FROM THE LARGEST COMICS PUBLISHER IN NORTH AMERICA AND PROFESSIONAL WRESTLING TO SUBSIDIZE MY OWN PUBLISHING EFFORT.

THE FIRST ISSUE OF "STAR-RAIDERS" CAME OUT ABOUT A YEAR AGO, AND IT'S BEEN DOING RELATIVELY WELL. OF COURSE THESE DAYS, THAT MEANS IT'S JUST NOT LOSING AS MUCH MONEY AS MOST SMALL PRESS BOOKS.

BUT YOU KNOW WHAT? IT DOESN'T MATTER. I'VE GOT HILDY AND THE GIRLS, I'VE GOT MY OWN COMIC BOOK... I'M LIVING THE LIFE I DREAMED OF.

BESIDES, I HEARD THE ADVANCE ORDERS FOR THE "METEON" VIDEO GAME ARE <u>HUGE</u>!

NIGHTSTALKER
CREATED
FOR ZOOM COMICS
by
BROOKLYN NATIVE
IRVING FLAVOR
1925 - 1997

I'd like to express gratitude to my cartooning friends Ivan Brunetti, Doug Cenko, Steve Conley, Wally Crane, Kieron Dwyer, Glen Garner, David Hahn, Dean Haspiel, Sam Henderson, Chris Kalnick, John Kerschbaum, Brent Kirk, Derek Kirk Kim, John Kovalic, Tim Kreider, Terry Laban, Pete Sickman-Garner, Colin Upton, Kurt Wolfgang, Joe Zabel, and Andrew Zaben, all of whom contributed fine drawings to the original Box Office Poison series. Please buy their comics.

Thanks to Chris and Brett for risking all that they have worked for by publishing this book. Please buy other Top Shelf books. Special bonus thanks to Tony Consiglio for his invaluable friendship and camaraderie. Please buy his comic Double Cross and new graphic novel 110 Per¢. Finally, eternal thanks to Kristen Siebecker, whose love and support made this book possible.

Alex Robinson graduated from Yorktown High School in 1987. He worked in a major metropolitan bookstore for seven years before finally quitting to draw comics full time. He is currently living in New York City with his wife, Kristen, and their two cats, Cadbury and Krimpet. His other books include the short story collection BOP!: MORE BOX OFFICE POISON and his most recent graphic novel, TRICKED, published by Top Shelf in 2005. Check out Alex's website: http://members.aol.com/ComicBookAlex